Speaking of Writing

Speaking of Writing

Selected Hopwood Lectures

Edited and with an Introduction by
Nicholas Delbanco

ANN ARBOR

THE UNIVERSITY OF MICHIGAN PRESS

Library of Congress Cataloging-in-Publication Data

Speaking of writing : selected Hopwood Lectures / edited, and with an
    introduction by Nicholas Delbanco.
        p.   cm.
     ISBN 0-472-09422-X (alk. paper). — ISBN 0-472-06422-3 (pbk. :
alk. paper)
      1. Authorship.   2. Criticism.   I. Delbanco, Nicholas.
PN151.S64   1990
808'.02—dc20   90-37448
                                                          CIP

Contents

Introduction:
"To the Young Writer"

Nicholas Delbanco

Avery Hopwood was born in Cleveland, Ohio, in 1884; he was graduated from the University of Michigan, Phi Beta Kappa, in 1905. Thereafter he went to New York. Although known as the "playboy playwright," he had a productive career; he was the author or coauthor of thirty-three plays. He wrote one novel also. In her memoir, *What Is Remembered,* Alice B. Toklas describes Hopwood and Carl Van Vechten as having jointly "created modern New York. They changed everything to their way of seeing and doing. It became as gay, irresponsible and brilliant as they were."

Hopwood recalled his own original impetus, and why he began work on his first play, *Clothes:*

> An intense admiration for the theater, a fondness for writing, and the ambition to make money, contrived to pave the way for my career as a dramatist; but the influence that focused my efforts was an article written by Louis V. De Foe, that appeared in the *Michigan Alumnus,* when I was a student at the University of Michigan. "The Call of the Playwright" was its title, and in it Mr. De Foe told of the fabulous sums that dramatists had made; the more I thought about it, the more determined I became to try my luck in this field.

He did, and his gamble paid off. By 1920, Hopwood could claim four shows running simultaneously on Broadway, and two years later the *New York Times* described him as "almost unquestionably the richest of all playwrights." He celebrated often, lavishly, and then his luck ran out. After a party in Paris, he sent a postcard to two of his guests, Alice B. Toklas and Gertrude Stein. He thanked them for attending. "But there was no stamp on the card," Miss Toklas later wrote. "It was Avery's little way of getting things done for him without any bother.

That very day we had news that Avery had been drowned in the Mediterranean."

He died at Juan-les-Pins, swimming, in 1928. Mouth-to-mouth resuscitation did not work. There were rumors: he had been drunk, he had been murdered, he went swimming too soon after lunch. The coroner's verdict, however, was coronary occlusion.

Hopwood's legacy, if not his writing, endures. "What is remembered" at present are the awards in his name. Under the terms of his will, and after the death of his mother, one-fifth of Hopwood's estate was to be left to the Regents of the University of Michigan. The will stipulates that prizes be awarded to students "who perform the best creative work in the fields of dramatic writing, fiction, poetry, and the essay." The terms of the bequest further state, "that the students competing for the prizes shall not be confined to academic subjects, but shall be allowed the widest possible latitude, and that the new, the unusual, and the radical shall be especially encouraged."

The first Hopwood contest was held in 1930–31. In each of the categories adduced above, the list of its winners is long. By now we have honored more than twenty-four hundred students and dispersed more than one million dollars in prize money. The successful author of "Nobody's Widow," "Fair and Warmer," "The Gold Diggers," and "Getting Gertie's Garter" is celebrated, today, for sponsoring young talent. His name has grown synonymous with the university writing awards program to encourage and then recognize "the best creative work."

All enduring language is in part a legacy; each effort to instruct is in some sense a bequest. Our anticipated audience may change. We may write for ourselves or for strangers, in the "creative" or "critical" mode, for a small selected gathering or as wide as possible a reading public. Sometimes this is conscious: a manifesto. Often it comes as response: an author or issue or attitude intrigues or delights or dismays us, and we write reaction down.

W. H. Auden puts it succinctly: "The ideal audience the poet imagines consists of the beautiful who go to bed with him, the powerful who invite him to dinner and tell him secrets of state, and his fellow-poets. The actual audience he gets consists of myopic school-teachers, pimply young men who eat in cafeterias, and his fellow-poets. This means that, in fact, he writes for his fellow-poets."

Implicitly always, and often explicitly the writer addresses other writers—a community of colleagues in absentia. Words demonstrate if only by assertion their own authority; an aesthetic framed in silence (if its medium be language) cannot but fail to persuade. We talk to keep silence at bay. Yet talk framed with the notion of and delivered to an audience of aspiring professionals is likely to serve as the writer's credo, the maker's considered mark. As the lady in the adage says, "How do I know what I think until I see what I say?"

The Hopwood Awards ceremony takes place in Ann Arbor in April. That occasion is further distinguished by a lecture, delivered by a prominent writer on a subject he or she considers of importance. These annual lectures have been, seriatim, compiled in three previous volumes: *The Writer and his Craft* (edited by Roy W. Cowden, 1954), *To the Young Writer* (edited by A. L. Bader, 1965), and *The Writer's Craft* (edited by Robert A. Martin, 1982). Singly and collectively, they are remarkable books. They speak to the apprentice author from the craftsman's vantage, and they do so with variety and force. All have been published by the University of Michigan Press; this work comprises the fourth volume of that series.

It differs from its predecessors, however, in several important respects. First, it is retrospective—reprinting some of the lectures from earlier editions, since they are now out of print. Second, it is selective; we could not hope to publish all the Hopwood lectures in a single volume and have settled for roughly half. Third, this selection reflects its editor's bias and may therefore bear some explaining.

The range astonishes. From Robert Morss Lovett to Francine du Plessix Gray—from the first speaker, in 1932, to the most recent, in 1989—those who composed the Hopwood Lecture have taken it for granted that their audience is literate, engaged. By and large these talks have been delivered by practitioners in a genre—though there are instances of "genre-crossing"; the poet Donald Justice, for example, titled his 1988 lecture, "The Prose Sublime." To claim a common denominator for these essays is to risk reductiveness; they deal with no single shared theme. Yet the speakers share an assumption that literature matters, and vitally, to the culture it reports on and sustains.

Inclusiveness would have been easy; the process of selection—exclusion—has been hard. Two artists (Arthur Miller—himself a Hopwood winner—and Stephen Spender) delivered two separate talks; I have chosen one from each. Several of these texts discuss an individual author and his or her particular merits; these I have excised. Here too, of course, the exception proves the rule; I could not bring myself to forgo W. D. Snodgrass's brilliant talk on Shakespeare (1974). When an author turns individual analysis inward, focusing on his or her own creative process, that discussion seems germane.

Excluded also, here, are several first-rate lectures on biography, drama, and the art of film. Had we space enough and time, the role of the artist in society might have emerged center-stage. Nadine Gordimer's assessment of modern African writing and Francine du Plessix Gray's "The Russian Heroine" strike me as signposts in this regard—essays that suggest analysis of world literature as telling as that of America. But most are "domestic" lectures, and their freely ranging subject matter stays nonetheless close to home. To the contemporary reader, that notion of "range" may seem circumscribed; the early lectures were almost without exception delivered by white male writers. Only in recent years have we begun to correct such disproportion and redress imbalance.

This volume finds its focus in a twinned discussion of the craft of prose and the art of poetry. The loss of what we cannot print is compensated, surely, by the yield of what we can.

The first director of the Hopwood Program was Professor Bennett Weaver. Roy W. Cowden succeeded him, serving from 1934 to 1952. Arno L. Bader served from 1952 to 1965, and Robert F. Haugh was chairman of the Hopwood Committee from 1965 to 1972. In the two subsequent years the committee was cochaired by Donald Hall and Sheridan Baker; John W. Aldridge held the position from 1975 to 1988. Andrea Beauchamp has served as administrative associate of the program —ably, indispensably—since 1979.

The Hopwood Room in Angell Hall holds hundreds of volumes produced by past award winners, and dozens of journals to which we subscribe; these lectures too sit on the shelves. Having been appointed chairman in 1988, I began to read. The first Hopwood Lecture has the authority of an inaugural address; it is therefore reprinted here. Yet there is a cobwebby feel to the language, the sense of an era far past. Robert Morss Lovett refers, for example, to "such contemporary writers as Mr. Aldous Huxley and Mr. T. S. Eliot . . . Dr. Santayana and Professor John Dewey." He established a tradition and began its continuity, but "Literature and Animal Faith"—delivered by a speaker born in 1870— suggests how long ago this program was conceived.

Among the writers mentioned in that inaugural lecture, however, is the author of the second. And this man, to my glad surprise, was someone I had known. The sense of colleagueship as "handing-on"—of membership in a community—became therefore immediate. What follows is a private account that may suggest in its public accounting what one writer owes to another and each of us to all.

Max Eastman was in his eighties when I was in my twenties. We met on Martha's Vineyard and grew close. He welcomed me, whether in Gay Head, New York, or Barbados; he was tolerance incarnate, with an amused abiding sense of how youth preens. I postured; I was working on a book (*Grasse 3/23/66*) that was recondite in the extreme. I'd labor in an ecstasy of self-congratulation, producing perhaps a hundred words a day, intoning the sybillant syllables until they appeared to make sense. One such passage, I remember, contained a quotation from Villon; a description of Hopi burial rites; an anagram of the name of my fifth-grade teacher; an irrefutable refutation of Kant; glancing reference to Paracelsus; suggestive ditto to my agent's raven-haired assistant; paraphrase of Cymbeline's dirge; and an analysis of the orthographic and conceptual disjunction between Pope and Poe. I took my time; I let it extend to ten lines. That night I brought my morning's triumph to Max and permitted him to read. He did so in silence. He tried it aloud; so did I. When he said it made no sense and I explained the sense it made, he looked at me with generous exasperation. "Sure," he said. "That's interesting. Why don't you write it down?"

I remember staying with him on Martha's Vineyard one October. His wife, Yvette, was off to New York for a shopping trip, and she asked me to stay in their house—a favor to me, really, since my own hut was unheated. I was full of beans and bravado then, and would get to work by six—waking up and clacking at the keys in my upstairs bedroom. In the first pause, however, I could hear his steady hunt-and-peck in the study underneath; he'd been at work well before. So we'd share a cup of coffee and a comment on the news, then I'd fuss at my novel again. At nine o'clock I'd take a break—tear off my clothes and run down the hill to the pond. The morning would be glorious: that crystalline light, those sizeable skies, the pine trees somehow greener against the sere scrub oak. And always, out there from the still warm water, Max would lift his hand to me, his white mane on the wavelets like some snowy egret's, grinning.

Time passed. He died at eighty-six, in 1969. But it takes no effort to see this again, see it always as tradition's emblem: an old man waving from the water at the youth on the near shore. They are naked, both of them; the sun slants over Lobsterville. A few day sailors might be on the pond, or someone in a kayak, or musseling or digging clams. The seabirds settle, incurious; the beach smells of seawrack and tide. There's a busy imitation of silence: the man in the water, bobbing, flutters heels and hands. The young one runs to meet him and it's all a perfect clarity until he does a surface dive and, splashing, shuts his eyes.

So I have been thinking, lately, of the notion of a guild. It has to do with the instructed awareness of tradition, and one's relation thereto. My model is that of the medieval guild, with its ordained sequential progression from apprentice to "master." These last must teach the first. They do so from the page when they have quit the stage. Their voices speak with undiminished resonance to a private reading audience, as well as to the public one gathered each April to hear.

As Roy W. Cowden observes, in his foreword to the first Hopwood volume, "The speakers have all been craftsmen who have shown an interest in young writers, and their choice of subjects indicates what they themselves have thought might be useful to the apprentice. In these talks will be found critical opinion as broad and varied as our American culture. Here also is a revelation of the ways of the writer as writers understand them."

Arno Bader, in the second volume, observes much the same: "Some of the speakers concern themselves with technique, others with literary genres, with the criticism of individual writers, or with problems of the writer's training, of his gaining recognition, of his attitudes toward experience. Yet despite much variety of subject and diversity of critical opinion, all the speakers have in common an interest in the young writer and a desire to be useful . . . ."

One cannot ask for better or require more. This is a great tradition, and one I am honored to share.

Literature and Animal Faith

Robert Morss Lovett

The Hopwood Foundation is the largest and most ambitious attempt to invigorate and sustain literature from without, through such aid, material and intellectual, as even a mechanized society can offer to its artists. Its establishment was a profession of faith in the importance of literature to the society from which this aid was derived. In associating the foundation with a university, the official guardian of inherited wisdom and of the aesthetic values which have arisen from the experience of mankind, the seat of scientific research and social criticism, the donor implied a belief that literature is not an esoteric and exotic product, an expression of the writer's emotion for his own release or healing, but a public enterprise, a part of the effort of humanity to live adequately, even richly and nobly, by employing all the resources of its environment; an effort which it is the object of the university to promote, and which is symbolized in its name. It is therefore not inappropriate on this occasion, when the fruits of Mr. Hopwood's beneficence are awarded, to devote some minutes to a reconsideration of literature as a contribution to society. This reconsideration has been suggested to me by reading the essays submitted in the contest, many of them sharing a certain distrust of material, a present tendency of literature to shrink away from reality into itself, which it is the purpose of my remarks to deplore. It is the more pertinent to press such an inquiry at the present time when it is beginning to be understood that humanity is in danger, when skepticism prevails concerning the structural strength of Western civilization to support its own weight, when defeatism is ringing changes on the decline of the West. Can art help a sorry world? The arts-and-craftsmen of the late nineteenth century had no doubt of the answer, and in the early twentieth we have had the affirmation of philosophers to whom I shall refer later. If the question be asked today, it is to literature that we turn most expectantly for answer. Of all the fine arts, literature is the most democratic, the least self-conscious, the least removed from popular understanding by an exacting technique, the best fitted to serve toward the appreciation of the other fine arts and as the introduction to them. Our culture is largely literary. Hence the question is asked more urgently of literature than of music or sculpture: Can it in a social sense help to save the world? But another question must be asked preliminary to this: Can such salvation become a source of aesthetic values? For unless this be answered in the affirmative, the literature of salvation will cease to be literature, and will become propaganda in the form of books, magazines, newspapers, moving pictures, or radio eloquence, which apparently it was not the purpose of Mr. Hopwood to subsidize.

Mr. Lewis Mumford remarked in a recent review of Mr. Max Eastman's book, *The Literary Mind,* "Any sensible pronouncement on the function of literature must be based upon a first hand study of the way it acts and works, not upon the way other critics may imagine it acts and works." Taking this pragmatic principle as a starting point, we may begin with the commonplace that of all the fine arts literature is most definitely based upon content. Great periods of literature have depended upon a body of material which invited the imagination of poets and prose men, and with which they could freely and confidently deal. Such material naturally resulted from man's sense of knowing, of conduct, of beauty; it included values drawn from all three, and represented, sometimes naively, sometimes with conscious striving, a unity among them. It is necessary only to mention as examples the age of the Greek epic and of Greek tragedy, the Augustan age of Rome, the Middle Ages, the Renaissance, the Age of Enlightenment. The existence of material endowed with a sort of prescriptive authority was clearly a boon to the writer. It determined the original intention whether of Homer or Aeschylus, of Virgil or Dante or Shakespeare.

The less illustrious nineteenth century differs markedly from these periods in possessing no material of authoritative prescription. It is true, it owed to Romanticism the discovery of one great source of original material in nature; but with this exception we find a growing uncertainty as to subject matter—a novel form of self-consciousness in literature. Matthew Arnold expressed it most definitely in the preface to his *Poems of 1852,* concluding that the poet must seek his subject in excellent actions "which most powerfully appeal to the great primary human affections," such material to be found chiefly in the heroic past. Other poets also felt the search for themes a hampering necessity before which inspiration wavered, and which Browning and Whitman alone seem to have escaped entirely. The past offered the common refuge. History was the chief subject of intellectual inquiry for the early Victorian Age, providing themes for works of first magnitude to Carlyle, Macaulay, Grote, and Buckle. Novelists wrote or conceived their masterpieces against the historical background, and the revival of the literary drama was based on historical characters. But equally characteristic of the age was a growing preoccupation with the present as the problems of man's life in society became more pressing and more menacing. The Victorian Age is a long descent from Parnassus. Almost every one of its great figures in literature emerged, under the compulsion of social necessity, from the romantic isolation of an art founded on the past. Carlyle, beginning his career as a critic of literature, became a master of applied history. Tennyson deserted the "Palace of Art" and converted the epic of the Round Table into a social allegory. Mrs. Browning passed through a series of transmigrations to confess at last—

I do distrust the poet who discerns
No character or glory in his times
And trundles back his soul five hundred years
Past moat and drawbridge, into a castle court.

Matthew Arnold turned from poetry to criticism and from criticism of poetry to criticism of life. Morris exchanged *The Earthly Paradise* for *News from Nowhere*.

It is a commonplace to assert that one reason for the uncertainty of the nineteenth century about the content of literature was the triumphant advance of science. The upholders of traditional culture found themselves, like the defenders of the Roman Empire, threatened by barbarian hordes pressing upon the frontiers. And, as in that historical parallel, they were afflicted by divided counsels. On the one hand they saw the values of authority, of "the best that had been thought and said in the world on matters that most concern us" reduced to mythology and allegory by a new body of factual truth. On the other hand, in recognizing the advent of new and vital knowledge which, according to precedent, should have furnished the inspiration and content of a new art, they were disconcerted by its recalcitrance to absorption in literature. It is rather cruel to recall today the cordial words with which Wordsworth in his Preface to *Lyrical Ballads* welcomed the science which was to destroy his God.

If the labors of men of science [he wrote] should ever create any material revolution, direct or indirect, in our condition, and in the impressions which we habitually receive, the Poet will sleep then no more than at present, but he will be ready to follow the steps of the man of science, not only in those general indirect effects, but he will be at his side, carrying sensation into the midst of the object of the science itself. The remotest discoveries of the Chemist, the Botanist, or Mineralogist, will be as proper objects of the Poet's art as any upon which it can be employed, if the time should ever come when these things shall be familiar to us, and the relations under which they are contemplated by the followers of these respective sciences shall be manifestly and palpably material to us as enjoying and suffering beings. If the time should ever come when what is now called science, thus familiarised to men, shall be ready to put on, as it were, a form of flesh and blood, the Poet will lend his divine spirit to aid the transfiguration, and will welcome the Being thus produced, as a dear and genuine inmate of the household of man.

The reasons for the failure of science and poetry to lie down together are two. In the first place, the "discoveries of the Chemist, the Botanist, or Mineralogist," while they have created a "material revolution in our condition," have never in the sense Wordsworth envisaged—that is, a complete, satisfying, and fruitful reorientation—become "manifestly and palpably material to us as enjoying and suffering beings." On the contrary, the relations under which the discoveries of science are contemplated reveal a cosmos indifferent and even hostile to man in his higher life of sensibility and aspiration. In the second place, these discoveries are tentative, depending on hypothesis, and liable to repudiation. Science refuses to speak with the assurance of revelation; it refuses to give the artist the certainties upon which his imagination has heretofore been able to build. The attitude of the scientist is indeed the opposite to that of the artist, or poet. According to Huxley, "The improver of natural knowledge absolutely refuses to acknowledge authority as such. For him, skepticism is the highest of duties; blind faith, the one unpardonable sin."

While science did not directly supply content to art, however, it provided an intellectual background and suggested a method. Realism or naturalism in art is the concomitant of science in nature. As science undertakes to give a complete account of the universe in terms of mathematical-mechanical relationships, so realism in its confident youth undertook to describe completely the phenomena which fall under our observation. Both scientist and realist, relying on the evidence of the senses, accept the objective world in the spirit of animal faith. Indeed no scientist could make a more robust confession of this faith than Chekhov when he declared that "outside matter there is neither knowledge nor experience, and consequently there is no truth." With Zola we find the novelist boldly taking his place beside the physicist and physiologist, and in his well-known manifesto announcing his graduation from the preparatory school of art into the university of science, indeed claiming the highest rank in that institution: "The novelist . . . gives facts or observes them and, through experiments, shows that their succession will be such as determinism exacts. . . . We continue by our observations and our experiments the work of the physiologist, who continues that of the physicist and chemist."

The sublime and arrogant audacity of that pronouncement testifies to the confidence which for a brief period the example of science gave to literature, and which accounts for the speed and scope of the conquest which realism achieved in Europe at the close of the nineteenth century, approximating the domination of the romantic mood at its beginning. The collapse of naturalism at the end of the nineteenth century resulted in part from those reasons to which I have ascribed the failure of scientific knowledge to impart substance and vitality to art. More and more it became evident that the cosmos of mathematical-mechanical relationships did not supply a sanction for the things in which alone consciousness has found significance. Hence the decline of literary values—not only those of sin, repentance, renunciation, but also of tragedy and romantic love, the passing of which Mr. Krutch chronicles poignantly in *The Modern Temper*. Science, after stimulating realism to emulation of its methods, revealed a *reductio ad absurdum:* if man is essentially meaningless in any terms with which his mind can deal, a negligible accident in the cosmos, what justification has the realist for conscientiously recording the phenomena of his existence?

In addition to this revelation of an unfathomable crevasse between the essential purposes of art and science, there has been the circumstance that science itself has, as it were, lost its way. Not only is man without meaning, but nature also. An article by Professor P. W. Bridgman a year or two ago included a statement of the so-called bankruptcy of science which contrasts sharply with Zola's optimistic declaration: "The physicist thus finds himself in a world from which the bottom has dropped clean out . . . he must give up his most cherished convictions and faith.

The world is not a world of reason, understandable by the intellect of man, but as we penetrate ever deeper the very law of cause and effect, which we had thought to be a formula to which we could force God Himself to subscribe, ceases to have meaning."

This pessimism, based on complete loss of orientation, is first of all an affair between the scientist and his God; but it challenges also the poet, and indeed every thinking inhabitant of the world which science describes. Long before it emerged, however, to convict realism, in addition to all else, of being unscientific, the psychological inadequacy of realism had become evident. Almost spontaneously, symbolism came to supplement and modify the method of the realist. For the human mind, in addition to demanding an inner reality behind the visible, has the quality of endowing realistic detail with extra-realistic significance; so that, automatically, the higher examples of realism took on a symbolical aspect. Ibsen, in his later prose dramas, turned naturally to symbolism; he was succeeded as the all-European dramatist by Maeterlinck, who stated as the third requirement of high poetry "the idea which the poet has of the unknown, in which float the beings and things he evokes, of the mystery which dominates them and judges them and presides at their destinies."

Symbolism is necessarily dependent on the intuition of a single mind; it lacks the authority of knowledge controlled by experience of external facts. Fascinating as guesswork, it is without any check upon the validity of the guess. Moreover, symbolism led to a technique in which substance and meaning suffered further attenuation in the interest of the artist's mood. As realism, in despair before its task of recording all the visible and all the audible, found relief in impressionism, the limitation of approach to a single point of view and concentration upon salient detail, so symbolism found its correlative method in expressionism, which deals with the external world, not directly, but through the state of emotion which it arouses in the consciousness of the artist. Again, the fascination of experimental technique led to increasing concern with the methods of art and emphasized the slogan of the nineties, "Art for art's sake."

Even for writers who continued to deal with the problems of man in his world, the emphasis shifted under the influence of Ibsen and Butler to an individualistic point of view. The novel became iconoclastic in its attack on social institutions, marriage, the family, the church, the state. But the individual himself under intense scrutiny revealed contradictions hitherto unsuspected. Human character was increasingly pictured as a

chaos of incongruities, the normal man evolving into a mass of pathological potentialities. Among the literary values more and more subject to
depreciation was the self. "Be yourself," was Ibsen's message. "Well,"
replies Mr. Aldous Huxley, "I try to be sincerely myself, that is to say, I
try to be sincerely all the numerous people who live inside my skin and
take their turn in being master of my fate."

This development was immensely forwarded by psychological research, emphasizing in human character the place of the unconscious,
defined by Lawrence as "that essential unique nature of every individual
creature which is by its very nature unanalyzable, indefinable, inconceiv-
able. It cannot be conceived; it can only be experienced in every single
instance." The effort of fiction to deal with experience in a detail which
eludes classification is indicated by Mr. H. S. Peterson in his account of
Mr. Conrad Aiken's novel *Blue Voyage* as "not so much a unitary work
of art as a melancholy *cauchemar* of ghosts and voices, a phantasmagoric
world of disordered sounds and colors, a world without design or purpose, and perceptible only in terms of the prolix and the fragmentary."

These are, of course, merely instances of a tendency which is obvious. Fiction has become increasingly introvert and disconnected from the
flow of general life. The natural sciences insofar as they have conditioned
contemporary writing have reinforced this separation. The author, returning to the ivory tower, shares the tendency of his material, which
more and more has become autobiographical, developing methods dependent upon private association and eccentric reaction. The result is
evident in techniques which impose upon the reader an effort unprecedented in fiction—the work of James Joyce in England and William
Faulkner in America are examples of the necessity laid upon the reader to
grapple first with the author's medium before coming to grips with his
import.

The willingness to be incomprehensible has been even more clearly
manifest in poetry than in prose. Mr. Max Eastman in his book, *The
Literary Mind,* scathingly likens exponents of what he calls the "cult of
unintelligibility" to children soliloquizing in public, in a jargon no one
else can understand. M. Lanson less violently observes: "The laws which
preside over the relation of words have had as their end, up to now, the
intelligible; the new schools have wished that they should have as their
end the emotional. To group words not according to logic, to realize a
sense perceptible to all, but according to sensation, to manifest an impression perceived for the poet alone, has been the end more or less

consciously pursued." So far as the mere facts are concerned, such criticism is valid. Even discounting the accelerating response of the public to new techniques, which makes the incomprehensible of one generation easily understood by the next, there is no doubt that communication between reader and writer is at low ebb in the writing labeled "modernist." The tendency is but a natural symptom of a psychological state induced by acute consciousness of frustration and bewilderment in a world where man is no longer at home.

This attitude of literature, its repudiation of material which connects the individual with the outside world, its attenuation of meaning, its indifference to communication, above all its preoccupation with itself, is a phenomenon parallel to that skepticism in philosophy which since the Renaissance has not ceased its disintegrating criticism of knowledge. Both are expressions of the same discouragement, rendered acute by disappointment with the results of science, the inadequacy of instruments to conquer the unknown, the lack of any positive relation between man's consciousness and the cosmic process which includes it.

Obviously one reaction to the unknowable is to ignore its existence; one reaction to an unmeaning universe is to mean as little as possible in dealing with it. Much modern poetry has direct affinity with the solipsism of the romantic philosopher cherishing his solitary dream of the world. But in any situation there are three ways of meeting the issue: to evade, to stand pat, or to attack. Already philosophy, schooled by the physical sciences, is preparing to enter the field: it is abandoning infinite assumptions, discarding absolute goals, and extending the experimental method to all human interests. "The function of perception and natural science," says Dr. Santayana in *Scepticism and Animal Faith,* from which I have borrowed my title this afternoon, "is not to flatter the sense of omniscience in an absolute mind, but to dignify animal life by harmonizing it in action and thought with its conditions. . . . What matters is that science should be integrated with art, and that the arts should substitute the dominion of man over circumstances . . . for the dominion of chance."

Such contemporary writers as Mr. Aldous Huxley and Mr. T. S. Eliot can by no means be convicted of failing to integrate science with art, though not to the end indicated by Dr. Santayana. Their integration of the two has only tended to confirm the tendency to helpless withdrawal. Mr. Eastman's reiterated complaint that the modern writer ignores science must be amended: he has heeded scientific data and been overwhelmed by them. Even for purposes of art the defeatism represented by the typical science-conscious writers of today offers resources that must soon be exhausted. In the realm of actual experience their point of view is yet more sterile. What is needed is not further study of scientific fact, but an emulation of the intrepidity with which the scientist meets the crumbling of the foundations on which the structure of his belief has been reared. The pendulum seems to have swung as far as possible toward the inaction of despair; the only direction left would appear to be a return toward something more constructive, whether the pragmatic acceptance urged by Professor John Dewey, or such a mellow stoicism as seems to be foreshadowed in the poetry of Mr. George Dillon. Either course indicates that it will be possible for man to accept the implications of science without renouncing the demands of his own nature for affirmation and action.

This is the consummation toward which Dr. Santayana looks in the passage quoted. The basis upon which it is to be achieved is the quality which he distinguishes from philosophic skepticism by the term "animal faith," which he defines as "the faith I live by day by day." This faith is part of human nature, depending on the fact that "man is an animal in a material and social world." He continues to expound this faith. "In regard to the original articles of the animal creed—that there is a world, that there is a future, that things sought can be found, and things seen can be eaten—no guarantee can possibly be offered. . . . But while life lasts, in one form or another this faith must endure." "All the animals trust their senses and live: philosophy would persuade man alone not to trust them, and if he was consistent, to stop living."

I trust that the application which I have in mind of this doctrine to the arts, and especially literature, will be clear without long exposition. It is, in brief, that there is a definite body of material prescribed to literature today. That material is the experience of man in the world. It is true that human experience has been the subject matter of literature in the past, but usually of minor forms and subsidiary to so-called higher interests. Today this subject matter, properly recognized as knowledge, is invested with a new and compelling importance. If theology and science alike have failed to sustain man in his sense of unique significance in the scheme of things, he has only his own experience as a body of material upon which his consciousness can work to elicit values of living. This pursuit of significance had taken place in the past in a world outside of experience, a world which no longer exists. Within experience itself must in future take place those activities which will give to man's career on earth the enrichment and dignity that justify it to finite ends. "By experience," says Dr. Santayana, "I understand a fund of wisdom gathered by living. . . . I think it mere mockery to use the word experience for what is not learning or gathering knowledge of facts. . . . Experience presupposes intent and intelligence, and it also implies . . . a natural world in which it is possible to learn to live better by practising the arts."

In this falling back of humanity upon animal faith, upon experience and its lessons, it is clear that literature has a function which cannot be fulfilled by abolishing substance, by repudiating meaning and avoiding communication, by dealing with experience at one remove or treating the individual as if he alone experienced in an isolated world. The contemplation of art in its relation to life leads directly to a contemplation of life in the living. If experience is to be the substance of art, then experience itself must be enriched; if experience is trusted to furnish meanings, then primary experience itself must be improved; and if the most imperative extension of experience, in the event that civilization shall be saved, is social integration, then experience must be communicated.

Enrichment of man's experience is a function of the fine arts. There is no doubt that the resources of mankind in this direction are, if not infinite, at least immeasurable. As I have said, our common culture is largely literary. The very obvious growth of appreciation of music, painting, sculpture, indicates that these other arts will share to a far greater extent in the culture of the future than in that of the past. Literature is peculiarly fitted to act as mediator between the other arts and man's apprehension of them, to introduce them more widely into his experience. For literature remains the art most immediate to his rational faculty: man is a thinking animal, and it is part of human nature to demand meaning.

It is not the mission of literature to impose its special form of intellectual imagination on the other fine arts—we have had too much literary painting, sculpture, and music. The literary imagination differs essentially from the pictorial, the sculptural, the musical imagination. To these latter, material is valuable in proportion as it lends itself to translation into the language peculiar to each. While it is certain that literature will constantly gain aesthetic values through its penetration by the other fine arts, examples of which come to mind in recent poetry and fiction, this is far from saying that literature, in subordinating its material to a technique borrowed from another art, can find justification in limiting itself to plastic values, or sound, or color—in seeking to become music or painting.

Enrichment of experience by art may take place in a declining civilization, in a dying world. The colors of autumn are more brilliant than those of spring; there is a fascination in decay. But such enrichment is temporary and individual, for it is in contradiction to one of the most masterful impulses of animal faith, that of survival. Experience for most men can never be satisfying except as it moves toward the realm of further experience, through more harmonious relations with environment. This again is the function of art, the organization of experience toward the improvement of man's lot on earth. Throughout the quotations which I have drawn so copiously from Dr. Santayana, you may have noticed the undercurrent of belief in improvement. He speaks of "the waxing faith of an animal living in a world which he can observe and *sometimes remodel.*" Particularly does he speak of living better by practicing the arts, and of using the arts "to substitute the dominion of man over circumstances for the dominion of chance." This is strikingly similar doctrine to that of certain philosophers with whom Dr. Santayana finds himself frequently in disagreement—the Pragmatists. "All art," says Professor Dewey, "is a process of making the world a different place in which to live." "The history of human experience is a history of the development of the arts." And again, "Art is the sole alternative to luck."

Mr. Havelock Ellis is more specific in attributing social force to the aesthetic impulse. Not only is art in his conception "the sum of the active energies of mankind," "the moulding force of every culture that man has produced"—more than this, art sharpens experience by bringing us into contact with "the reality of things behind the veil of convention which is the result of simplification and classification for intellectual purposes." And what is greatly to the purpose of the world today, it trains the aesthetic instinct to counteract the possessive, for the aesthetic instinct gives us "the power of enjoying things without being reduced to the need of possessing them."

In promoting this social function of art, literature again has a primary responsibility. Indeed Ruskin when he began to teach art at Oxford found it his first work to set about the creation of a society in which a worthy art was possible, and his tool was literature. Nor can it be doubted that literature will profit by contribution to the value of life through social integration. If experience is the proper subject of literature, the enrichment and improvement of experience will be of direct benefit to literature, which will move to its own fulfillment as activity by bringing along with itself a release of further activities.

I am not speaking especially of the literature directed primarily to social criticism, though I am far from admitting such direction as a shortcoming and a reproach. In the late nineteenth century that impulse was one of the strongest motives behind the literature characteristic of the period represented by Carlyle and Mill, by Ruskin and Matthew Arnold, by Disraeli, Dickens, Kingsley, and Mrs. Gaskell among the novelists, by Mrs. Browning, Swinburne, and Morris among the poets. It is the notable distinction of the Edwardians, of Mr. Wells, Mr. Galsworthy, Mr. Shaw, to have revived that tradition. I do not feel that literature has in the long run lost literary values by the effort, consciously put forward, to spread a sense of these values and of other values of living more widely among men. I believe on the contrary that it has gained in robustness and energy by the possession of purpose. I think it a hopeful sign for literature and for society on which literature depends that the younger literary people in the United States are becoming a social force.

As the line is drawn more sharply between the writers who have a social point of view and those who aspire to a purity of aesthetic which excludes not only purpose but meaning, I am forced to ask myself whether, in event of the social changes which it is granted on all sides are imminent and necessary, the future historian of literature will not consider the former group of more importance than the latter. I am speaking, however, not specifically of novels of purpose or poems of social protest, but of literature in general, which accepts the reality of the world of human beings and experience and knowledge. To literature in this sense the primary function will be communication. And "communication" as Professor Dewey reminds us, "is an immediate enhancement of life enjoyed for its own sake"; and again, "shared experience is the greatest of human goods."

That communication is fundamental in the enjoyment and improvement of our lot in this world, which we perceive and live in by virtue of our common animal faith, who will deny?

At present for most of us the faculty of communication does not extend even to our fellow men beyond the bounds of our race, our nationality, especially our class. Disraeli, in his famous and terrible arraignment of class division, points out that the two nations over which

Queen Victoria ruled, the rich and the poor, are as ignorant of each other's habits, thoughts, and feelings as if they were inhabitants of different planets; that there is no intercourse between them, and hence, no sympathy or understanding. Class separation is the wound in the side of civilization from which the lifeblood of humanity is ebbing. Readers of Tolstoy's *What to Do?* will recall his statement of the difficulty he found in meeting men of another class than his own, how "on looking at our lives, or at the lives of rich people, from without, I saw that all that is considered as the *summum bonum* of these lives consists in being separated as much as possible from the poor, or is in some way or other connected with this desired separation."

That art may be one of the forces which keep classes apart is unhappily true. As Morris declares in one of his lectures: "Until something or other is done to give all men some pleasure for the eyes and rest for the mind in the aspect of their own and their neighbors' houses, until the contrast is less disgraceful between the fields where beasts live and the streets where men live, I suppose that the practice of the arts must be mainly kept in the hands of a few highly cultivated men, who can go often to beautiful places, whose education enables them, in the contemplation of the past glories of the world, to shut out from their view the everyday squalors that the most of men move in."

But that art may be the means of bridging the gap between classes, nations, and even races, is the revelation of the period after the World War. In Russia, Germany, Austria, Great Britain, there is today a proletarian art which shows its potency in the breaking down of class barriers, in bringing people of different backgrounds to speak the same language, to share experience on a common basis. One of the most notable examples of a shared experience and a common understanding among nations is seen in the literature of the war. From every country there comes the same cry of disgust and horror, from Barbusse, Rolland, Latzko, Remarque, Arnold Zweig, Markowitz, Montague, Mary Lee, and many more. The Honorable Frank Kellogg has not outlawed war; it may be that literature has done it. Again, in such progress as we have made toward bringing together two races in this country, it is not the material advance of the colored that has counted most, but their art. I am not prepared to defend Tolstoy's definition of art, with all its rigorous exclusions; but I submit that in the present crisis of humanity his emphasis is right when he says: "Art is not, as the metaphysicians say, the manifestation of some mysterious Idea of beauty, or God; it is not, as the aesthetical physiologists say, a game in which man lets off his excess of stored up energy; it is not the expression of man's emotions by external signs; it is not the production of pleasing objects; and above all, it is not pleasure; but it is a means of union among men, joining them together in the same feelings, and indispensable for the life and progress toward well being of individuals and of humanity."

The material of literature is derived from humanity and human experience. It returns, revitalized and reinterpreted, to be received again by human beings and to become once more a part of their experience. In this process the artist is mediator and agent. Surely neither artist nor art can profit by being divorced from the great community which is for both, and in a double sense, the source of life.

Literature in an Age of Science

Max Eastman

I think I would better begin this speech by telling you that I won't keep you waiting long. I know how you feel. There are probably several dozen of you poets counting on these prizes to enable you to pay your bills and get out of town. That was how I managed to leave college. Moreover, one of the prizes that I was particularly counting on, and that I won, and that belonged to me in all right and justice, fell into the hands of some warped and prejudiced and crooked-minded judges, congenitally incapable of delivering a just and honest decision about anything, and instead of giving me the prize, they divided it between me and another man who had no right to it whatever, except that he worked harder than I did, and hadn't run up any bills, and didn't need it, and moreover wouldn't even lend me his half after he got it. That mistake of those judges gave me a bad start in life financially that I've never got over. And so when a majority of you poets go out of here, as you are inevitably bound to do, saying that I have no taste whatever in poetry and am constitutionally blind, deaf, dumb, dishonest, and reactionary, please remember that I agree with you. I think all prize judges are like that. And I realize now that if I had any sense I would never have come up here after judging your poetry, and submitted my own feeble oratory to your withering criticisms. It was, to tell you the truth, an act of weakness. I could not resist the temptation of the peculiar opportunity afforded by this occasion for making a few timely and appropriate remarks about my own books.

My latest book is called *The Literary Mind: Its Place in an Age of Science*. And it starts off by drawing a few teeth out of the ogre that is called up in the minds of a good many people by that word *science*. If you have a brain and a certain amount of energy and make a systematic effort to find out what is the cause of any event, or what are the properties of any object, and your effort is successful, why that is science. It does not matter whether you are moved by pure curiosity or by some purposive interest. It does not matter how important or how trivial the problem is in which you are interested. If you sincerely want to know, and go at it persistently and systematically, and with the only means available—observation, study, reasoning, and above all experiment—that is science. Science is merely the mature and disciplined use of the mind and the stores of human knowledge about any problem.

This first chapter about science is very important. Very important that it should stand first. If you carry into my book any of those old-fashioned, credulous, fairy-story views of what science is that were so popular with people who thought they were hardheaded thirty or forty years ago, you will go utterly astray on my argument. That is what a lot of my extremely learned critics have done—they have read only the title of this first chapter, "The March of Science." "Oh, yes, the 'march of science,'" they have said—"he belongs to the period of Spencer, Huxley, Haeckel. He still believes that the world is a machine, that all knowledge is quantitative, and that an absolute determinism prevails throughout nature which makes human choice a delusion. He is doubtless also a Behaviorist." If these extremely learned critics had happened to read my chapter on the march of science they would have found all those opinions listed as credulous metaphysical fabrications which science has left behind on its march. They would have found Behaviorism listed there. These views are not scientific findings but wild jumps at emotional conclusions. And jumping at conclusions—whether you take science for your springboard or whether you take religion or poetry—is not science. It is the opposite thing. Science consists only one-half in knowing what is known: the other half is never pretending to know what is not.

Now this attitude of skeptical and disciplined experimental inquiry, born, you might say, about the middle of the sixteenth century, has for four hundred years been steadily advancing into one department of human experience after another. In the sixteenth century, astronomy and geography and physiology; in the seventeenth, physics and chemistry, optics and mechanics; in the eighteenth, economics and political science; in the nineteenth, biology and sociology; in the twentieth, psychology. This is a mere rough suggestion of the general course of development. But you see how this organized and mature technique for getting reliable knowledge has very gradually spread over the whole field previously occupied by emotional guesswork and literary eloquence. And the process is only just now, in our own days, complete. I do not mean that scientific knowledge is complete, but only that scientific knowledge exists, and is distinguishable from amateur opinion in every field. You may say that with the development of a psychology and sociology of religion this four-hundred-year triumphant march of science came to an end. Science has now pitched its camp in every field in which men have opinions.

I will not try to convince you that this is the most momentous change that is to be found in the whole history of human culture, although I think it is. I only ask you to believe that this steady, relentless, step-by-step invasion by verified knowledge of all the fields heretofore occupied by literary eloquence is the most momentous thing that has happened or could possibly happen in the history of literature. The whole literature of our modern epoch ought to be read and studied primarily, although not of course exclusively, in the light of its relation to this change. Particularly the literature of these recent years, when, with the development of psychology and sociology, science has overthrown the last bulwark and invested the last field that was still held sacred to the poet and critic—the field which used to be described as "humane letters" or "the humanities."

In the next section of my book, therefore, I take up one or two of the outstanding literary schools or tendencies of our day and I show that in their main outlines they are either defense reactions, or reactions of retreat before this invasion by verified knowledge of the fields which used to be occupied by literary eloquence.

The efforts of T. S. Eliot and his very British and very priggish friends, for instance, to revive a regime of what they call "intellect" in literary criticism—their attempt to go back, as they say, to seventeenth- and eighteenth-century tradition—is a mere maneuver in the defensive warfare of literary truth against science. It may seem strange to you that people should be resisting science in the name of intellect, but that is because you belong to an age which has so completely embraced the viewpoint of science as to have forgotten the meaning of the word "intellect," or come to look upon intellect as a slightly comic affliction. On the lips of Emerson and Matthew Arnold the word *intellect* was consciously opposed to the exercise of the mind in experiment and investigation. It meant literary as opposed to scientific thinking. T. S. Eliot is trying to head off the advancing prestige of science by making literary truth look very cool and rational and unemotional and extremely scholarly and high-brow. He is yearning back to the seventeenth and eighteenth centuries, in which literary intellectuals still had a social prestige higher than men of science.

The New Humanists, on the other hand, are trying to head off the march of science with a moralistic propaganda. At least they were a year or so ago. They seem to have given up the sponge for the time being. It is a notable and surprising fact, at least, that their central fortress and arsenal and mighty organ of propaganda, the *Bookman,* has never yet printed a word of reply to the attack on them contained in my book. Of course these literary battles are not carried out under the Marquis of Queensberry rules, but I have already counted nine issues of the *Bookman* since I landed my blow, and I maintain that if I count ten it is a knockout.

Here, at any rate, is what I said: I said that with all the expert writers writing about it, and the expert teachers teaching it, it remained an insoluble riddle and mystery just what the New Humanism really is. The New Humanists believe in some eighteen different principles or points of view, all held together by the fact that the New Humanists believe them, but not in any other way that anybody has ever been able to discover. I asserted that I had discovered what it was that held these eighteen hetero-geneous things together, and that I could prove it. Every single one of them was either a direct defense of literary eloquence as against scientific knowledge, or else a strategic position which enabled them to direct some sort of cross-fire on the advance of scientific method into the field heretofore dominated by literary eloquence.

The humanists pretend, for example, to be very much interested in something which they call the "inner life." In the name of the "inner life" they attack psychology, which is a serious attempt to find out about the inner life. In the name of Socrates, who adopted for his own the motto written over the temple of the Oracle at Delphi, "Know thyself," they attack Sigmund Freud, who—with all his mythological propensities—has perhaps contributed more than any one man since Aristotle to the knowledge of the self. And this "inner life" about which our humanists make such a fuss that you might think they would be ready to abandon father and mother and go sell all they have and give to the poor, and turn their backs on all the advantages of place and position and property in this exterior world, in order to achieve it—this "inner life" turns out to be nothing more illuminating and, for that matter, nothing more "inner" than decorum, or the art of behaving like a gentleman or a lady with a proper amount of money in the bank. Those humanists are not interested in morals, and they are not interested in the inner life—not any more than the rest of us. What they are interested in, like so many of the human beings around them, is their own profession. They are defending the right of literary critics and essay writers to talk loosely and yet be taken seriously in a scientific age. They are defending the profession of humane or polite letters against the inexorable advance of a more scientific study of man.

After discussing these critics and professors of literature who are fighting science in the name of "intellect" and "morals," I take up those poets and creative writers whom we group under the general term *modernist*. Their literary character also is fundamentally determined by this advance of scientific knowledge. But instead of a defense reaction, theirs is an attitude of retreat. Instead of opposing the advance of science into the field of literary truth, they have abandoned the field. They have ceased even to pretend to make any serious comment upon life, or give us any important thought, counsel, or direction as to its conduct. They have taken refuge in what I call a "cult of unintelligibility" on the one hand, and in a tendency toward "pure poetry" on the other. Under these two chapter headings, "The Cult of Unintelligibility" and the "Tendency toward Pure Poetry," I have summarized the outstanding features of those modern kinds of writing which are to be found so often upon people's drawing-room tables, but so rarely in anybody's hand when he reads.

If you pick up a book by Wallace Stevens, or E. E. Cummings, or Hart Crane, or James Joyce, or Gertrude Stein, or Edith Sitwell, or T. S. Eliot as a poet, and read a page innocently, the first feeling you will have is that the author isn't telling you anything. It may seem that he isn't telling you anything because he doesn't know anything. Or it may seem that he knows something, but he won't tell. In any case he is uncommunicative. He is unfriendly. He seems to be playing by himself, and offering you, somewhat incidentally, the opportunity to look on.

Here for instance is a book of poems by Wallace Stevens. Let us open it at random and read a poem. I am not really opening this book at random—I have it trained so it will open where I want it to. I have read this poem aloud forty-four times, and no one has ever been able to tell me what it is, or what it has to do with. Let's see if you can do any better.

Jasmine's Beautiful Thoughts underneath the Willow

My titillations have no foot-notes
And their memorials are the phrases
Of idiosyncratic music.

The love that will not be transported
In an old, frizzled, flambeaued manner,
But muses on its eccentricity,

Is like a vivid apprehension
Of bliss beyond the mutes of plaster,
Or paper souvenirs of rapture,

Of bliss submerged beneath appearance,
In an interior ocean's rocking
Of long, capricious fugues and chorals.

Did you get it? It's a simple poem, you see, and from a distance beautiful, but if you come up close and try to make friends, it won't confide in you. It won't tell you candidly and exactly what it's thinking about. I have read Wallace Stevens's book through, and with the exception of one or two brief moments I do not feel that I have ever been in communication with him.

And that is typical. I think you might say that the dominant tendency of the advanced schools of poetry—and of art in general—for the last twenty years has been to decrease the range, the volume, and the definiteness of communication. I should put that simple statement, which has the advantage of really meaning something, in place of about one-half the misty "literarious" talk of the poets and poet-critics of the modern movement. They are not abandoning romanticism, or going back to an eighteenth- or seventeenth-century tradition. If the words *romantic* and *classic* mean anything at all, which is subject to question, then the height of the romantic movement is the idea of these modernist poets that they are classical.

Let me read you something from T. S. Eliot's famous poem *Ash Wednesday*. This is said to be a religious poem, and it was first published in a tiny, thin volume containing only nineteen pages of ten-point Caslon type, and which nevertheless sold for five dollars—a point relevant to my argument that this modern poetry is distinguished by a decrease not only in the volume and definiteness, but also in the range, of communication. Let me give you a small sample of this expensive religion— about sixty-five cents' worth, as I figure it. And do not forget that T. S. Eliot considers himself a neoclassical poet. He thinks that he represents a return to the manners in poetry established by John Dryden, who said "The first object of a writer is to be understood."

If the lost word is lost, if the spent word is spent
If the unheard, unspoken
Word is unspoken, unheard;
Still is the unspoken word, the Word unheard,
The Word without a word, the Word within
The world and for the world;
And the light shone in darkness and
Against the Word the unstilled world still whirled
About the centre of the silent Word.
    O my people, what have I done unto thee.

Now I don't say that that is weak, unctuous, and invertebrate poetry, a mere oily puddle of emotional noises, although that is what I
think about it. I merely say that anything farther away from John Dryden, or what is generally called classical in poetry, or the kind of poetry
that prevailed in the later seventeenth and eighteenth centuries, would be
impossible to find. And I say that the number of people to whom Eliot is
going to communicate this religion at five dollars a shot is very small.
These poets are not returning to an eighteenth-century tradition. They
are not returning to any tradition at all. They are not going anywhere.
They are withdrawing into themselves. They are communicating with
fewer readers; they are communicating less; and what they communicate
is less definitely determined.

The cult of unintelligibility might be described as a tendency toward
privacy in an art condemned by its very nature to employ as materials the
means of social communion. However, this cult of unintelligibility is
only a part, and probably a transient part, of the modern tendency in
general. Indeed, some people tell me it has all but gone out of fashion. It
might be described in medical terms as an "exaggerated reaction" to the
march of science. "All right, if you won't let us be fountains of truth any
longer"—the poets say—"why, we won't communicate at all. We'll
have nothing to do with you. To hell with the reader." And so they have
climbed way upstairs and are sitting there in the middle of the nursery
floor playing with words and ideas all by themselves, with an egotistical
pout on their lips. The cult of unintelligibility is a sulk on the part of
poetry brought on by the greater attention which is being paid to science
in these modern days.

The other aspect of the modern tendency is more serious, more
long-lasting, a more adult and inevitable reaction to the march of science.
That is the tendency toward pure poetry. By pure poetry I do not mean
anything mystical or queer. I merely mean poetry that is free from the

motive to persuade, or educate, or give advice, or point a moral, or convey knowledge, or "criticize life," poetry which is solely concerned, as music generally is, to communicate an experience. The most important thing in my book is an essay right in the heart of it entitled "What Poetry Is." In that essay I show that poetry differs from prosaic language in that it dwells upon the qualities of the things it mentions more than is necessary for practical understanding. And pure poetry is poetry that mentions things solely in order to convey qualities, and not in order to interpret them or tell you anything *about* them.

I have explained this in that chapter in a psychological manner. In another I have approached it historically, and I want to repeat my historical outline—to make you realize what poetry is in its own nature by imagining it originating, as it doubtless most often did, in the incantations of medicine men and magicians. Names are supposed by all primitive people to have an occult power over the thing named. They have the power of evoking the being of that thing and compelling its obedience. But in order to do that they have to be just the right names. And the medicine man or shaman or poet-magician would get the idea spread abroad that he knew the right names of things. He could bring rain, for instance, by standing out under the sky and saying the right words. That is a very wonderful and exciting way to use words, you see, and yet totally unrelated to science or everyday practical communication. The ordinary way to use words when the garden gets dry is to say, "Well, don't you think we'd better find the old sprinkling pot?" And the scientific way is only a little more elaborate: "Let's build a dam and dig ditches and irrigate the whole valley." But the sorcerer, the poet, this wonderful and deep-eyed man who is in touch with the heart of reality through language, gets out there in the middle of the valley, and spreads out his hands, and says words which do not mean a thing. And then the rain falls. Or else it doesn't! In any case it ought to. And among all primitive peoples, all human tribes who have not yet passed under the affliction of statistics, the opinion is that if the poet has got the right words, the rain does actually fall.

That was undoubtedly the principal mother lode from which poetry arose. But that is not what poetry is. In the mind of that wonderful-tongued magician, naming the raindrops out of the sky, there was an actual vision of the drops he named. His words did have the power to evoke the being of things—in his imagination. For him, moreover, the line between imagination and sense was not too clearly drawn. He was not entirely a sorcerer, but something also of a child. And he had an *interest* in raindrops, an absurd and altogether important interest in raindrops, which had nothing whatever to do with agriculture or the problem of watering the soil. He had a like interest in the sky. It is not too much to say, in view of what we know about his successors, that he sometimes loved the sky, in a mournful way, even when it failed to rain. He loved, whether with joy or sorrow, the whole business of "being" in this world. And, like all people who love a thing, he enjoyed calling it pet names. Set free by his profession from any other very steady occupation, he developed a great habit of sitting around thinking up pet names for things—the names that would most exactly and vividly evoke them into his imagination. That was how he kept awake when he was not working. And that was pure poetry.

It is to this original and pure form of poetry that the modernists, with all their sophistication and their city things, are tending back. They are abandoning practical meanings, themes, preachments, all that stuff of education and edification that led Wordsworth to describe poetry as "the breath and finer spirit of all knowledge," and Matthew Arnold actually to define it as a "criticism of life." In place of a criticism, these poets offer us in each poem a moment of life, a rare, perfect, beautiful, ugly, grotesque, or intense moment, and nothing more. They offer us awakening—they even offer to keep us awake for the few moments while we are reading their poem—and that seems to them enough. Poetry is a thing like music or the morning, which stands in no need of ulterior justification for those who are sensitive enough to perceive it.

And the reason why they are doing this is that their former function, the function of interpreting things and criticizing life, has been taken away from them by the advance of scientific knowledge. To put it crudely, the reason the poets don't teach us anything is that they have become aware of the fact that *as poets* they don't know anything. The business of knowing things has become a highly specialized technical function in the hands of scientific experts. Where our fathers consulted Browning and Tennyson for actual guidance in the moral and social crises of their lives, we consult the psychoanalyst or the expert in home economics or the theory of business cycles or the class struggle for the seizure of power. That is what is happening. Just as in the seventeenth century Galileo and Isaac Newton and Robert Boyle were driving poetry out of the books which interpret physical and chemical experience and show us how to deal with external nature, so in our day the physiological psychologists, and the Freuds and

the Marxian Lenins—to mention only a few—are driving poetry out of
the books which interpret mental and social phenomena, and show us
how to deal with man.

I think it is very important that this fact should be clearly faced, and
that is why I express it in these crude terms. Poets *as poets* don't know
anything. Men of letters *as men of letters* are not to be looked to any longer
for reliable knowledge in any field. Such statements as this which I am
going to read from John Masefield, the poet laureate of England, are the
feebly extravagant gestures of a dying belief: "There is another way to
truth: by the minute examination of facts. That is the way of the scientist:
a hard and noble and thankless way. It is not the way of a great poet, the
rare unreasonable, who comes once in ten generations. He apprehends
truth by power: the truth which he apprehends cannot be denied save by
greater power, and there is no greater power."

And such statements as this from Archibald MacLeish—politically
backward enough to be our own poet laureate!—are equally moribund
to any man of clear intelligence with the courage to face facts: "The
contemporary critic who sees nothing significant in a poem unless it uses
the word dynamo, waves a submachine gun and draws its symbols from
New York morning papers of even date will eventually die—as the
esthetical critics and the moral critics died before him. And his grand-
children will find in 'Anabase,' with its biblical and Asian images, and in
'The Waste Land,' with its Eastern references and its Elizabethan phrase,
the understandable answer to questions neither Mr. Keynes nor Major
Douglas nor the whole literature of Marxism will be able to resolve."

That is not the way to defend poetry, or assert its future possibilities
or independent rights. That is the way to destroy everybody's respect for
it. *The Waste Land* does not give an understandable answer to any question, and every man of clear sense knows it, and will know it from now
on. There is no use trying to defend poetry with this old, elevated jabber
about truth come at by Power with a capital *P* any longer. There is no
use. The facts to the contrary are too obvious.

I am as much concerned to defend poetry, and assert its independent
rights and future possibilities, as these poets are. For that very reason I
insist that poetry—whatever it may at times be used for—be defined as a
communication of experience, and that we fearlessly acknowledge that
the progress of intellectual culture has demanded a steadily growing
separation of the function of communicating experience from that of
communicating knowledge about experience. The limit to which this

separation will go is defined only by the limit to which exact and reliable knowledge will go. And the fundamental way to defend poetry, even in the face of an infinite progress of science, is to point out that in devoting yourself to the cultivation and communication of knowledge *about* life, you fail to cultivate and communicate life. The scientist is as much lamed and crippled by the division as the poet. Poetry is not knowledge—no, but it is life. Is it so small a thing to live? And to live vividly? And to live *together?* That is what poetry is—living vividly and living together.

This point of view always makes my Marxian friends a little angry. They think I am deserting the banner because I do not affirm that all literature and all art is a mere reflection of that economic evolution which lies at the basis of social life, and point out that this tendency toward pure poetry and this cult of unintelligibility that I have been discussing are reflections of the approaching breakdown of the bourgeois-capitalistic regime. I cannot repeat these dogmas of the philosophy of dialectic materialism, because I know that they are not true. I have explained at length, in a book which you never heard of, that Marx confuses the conditions which make a thing possible with the causes which determine its nature. He does this because, being a German romantic philosopher, he thinks he has to prove communism is historically inevitable, and not merely that it is possible—which is all that any scientific revolutionist needs to know. It is true that we could not have had the literature we have if there had not been a certain development of the technique of industry. But that is not saying that the developing technique of industry determines what kind of literature we have.

However, I am not going into that philosophical question just now. Suffice it to say that I have taken upon myself the task of keeping the philosophy of dialectic materialism out of America while helping to bring the Marxian contribution to science in. This subject of the relation of art and literature to social movements in general, and more particularly to the Communist dictatorship in Russia, will be treated in my next two books.

Meanwhile, I will say only this—that it is just as true in the sphere of social engineering as it is anywhere else that science, or the communication of knowledge about experience—knowledge of its relations—is separating itself from poetry or the communication of experience itself. And it is because their philosophy does not recognize this fundamental and inevitable division of labor that the Bolsheviks under Stalin have found it so easy, and made it appear so noble, to strangle poetic literature in Russian.

When this fundamental division is recognized—when poetry, I mean, is defined as a communication of experience and it is recognized that with the advance of human culture this function becomes increasingly set apart from science, or the communication of knowledge about experience—then, of course, you have to make some qualifying statements. And here my friend Professor Boynton, of the University of Chicago—and your friend, too, undoubtedly—who is one of my most kindly and understanding critics, succeeds in poking a little fun at me. He calls me the "Angel with the Flaming Sword," and says that after I have driven the poets and literary professors out of the Paradise of truth-seeking with what seems a terrible wrath and ruthlessness, I relent in a most gentle manner—in fact in the manner of an anticlimax—and let them back in on certain conditions. And that is quite true, and I am very proud of it. There is in fact only one virtue, only one genuine old-fashioned virtue, that I have ever laid claim to, and that is that I am really interested in finding out and stating what I believe to be true, and I am more interested in that than I am in building up an imposing argument.

I could have made quite a sensation, perhaps, if I had concluded this book by saying that everything except pure poetry is now dead, and the professors of literature can go and shoot themselves. Instead of that I turned round and pointed out some obvious facts which qualify the increasing separation of poetry from science, and make the future of poetic literature and of teaching literature a gorgeously exciting prospect.

One of these obvious facts is that the same single individual, if he is big enough, can be both scientific and poetic. That is, he can learn the scientific point of view, understand the validity of science, lay up a certain store of information, and so, without ceasing to be a poet, win back, or retain, his old place in the forefront of human culture. For that purpose, however, he will have to be very big.

Another of these obvious facts is that in certain fields in which scientific knowledge is not very specialized or mathematical, truths *ascertained* by the methods of science can be *expressed* in poetic language. I cannot go into all the ways in which this can be worked out, but for one thing a general statement can often be conveyed to your mind—and conveyed with weight and living warmth of color and convincingness—by a particular instance or concrete example. That is the most simple and natural reunion of poetry with science, and probably the most simple instance of that is the significant story. Telling tales that teach or convey an attitude of wisdom essentially based upon science—tales of which Goethe's *Faust* is an example—will, I think, be one of the prevailing forms in which *Dichtung* and *Wahrheit* will be united in the future.

Another of these obvious facts is that verified knowledge, although it now exists in every field, is nevertheless extremely limited in content. There is still a vast kingdom of ignorance in which the man of letters has as good a right to make imposing guesses as the man of science. Indeed he has a better right, for he will not be misusing the authority of science, which derives from an opposite procedure, in order to give more weight than they deserve to emotional guesses. Moreover, these literary guesses stand a chance of planting some seed of a new hypothesis, which will be nourished by men of science and bear fruit of verified knowledge.

In short, the division of labor I am talking about can never be absolute, either among people—as to say, these men are wholly poets, these wholly scientists—or among books—these books are poetic literature and contain no knowledge about experience, these are science and contain no communication of experience to the imagination. But nevertheless it is a fact that these two *functions* are separating, and their separation is an inevitable accompaniment of the progress of civilized culture. It inheres in the very nature of experience and of our knowledge about it. The important thing is to recognize the fact. Literature, and also the teaching of literature, have a great future. But the great future of literature is in the hands of those who understand what has happened and accept it, not of those whose writings are a blind reaction to it, whether of resistance or of flight.

Literature versus Opinion

Henry Hazlitt

The will of the late Avery Hopwood expressed the desire that the literary prizes for which he so generously provided should be especially used to encourage "the new, the unusual, and the radical." It is interesting to recall that the will was made in 1922. It was about that time that those whom we now think of as the older generation in American literature, symbolized by such figures as Theodore Dreiser and H. L. Mencken, emerged into real prominence. Just before that period the waters of literary discussion had been relatively stagnant. Mencken and his disciples, deserting the genteel tradition, began calling their opponents harsh and extraordinary names, and the attention of youth was arrested. A fight is always exciting: moreover, if literature was something worth fighting over, it might be worth looking into.

That particular battle has not continued, but a series of battles have followed each other with only the briefest intermission. Meanwhile the issues have altered and even the sides have changed, so that many of those who were previously on the left now somehow find themselves on the right. The battle lines, moreover, have become so widely extended that it is no longer clearly possible to tell the literary front from the political front. Whatever one may say of the present era, it is not stagnant. One result, at least, is that "the new, the unusual, and the radical" are today much more certain of a hearing than they were thirteen years ago. But another result, less happy, is that the growing bitterness of the battle, and the extent and depth of the issues involved, have placed the most serious obstacles in the way of a sober objective evaluation of the current literary product, whether new, unusual, radical, or otherwise.

The tone of political discussion in the last few years has been increasingly acrimonious. It is not merely that arguments have been growing more passionate and less reasonable; the extremists on both sides have been losing faith in the efficacy of reason itself. One should not attempt to persuade one's opponent; one should suppress or imprison or execute him. This is the philosophy of the rulers of Germany and of Russia; it is

shared only to a lesser degree by other rulers who have not yet consoli-
dated their power, and it has influenced the tone of political discussion
even in the great democracies. It has spread to the field of letters, and it
emerges there as the theory that no such thing as an objective judgment
of literary work is possible: there are only proletarian, bourgeois, or
Fascist judgments; and writers are praised or denounced in accordance
with their political or economic sympathies and doctrines.

Now I cannot believe that this attitude is either a salutary or a lasting
one. It is, of course, the most natural thing in the world to praise those
who are on our side of any question and to denounce those who are
against us. Some of the so-called Marxist critics have built up elaborate
rationalizations of the process. But the critic of literature who yields to
this temptation, whatever good he thinks he may thereby be doing for
his particular "cause," betrays his function as a literary critic.

The great critics of the past have always recognized this fact, and
have been great critics partly through that very recognition. One of the
most interesting examples is William Hazlitt. Now few writers have ever
had more violent and uncompromising political opinions than he had.
He was an ardent and tireless defender of the French Revolution; the
uncompromising vehemence of his Jacobinism, indeed, led him into
constant quarrels with most of his friends. But these differences of opinion, or even violent personal antagonisms, seldom perverted his literary
judgments. No better illustration of his sanity and insight in this respect
appears than in his numerous discussions of Edmund Burke. Here was a
writer who had thrown the whole weight of his eloquence and passion
against that French Revolution which to Hazlitt was one of the great
historic landmarks in the eternal struggle for human liberty. Yet Hazlitt
almost never wrote of Burke except in terms of the most ungrudging
praise. In an essay devoted to him in 1807, Hazlitt tells us that Burke
"enriched every subject to which he applied himself"; that "he was the
most eloquent man of his time, and his wisdom was greater than his
eloquence." "It has always been with me," he added, "a test of the sense
and candor of any one belonging to the opposite party, whether he
allowed Burke to be a great man." Hazlitt apparently had never met
more than one or two political opponents who would make this concession; and he set their reluctance down either to the fact that party feelings
ran too high to admit of any real candor, or to "an essential vulgarity in
their habits of thinking."

Hazlitt's praise seems to have been misunderstood. In a later print-

ing of his "Character of Mr. Burke" he inserted the following explana-
tory footnote: "This character was written in a fit of extravagant candor,
at a time when I thought I could do justice, or more than justice, to an
enemy, without betraying a cause." But the truth was that Hazlitt was
always subject to such "fits of extravagant candor," and seldom had fits
of any other kind. In his essay "On Reading Old Books," he tells us that
when he first encountered Burke's writings he exclaimed to himself:
"This is true eloquence: this is a man pouring out his mind on paper."
"The most perfect prose style, the most powerful, the most dazzling, the
most daring . . . was Burke's." It was "forked and playful as the lightning, crested like the serpent." And here Hazlitt wrote the sentences that
may serve as a sort of text for the present lecture: "I did not care for his
doctrines. I was then, and am still, proof against their contagion; but I
admired the author, and was considered as not a very staunch partisan of
the opposite side, though I thought myself that an abstract proposition
was one thing—a masterly transition, a brilliant metaphor, another. I
conceived too that he might be wrong in his main argument, and yet
deliver fifty truths in arriving at a false conclusion."

Let us look at some of the implications of this attitude, and see to
what extent we can apply them to the literary controversies of our own
day. One of the favorite slogans of the Marxist critics is that "art is a
weapon." We need not ask, at the moment, in what sense or to what
extent this is true. But I should like to point out that even if art *is* a
weapon, and even if we grant also that we must all line up on one of two
sides in wielding it, it is still possible for us to judge it objectively.
Machine guns are certainly weapons, and we should prefer to have them
all on our side, but a sensible man's preferences have nothing to do with
his realistic observation. Allied military commentators during the World
War were able to say quite objectively whether the Germans had better
or worse rifles, artillery, airplanes, or gases than they had, or whether
they made more or less effective use of them. An objectivity that is
possible in a war of bullets ought surely to be possible in a war of
pamphlets. A Communist critic ought to be able to discuss the ability of
a bourgeois or a Fascist writer with the same cool detachment with
which the high command in a war must estimate the ability of the
opposing leadership. Wars are not won by dismissing all the enemy's
generals as scoundrels and fools.

Here, then, is one form of critical objectivity of which even the most
embittered class-conscious critics should recognize the need. We must

correctly estimate the skill and ability of our opponents. This correct estimate is one of the primary functions of literary criticism. The important question for such criticism is not which side a writer is on, but how able he is in the service of that side. For estimating him it is not the bald conclusion at which he arrives that counts, but the mental process by which he arrives at it. It is not what he nakedly contends; it is the persuasiveness with which he states it. There are dull minds on both sides of every great controversy—minds that deal only in stereotypes and clichés, minds that can only repeat, parrot-like, the phrases the leaders have coined. But there are also brilliant minds on both sides of every great controversy; it is these that develop the new arguments and put them forward with the greatest force. The cardinal business of literary criticism in such a situation is not to declare that side A is right and side B wrong; it is to distinguish, on whichever side, the brilliant and original writers from the empty ones.

In brief, it is the paradoxical function of the literary critic, as critic, to detach himself as completely as possible from the actual merits of the controversies of his own time. In appraising the comparative qualities of individual writers, he must judge not the controversies but the controversialists. He will sometimes be obliged to say, at least to himself: "What A writes is perfectly sound, and I agree with it passionately; but I am obliged to add that it will be completely forgotten ten years from now." At other times he will have to say: "This man B is utterly wrong; his perversity sometimes infuriates me; but, damn it all, there is some quality in what he says that leads me to fear that a century from now it will still be quoted." Few people could be more thoroughly wrong-headed, according to most of our current standards, than Dr. Johnson, but his aphorisms live because they have this quality. As for the philosopher, there is almost as much disagreement today as in his own lifetime whether Berkeley, or Kant, or Hegel was right or wrong. It is not being right or wrong that counts: it is having an interesting and original and powerful mind.

But this brings us to a further question. There is a certain ambiguity about the phrase "being right." For there are several kinds of truth, and the truth of literature is not necessarily the truth of science. We recognize this as soon as we come to deal, in fiction, with the differences between realism and romanticism, naturalism and fantasy. *Gulliver's Travels* is a true book; but it is not true that there are midgets of six inches, or giants seventy feet high, or nations of horses. The truth of *Alice in Wonderland* is not the truth of Main Street. The truth of poetry is not the truth of prose. Departures from fact, even when not purposely made for a certain effect, must be judged by different standards, depending on where they occur. The recognition of this principle is as old as Aristotle. When an error has been made in poetry, he remarks, it is important to ask whether it is a matter directly or only accidentally connected with the poetic art. For example, he tells us, it is a lesser error in an artist not to know that the hind has no horns, than to produce an unrecognizable picture of one. To speak of stout Cortez and all his men, silent, upon a peak in Darien, may be bad history but excellent poetry.

What all this comes down to is that we cannot apply ordinary fact-standards or opinion-standards in any crude or direct way to the judgment of literature. We have first of all to recognize that the elements of literature are so various and complex, as Lytton Strachey once reminded us, that no writer can be damned on a mere enumeration of faults, because he may always possess merits which make up for everything. If this is true, as I believe it is, then it is surely still more absurd either to dismiss a writer, or to regard him as important, merely because he holds or rejects some specific doctrine.

I am afraid that most Marxist critics would disagree with this. They might say that this would doubtless be so if the doctrine were one of secondary importance, but that the question of the class struggle happens to be paramount and central. A writer must align himself either with the proletariat or with the bourgeoisie, either with the forces of light, or with the forces of darkness. In the first case, the effect of his work will be beneficent; in the second it must be pernicious. They might go even further, and hold that the abler a bourgeois or capitalistic writer is, the more harmful the effect of his writing will be.

Now when we examine this reasoning it begins to strike us as strangely familiar. The class struggle is not the first so-called paramount or central question to divide mankind. Historically there has always been some issue that partisans have declared to be the central one, and historically it is always a different issue. For centuries writers have been damned for not holding the correct religious or theological beliefs, or for not belonging to the right political party, or for not having the correct attitude toward sex. In the Victorian period, and during the 1920s, we were accustomed to having novels judged by so-called moral standards, which usually referred to sexual morality. The Victorians condemned their predecessors, from Rabelais and Boccaccio to Wycherly and Congreve, for their indecency, and disapproved of the Voltaires and Swifts for their cynicism. Our critics of the twenties dismissed the Victorians for their prudery and puritanism, and derided them also because they were sentimental, and not, as they should have been, cynical. Our new Communist critics now dismiss contemporary writers who have only a "sterile cynicism" in place of a fighting faith.

There are two ways of dealing with Marxist criticism. One may begin by questioning its premises. Is it true that there is an inevitable class struggle? Is it true that social and economic classes divide themselves basically into just two? Is it true that this social cleavage is more important than any other? Even before we begin any close scrutiny of the matter we are entitled, certainly, to our suspicions. For it would be astonishing if the objective facts were to fit in so neatly with the requirements of drama. Immemorially playwrights have recognized that audiences want to see a clash of just two great contending forces. If the contending forces are three, four, five, or twenty, the audience is distracted and confused. Its attention is scattered, its sympathies dispersed. To economize attention and sympathy, it is necessary that there be essentially just two contending forces, and that the audience should wish to see one triumphant and the other crushed. The theory of the class struggle conforms providentially to this law of the theater. It is obliging enough to conform also to the requirements of Hegelian logic. This second conformity is perhaps not so surprising, because the Hegelian logic, by which Marx was so deeply influenced, was itself unconsciously created by Hegel to accord with the rules of dramatic appeal. Marx acquired from him the habit of looking in the actual world for the embodiment of logical categories, with sharp boundaries, clearly opposed to each other.

So we have presented to us in the Marxist drama a world consisting essentially of just two classes engaged in a death struggle: on the one side the capitalists and their hirelings; on the other the onmarching proletariat. When we look at the world, however, unencumbered by this rigid theory, we see that the border line between economic classes, particularly in America, is vague and shifting. We see that the president of a great steel corporation, working on salary and holding little or no stock in his company, is technically an employee, while the owner of a fruit stand with one assistant is technically a capitalist and an employer. More importantly, we know that, for all the appalling contrasts in wealth and income at the two extremes, income classes in the United States shade gradually into each other. The National Bureau of Economic Research, a statistical organization of the highest standing, for example, recently divided the country, not into two, but into seventy-four separate "income classes."

Space will hardly permit an extensive examination of the postulates of Communism, and fortunately such an examination is not necessary. Let us for the moment, instead, accept some of the premises of Marxist literary criticism. Let us accept the premises that there are essentially just two economic classes, that the division between them is real and sharp, and that membership in one of these classes affects our whole point of view. Even if we cannot believe that our opinions are mere rationalizations of our class status, let us grant at least the large element of truth in the contention that our class status influences the opinions of nearly all of us in various unconscious and subtle ways—and sometimes even in pretty obvious ways.

The question we must then ask ourselves is this: Is it impossible for the exceptional writer to surmount these limitations? Is it impossible for him, once he has been brought to recognize this bias, to guard against it as he tries to guard against other forms of bias? For the limitations and biases that may affect the human mind are almost innumerable. There is the limitation imposed by a man's language and nationality. What can Thomas Mann and Spengler, and Proust and Gide, and Pareto and Knut Hamsun, and Dostoyevski and Tolstoy, have to say that could interest Americans with their so different experience? Yet somehow they seem to have a great deal to say to us. There are Americans who feel that they get more of value from some of these foreigners than from any of their own writers. Anatole France once regretted that we could not, like Tiresias, be men and remember having been women, that we are shut up in our personality as in a perpetual prison. But his own works, and the works of hundreds of other writers in all ages, of Shakespeare, of Flaubert, of Hardy, of Dreiser, prove otherwise. The great male writer, by the power of his imagination, can portray the soul of a woman more fully and truthfully, even in the opinion of women, than the overwhelming majority of women writers can. And the great woman novelist can tell us more of what goes on in the mind of a man than most men can.

To take but one more example, there is the limitation imposed upon a writer by the historic era in which he lives. If any limitation seems absolutely insuperable, this one does. How can Karl Marx, who died fifty years ago, who knew nothing of the immense social, political, scientific, and technological changes that have taken place in the half century since then, how can Marx possibly have anything to tell us that is still of value? How can Shakespeare and Montaigne, in their graves three centuries and more, possibly have written words that we can still cherish for their wisdom or beauty, that may even come to us with a shock of delight? What could be more absurd than to suppose that Aristotle and Plato and Homer, who knew nothing at all of the knowledge and experience that a hundred generations of mankind have garnered in the years since they passed on, what could be more absurd than to suppose that any of them could have written works that can still give us intense pleasure, or a sense of encountering flashes of penetrating wisdom for the first time? Yet this miracle is achieved.

In brief, the great writer, with supreme imaginative gifts, can universalize himself. He can vault over the apparently insuperable barriers of race, sex, and time. And yet there is a new school of critics who tell us, in effect, that he cannot vault over the barrier of his class. This contention is an astonishing one. For while no writer can, in any literal or physical sense, change his race, his sex, or his historic era, the one thing he can and frequently does change is precisely his economic status. He can have the experience of being poor, as well as of being "comfortably off," not merely in imagination, but in actuality. Economic class boundaries are so uncertain, indeed, that even Marxists have difficulty in deciding upon which side of "the coming struggle for power" certain great groups will be aligned, or which "ideology" controls them.

We are obliged to conclude, then, that it is surely no more difficult for the great writer, in a functional sense, to transcend the barriers of class than to transcend those of nationality, sex, and time. And we are also entitled to conclude that the great upper- or middle-class writers of the past, or even of the present, have as much to say to the intelligent proletarian as they have to the intelligent bourgeois. We may acknowledge that class bias sometimes enters into what these writers have written. Where it does, it is the duty of the critic to point to the extent and nature of the bias. The positive contribution of the literary Marxists is that they have sharpened our eyes in this respect. But it is not the duty of the critic to declare a priori that this class bias necessarily affects and invalidates everything that a middle-class writer has written; or to point to this bias to the exclusion of all others; or to make it the central theme of all his criticism. Such criticism merely rests on the ancient fallacy of the *argumentum ad hominem*—of trying to discredit an argument or an attitude (and thus to seem to prove the opposite) by abusing the one who advances the argument or who holds the attitude. Such criticism, moreover, must miss all the infinitely rich and subtle values that literature has to offer. It must end by being dreadfully monotonous and tiresome.

Now I must confess that some of the views I have been discussing up to now are extreme. They are by no means held by all critics who call themselves Marxists. For the more intelligent Marxists have been uneasily aware of the narrow and absurd judgments into which this type of reasoning must lead them. So they have sought to rescue themselves from their dilemma by making a distinction. They have, in fact, sawn literature itself into two sharply contrasted aspects, as they have sawn society into two sharply contrasted classes. This might almost be called the official cleavage. The resolution on literature, for example, adopted by the Political Bureau of the Communist Party of the Soviet Union in 1924, begins by declaring that "such a thing as neutral art in a class society does not and cannot exist." It then divides literary works, however, into their "social-political contents" on the one hand, and their "form and style" on the other. On all questions of "content," it holds, the Party must take a firm and positive stand; but on questions of "form and style" it may permit considerable freedom. A similar division is made by a number of American Marxist writers when they distinguish between the "social significance" or the "ideas" of a literary work, and its "craftsmanship." Something of the same sort seems also to be in the mind of the English Marxist, Mr. John Strachey, in his somewhat confused volume called *Literature and Dialectical Materialism*. After praising Mr. Granville Hicks, for example, as "the foremost Marxist literary critic of America," he adds that Mr. Hicks "hardly seems to pay enough attention to the merits of writers as writers."

This whole attempt to split literature into its "ideas" or "social significance" on the one hand, and its "form and style" or "craftsmanship" on the other, seems to me mistaken. Literature will simply not submit to such a violent bifurcation. "Style" and "form" are not separate qualities that can be thrown over "content" like a raincoat: they are determined by content. A work of literature is an organic whole. It is true that, for convenience of discussion, either "craftsmanship" or "social significance" can be discussed as if it existed in isolation—provided the critic always remembers that it does nothing of the kind. What is even more important for us to keep in mind, in relation to the present point, is that after we have discussed the "social-political contents" of a literary work on the one hand, and its "craftsmanship" on the other, we may still have left out what is chiefly important about the work—unless, of course, we happen to have stretched one or the other of these two terms far beyond its legitimate meaning.

Let us see what would happen if we applied these standards, for example, to *Hamlet*. I am afraid that on the question of social-political content a Marxist critic would give that play a very low rating. For in the usual sense of the phrase, it seems simply to have no social-political content. It aims at no reform; it does not imply the need of any change in social-political institutions. It takes for granted the institution of monarchy, and the class relationships and moral code of Shakespeare's time.

Ah, says the sophisticated Marxist critic, but the value of *Hamlet* lies in its "craftsmanship," in its "style and form." Now, certainly, part of its value does reside in these qualities. To take but one example, in the way in which he leads us up to the scene in which Hamlet first sees his father's ghost Shakespeare reveals a masterly technical adroitness. But if the reputation of *Hamlet* rested wholly on its "craftsmanship," as that word is ordinarily used, it would not be higher than that of hundreds of other plays. For it is full of what today would be thought of as technical crudities. It is a sprawling drama of five acts and twenty scenes, overloaded with improbable accidents and coincidences. Any second-rater today could probably do a neater job of mere carpentry.

In what, then, does the greatness of *Hamlet* consist? We might, if we wished, here begin to introduce further criteria. We might speak of "character delineation," which is not "social-political content" and which is surely something broader than mere "form and style." We might talk of the magnificent poetic imagery, which may mean "style," but which implies a good deal more than that. We might talk of the truth or wisdom of the ideas in the famous soliloquy, or in the advice of Polonius. But whatever our detailed analysis, we should be obliged to say, finally, that what made *Hamlet* great was the whole range and texture and quality of its creator's mind.

This is what counts, in the end, in literature—the quality and nobility of the author's mind—and not either mere technical excellence, or the author's social and political sympathies. If we were to judge authors by our agreement or disagreement with their leading doctrines, a very strange sort of criticism would result. But in recognizing this, as the more intelligent Marxist critics do as well as the rest of us, it is unnecessary to fall back upon so narrow a standard as "craftsmanship." We can, instead, recognize more completely than before the wisdom of William Hazlitt's criticism of Burke. "Burke must be allowed to have wanted judgment," he wrote, "by all those who think that he was wrong in his conclusion. . . . But if in arriving at one error he discovered a hundred truths, I should consider myself a hundred times more indebted to him than if, stumbling on what I consider as the right side of the question, he had committed a hundred absurdities in striving to establish his point."

So far we have been discussing the duty of the critic in the present situation. What shall we say of the duty of the creative writer? Supposing his sympathies to be radical, shall he devote himself to writing propagandistic novels, propagandistic plays, propagandistic poetry? Shall he plunge into the center of the fight, or shall he stand "above the battle"?

These questions are by no means easy to answer. There is, to begin with, the difficulty of determining exactly what "propaganda" is. There is a sense in which all art is propagandistic because it reflects and propagates some vision of the world. Propaganda, it has been argued, does not need to be conscious; it may express itself through the unconscious acceptance of existing values and institutions that have been taken for granted. And it is on this basis that Marxists hold that all "bourgeois art" is propaganda for capitalism.

Now while there is perhaps an element of truth in this contention, it seems to me that it does make a difference whether propaganda is conscious or unconscious. To say this, however, does not solve the problem, for it is sometimes difficult to say to what extent propaganda is conscious. Perhaps we can get at the question best by looking first at propaganda in the strict sense, then at the examples of literature which are difficult to classify in this respect, and finally at literature which can be called propagandistic only by the greatest possible extension of the term.

Strictly propagandistic art may be provisionally defined as art which is not regarded by its creator as a sufficient end in itself, but merely as a means of achieving some further end which its creator considers more important. It aims usually at some specific social or political reform: the abolition of capital punishment or of vivisection, a revision of the divorce laws or of sexual mores, the need for revolutionary action. Thus *Uncle Tom's Cabin* is clearly a propagandistic novel, as are most of the novels of Upton Sinclair and the later plays of Elmer Rice.

But now we begin to move into more doubtful territory. As the implied reform becomes broader and vaguer, as the implication itself becomes less definite, the propagandistic nature of a work of literary art becomes more doubtful. The mere fact of whether the work under consideration is good or bad does not always help us in deciding upon its propagandistic nature. Horatio Alger's novels seem propagandistic enough, for they very clearly imply the importance for material success of the virtues of ambition, pluck, hard work, and thrift. But there is a question even here. Alger was certainly not, in the ordinary sense, *advocating* material success; it was a value that he took for granted and assumed that his readers took for granted. Further, the question may be raised whether he was deliberately advocating these means toward material success, or was again merely utilizing the values he assumed his readers already to believe in, in order to secure the undivided sympathy for his heroes and the undivided hatred for his villains deemed essential to create interest and suspense.

Most of the plays of Shaw are propagandistic, as are many of the dramas of Ibsen; *Pillars of Society, A Doll's House, An Enemy of the People, The Wild Duck,* all imply a definite social philosophy, and the need of some sort of social renovation. But clearly we have begun here to move toward works that it is getting to be more difficult to classify. This doubtful field is a very broad one. It includes many of the novels of Dickens, which helped in the movement toward prison reform and the alteration of the debtor laws; it includes Hugo's *Les Miserables,* which affected the French attitude toward criminals. And almost too propagandistic to be doubtful are the novels and plays of Dumas *fils,* which inculcate such morals as the duty of a seducer to marry the woman he has seduced, or the right of a husband to take the law into his own hands and kill the wife who has been unfaithful and worthless. The propaganda in a novel need not necessarily take the form of solemn advocacy of a given attitude: it may consist merely in derision of its opposite. Thus Voltaire's *Candide* is a clear piece of propaganda against the philosophy of optimism.

We come at length to those works of literature which are as free from propaganda as it is possible to imagine. They include some of the greatest works in the language and some of the worst. It would be a rash critic indeed who would venture to say that there is much propaganda in the poetry of Keats, or who could find much more than a shade of it in the plays of Shakespeare. Shakespeare, it is true, sometimes reveals a social attitude; he had, for example, a hardly disguised contempt for the mob. But for the most part his work merely reflects an acceptance of, or

an indifference to, the dominant social values and institutions of his time;
he portrays no interest in changing them. The average detective story of
our own day is just as nonpropagandistic.

What conclusions can we draw from this casual survey? We are
entitled to conclude, I think, that no clear-cut division can be made
between propagandistic and nonpropagandistic work. But this absence
of a clear boundary line does not mean that the distinction is unimportant. On the spectrum it is impossible to tell at precisely what point blue
becomes green or green becomes yellow, but this does not mean that
there is no difference between blue and yellow. And it is pointless in
view of this survey to continue to argue that *all* literary work is basically
propagandistic, whether definitely or vaguely, consciously or unconsciously, aggressively or passively, because even if we were to grant this
it would still be necessary, for purposes of intelligible discussion, to
distinguish between definitely, consciously, and aggressively propagandistic work and vaguely, passively, and unconsciously propagandistic
work. It saves time to call the first propagandistic and the second nonpropagandistic.

Making this distinction, then, what can we say about the duty of the
writer? Shall he write propaganda or unflinchingly eschew it? I think we
are obliged to say, after our perfunctory glance over the field, that it is
folly to lay down any general rule. We can merely point to some of the
possibilities and dangers of the alternative courses. The dangers of writing propaganda are almost too numerous to mention. At its lowest level
the propagandistic novel or play is too unreal and mechanical to be
convincing or even interesting: the sheep are all on one side and the goats
on the other—the characters are either white or black. Close to this is the
danger of falling into a shopworn formula: there is a picture of the
oppression of the working class in the first two acts, for example, with a
triumphant revolution or strike or a sudden outburst of proletarian consciousness in the third act. Even the best writer runs the danger of
subordinating his characters to his thesis: instead of being interesting for
their own sakes, instead of impressing you as living, breathing people
that act on their own account, they then become obvious marionettes
built to fit the plot and to prove the equation; and one is always conscious
of the author pulling the strings. For all his cleverness, most of Bernard
Shaw's plays suffer from this defect.

"I hate poetry," said Keats, "that has a palpable design upon me."
That line points to the central difficulty of propaganda in all art. It has a

design upon you, and the task of the writer is to prevent it from becoming a palpable one. It requires the highest skill to succeed in that task. It would be unfair to condemn all propagandistic work merely by pointing to the innumerable examples of bad propagandistic works, but they must forever stand as awful warnings to the new aspirant. He must never forget that he always has the direct pamphlet in which to agitate specific reforms, and that it is possible to keep them out of his art.

There are, on the other hand, especially in an eruptive period like the present, also dangers in avoiding propaganda. The artist has every right, if he wishes, to ignore the social and political upheavals of his time, and if he is a great artist, he may increase his chances for immortality by doing so. "The world," as Joseph Wood Krutch has eloquently reminded us, "has always been unjust as well as uncertain. . . . It is too bad that men had to be hungry and women had to be dying at the very moment when Newton was inventing the method of fluxions or Gibbon was composing the history of the downfall of Rome. It is too bad that these things had to be done then; but it was far better that they should have been done then than that they should never have been done at all."

There is only one rule: the writer should write about what most interests him, and in the way that he prefers to do it. Good literature is any literature that intensely interests his fellow man; and that is likely to mean, whatever most intensely interests the writer himself. A more narrowly propagandistic literature may interest more men now and fewer men later. A literature with broader aims, without conscious propaganda, on some theme that has little to do with economics or politics, may be neglected today but widely read by the next generation. But what in any case will finally save a work of literature, and make it worth reading, is not the specific doctrines held by its author, but the whole quality and texture of the thought and imagination that go into it.

The American Tradition in Contemporary Literature

Henry Seidel Canby

Too much has perhaps been said of new departures in American literature. Like the New Deal, they are new in America only insofar as
twentieth-century man has encountered new problems and invented new
ways of thinking about them. This nation has been incredibly urbanized
by the factory, the automobile, the moving picture, and the radio. Racial
minorities, with traditions other than Anglo-Saxon, have become articulate and given to American literature, not so much a new accent, as new
materials upon which the imagination can work. Yet it is questionable
whether American literature owes much that is distinctively American to
these influences. Joyce has worked more powerfully in our fiction than
the radio broadcaster; New York Jews, Minnesota Scandinavians, Mississippi Negroes, Boston Irish, when they begin to write, prove to be
more American than foreign, sometimes, I think often, more American
than the Anglo-Saxon strain. If we are to seek for a national character in
American literature, giving it qualities not dependent upon its English
backgrounds and the doctrines of the twentieth century, it must be in the
American tradition. This is not a dead hand reaching from out of our
past, but a force that is alive and, like all living things, growing and
changing, while preserving a pattern that can be recognized and defined.

There have been many attempts to define the American tradition,
but the best have been protests against some other definition, and have
suffered from oversimplification. Turner's famous exposition of the
frontier spirit was a correction of an overemphasis upon our European
origins; Parrington's study of democracy in American literature was an
attack upon the New England successors of the Federalists, who had
been indifferent to democracy. The recent Marxian school has lit obscure
corners of economic influence without supplying any formula broad
enough for an Emerson, a Cooper, or a Whitman. In a brief paper like
this one, I cannot hope to analyze, and much less to challenge, all these

explanations of what it means to be an American. Yet it is possible to break down some of this conflicting testimony, and describe a group of traits that we can all agree are distinctively American, and then see how far they continue to live in the vivid, vigorous, if often disorderly, and sometimes noisy, literature of our own contemporaries in the twenties, thirties, and forties.

I shall not try to be original in this portrait of the American tradition, unless in a fresh application to books and people of our time. Probably the job could be done with different classifications, and certainly more classifications are possible. That is not important. If the traits I describe are true and significant, they are enough for an experiment in literary criticism. If anyone wishes to deny that the categories that follow are intensely American he will need a powerful argument. Some of them are English or French or Russian traits, also, but not to the same degree, not in the same way, not so significantly. Taken together, they spell in outline the name of our country when it thinks, feels, imagines, judges, expresses itself in literature.

The first and probably the most deep-lying of these characteristics is expansiveness. Naturally, our conquest of a continent conditioned us to expansiveness, but the inheritance goes much further back. It is probably true that the vast majority of immigrants to these shores, from the seventeenth century on, came because they felt they had to come. But it is not so often remembered that an equal, and perhaps a much greater number of Europeans, under like compelling circumstances, stayed at home. We got the restless, we got the seekers, we got the rebels, we got the oppressed who were willing to escape. When the first Swedish colonists landed on the Delaware, they brought with them some Finns who had been jailed for their undue energy in girdling and burning Her Majesty's forests in Sweden. Criminals at home from too much expansiveness, they became ace settlers on the Delaware, where burning, girdling, and chopping were the preliminaries to every crop of corn. The story is typical. And if, by the eighteenth century, expansiveness on land had subsided east of the Alleghenies, the burst through to the West, and the conquest of sea routes, renewed it in full vigor. Franklin's *Poor Richard* is intended as a brake on expansiveness. With Jonathan Edwards, hell itself became expansive. *Rip Van Winkle* is a serio-comedy of expansiveness. Cooper's Natty Bumppo symbolizes the conflict between the expansive soul seeking the freedom of the wilderness, and an expanding civilization always at his heels. Emerson is a spiritual expansionist. Thoreau wrote

Walden to turn expansion inward. Mark Twain's boys are always going places, and Whitman's *Song of Myself* links Brooklyn, human nature, the West, and the universe.

But how vitally this trait persists in our literature today! If there is one trend, for example, in American fiction that has amounted almost to a folk lore in this decade, it is the historical novel, which has pushed for its sources backward and left and right across the continent. And note that these novels, from *Northwest Passage* and the innumerable narratives of prairie settlers to *Gone With the Wind,* have been stories of expansion, of conflict, and of building. It is the re-creation, the expansion, of the new South after the war that is the original and memorable part of *Gone With the Wind,* and both hero and heroine are identified with salvage and reconstruction, not with memory and loss. Note again the contrast of this school of history in fiction with the great European novelists of a century earlier. It is lost causes, defeated countries, or heroes in their last stand that Sir Walter Scott chooses for subjects. With him and with Dumas the vane points always to the past. The theme in the American books is preparation for a future expansiveness.

Or let us choose an individual writer, regarded by many of the younger generation as their leader, Thomas Wolfe. Here is expansiveness incarnate, even as in Whitman, even as in the westward pioneers who lived for frontier experience and moved on when stability caught up with them. Wolfe could write only one book and that was his whole expanding life. His work has a beginning and many middles but no end anywhere. Its faults are apparent, its virtue is an insatiable zest for experience, an expanding ego to which every happening seems important because it happens to Tom Wolfe. Asheville, the railroad, the Harvard library, New York, and love and hate and human nature, all open illimitably when he reaches them. Everything is continental to his view, and he is as immune to classical restraint as a Mohawk chieftain, or Anthony Wayne, or Colonel Sellers, or Moby-Dick. He ravaged his country for words, as the lumbermen ravaged its forests—leaving desert wastes and blacked confusion behind, but also roads and magnificent vistas. This is expansiveness run wild in the fourth century of our exploitation of a continent, in the second century of our national literature.

I could add many more examples, John Dos Passos, Faulkner in his way, Hemingway in his, Benét's *John Brown's Body* in its way, Hervey Allen, Robinson Jeffers emphatically and, like Wolfe, to his own damage, Marc Connolly's *The Green Pastures,* or Richard Wright's recent

Native Son, a study of expansiveness thwarted and poisoned by racial prejudice.

I dislike applying a term such as *equalitarianism,* with its strongly European connotations, to the next American trait to be discussed, but I can think of no other word so applicable. Nevertheless, American equalitarianism is very different, both in origins and in results, from the European variety. It had to wait for no French Revolution in order to flourish. The first Swedish governor in Delaware complained that he could not keep his peasants within the stockade: they insisted upon establishing themselves in the forest, where they could become landholders like their superiors at home. The Quakers of Pennsylvania were radically equalitarian, and even when many of them grew rich, remained so within their own sect. The eighteenth-century aristocracy of Virginia and New England came from small people seeking equality with their betters in the old country, and was submerged in New England and segregated in Virginia by new waves of equalitarians. Given easy access to land and water, if not at home then just over the hills, an equalitarianism was as inevitable as an increase in national wealth. We have been conditioned by it in our formative centuries.

One result of this long-continued and dangerously successful attempt to make the Smiths as good as the Joneses is the dominantly bourgeois nature of the American tradition. Where so many have had— in the past at least—an opportunity to rise in the economic scale, there will be neither an aristocracy nor a plutocracy with that sense of security which produces a class. Equalitarianism and exclusiveness are mutually incompatible, and privilege, which has supported aristocracies elsewhere, becomes a reward of ability, not a heritable right. Plutocracy is less vulnerable here than aristocracy, but it is clear that even our plutocrats have been forced to establish foundations rather than families, in order to perpetuate their names.

But I am using *bourgeois* in no unfavorable sense. *Middle class* is the more usual term, and, indeed, fits perfectly the economic aspirations of the American millions since we began. It is too narrow a word, however, to apply to literature. Our literature has had the bourgeois virtues, which are real and valuable. It has never been successfully heroic, although intellectually it has reached, especially in our earlier New England, formidable heights. But on the austere pinnacles of thinking an Emerson and a Thoreau, if not a Hawthorne, wrote definitely for the community of all men of good will, and believed them capable of good will. So did

Jefferson, although himself a product of our Southern experiment in making an aristocracy by the plantation and slavery system, an experiment already failing in his time. It was, indeed, the so-called Virginia aristocracy which founded the political party which has made a political program of equalitarianism.

Could anything be more bourgeois in a good sense than the books of Mark Twain? I do not refer to the obvious leveling of *A Connecticut Yankee in King Arthur's Court,* but to more instinctive because less conscious expressions of equalitarianism. Consider the theme of *Huckleberry Finn,* which must certainly be regarded as one of the most typical as well as one of the best creations of the American imagination. The theme of that book is the conversion of Huck to the bourgeois virtues. He has inherited an outmoded equalitarianism, the faith of his poor-white father that he is as good as any man—and indeed he is, in a frontier society where good hunting and good fishing and a body inured to cold and bad whiskey guarantee independence. But Hannibal is not frontier any more. The border ruffian is out of date. All he can do is to boast and go to the lockup. If Huck is to climb on the American bandwagon, he has to learn how to keep up with a new set of Joneses, and his difficulties and backslidings make the story. Mark Twain doubts the values of Hannibal society, and it is possible to read both *Tom Sawyer* and *Huckleberry Finn* as satires of that society, but he never doubts—or never doubted until toward the end of his life—the duty and privilege of every good American to become as rich and independent and successful as the Judge Thatchers, whoever they might be, of the time. Huck grown up will be a better bourgeois than the rest.

How strong this equalitarian *motif* is in the majority of American books need not be emphasized here. The difficulty is to find American books of vitality in which it is not a moving force. Poe, who belongs to another phase of the American tradition, is one example. Melville may be regarded as another, Hawthorne as a third, Henry James as a fourth. But Poe was a pathological romanticist, Melville and Hawthorne were skeptics, and James an internationalist. And even these men were all specialists in that inevitable accompaniment of bourgeois equalitarianism, the emphasis upon the individual and individualism. Far from having subsided with the closing of the frontier and the economic changes which have so clamped down on American opportunity, this trait has merely changed its metabolism in the imagination.

The novels of Sinclair Lewis, for example, are essentially studies in the pathology of American ambition. In every important story, from *Main Street* on, he has described the American passion to get on, to be as good as the current Joneses, to conform to success and share it. But the societies that Lewis describes have got their values wrong. They want, like Babbitt, tokens of success, which prove to be only tokens. They have lost sight of valuable ends in contriving efficient means. Or, as in *Arrowsmith* or *Elmer Gantry*, they have paid a heavy price for an equality of low ideals and an unworthy success. It is never the right of the American to have what the best have, which Lewis questions. His heroes are all go-getters in their own right. But Americans have gone after the wrong values. He scorns them, not because they are going places, but because they have lost their way. In all of this, though with less satire and more philosophy, Thoreau, in *Walden*, was his predecessor.

A less important but very cogent instance may be found in a book just published, which, with its renewal of the theme of *Huckleberry Finn*, shows how heavily this national problem still weighs upon our imagination. Jesse Stuart, the Kentucky poet of the mountains, has written a novel in poetic prose called *Trees of Heaven*. It is a notable contribution to those books sprung from the American soil, styled by it, and rich in essential character, which prove that the virility and energy of the new American fiction are not to be confined to ideology, sophistication, or fictionized history. But *Trees of Heaven*, unlike *The Yearling* with which it may be compared, has a theme. Anse, the mountain farmer, is an equalitarian determined to lift his family to economic security. In contrast, the squatters, who once had been free pioneers, are poor whites on the way out to relief or vagabondage. Boliver, whose daughter is so beautiful, is Huck's father over again, with a difference. He can work, he can create a good life, but the particular bourgeois ideals that Anse has acquired from the Joneses of his neighborhood send Bolly back to drunkenness, with his bare feet hanging over the porch. This American type must have freedom to enjoy life, as his ancestors had freedom to live their own life in the woods. The wrong kind of equalitarianism makes him into a bum.

The will to be equal, which is so strong in the American tradition, has become a critique of equality; but the will is still there. You will find it as the motive of Richard Wright's Negro story, *Native Son*. You will find it, subtly displayed, in Thornton Wilder's *Our Town*, you will find it dramatically spoken by Mrs. Joad in *The Grapes of Wrath*. We are mature as a nation, but this obsession is the same as in our youth.

Picking and choosing among the other outstanding attributes of the American tradition, I take next its most puzzling element. Not puzzling in how and why it came about, but puzzling in its action and its unexpected strength and weakness. We are a humanitarian nation, even more so than the British—one might say, the tougher we are, the more humanitarian.

Our record for tough ruthlessness is not a pretty one. If fewer Indians were massacred in Anglo-Saxon than in Spanish territories, it is chiefly because there were fewer Indians to massacre. If we did not reduce the remainder to slavery, they were equally exploited and much more thoroughly dispossessed. The type badman of modern literature comes from our West. The gunman and gangster were American specialties until Germany capitalized them for political purposes. If the factory system at its beginning was more ruthless in England, that was simply because British men, women, and children were more helpless. There was less room and less food. The most influential humanitarian book in English, one of the most effectively moving books of all time, *Uncle Tom's Cabin,* was inspired not so much by slavery as such, as by the ruthless exploitation of the Negro for quick profits in the cotton lands of the frontier. We have never been slow with knife, pistol, or whip.

And yet never was a nation so readily touched emotionally to humanitarian ends as the American since the nineteenth century made the idea of humanitarianism familiar. The North took back the South after the Civil War without a proscription, an unheard of thing then, before, or after, in a civil war. If there was oppression and exploitation later, that came from the other strain in our make-up. Our foreign-mission effort, of which at least two-thirds was humanitarian in its appeal, has been vast in proportion to means and population. No cause that awaked pity or sympathy has ever failed of support in this country, and, as we grow rich, our contributions to world suffering have expanded out of proportion. The type political machine of the United States, Tammany, to whose methods the Nazis owe much, was built upon a basis of genuine humanitarianism combined with exploitation without scruple.

The cause, of course, of this deep-set trait is no superior quality of mercy in the stocks that settled America. The fact of settlement itself made them will to re-form themselves and their circumstances. Newcomers, torn from a settled environment, facing new conditions of living, separated from the tradition of stable communities upon which law and custom are based, they *had* to re-form themselves, and sooner or later re-form their neighbors. The frontiers of the United States have usually been advanced by pioneers who, having re-formed themselves once to the freedoms and necessities of the wilderness, did not choose to re-form themselves again to suit an approaching civilization. Reform in its broadest implication is in our blood because we have been conditioned by it for generations. It has become traditional, and this tradition the experiences of the latest immigrants into our industrialized society has not invalidated. They also have had both the opportunity and the necessity of re-forming themselves.

But this reforming habit of mind did not have to become humanitarian. It did not have to become moral. It was the influence, undoubtedly, of the strong Protestant tradition of a reforming ethics which made our tradition of reform so moral in its implications. An interesting comparison can be made here between the re-forming of Latin civilization in both North and South America, and our own. With the Latins, the ethical element in reform was weak, even though the religious element was durable. They sought a rich life rather than a good one.

And it was the influence of abundant opportunity in a continent working upon this ethical prepossession that seems to have made the peculiarly American blend of humanitarianism. It is more sentimental than the English because, except perhaps in the area of slavery, it has never been harshly tested. It is notably more widespread, being not confined to a class, as in the humanitarianism of the Victorian middle class, but even more characteristic of the worker than of the *rentier* or successful exploiter. It is more generous among men and women of small means because our opportunities have been more generous. We have never had to be stingy or mean, at least as a nation. Economically it may ruin us yet, for it is behind the easy good nature that, quite as much as predatory politics, is responsible for such disastrous handouts as our pension system and the uncritical character of much of our relief.

To stretch out the long list of notable American books which carry on the tradition of this humanitarianism is quite unnecessary. There are, as a matter of fact, few really hard-boiled books in the American tradition. Those which appear to be so, usually under scrutiny show, like Poe's stories of terror, a shrinking sensitiveness to pain, or like Hemingway's tough episodes, a defensive mechanism against fear. But in the main stream of tradition, the trait is self-evident. Curiously enough, the two great men of Concord, Emerson and Thoreau, have the least of it.

They have good will toward all good men, yet—Thoreau especially—
are not easily moved to emotion by ills not spiritual in origin. But there
is passionate and uncritical humanitarianism in Walt Whitman. There is
sentimental humanitarianism in Bret Harte, whose stories of the easily
aroused pity of gold-diggers and camp prostitutes seem to have had
sufficient base in reality. There is a passionate and unsentimental humanitarianism in Mark Twain—at its best, I think, in *Huckleberry Finn,*
where it is veiled by irony. And, coming to our own times, regard again
for an instant Sinclair Lewis, whose *Babbitt,* felt at the time of its publication to be a document in reform, seems now to be not so much a satire as
a lament for the good American warped by the irresistible pressure of
commonplace ideals. Or consider Theodore Dreiser's *American Tragedy,*
which, for all its appearance of callous documentation, is at base pity
for an ordinary man caught in tragic circumstances and doomed by
his public's pathological craving for sensation to relieve its own dull
lives.

No better example, however, could be found of the persistence of
this tradition in what we profess to think is a new and different America,
than the resounding success of John Steinbeck's *The Grapes of Wrath.*
Here is a book which breaks the laws of the genteel Medes and Persians
who, until this decade, have always dominated our literature. It offends
decency, not only by deeds, which has always been permissible, but by
words. Its language sets new standards of realism for the American
novel. Here, also, is a book which attacks the economic theories which
have been orthodox in American literature, and attacks them, not by
argument, but by precisely that kind of sentimental generalization upon a
society of mutual love and help which has always driven the practical
American business man into a contemptuous fury. Nevertheless, in spite
of some natural local objection in the communities described, the book
has made its way wherever a book can in America. And why? Its sometimes uncertain art aside, I am sure its success is due to a reforming
humanitarianism in the exact American tradition which produced *Uncle
Tom's Cabin.* We may shrug our economic shoulders over the problem of
migratory labor, but we cannot guard our imagination against ·Mrs.
Joad, who wanted only to make good Americans of her family, and
could not. We are sorry for the Joads because they were deprived of what
has made our tradition a generous one—opportunity. And this pity stirs
on to reform.

I shall choose for my last earmark of the American tradition—

youth. With more time and analytical shrewdness, it might be possible to distinguish a dozen more, but this one cannot be neglected. Perhaps it is the most important, probably it is the most determining characteristic of all. I am not so naive as to speak of America as a young nation politically and economically. Politically we are matured, though, one hopes, not crystallized. Only the British regime shows an equal correspondence between the will of the people and the direction and control of government. And this constitutes maturity in politics, even though strains and stresses show the vital need of more growth and adaptiveness. France is still experimental by comparison. The totalitarian states are in the crude youth of violence and compulsion, where evolution has scarcely begun its work, and order comes from forced obedience, not from custom and free acceptance. Nor are we young economically. On the contrary, our capitalist system, slowly absorbing ideas and practices of socialism, is certainly the most developed of its type, and, if it lags behind the industrial revolution, has not found it necessary to change our ways of life in order to survive.

But in literature—and the arts in general—we are still extraordinarily young. In fact, it is obvious that we have been growing younger and younger as decade by decade we have wrenched further and further away from European, and especially English, tradition. Jonathan Edwards and Benjamin Franklin were European minds only slightly affected by a new environment. Irving and Cooper are still old minds functioning with new material. Emerson and Thoreau are full of new sap, but their youthfulness is not in manner; it is hope in the one and rebellion in the other. With Mark Twain and Whitman a raw kind of youthfulness appears—brash, vulgar, disregardful of the rules. They write like youngsters even when they are old. Energy begins to be the chief attribute of great Americans, a crude and wasteful energy, not regardful of the labor-saving devices of classicism. Such men write both badly and well, and on the same page. The vigorous, pushing imaginations grow more and more experimental, more and more indifferent to anything but quick expression. It is not literature that excites them any more, but the country. They go to it for news, and their reporting in prose or poetry is news, with the quality of journalism, which becomes an American art. The proportion of the writers who work in the great literary tradition to the innovators and expressionists grows steadily less. Finally, in our own time, the public taste itself changes and readers fall avidly upon the sensations of their own land.

What is young here is, of course, the imagination, which at last is beginning to construct its images in terms of a new continent. And there are many other signs of youth in this imagination besides its reckless and untiring energy. American writing for a half century has tended to begin everything and finish it fast. In fiction, the short story has been its chosen form, and its very best writers—even such classicists as Willa Cather— have been at their best in briefish stories. Others, like Caldwell, Faulkner, Hemingway, Wilder, Steinbeck, Sherwood Anderson, have begun to falter every time they have tried to sustain their work in the dimension of a complete novel. Their great success is in the short story, single or compounded. It may be that this results in part from the un-heroic character of the equalitarian American mind, but that is not enough explanation. Our social structure is, apparently, still too youthful, too fluid, to bear the weight of a great reconstruction in terms of art. Light craft go better.

Another trait which seems to me characteristically youthful is the curious duplex quality of the American imagination. Ever since the beginnings of our national literature this has been manifest. In the upper story we tend to be cheerful, generous, optimistic, humorous. But downstairs, writer after writer has been caught, sometimes fatally, by the macabre, the satiric, the sardonic, the horrible. It is surely strange that Poe and Ambrose Bierce and the Twain of *The Mysterious Stranger* and James of *The Turn of the Screw,* and Faulkner who wrote that terrible book *Sanctuary,* and Hemingway who specialized in cruelty, should all be Americans! Not strange, however, if one remembers the contrasts between freedom, success, degeneracy, and violence, all existing on the frontier, or in a boom industrial city. Not strange either, if one considers the hurry of our development, which has been built over bog and cesspool, as well as good firm ground.

And, indeed, these almost hysterical relapses into fear and disgust, so characteristic of American writing, are certainly aspects of a youthful imagination that, until recently, has never had to take stock. If it assumed a culture as its basis, it was a European culture, and in this it was like a youth who assumes his parents' stability as groundwork for his own activities. And as with that youth, when America showed itself as not according to European specifications, there has been a quick disillusionment and a tendency to rush into extremes of despair or abuse. It is hard to tell where one gets the most untrustworthy pictures of American life—in the too wholesome, too complacent books of the Age of American Confidence, or in the hysterical studies of disorganization, depression, exploitation, and violence, so current today.

The truth is, that since the American imagination really began to busy itself with America as a subject for literary interpretation, it has been going places with such youthful and nervous rapidity that relapses into pessimism or distrust or plain hysteria were inevitable. It has, as I have said, been primarily engaged with news, and what has been found has been described more often than interpreted. Mark Twain and Whitman were like that. Thoreau's *Walden* was a protest against going places until you know your own, and if there had been a more vigorous literature extant might very well have been aimed in that direction instead of at mercantilism. Much as he admired Whitman's passionate individualism, Thoreau took issue with him on just this point. Why praise the hurrying crowds until we know the man?

Look once again at Thomas Wolfe. Could anything be more youthful in good and bad senses, or more illustrative of the American way of attempting a great theme, than his work? His achievement is to describe Tom Wolfe going places and recording his reactions in contact with a continent. His writing boils with energy, it is all news, it descends from ecstatic enthusiasm to the macabre or the despairing, it has, as I have said, beginning and middle, but no sign of the ending which to an older imagination would have been implicit in the first chapter. Not a truly successful writer, Wolfe, in his faults and in his virtues, is symptomatic of what we are imaginatively, and that is the reason for his powerful grip upon young artists of this generation.

I might add, of course, to this picture of youth, the moving picture, an American art, still dominated by Americans, as a more complete and even more cogent example of the young imagination of America, although the tight grasp of profit makers has almost, but not quite, suppressed relapses into disgust or despair. Particularly when the American movie is not literature at all, which is usually, the mental age of its imagination can scarcely be more than twelve. And that, of course, is because the producers, however sophisticate in techniques, have spiritually and morally not yet reached adulthood, and so welcome the immature as well as the energetic in the American imagination.

The moral I have tried to draw in this paper is a very simple one. In our culture, we are definitely a nation in the making, and this is our tradition, and still governs us. This culture has had two climaxes. The first was just before the Civil War, when, still largely English in civilization but feeling our new environment, we broke into extraordinary waves of duplex energy, some material, some spiritual. The second climax, I suspect, we are living in now, and European chaos may hasten its movement.

In both climaxes the formative elements of our tradition are powerful. We have lost little from these, and are steadily adding to a distinctive heritage. It is not a literary culture to boast about yet, as one can boast of our political and economic progress even while deploring our errors. But it is still expansive, and perhaps never so interesting to a student of criticism as now.

You get one aspect of it today in the cheaply optimistic magazine, which is all wish psychology, like the pioneer. You get another in our ironical, sophisticated books, and magazines like the New Yorker, where idealism is handled skeptically by a good-natured fellow who does not intend to be fooled. You get still another in deadly serious reformers, like Steinbeck. You get still another in brutal tough guys, who easily turn tender. Still another in the vulgar smartness of gossip columns, the trim emptiness of Broadway plays, the mechanical short story.

But make no mistake. The expansiveness of a hearty America, good-willed, hopeful, energetic, is not dead. Tom Wolfe echoes Whitman; Steinbeck, Harriet Beecher Stowe. When this generation gets through with going places, we may expect another period like that really great New England stir of the imagination which was frustrated by materialism and war. Unfortunately, there is another war on, but I doubt whether any European involvement can now change the direction, though it may add to the qualities, of our American tradition.

On Counting Your Chickens
before They Hatch

Edward Weeks

You remember the story of the chicken farmer? One night he heard a fearful rumpus in his chicken yard. Seizing his shotgun, he ran out to the wire, where he thought he saw a figure lurking in the corner. "Who's there?" he shouted, "Come out! Come out, or I'll shoot!" Dead silence. Then a soft voice said, "Ain't nobody here, boss, 'ceptin' us chickens." On this occasion I knew that I should have the opportunity of speaking face to face to a group of people who were just as interested in writing as I am. There would be nobody here but us chickens.

I have noticed that writers and editors have this much in common with people who raise chickens—they love to count their chickens before they hatch. I believe it is second nature for writers to do so. When I was in college I wrote what I thought was a good story in which my parents were the central characters. My teacher in composition said it should be published, and after the manuscript had been returned to me by the *Saturday Evening Post,* I contributed it to the *Harvard Advocate.* But even before it appeared in print I was receiving congratulations—at least in my mind—not on that particular short story but on the volume of them which at that moment I was confident I should write in the next six months. If I had written such a book, I am sure you would have heard of it, but it still remains one of those chickens I haven't had time to hatch.

All writers, small and great, are nourished by such illusions. I don't think they could live without them. When John Keats realized that he was in love with Fanny Brawne and could not afford matrimony, he decided to get away by himself and write for money. We know from his letters that *La Belle Dame sans Merci* was almost the least of the arrows he thought he had in his quiver. He was going to write plays, great smashing tragedies which would make his reputation, and he thought he already heard the applause before he had finished the first act of *Otho the Great.* The notebook of any honest writer will tell you the same thing.

Think how often Samuel Taylor Coleridge got set for some great, ambitious project—and how seldom he laid the egg. Xanadu stands for that superb but fleeting vision which entrances every one of us who try to write. While the spell is on us we see our short story instantaneous, vivid, and complete; we see our poem an epic to stir the country; we see our novel so thick—and over 100,000 copies! We all share in this experience when we have the vision and feel the power that goes with it, and our only wonder is whether we shall have life enough to accomplish the limitless and magnificent work we see ahead. Were it not for this recurring illusion, writing would be a drudgery too disappointing for most to endure.

Those of you who have been competing for the Hopwood Awards this year must have had moments when you asked yourselves whether it was worth the doing. What chance is there for a beginning writer in a world so full of tension and belligerency? Or, to put it specifically, what chance will you have to practice what you have learned when a year from now you may be in a training camp or up to your ears in defense work? It seems to me that perhaps the friendliest service I can perform this afternoon is to describe the climatic conditions under which I see writers working today and to foretell as accurately as possible the demands which any young American author will be expected to meet in the near future. I am not speaking as a prophet but as an editor of a magazine who has been trained to observe the changing currents in literature.

In the first place, what effect has the emergency upon those who are going to read your work? To what extent have the tastes and needs of the American reader been altered since the summer of 1939? Let me give you a close-up of the American reader in action. Fresh from his shave and with all the vigor of the early day, he comes down to breakfast to be greeted by the morning newspaper. After some quick sparring with the headlines he reads the baseball scores, follows along with the local murder case, and then, since he can't escape it, he stands up to the war news as delivered by the A.P., the Berlin dispatch, Walter Lippmann, Alsop and Kintner, Boake Carter, Pearson and Allen, Dorothy Thompson, and Westbrook Pegler. Round One. The challenger is still fresh, but a little off-balance. On the way to the office he is asked what he thinks of the President's speech. He puts up the best defense he can by quoting what he can remember from Walter Lippmann, Alsop and Kintner, Dorothy Thompson, and Westbrook Pegler. Round Two. On his desk at the office is the Whaley-Eaton Foreign Letter, and the Kiplinger Letter from Washington—full of portentous details about the defense program. The challenger is still boring in. Round Three. On the way to lunch he sees a scare-head and buys the extra. At lunch he is asked what he thinks of the British chances in the Middle East. He leads with his chin. Round Four. On the way home from the office he reads the afternoon edition, and before dinner his wife turns on the broadcasts from the foreign capitals. Round Five. Challenger still upright but wobbly. After dinner he looks through the illustrations in *Life*—which dent him a little. And as he is trying to get up courage to read the *Atlantic,* the family says to come along with them to the movies. When he gets there, the first thing he sees is the newsreel. Round Six—and the challenger is on the ropes. Joe Louis would be child's play for a mind that goes through such daily battering— and that is the kind of mind you've got to cope with for the duration!

Most Americans I talk with today are groggy from the effects of journalism. But that's not the only reaction I observe. In their self-defense they have become much more determined about what they want to read in their free time. What I mean by determination is this: the American reader is impatient with big words—those India-rubber words which have been stretched too far and too often by propagandists, orators, and politicians. It is my custom to make at least two long trips from East to West each year, and always I return from them with an amazement that a nation so widespread and composite can manage to settle its local problems and at the same time pull together. I think that is the kind of thing our American reader wants to know. The word *democracy* is not enough: he wants to be told how it works.

Second, he knows he is living in a world of violent change and that, like a gambler, he must take his chances with the rest of the country. He has learned to be much more resilient since That Man in the White House showed us the need. Third, he is eager for leadership. He is hopeful of finding a way out of this mess. He is waiting for a Democrat to provide a better solution than Hitler's. But he is not prejudiced—it might be a Republican.

And, finally, the American reader has more respect for his way of living. What do I mean by that? Well, let me show you. My office is a five-minute walk from my home on Beacon Hill. To get to it I skirt the Boston Common and cut a diagonal across our Public Gardens. On these late spring afternoons I find myself looking up into the sky and thinking, "My lord, what an easy target this open city would be for a bomber."

The contrast between the pond with its swan boats, the blazing beds of tulips for which our Gardens are famous, and the fine old trees which were planted here on the clam shells by Charles Sargent—the contrast between this serene picture and what the place might look like when a squadron of heavy bombers had done their work has this effect upon me: it makes me realize how much I love life and how much I want to remain the kind of individual I am. I have been bombed before, and this new approach of danger sharpens my respect for individuality. I know that in my own case I am reading novels with avidity these days because I find they refresh my mind and restore my confidence in what the individual can do. In our novels it is the individual, not the system, which carries our hopes of the future. That is certainly true of Ma and Tom Joad as they are revealed to us by John Steinbeck. It is equally true of old Pilar in *For Whom the Bell Tolls.* No civil war, no cruelty, will ever shake her faith in life.

If these changes are apparent in the American reader, what can be said of our writers? The first thing an editor notices is that our chickens have all come home to roost. Novelists from Wisconsin and Ohio no longer need the sunlight of the Riviera in which to do their work. The expatriates who were once so busy finding—or losing—themselves in Paris have come home. With them have come many talented exiles who, as they struggle to adjust themselves to American life, may help us to a better appreciation of what American life should be. One result of all this is that the condescension toward things American has disappeared, I suspect for good.

With the disappearance of the expatriate there has also disappeared that by-product of the cosmopolitan, the book which was fashionable because it was odd. I am sure that there would be no incentive today which would prompt Gertrude Stein to write that first freak of hers entitled *Tender Buttons.* The impulse which led James Joyce away from *Dubliners* and into his maze, *Finnegans Wake,* is dead and buried with the past. So is the fashion which produced *Gadsby,* a novel of over 50,000 words, written without the letter *e.* The author, E. V. Wright, tied down the *e* key on his typewriter before he began to compose. For your own fun sometime just try to write an engaging sentence of twenty-five words without once using the letter *e.* Oddities like these shrink to the size of very small buttons indeed when writers are faced with the magnitude of what is now going on. There will always be need for experiments. There will always be a proving ground in literature for those young writers who must seek new directions. But, for the time being, the cult of unintelligibility finds no takers. That cult has gone with the silly sophistication which once made it popular.

And going, going, gone is that much more serious influence, the cult of the negative, a philosophy with which our novelists lived for twenty years, a philosophy which urged them to point out what's wrong without the glimmer of hope for what's right. "A mood of desperate unhappiness reigns in the world," says Van Wyck Brooks in his recent address "On Literature Today," "and this is marked especially in most of the writers. The temperamental cards of our time are all stacked in favor of despair. It seems as if our writers passively wallowed in misery, calling it fate; as if the most powerful writers, from James Joyce to Hemingway, from Eliot of *The Waste Land* to Eugene O'Neill and Theodore Dreiser, were bent on proving that life is a dark little pocket. Even where, as in many cases, these writers are fighting for social justice, they still picture life as hardly worth the trouble of fighting for it. You know the picture of life you find in the novels of William Faulkner, Dos Passos, James T. Farrell and so many others, who carry the day with their readers because they are writers of great power. They seem to delight in kicking their world to pieces, as if civilization were all a pretence and everything noble a humbug." I agree emphatically with Mr. Brooks. This attitude began as a direct reaction to the First World War, it settled into a habit, and it ended by becoming a pose. I do not mean for a moment that our writers will cease to be realists. But I do mean that writers and readers both have had a bellyful of despair and that as a daily diet it is simply not good enough.

You won't remember the books on which this country was feeding as it made ready to take part in the First World War. But I do. I remember them vividly, because they were the books which eventually inflamed my mind and propelled me into the French Army. When I volunteered at the end of 1916, I stood five feet five and weighed exactly ninety-eight pounds. The French Army was the only army then willing to take a soldier of that size. Let me give you a bird's eye view of what our literature was like at that time.

Begin in the spring of 1914—we were perfectly oblivious to the thunderstorm that was coming. We were like cows in a happy pasture, munching on lush novels which, I suspect, would turn your stomach if you tried them today. Remember that 1914 was the end of an epoch, the climax of peace and prosperity. In 1914 a struggling young American poet named Robert Frost published his collection of poems, *North of Boston,* but he did not publish it in Massachusetts. He published it in England, where he had gone in search of the recognition and encouragement denied him in America. In 1914 a young man who was having a hard time trying to write plays, a young man by the name of Eugene O'Neill, brought out his first book, *Thirst and Other Plays.* In 1914 Theodore Dreiser published his novel, *The Titan,* and I doubt if two thousand people in this country took the pains to read it. The reason we did not have time to discover the talent of Robert Frost and Eugene O'Neill and Theodore Dreiser was that we were absorbed in the best sellers. We were reading *Pollyanna* by Eleanor H. Porter, which sold more than a million copies; *Laddie* by Gene Stratton Porter, which sold a million and a half copies; *Tarzan of the Apes* by Edgar Rice Burroughs, *The Eyes of the World* by Harold Bell Wright, and *Penrod* by Booth Tarkington—all in half million lots. I don't hold these up to you as models for imitation, but if you will compare those titles with our 1940 best sellers you will see how our taste has improved.

The outbreak of the war stunned our writers. But not for long. The same prevailing optimism, the same belief that right would triumph, and that life would always have a happy ending, rose again to the surface in the first crop of war books, and it was reinforced by the passionate belief that the Hun was all black and that we were all white and that no personal sacrifice was too great for Democracy. I read every one of those war books I could get my hands on. I read Guy Empey's *Over the Top.* I read *The First Hundred Thousand* by Ian Hay, in which you saw the eager spirit and good humor with which English civilians were converted into fighting men. I read *Kitchener's Mob* by James Norman Hall who was one of that Mob—and that second book of his, *High Adventure,* in which he describes the almost idyllic chivalry of a war pilot. There were no dive bombers in those days.

It would be impossible to make you feel the electricity which passed from books like those into the minds of us who were still under twenty. If you write those books off as English propaganda, you miss the point. They were written by men who were actually in the fighting, not by bureaucrats in the Home Office. They were written by men who volunteered to fight because they believed it was the only way to save what they valued. Later, as the novelists swung into action, I read *Sonia* by

Stephen McKenna, one of the great best sellers in England, in which the
hero comes back blinded—but he does come back! And I read *Mr. Brit-
ling Sees It Through,* the novel by H. G. Wells which typified what the
head of any household should be willing to sacrifice. I cannot over-
emphasize the importance of that word *sacrifice.* The men in the Army
never used it. But it meant something to them, and even more to the
people back home. And if any one word was ever a seed, you can say that
this word *sacrifice* was the seed from which grew the novels and poems
which were written during the war. It is the idea which lies behind Edith
Wharton's *A Son at the Front;* it is the idea which Edward Streeter kidded
and made laughable in his *Dere Mable;* it is the idea which runs through
that exceptionally good novel of Willa Cather's, *My Antonia.*

But by 1918 a change was discernible. The poets were the first to
reveal it, being, as I suspect, thinner-skinned than most novelists. At the
outbreak of the war the poets had marched off singing. They could not
wait for commissions—the war would be over too soon. They were like
Rupert Brooke. And his war sonnets stand for the ardor of that time as
no others we have:

> If I should die, think only this of me:
>   That there's some corner of a foreign field
> That is for ever England. There shall be
>   In that rich earth a richer dust concealed;
> A dust whom England bore, shaped, made aware,
>   Gave, once, her flowers to love, her ways to roam,
> A body of England's, breathing English air,
>   Washed by the rivers, blest by suns of home.
>
> And think, this heart, all evil shed away,
>   A pulse in the eternal mind, no less
> Gives somewhere back the thoughts by England given;
>   Her sights and sounds; dreams happy as her day;
> And laughter, learnt of friends; and gentleness,
>   In hearts at peace, under an English heaven.

Siegfried Sassoon wrote in the same vein. But Sassoon survived the
first two years of the war, as Brooke did not. And it was he who first
marked the change. It was Sassoon who came out flatly with the statement that the sacrifice was too great; it was wanton; it was more than
civilization could endure. Sassoon was an infantry officer who had been
awarded the Military Cross and who, so rumor has it, had been recommended for the Victoria Cross. But at that moment he did what every

hard-driven Englishman is prompted to do under stress—he wrote to the *London Times*. His letter was an eye-opener, and after its publication he threw his medals away and withdrew from the British Army. His friends kept him as quiet as they could. But Sassoon was aching to say then— and did say later in his poetry—what another infantry officer was already writing in his notebook. I mean Captain Wilfred Owen, who died of wounds just before the Armistice, and whose poems in their bitter beauty mark the despair which had risen in men's minds since Rupert Brooke:

> Let the boy try along this bayonet-blade
> How cold steel is, and keen with hunger of blood;
> Blue with all malice, like a madman's flash;
> And thinly drawn with famishing for flesh.
>
> Lend him to stroke these blind, blunt bullet-heads
> Which long to nuzzle in the hearts of lads.
> Or give him cartridges of fine zinc teeth,
> Sharp with the sharpness of grief and death.
>
> For his teeth seem for laughing round an apple.
> There lurk no claws behind his fingers supple;
> And God will grow no talons at his heels,
> Nor antlers through the thickness of his curls.

Coming back to this country for our demobilization, what did we veterans read? We read *Through the Wheat* by Thomas Boyd, *Toward the Flame* by Hervey Allen. We enjoyed *What Price Glory?*—the play which was so shattering to our parents—and eventually we read the greatest novel of the war, the story brewed from defeat, *All Quiet on the Western Front*. By that time the transformation was complete. Germans and Americans alike, we had been through the mill: the ardor had gone, we had seen what the sacrifice was worth—and despair was creeping in.

Today the habits of twenty years are still with us. It is still the method of our writers to shock the reader into awareness. The ingrained skepticism still makes our Zolas report what they see and question what they know. It also makes them slow, perhaps it makes them incapable of being sure that a better way is available. In short, we face this new war with the despair left over from the last. If we are to have any feeling of ardor, any self-confidence, any exhilaration about what we are to do, that feeling is still to come. Can despair sink any lower in literature? Can the attitude of our writers be any more discouraging than it has been in the past two years? Why, of course it can. You have only to look at France today to realize how far the tide has ebbed in that silent country. But even in France there must be people who take consolation in the thought that men have been through this despair in times past and have risen from it. At the end of the French Revolution, a Frenchman said something like this: "Now we must begin to build again on the bedrock of despair; we must entertain no illusions, we must recognize the worst—and then build."

On this side of the Atlantic writers are trying to shake off their gloom. They are trying to write constructively about what is to come. But, you will ask, what is there that we can positively believe in at this moment? There is a new feeling of responsibility in the air and this will inevitably affect your writing. First, I am positive that as a nation we can do the things we set our minds to. We are a dynamic people and we hate to mark time. We have set ourselves an enormous job and I am confident that we can do it. If some of you go into defense work, you will have a chance to see the job at first hand—and there may be books in it. Secondly, don't forget the millions of middle-aged and elderly people— your parents and mine—people who run out of breath, who find it hard to keep up with what's happening. Someone has got to bridge the understanding between your generation and theirs—and that bridge will be built of books. Thirdly, we have got to decide for ourselves whether we really are a united people. I am positive that we are. But according to Goebbels we are divided. Where does the truth lie? Have we been able to absorb thirty-eight million newcomers in a hundred years? Are they Americans? No one man knows enough to say. The truth can only be testified by hundreds of writers in their short stories and novels about our American communities.

"Sure, sure," you say to yourself. "I have heard something like that before. What I really want to know is how I am to get any writing done if I am packed off to a training camp." Well, that is up to you. T. E. Lawrence—Lawrence of Arabia, only he then called himself T. E. Shaw— managed to translate the *Odyssey*, write his forbidden novel, *The Mint,* and carry on the most voluminous correspondence—all this as a private in the English Tank Corps. James Norman Hall, who graduated from Grinnell College, Iowa, wrote his first two books in intervals between being a machine-gunner and a pursuit pilot. They had no more time than you will have. Nor should you dismiss the possibility of what can be

done in a letter. I remember reading last winter a famous letter in which
W. T. Donald, the Australian adviser to Chiang Kai-shek, describes the
enormous tenacity and infinite patience with which the Chinese transported their factories, their schools, their hospitals, and their homes,
brick by brick, object by object, all the way up to Chungking, knowing
even while they rebuilt their capital that it would be a target for the
Japanese bombers. Letters with a tenacity like that will live. So may
yours, if you are part of a great movement.

If writing is really in you, you will not lose the habit of counting
your chickens before they hatch. Your real problem, it seems to me, is
not whether you will be able to write, but rather what form of writing is
best suited to the nature of your work and the time you have available.
For example, if you are going to camp or if you are going to be tied up
for nine hours a day in some heavy industry, then obviously the kind of
writing which you can most readily putter along with is that which
grows out of the first person singular. Read your own experience, see
what it is good for, and then see how vivid you can make that experience
to the stay-at-home. That's what Jim Hall did. That's what John Dos
Passos did. That's what Hervey Allen did.

If you are a poet, you are in luck, because poetry hits quickly and a
whole poem can often be captured in an afternoon off. If you are a poet,
remember what I said about the cult of unintelligibility. If you have got
something worth saying, make it count. And if you are a poet, don't
spend all your substance on the lyric or the didactic. Remember that not
since *John Brown's Body* has anyone really taken the trouble to exercise
the narrative poem. People are hungry for narration today—just as hungry as they are for poetry they can understand.

If you are a novelist, I suggest that you do not burn up your free
time trying to write a long novel. If you have got to make every minute
count, and if you are weary—as I am—of that novel which begins with
the hero in his cradle, carries him through his school days, through his
college years, through his unhappy marriage and finally pushes him into
the grave, take a day off and refresh your knowledge of what can be done
within the compass of the short novel. See what Conrad Richter did in
that intense and lovely story of his, *The Sea of Grass*. All told it measures
less than 36,000 words. See what Willa Cather did with her *Lost Lady*.
See what Wilder did in his *Bridge of San Luis Rey*—that story is less than
50,000 words. See what Steinbeck did in *Of Mice and Men*. See what
Robert Nathan does, year after year. These are brilliant performances,

these short novels, and the form is a very exciting one with which to work. You haven't room to build year upon year; you haven't room for any elaborate descriptions. You have got to begin in the middle of things and then, shuttling your story back and forth, by balancing your passages of introspection against the forward movement, you shape a story which, if it be really good, will carry the reader's thoughts far beyond the last period.

I know no more than you do whether we shall go all the way down the road to intervention until we are at last openly and irrevocably at war. Or whether by some surprising turn we may be able to tip the scales in favor of a negotiated peace. If peace comes now, I wonder if it can be any more than an armistice until our job is done. For whether we like it or not, we have been challenged to stand up and tell the world what we mean by American democracy. We can't do that overnight. It will take time. And as we work out the proof in our own way, there will come with it, I firmly believe, an upsurge in American writing. I look for good historical novels; I hope for a revival of the Mark Twain–Will Rogers humor we need so badly; I expect contemporary novels with courage and zest for the present. Where is the man who will write the novel that ought to be written about skilled labor? Will Steinbeck do it, or will someone we have never heard of? I have often speculated as to how it might be done. Suppose the father of the family was a railroad engineer and a member of the brotherhood. Suppose his son has thrown in his lot with motors, and is just as rabidly C.I.O. Here are men drawn together by their love of machines and their love of doing things with their hands, and yet set in opposition by systems over which they have little control. Were such a story told in human terms, it would stir us as no novel about our mechanical genius has yet done.

Or looking still further ahead into the future, who will tell the story of the resettlement of this country as it is now going on, as the new factories spring up and the boom towns grow? We are doing more than simply forging new weapons. We are forging new communities, many of which will become permanent when at last the time comes to live in peace.

I have often wished that I might have seen this country as Audubon saw it, when the trees were in the forests and the birds were in the trees. And kindred to that desire is a hankering to have lived at the time of the American Revolution and to have seen our first great leaders in action, to have seen Washington's farewell to his officers at Fraunces' Tavern, to have heard what Thomas Jefferson thought of the French Revolution, to have known men like John Adams and Hamilton. These men pulled the country together; to have lived in their time, we think, would have made bigger men of us. Time is kind as we look back. We remember the clear thinking, the manliness, and the grandeur of the old days; we forget the uncertainty, the persecution, and the despair which made them dark. Again as we approach the perspective of a full century we begin to appreciate the size and the depth of the men who came, most of them from nowhere, to wrestle, in the 1860s, with the problem of whether this country could be united: Lincoln, Grant, Sherman, Jackson, and Lee.

Now for a third time the country is being put to the test. Seventy-five years from now will people say to themselves, "By God, that was the time to have lived! How I'd like to have had a hand in it!" It could be.

Poetry as Primitive Language

John Crowe Ransom

A friend of mine said he had been driving in the neighborhood of Memphis. The new highway was in places a sort of causeway built up above bayou water, and right at the base of it on one side an old Negro was fishing. Thinking that the water was too near the slag and the noise of the highway for this sport, my friend stopped his car and had the following conversation with the fisherman:

> Good morning, Uncle, are you fishing?
> Yessir, Cap'n, I'm fishin'.
> Have you caught any fish yet?
> Nossir, I ain't yet.
> Have you had any bites?
> Nossir, I don't believe I has.
> Have you had any nibbles?
> Nossir, I can't say I is.
> Do you think there are any fish in that hole?
> Cap'n, I don't much reckon there's any fish there nohow.
> Well, Uncle, why do you keep fishing there?
> Well, Cap'n, this is the hole I'se always done my fishin' in, 'cause that's my house right up yonder on the rise.

This anecdote has several possible morals, and I may have used it in the past to suit the occasion. The one I read from it today is the truest of all its meanings, and has to do with a spiritual affinity between the fisherman and Mr. T. S. Eliot of *The Waste Land*. The big new road symbolizes modernity. It had killed out the fish in this particular hole, but the old man went on fishing there just the same. The fact is that fishing is not a single action like a science, but an ambiguous activity like an art. It means to take fish and be effective, just as poetry means to carry on a rational argument and say something. But it means also to sit on the ground, smell the water, watch the snakes and dragonflies, slap the

73

mosquitoes, feel the sun, and smoke a pipe—all of which together amount to a diffuse, delicious context which goes with fish-taking, and parallels most precisely the splendid contextual detail of poetic language. But in the forms of modern life the colored man and Mr. Eliot have found it so hard to attach the old familiar contexts to the new effective actions that they have decided to take the contexts and let the effective actions go. Modern art tends that way. It does a pretty piece of fishing, and allows for all the business that belongs to fishing except the taking of fish.

Let that wait a moment. My topic is not the ineffectiveness but the primitivism of poetry, and they do not necessarily come to the same thing, though sometimes they may. By primitivism I mean an antique or outmoded cast of thought, so that the poetry is likely to seem heroic as compared with contemporary thought, or to seem pastoral, agrarian, medieval, Pre-Raphaelitish, or merely old-fashioned and quaint. After some progress of civilization comes a movement of regress, with poets in charge of it. But I have generally labored this point in large or philosophical terms, with the result that I seemed to myself profound but not very pointed, and academically correct but, as a student of poetry, not really close to the topic. Today, in your honor, I will talk about the primitive quality that appears in poetry as language. This version of critical theory is brand-new for me, and experimental, since I have not worked it out, but it seems more streamlined and presentable than any other I have hit upon.

Literary criticism is not identical with philosophy at large, but it occurs to me that it may well be identical with linguistic. Or, if you prefer the term, it may be identical with semantics, one of the newest, most capable, and sharpest of analytic tools. The advantage is that in applying it, whether to a poetry or to a science, you can uncover a lot of philosophical elements that belong to your topic, and escape from uncovering a lot of philosophical elements that do not belong to your topic. I am at the moment a sort of convertite to linguistic, and am trying to translate into its forms such theoretical notions as I have otherwise arrived at.

I have assembled my observations not too systematically under the head of a numerical series of "points." This is logically a bad style, but it is a fast one, and great statesmen have recommended it to your favor. I will not say how many "points" appeared in my notes, but they were too many; they greatly exceeded fourteen. I have now reduced them slightly below that number. I proceed:

1. A primitive language is one whose standard discourse, in trying to be *conceptual* (or rational), is obliged also, and whether or no, to be *imaginal* (or substantival). That is, in trying to make useful formulations about things, relating them by virtue of some common or class property, it is obliged to refer to the many propertied or substantial things themselves, the things as wholes. Primitive languages are sometimes called *radical* languages: they consist almost wholly in root words, each one denoting a whole thing or whole event. In discourse these roots are jumbled together, and it devolves upon the hearer to figure out the properties in which the things named are related, and by elimination to read into the jumble a consecutive argument. Here is the famous ambiguity of language. You still have it in poetic metaphor, for example, and in all unskillful speech. Does your metaphorical word refer to the single property which makes it logically fit for the argument, or does it also evoke an image and refer to the independent substance? Homer was fond of the "wine-dark" sea, and used the locution again and again; ostensibly he meant a shade of color, but incidentally his readers and singers were sure to receive a fleeting image of the substantial and very good thing named wine.

2. A language develops out of its primitive or radical condition in at least two ways. First, it improves its vocabulary, finding words which denote the several properties of the thing and not having to keep on denoting every time the whole manifold of properties which make up the substance—adjectives for the leading aspects of the thing, adverbs and highly restricted verbs for aspects of the event. They are relatively abstract, technical, scientific, and useful. Second, the primitive language develops syntactically. It learns to place the parts of predication in a definitive order expressive of their relation; it invents inflections, prefixes and suffixes, and relational words like the conjunction and the preposition. It is improving the precision of discourse, and more and more squeezing imagination, which looks for its substantial images, out of the action. I do not mention as a syntactical development the device of compounding or hyphenating words; that is generally the crudest primitivism, though poets are given to it, and it either antedates or repudiates the close syntactical articulation.

In short, suppose an American Indian plenipotentiary, knowing his English only to the extent of a few root words like those of some primitive language and treating with the white invaders, who know even less than that about his language, as follows: "Heap big Indian hunting go,

heap big paleface firewater come." Against its particular background this
discourse might just be intelligible. But now conceive the plenipotentiary as having behind him a modern Indian's college studies and the
whole recent development of the English language, and phrasing his
proposition like this: "The designated territories are obviously extensive
and valuable, and my government would require in compensation for
them a fully proportionate volume of distilled liquor of acceptable alcoholic content." But to phrase the bargain in this way seems to insult the
intelligence of the party of the first part and the honesty of the party of
the second part, and we should remark that linguistic precision illuminates the values offered in a bargain, or anywhere else. I do not think
poets, Indians, heroes, demigods, or any other primitives could look out
for themselves in a society whose advanced prose precision they could
not master.

3. An advanced language is one in which the standard discourse is
perfect or nearly perfect conceptually, and the imaginal or substantival
range of meaning has all but disappeared. At this stage language conquers its involuntary ambiguity. It becomes fit for big business, technical
science, and all other abstract forms of thinking. This is the kind of
language that seems exclusively to be coveted by some semanticists, such
as Korzybski. Kenneth Burke wrote to me that all semanticists of his
acquaintance were naturalists, meaning that they tolerated only discourse
after the scientific ideal, and in his view were bad people; that is, they
would like to impose this ideal upon all discourses regardless of its suit-
ability. I for my part just now referred to conceptual discourse as the
standard of language; and certainly, as language improves its prose, it
approximates more and more to that standard; even if we include its
literary prose. Sir Thomas Browne sustained his imagistic magnilo-
quence proudly as something that in his day would be set to the credit of
a writer. It is significant that we have no Brownes today; but we do have,
for instance, Mr. Logan Pearsall Smith, whose phantasies are one sentence or at most several sentences long, whose mock seriousness represents an author with tongue in cheek, and who denominates his pieces as
Trivia. But I think not all semanticists are uncompromising partisans of
science for all occasions, and my acquaintance with them has been a little
more fortunate than Mr. Burke's.

4. As a language develops, and discourse becomes more rigorously
conceptual, and the imaginal fringe of substance is obliterated from
view, poetry intervenes. Poetry recovers to language its imaginal or

substantival dimension, almost as fast as language loses it, though of course not quite. That is probably what poetry is for, as nearly as we can state it. It is a special and artificial kind of discourse fighting for excuse to live in a society which has proscribed it. Naturally it might court the more primitive groups of this society and claim to speak their language, and Wordsworth offers a doctrine of poetry as the language of common men. But if it is not more regressive and braver in its diction than that, it will not have for common men the value of a poetry, and on the whole I think it needs to be maintained that poetry has a value only for those who are familiar with the advancement of contemporary language and disaffected by the failure of its imaginal dimension. The imaginal dimension in language is something you did not know was there till it is gone, and then you turn to poetry in order to get it back. The primitive character of the poetic language will show, of course, in the radical quality of its terms and in the looseness of its syntax.

5. Our own present language is highly advanced, so that its prose standard enforces a conceptual purity that would be simply fabulous for a primitive mind. The need for poetry is probably all the more imperative. But evidently the difficulty is greater than usual, perhaps greater than ever. It is harder to go primitive in your language when you are bred up to maintain its rationality; and at the same time it may be harder to palm poetry off upon a public that has come under an aggressive educational establishment and learned something about linguistic duty and linguistic destiny; the whole artifice of poetry becomes transparent, and a little shabby. What will the modern poet do? Mr. Eliot has advised him to "dislocate language" if necessary, and in his own verse has practiced many violences. That is a bold strategy, and does not appeal to the middling public, which, from its casual acquaintance with older poetry, is not used to outraging the contemporary modes of discourse so recklessly. But Mr. Eliot is a wise man and a veteran of the wars, and we should not dismiss his counsel hastily. Poets appear to be faced with a crisis of language, the critical difficulty being that the imaginal element of language is now so slurred and abridged that there is not room enough in reputable discourse for poetry to begin its usual procedures.

6. The style of poetic discourse has always been outwardly loyal to the purpose of primitive language (indeed to the ruling purpose of any language) in preserving the impression of being a conceptual discourse intending to say something rather clear and useful. But now there appear exceptions: poems in which no binding argument is visible supporting

the images of the poem. There are, for example, the poems of Eliot, of
Hart Crane, of a school of surrealists, and there is the poetic prose of
James Joyce. In France, where there is more consciousness of language
than elsewhere, the exceptions began with the Symbolists far back in the
nineteenth century. But in general these poems are highly modern, and
still under question. I advert again to my colored fisherman who
achieved the fishing without the fish: they are trying to provide the body
of poetry without providing a skeleton to hold it together. On the whole
I think the tactic is wrong. But that does not mean that the situation is
not desperate, and I hesitate to offer a general judgment because the poets
may really be more subtle and penetrating than I am in their analysis of
the poetic situation. I tend to take comfort from the example of William
Butler Yeats. His understanding was deep, his strategy perfectly adven-
turous, so that he tried many experiments that failed; but I am very sure
he found an area of language in which images and definitive arguments
accommodated themselves to each other. I am not yet sure how big this
area was and how much room remains there for further poetic farming.

7. Modern psychology seems to enforce point 6—especially Gestalt
psychology, with its studies of the process of attention and the process of
learning. I believe it admits scarcely any such thing as a pure image, that
is, an image in which our attention diffuses equally upon all the properties. On the contrary, we achieve the image of a thing only in the process
of recognizing the thing, and we recognize it by virtue of detecting in it
some dominating surface property or facet property which is obviously
valuable. We then apprehend the other properties of the image in a sort
of *sub rosa* fashion, thinking we are engrossed or pretending to be engrossed still with the dominant property, but really rioting in that territory of the image which is relatively out of focus and forbidden. However, it remains true that we attend to the image by focusing it, and when
it falls out of all focus we cannot attend to it. We get the fringe items by
looking out of the corner of our eye; or we turn our eye straight on them,
but not for long. Such a technique is probably the one employed by
poetry; a way of indirection, but perhaps the only way on earth of
realizing the vividness, magnificence, and beauty of the world. A psychology of poetry would work along these lines and show the devices by
which poetry permits us to have this truancy without offending the
public censor, or even the Freudian censor who presides over our own
consciousness. But the Freudian allusion may be misleading. I think the
remarkable property of the poetic image, aside from its existence at all, is

its innocence. There is no chance of accounting for poetic beauty as a libidinous gratification, nor even as something useful, nor even as something moral. Such accounts have been pushed hard and ingeniously, but they have failed. But perhaps I do not need to declare to you that the poetic beauty survives all the failures of our crude analysis, and we continue to receive it after we confess that it cannot be isolated as easily as we had thought.

8. There is no primitivism in poetry so ubiquitous, so atmospheric, as the primitivism of its language, which is almost identifiable with the process of consciousness itself. But there are primitive characters in it more obvious than this—and, for example, that of its cosmology, theology, or ideology. To be completely contemporary you must give up the Oxford *Book of English Verse,* and you must expurgate large tracts from the corpus of most of the famous poets and some of your favorite poets, because in respect of their ideas you come upon the primitive. Even in their own day they were prepared to commit anachronism. Think of the Christian poets who have restored the Olympian deities, and the Copernicans who have reverted to the Ptolemaic cosmos—a notorious infidelity on the part of the poets, and they must rate broadly and ideologically, as well as in ways much subtler and harder to remark, as apostates from our achieved culture. We are obliged to remark that there often appears in poetry precisely the mode of primitivism that has the official sanction of the religious establishments. Religion seems fundamentally to be a resistance to the purification of our cosmic conceptions, and in the face of progress a regression to beautiful but primitive dogmas. The new concepts are too pure and emasculated; the old dogmas registered better the contingent density of the actual created world; the concept and the dogma stand for different modes of knowledge. Construed philologically (*religio* = a tying back), religion may be expected, when the issue is joined, to espouse the dogma against the concept. The poetic ideas may likewise show very well the general direction that poetry takes, but they are not strictly my topic. They are a topic for poetic criticism unquestionably, and we know that while it is easy to spot the ideas it is not easy to trace them with precision. But what is still harder, and of a more enveloping importance, and probably more fascinating, is the analysis of the poetic language.

9. Returning to language. It must not be supposed that the poetic regression is merely a matter of finding some actual historic idiom that is now archaic and outmoded. That would be a defiance comparable to the

religious recital of the old dogma; but poetry lacks the support of a great institutional establishment to approve an overt defiance, so that would be too bold to succeed, and too simple and literal to rate as a technique. It is true that archaic diction figures in poetry, but it is also true, in my estimation, that the effect is bad. It is possible for poetry to cover up its tracks, and to seem contemporary without conforming to the level of conceptual attainment that is in vogue. Consequently it would be a poor critical project to plan, for example, to discover in the poetic diction of the eighteenth century a diction recovered bodily from the seventeenth century after the latter had vanished from eighteenth-century prose. Poetry must preserve "face." It should sound contemporary, and with the accomplished poets I think it does; it even sounds felicitous, elegant, and fashionable. This requires of the poet the greatest linguistic ingenuity.

10. The diction of fine poetry is always fresh and individual, but there are several broad techniques or strategies which poets have handed down to their successors since time immemorial. They have become publicly licensed, and no public has been querulous enough to challenge them, unless it is very recently. They make up the only objective institutional establishment there is for poetry to shelter under. I do not know what would happen to poetry if it should be deprived of them, and its tenuous establishment should collapse. I do not know what would happen, but perhaps there is a chance of my finding out before very long, if there is no shift in the linguistic climate. They are rank solecisms, either by nature or by the extravagant manner of their practice.

The first of these strategies is meter. It is a way of enforcing a phonetic imagery upon attention, which otherwise might be completely occupied with the semantic character, or meaning, of the words. That makes a dispersal of attention, enough by itself perhaps to be decisive and to convert reception into an aesthetic experience; the phonetic effect becomes a context round the semantic action. But it has a strange effect upon the semantic action itself which it is important to consider. The meter works upon the poet when he composes, and alters his composition, and then it works upon the hearer, and alters his sense of what he is reading. Look first at the poet. He is not quite free to use the words that express his intended meaning, because these do not automatically fall into the prescribed meter; so he must tinker with them, and try substitutions, till the meter has been realized and the meaning is not too remote. In this process the meaning gets loosened up. He has sacrificed the conceptual precision of his vocabulary, and the cogency of his syntax. If it was difficult to know how to escape from the bondage of a conceptual discourse, his metrical necessities have driven him to do just that, one little step at a time. And now observe the reader. I have observed the reader, many times, and professionally. I have observed that often the reader of a poetry that is perilously on the loose, imaginal, and primitive side is unaware of the fact, because he is fooled by the tidiness of the meter. It takes a reader from one of the science departments of the college to ignore the meter and dig into the obscurities of the discourse. The student from the science department has a harder head than one of our students and is useful to have on hand during poetic studies; but he is rather at the disadvantage of being committed to attending to one thing at a time—first the meaning, then the meter, hardly the two together. Perhaps he has lost his rugged primitive constitution, and is effete. On the other hand, the prejudice of the arts trained student is all against picking a good thing to pieces; but his habit of taking the whole thing in stride exposes him to blind spots as to just what he is taking. You can hardly persuade him that the elaborate musical development in Swinburne for example, or even in Shelley, went along with, and indeed necessitated, a serious deficiency in the meaning.

11. Another licensed poetic convention, whose loss poetry could hardly survive, is figure of speech, or trope, in all its luxuriant variety. I believe linguistic is prepared to lay down the general rule that any trope represents an aberration from the conceptual ideal of discourse. It is surprising that in collegiate departments of English literature the tropes are not systematically studied as logical or a-logical devices. In this respect the moderns have lapsed from the critical scholarship of the ancients. I would like to write a critical note entitled, "From Aristotle to Longinus to Genung." The point would be that Aristotle made a very close analysis of a great group of tropes under the general head of metaphor, classifying its lawless procedures with at least a show of system; it might be said that he was examining the dodges, or the devices, by which reputable poets, who knew better, imported radicals or imaginal terms into an argument expecting conceptual or abstract terms. Longinus also was more than an ordinary analyst, and should be useful to us because his interest, in part at least and perhaps chiefly, was in the tropes which are purely syntactical and which obscure discourse by jumbling words together without showing their articulation—waiving conjunctions and mixing up tenses, for example. The Greeks recognized both

kinds of trope, and a regressive poetry needs both, though we hear today
almost exclusively about the first kind, and find the second kind isolated
from their poetic occasions and held up to detestation in freshman man-
uals under such heads as "Uncoördinate Series" and "The *and* Fault."
And, last, Genung, American author of a famous textbook of rhetoric,
who names and defines most of the tropes with a very pretty scholarship,
and appears innocent of any suspicion that the tropes of honored poets
were acting with insubordination against the sequence and the unity of
their discourses. But Genung flourished years ago, when official studies
in English literature were new. The collocation of Aristotle, Longinus,
and Genung might prompt the query: What are the English studies
doing? And when will intelligent linguistic come into them?

12. This will be my concluding point. It concerns the over-all or
generic motive of the poet, and in the light of his record of apostasy,
aberration, sabotage, and furtiveness I should not want to waive that
question. I do not like to surrender to that ingenious motive-hunting
which finds us doing everything for the sake of something else. We do
many things because we must do them, and it only occurs to us later that
we probably did them because we wanted to and must have had some
"reason." Poetry is a discourse ordinarily in the indicative mode, therefore a mode of knowing, and probably one could say with touching piety
that its motive is Truth. But who will tell us what that means? The truth,
for the linguist at any rate, is what we know. Poetry is therefore a mode
of knowing whose motive is to know. But some illumination is gained if
we contrast the poetic language with the scientific language.

If my linguistic orientation is correct, poetic language arises historically because we are not happy over the improvements we make in our
scientific language. We are not happy because these improvements require us to abandon progressively the imaginal or substantival elements.
But the imaginal or substantival elements characterized a kind of language with which we were familiar by inheritance from our primitive
ancestors—an actual and evidently a satisfying kind of language. The
linguist will remark, perhaps by a slight departure from his professional
duties though with all the more weight because of his disinterest, that
there seems to be no testimony on the record to dispute the overwhelming agreement of the poets that these words refer to aspects of the world
which are still there and visible in the world, though it may be that our
modern linguistic training encourages us to pay little attention to them
any more. As a man uses language, so is he. But I do not mean to abuse

scientific language in order to praise poetic language. There is as much impulsion upon us to develop our scientific language as there is to protect our poetry. These are two actual and valid languages, though the one is in protest against the other and their fraternal relations become more and more uncomfortable.

I do not know anything further to say on this point, unless I should import into a linguistic discourse for the sake of a final flourish a big word from formal philosophy. The word would be: *ontological*. The poet's motive is ontological, just as is the motive of what we call the pure scientist; he is predicating about a character of the natural world, and it is not the character about which the scientist is predicating—though both might be said to be predicating about some character of The Way Things Are. But *ontological* would add little to the linguist's own nice sense of the poet's strategic situation except an impressive polysyllabic phonetic item. Suffice it to say that for linguistic the poet is in his duty.

Popular and Unpopular Poetry
in America

Louise Bogan

This subject, it is to be hoped, will not bring to mind the idea of "popular" in the sense of "successful" and "unpopular" in the sense of "unsuccessful." It is not a question of looking forward to a set of rules guaranteed to produce the kind of poetry that a great many people will read,
although, as a matter of fact, one could formulate just such a set of rules.
Rules of that kind, it can be demonstrated, are not worth learning, or
worth putting into action once they have been learned. Here the words
popular and *unpopular* will be used in a different sense: in the sense that
came in with the great changes that occurred in Europe at the beginning
of the nineteenth century, when the great Romantic and Industrial Revolution broke through the classic line that had endured for so long, and
with so much seemingly unbreakable strength, in England as well as on
the Continent.

To put the thought rather simply: What has happened to what was
once called "folk song" or "folk poetry"? Into what has it been transformed, if it no longer appears before us in the colors it once wore, in the
situation it once held? And then: What has happened to "formal" poetry?
Why is it the subject of so much suspicion and even so much contempt?
Why do some people seem to hate and fear it? Is it possible that formal
poetry must disappear, or has it indeed already disappeared in America?
Or is it possible to look forward to a development of formal poetry in
America analogous to the past development of this art in Europe?

It is necessary to go back a little and go over familiar material, so
familiar that, perhaps, it has been taken for granted. It is the historic
background of the textbooks; but here it can be approached from a
slightly different angle in the hope that it can be rid of the opaque quality
that everything taken for granted tends to assume.

In poetry the first thing to be noticed in the Romantic Revolution of
the arts, with its background of actual revolution, is that formal poetry

84

transformed itself by means of contact with folk song. The formal art-ists, in England and Scotland, with Wordsworth, Coleridge, and Robert Burns, and later, in France, with Victor Hugo, managed to re-connect their art with ordinary speech; managed to get back into their rhythms the hauntingly lovely, yet exquisitely simple, rhythms of the folk ballad; and managed, as well, to widen their field so that they could treat many subjects that had been for a long time closed to formal writing. New material techniques appeared almost immediately to aid the wide circula-tion of this new literature.

These techniques were those of the press (the newspaper), the new magazines and periodicals, and new methods of advertising and selling books. And not only lyric poetry, but dramatic poetry, the form hitherto encased in the most rigid tradition—that of the classic tragedy—began to break from the classic mold. Painting, too, turned away from the cele-bration of official occasions, either religious or secular, and the artist's canvas now had to compete with the lithographer's block, which, with Daumier as its master, was to bring in a whole new body of popular illustration. What was to become the most popular form of literature came into being almost overnight with Walter Scott's historical novels. The novel soon began to absorb creative energy on all sides. Poets, no matter how little vocation they possessed for the art of fiction, were by some obscure necessity compelled to write novels.

Dramatists, and even critics, tried their hand at this fresh and all-embracing, all-accommodating form. And in the truly miraculous way that Nature immediately supplies genius and supreme executants when-ever a new form or a new apparatus appears—we think of the millions of years that mankind did without the pianoforte keyboard and the rush of great virtuosi, from Mozart through Chopin and Liszt, that promptly appeared directly it *was* invented—in this extraordinary fashion the novel was at once supplied with novelists of the most exuberant talent and unflagging energy: Scott, Balzac, Victor Hugo, Dickens.

While here it is a question of poetry, we see at once in the world rising out of the Romantic Revolution, that it is difficult to speak of poetry alone; many other arts come rushing in. And we see that even in its early phases, the world of the Romantic Revolution is already our world—so filled as it was with dynamic force, so eager as it was to break through old forms, so resourceful at pulling over from the past and at conjuring up from the future what it needed, without thought of break-age or without fear of making irreparable mistakes. It is a world we recognize as we do not recognize the eighteenth century, or the seventeenth, or the sixteenth. It becomes our world with incredible swiftness; and one of the strongest elements we recognize in the whole is the emergence of "popular art."

"Popular art": something quite different from the folk art of feudal times, or of any time preceding 1789, in Europe. The former folk art was based on the peasant; the new folk art was based on the citizen of the town. The evolving modern techniques began to feed this citizen all sorts of assorted amusement and information. The new daily gazettes, the new *romans-feuilletons,* the impressively thick works of fiction, the illustrated periodicals, shared this citizen's attention with the new and exciting popular theatrical performances, the new and exciting popular music. All sorts of influences began to shuttle back and forth, from England to France and through Europe in general. The world was made new again, artistically, politically, technically. The young and vigorous had ousted the rigid, lifeless, and outworn. There seemed no limit to the hopes that one could have for the future.

The early nineteenth century, then, lacked only the moving picture, the radio, and some forms of nationwide advertising to be the world filled with various pastimes for the citizen, almost exactly as we know it today. It is important to look at it in its full freshness. That freshness faded, became transformed. The last thing one wanted to do, early in the twentieth century, was to look back at these rather outmoded writers and artists and musicians. The great writers had been transformed, as it were, into crowds of bronze statues; avenues and streets and squares had been named after them. Other things had happened; later technical devices had rendered the earlier ones obsolete. But we look back upon these beginnings now because we are looking for some help in present bewilderment. Something was wrong in all that surging creativeness; something was left out; something was neglected. Some false emphasis was already pulling the pattern askew, even while it was forming. We know this now, because we are still living in what remains—and, as has been suggested, a good deal remains—of that world.

A new popular art had rushed into being. But what had happened to unpopular—formal, "high," classic—art? And what was this new thing that had inserted itself, without any outward show and insidiously, between the two: this poetry, criticism, fiction, painting, music of a kind never seen in quite this form at any previous time? This thin, sentimental—this cheap and raucous—or this heavy and pretentious—or this rather hypocritical, florid, and bedizened literature (poetry, drama, and prose), painting, and even music?—What it was, and what it is, was middle-class literature, painting, and music. It spread about and absorbed matters on all sides so quickly that, even at the outset, it was difficult to know where it ended, and where true literature (or painting or music) began. Had true popular art—the expression of the folk, urbanized or peasant—totally disappeared? Had formal art totally dissolved? Where was the line of demarcation between bourgeois letters and the crumbling facade of formal writing? In England not much attention was paid to the situation. But in France, in the generation following the first Romantic generation, two men appeared who analyzed the problem with the most bitter and caustic insight. Of these critics, Flaubert was the most uncompromising, the most clear-minded. And Sainte-Beuve, in an article written in 1838, "La Littérature industrielle," denounced the entry of industrial practices into literature. But let us leave the historical background for a moment.

Let us consider folk literature, especially American folk literature. What folk art have we? where can it be found and how can it be used? We know that creative aridity sets in at certain periods due to rules clamped down over a culture, or due to some spiritual or physical exhaustion. Then the fresh and strong touch of folk art, if a submerged folk art exists in the given culture, often brings about a new upsurge of energy, a new depth of emotion, a new lyrical awakening. We remember that the daffodil, that particularly fresh and simple "folk" flower, disappeared from English poetry for almost a hundred years; it went out with the late Restoration and came in again with Wordsworth. It seems to be a recurrent phenomenon, this turning away from nature for a period; and no one notices particularly, or sheds any tears about the matter, when the daffodil disappears. But what shouts of rejoicing are heard when the daffodil comes back!

Something magical has come to be associated with the pure powers of creation residing in the folk. Highly artificial cultures have tried to get back to simplicity by *playing* at simplicity, to touch this magic by imitating the surface manners of the folk tradition. But this play acting never really works; it results in some charming "pastoral" decoration, but in no profound art. A real break-through must be made. We remember that all sorts of revivals and collections of folk ballads began to appear in the exact center of the eighteenth century. Then came a period of enthusiasm for the medieval, then came forged "romantic" poetry and counterfeit ballads; these were mixed in with the authentic songs and ballads that were being disinterred and revived. It is important to remember this point: that during certain uncreative periods, the taste and the need for folk expression become so strong that people begin not only to *play-act* "folk," but to *manufacture* it artificially.

At present there exists in America a real desire to return to our more primitive art. There is a definite suspicion, in the minds and hearts of many Americans, that something we once had—something we once were—has disappeared. Some refreshment we could once draw upon has dried up. Folk art is always "romantic." And it is the kind of "romance" that can be trusted: it is based on real human anguish, and upon real human joy, and upon real human energy and passion. Our rural and primitive past, with all its richness of song and story and tall tale and picaresque narrative—it is so near us, and yet it is so difficult to conjure up, to tie in with our mechanized and urban present. It is so difficult to make it the basis for our creative work.

The turning toward the folk at the end of the eighteenth century was preindustrial as well as prerevolutionary. In our own times, two poets succeeded in getting back to a folk tradition in their respective countries: Yeats in Ireland and García Lorca in Spain. But in these two countries, these two poets were dealing with cultures that had escaped, in a large measure, any true industrial development. There was no rigid barrier of industrialized attitudes to be broken through. Yeats in Ireland went back to the peasant songs and stories; Lorca went back to the *flamenco* tradition. Both of these poets received the experience of poetry *still attached to music* and still at an *improvisatory stage;* both were refreshed by the experience of an audience creatively involved (actual listeners and, at times, actual collaborators—not mere readers) in what these two men, as poets, produced.

We turn to examine our own folk tradition, and what variety and abundance we find! We can trace the line of the American folk songs through the ballads of English, Irish, Scotch, Welsh, and, sometimes, French and Spanish origin—broken away from their original background and variously transformed. Then come the work songs of all kinds—sea chanteys, songs of the plantation, the rivers, and the cattle range. Developing along beside these secular songs come the spirituals and hymns, elaborating out of a few basic tunes into countless variations.

Then the culmination and the turning point of American folk song appears in the person of Stephen Foster. This untrained and greatly gifted writer of popular songs managed to express fully the emotions common in a period of transition. On the one hand, through him, the loneliness as well as the rough gaiety of a primitive society found its voice. On the other, Foster gave expression to something quite new: to an emotion that was to become increasingly persistent in the American spirit—the emotion of profound nostalgia for an already disappearing rural way of life. The strong sentimentalization of Foster by his modern audience proceeds from the holdover of this crucial, though fairly well dissimulated, nostalgia into our own time. Clearly, Foster was the end of one kind of American folk, the point beyond which no pure development of his kind of material was possible.

We then begin to hear, after the hymns and marching songs of the Civil War, the beginning of what may be called *urbanized* folk music. The railroads building and having been built, we get the railroad songs. The cities once made, we get the hybrid genteel almost at once: the songs of the upright piano and the sheet-music era, along with songs a little nearer the bone of life, those of the minstrel show and vaudeville; and finally, the songs in which life shows up coarse, strong and wild and tragically clear—the songs of the cities' "underworld." Now it is becoming more and more difficult to get back to origins; the road back is falling into neglect. The Gilded Age is beginning—the influence of which persisted up to the time that we entered the war in 1917. After 1919 the earliest traditions began to possess interest once again. Interest in American folk began to be channeled into real research into Americana. The rural tradition in literature began to be of interest for novelists and poets again; it came back with the fashion for the earliest form of antiques.

People began to bring pine blanket chests and hooked rugs out of the attic or the dealer's showroom into their rooms, and collectors of folk song went into mountainous regions after folk ballads. In spite of the accusation recently made by certain American critics that Americans in the 1920s neglected and denied their own land and its folk art—that they chased after strange European gods and took no notice of anything that had ever occurred west of the Mississippi—the fact remains that the folk tales, the folk poetry, and the folk crafts of America received a great deal of attention in the 1920s. The songs and the literature were sung and read widely and made into anthologies. All this was brought over into urban life; it was incorporated into the industrialized culture of the time.

This last statement should be emphasized. Is it not true that our most primitive folk art has been pretty thoroughly absorbed into our middle class mores, our bourgeois tradition? Is it not true that when we feel baffled by its elusiveness and uncomfortable about some of its translations into "formal" literature, we dimly realize that it has been carried into a region where the artist cannot get at it, into the middle region, where nothing living or nutritious for the artist's purposes exists? Has not this material been, so to speak, genteelized and sentimentalized so that at present it bears little relation to the rough, living stuff it once was? We can look at its forms, listen to its music, admire and imitate its sound, but can the artist, at present, call upon it to perform any important task? I, for one, feel that our early "folk" has been almost entirely absorbed into our industrial culture. Here we come up against that kind of industrial and commercial form of literature, that, let us call it, bourgeois form of literature, against which both Flaubert and Sainte-Beuve fulminated when it first appeared more than a century ago. It is not necessary to hammer on this bourgeois form of art in a fanatical way. But we can look at it without too much tension, consider it as a fact, try to define it, try to trace its boundaries, try to understand where the imitation leaves off and the real begins. We will get nowhere, as writers, if we take to play-acting pastoral or imitating—counterfeiting—folk.

Perhaps it is true that folk art can only be used by those artists who are in themselves part and parcel of folk life, who have really lived in its vigor and been part of its fabric. We think of Mark Twain and of his direct use of his own experience as a boy and a young man. If direct experience of folk life is necessary, where is the writer to find that direct experience at the present time? Not, surely, by going back to frontier days that have long been closed or by duplicating any form that has already been absorbed into a sentimental legend. Where can the writer find a contemporary folk art? Well, we are surrounded by folk vigor of all kinds. Because we cannot seem accurately to ascertain just where or what it is, we must be all the more searching in our analysis of the contemporary scene. The whole trend, at the moment, is to take what surrounds us more or less for granted; but this situation cannot last forever, and young writers are the last people who should be taken in by the seeming opacity of their surroundings. Young writers should be filled with both vigor and curiosity, as well as with talent; and many of them have instinctively and with enthusiasm picked out certain phenomena that lie near the creative center of urbanized folk. Other young people may be a little frightened of what they see and hear when they look beyond their own safe and normal backgrounds. They cannot be sure what is folk and what is mere cheapness and vulgarity. Many people, other than the young, are not quite able to make up their minds whether "swing" and "name bands" and "popular songs" are folk art or merely manifestations of vulgar energy that quietly enlightened people have no relation to, no taste for, and, perhaps, should have no dealings with.

We all have heard, perhaps with a certain amount of amusement, the claims of the extreme enthusiast who would have us abandon all music produced up to now and listen to nothing but his record collection: to his marvelous recordings of Louis Armstrong in his good period, to the subtleties of "boogie-woogie" piano playing, to the development of Duke Ellington or the nondevelopment of Bing Crosby, or whatever. This sort of enthusiasm is held with heat; it is filled with intolerance for people outside the magic circle; and, in many ways, it is all to the good. For these extremists have actually touched the center of the urbanized folk music and folk poetry by which we are surrounded on all sides. But we should not be extremists. And the problem remains complex. We should hold a steady interest, no matter what fashion or fashions sweep over the enthusiast, in finding and recognizing what is real folk and what is not. We listen to the radio, and hear the greatest mixture of genres that it is possible to imagine. We decide, perhaps, that the radio has its distressingly meek and namby-pamby side, even so far as popular music is concerned. We listen, then, to the juke-box favorites and sometimes we find that this repertory is quite different from what is being unfolded in the repertory of the radio at any given moment. The juke-box patrons know what they want and get what they like; the tone is at once rougher and more primitive—but more sentimental, too. Or, perhaps, we decide, tentatively, that anything "popular" must be folk song.

Stripped of its commercial coloring, and divorced in our minds from its Tin Pan Alley origin, perhaps every popular song, from the hillbilly tunes—or their imitations—through the sentimental ballads to the words and music of the "slick" revue, is authentic, is the material for which we search. But immediately we begin to cling to this notion, an expert tells us that we are completely mistaken. The brilliant and informed Mr. Virgil Thomson, music critic of the *New York Herald Tribune,* remarks, icily, in a critique: "Mr. X [a composer who had used 'popular' and 'commercial' usages in a formal composition] seems to think that the music called 'popular' is a style, a domain in itself like folk-lore, and hence material for art. He is wrong. It is the last stage of art-music's natural decomposition. It is all bromides and means nothing. There are musical raw materials among the folk, and hot jazz is one of them. But the commercialized 'popular' music that is Mr. X's world is not worth sympathetic re-working. Its stuff is worn too thin already."

How baffling the whole question becomes! For here we are confronted with a kind of "popular" music that perhaps we had overlooked: the broken-down high art form. I agree with Mr. Thomson that such a thing exists. That it has spread over all "popular" music—over all popular songs—I very much doubt. I could quote the names of a dozen popular songs that are indubitably tainted with this worst of all influences: the influence of high or formal art in deliquescence. But let us consider a moment longer commercialized, urbanized popular music as it exists today.—We are disturbed to find it more primitive than we expected. To a cultivated taste much of it is silly and maudlin; it is so repetitive in theme that very little of it can be listened to at one time. It is also repetitive in beat; the underlying rhythm does not change. The beat is the thing, and all the elaborate harmonic tricks serve only to embellish the beat. And it never gets much beyond the form, as someone has pointed out, of theme and variation.

Again, it is combination of words and music that leaves out whole areas of human emotion. The tragedy and lamenting and sense of death and dissolution—of violent death, of accident—never come into it. Violent people appear in it very seldom. Its roughness is oddly mixed with smoothness; its wildness keeps slipping over into something quite tame. It lacks, in spite of its range between nervous gaiety and a kind of dolorous "blue" quality, any real subtlety of joy, such as we find in the great art songs on the one hand, or any real tragic depth, such as once resided in truly primitive music. But—and this is the point to remember—the words are attached to music, are, rather, fused with the music, as in all primitive states of poetry and music.

We use here terms of music as well as of poetry because the material I have been dealing with is at that primitive stage when it is inextricably both. And if there is any doubt about the vigor of this folk art, witness the inexhaustible fertility of its inspiration, and witness as well its powers of improvisation. (Here we get into a purely musical phase of the matter, it is true, but how interesting it is to see pure spontaneous creation of this kind actually at work around us.) Granted that the line between the real and false is wavering and unclear. Surely we are surrounded nevertheless by a living folk poetry and music of extreme variety and vigor, compared to which the songs of the sheet-music era show up as awkward, saccharine, and devitalized. We are in a cultural period when folk is in a good creative era of *its own:* a period that should develop to the point where it can express anything, from simple to complex emotion, and express these things well.

Whether or not the formal artist can use folk in its present unmalleable stage and whether this folk art will ever manage to get completely clear from all sorts of commercial and middle-class influence that certainly cloud and hamper it at the moment, I do not know. Time must pass, and our formal art must clear itself of its myopic vision, its lack of insight, its shyness of self-analysis, and other weaknesses and defects, before the two lines of art that, perhaps, need to intersect before great literature can be expected, can meet.

We now come to that most unpopular art at the moment in America: formal poetry. Formal writing in general receives little enough attention, but when we come to the two words *formal poetry,* we come to a subject the discussion of which is dangerous in the extreme. For we have been confronted, for more than a decade, with the spectacle of writers defaming their own vehicle; insisting that it be put to some use; of men and women bringing to bear on the worth of their own talents, and the literary form in which those talents are expressed, all kinds of moral and even, one could say, evangelical disparagement. The incomprehensibility of modern formal poetry comes up frequently; the charge that it is unscientific also is heard. That we have been "betrayed" into one state of mind or another by our formal poets—even into a kind of treason against real American values—has been dinned into our ears for a considerable length of time.

This bitterness followed closely, let it be remembered, on a period in which Americans were delighted to discover not only the number of poets they were producing, but also the number of varieties of poets. Beginning around 1912, we had a "renaissance." We suddenly saw about us American satiric poets and American naturalists; American pastoral poets with a tragic sense of the past; bitter and witty elegiac poets; poets with a gift for sustained narrative; as well as men and women with poignant lyric gifts, and men and women with a talent for poetic drama. We produced, in some quantity, poets whose subtlety matched the subtlety of their French

Symbolist masters; and in Eliot and Pound we realized that we had
nurtured true virtuosi: men whose poetic influence affected a whole generation of English writers as well as a generation of Americans. For a
time it seemed that we had managed to throw up a poetic generation that
could compare with any recent creative generation in England or on the
Continent.

What happened to this enthusiasm? Is it possible that economic and
historical accidents and letdowns can wipe out, almost at one stroke, and
in the short time of ten or fifteen years, the whole enthusiasm of a people
for an art in which they, for a time, brilliantly excelled? Is it possible that
moral pressures, which always appear in periods of material disorganization, can become so strong that they destroy the interest and the happiness of many people in what has been so vigorously created? If this
revulsion on the part of Americans who admired formal poetry could
come about with such a cutting effect of disowning one's own, of throwing the erring child out into the blinding snowstorm, what hope is there
for formal poetry in America in the future? Have we not proved ourselves full of a kind of dislocated bigotry and, even, of ingratitude for our
own gifts?

We must now face a fact that is a little irksome to face. We are a
great nation, but we are a romantic nation. Victor Hugo, in the preface
to *Hernani,* defined romanticism as the spirit of liberalism in literature.
Fortunately, the spirit of liberalism in government has this same romantic base. The industrial pattern of our society, the commercial infiltra-
tions into our culture, cannot change the fact that the Colonies became a
nation during the Romantic period; and many Romantic faults, as well as
many Romantic virtues, are fundamental in our nature. Being, at bottom, romantics, we like change. We tend to veer about. We are impatient; and we do not, so far, show any signs of ever wanting to go over
into a rigid classicism or to subject ourselves to a series of canons and of
rules.

The sharp criticism to which Flaubert subjected certain bourgeois
tendencies of his day has been mentioned. His unfinished novel, *Bouvard
et Pécuchet,* has puzzled many people. To some, it has seemed a crushing
indictment of middle-class foibles; to others, it represents a poisonous
attack on mankind itself, somewhat in the manner of Swift. Or it can be
considered a dissection of the Romantic temperament; or it can be considered a combination of all these things. "Flaubert's design," says Albert
Thibaudet, "is not absolutely clear . . . but in the large, one can say that

Flaubert wished to give a synthesis and a sum of all that pertains to automatism and to the grotesque, in the thought and life of the ordinary middle-class man—the man in the street—the conformist in society."

The main theme of *Bouvard et Pécuchet* is one of enthusiasms continually changed. These two well-meaning copyists are afflicted with a series of unparalleled manias. They rush into a passionate absorption of one thing after another. They rush into the collecting of antiques; then it is scientific farming; then the distilling of liqueurs; then chemistry, anatomy, medicine, geology, archaeology. Then comes a passionate interest in history, in historical novels, in grammar. Soon, urged on by contemporary events, they are fascinated by politics and social theory. A little later they are involved in gymnastics and physical culture, in magic, in spiritualism. All the while their lives become more and more absurd, farther and farther removed from normal realities. Everything natural and human they touch becomes mixed up in the most alarming way. Toward the end of the book they are violently seized by religion: religion of all kinds, including Buddhism. Then come educational theories, sketching, public speaking. And in Flaubert's notes we find that the two friends will try to work out a theory of the future of Humanity, of the future of literature, of the future of science. They will be interrupted from time to time by the arrival of outraged authorities, but they will keep on trying, until at the end they will have to acknowledge that the matters into which they have plunged themselves are a little beyond their full grasp. They had better go back to the job of copying from which they had emerged.

The most striking characteristic of these two figures is, of course, their lack of maturity. They are childish. They have no sense of proportion. Then again, they rush into things with complete singlemindedness, explore them—to the point of satiety, and then reject them utterly, because they have lost so many traditional links with reality. They have no religion, no fixed material basis in life. They are floating men.

The point to make most strongly to young writers is that in some way, if one wishes to belong to a free and creative future, one must get outside this repetitive pattern of enthusiasm, satiation, repudiation, whether it be a fashion of thinking, of feeling, or of action. Let us call this tendency to reject only to embrace elsewhere, middle-class or Romantic or what you will; it is certainly not the approach of the artist. But, we have recently been told, the staying powers, the nervous organization, the quality of brains, in mere writers, cannot in any way compare with the same attributes in the man of action, the scientific investigator, the explorer. The 1920s were excited about literature; but how much of that literature can stand up against this, that, or the other exploit of men of action or scientific achievement? Do we hear Bouvard and Pécuchet speaking out of one of their enthusiasms when we hear this sort of statement?

I have read, as a reviewer, along with all the good poetry, practically all the bad poetry published in English since 1931. So that I can tell you exactly why the dullest poetry is dull; and I can trace for you the falling line down which bad, worse, and worst poetry sinks. Thoroughly poor verse, really "bad" poetry, is remarkable for two things. It is not a question of its being written to this rule or that, or in this fashion or that. It is a question, first, of its conformity to the middle and accepted view of things. It tends to pull every subject treated, from love to the starry heavens, comfortably and cozily into that view. The bad poet is not to be shaken from his smugness. Everything comes into his house, as it were, and puts on slippers and sits in his armchair and pats his dog. The winds, whether of nature or of doctrine, may howl as they will; he has every-thing quietly under control because he is on the side of the received idea, the conventional concept. It is remarkable how this middle tone can pervade the most diverse forms. I have seen imitation Elizabethan son-nets filled with it, as well as the most revolutionary calls to action.

The second sign of really bad poetry is its author's tendency to laugh things off—to transform tragedy into, if not exactly a joke, then at least into something that can be managed with sentiment rather than passion. The middle poet, like the middle painter and prose writer, tends to hush things up, smooth things over, transform the wild into the tame, the exact truth into the approximation, the terrible fact into the commodious fact. There is a kind of lulling rhythm, a peculiar turn of phrase, a refined and limp vocabulary that goes into this middle kind of expression. We laugh at the graveyard verse of the eighteenth century and at the lame imitators of Pope. We think Felicia Hemans and her like delightfully "period" and definitely dead. Not at all; their kith and kin are around us on all sides. Because we are their contemporaries, it is difficult to hear their debased tone unless we are trained to hear it.

The young writer, then, must in some way stand outside middle-class art. Then, I feel that the time of experiment, as experiment, is over. There are no more stiff forms to break, and no more virtue in writing

gibberish, and no more sense in "plumbing the depths of the subconscious" in a theatrical and artificial way. The depths of the subconscious appear in any work of art. Salvador Dali reports a remark
made to him by Freud: "When I look at a formal work of art," Freud
said, "I look for evidences of the subconscious. When I look at a surreal-
ist work of art, I look for evidences of the conscious." How many tasks
are waiting for the young writer—tasks that require a sensitive, under-
cutting perception, and a penetrating, informed wisdom! So much has
had to be passed over or neglected. So many weights and tasks have been
put upon literature that could not be put upon other forms of creative
expression. Literature is the most useful carrier for ideas. And when
materialists take it over for their own purposes, they must clear literature
of much of its meaning; they must make literature's imaginative and
spiritual residues as small as possible, so that literature's useful side may
function without too many hitches and jars.

The young writer should understand, at any given moment, at least
some of these manipulations. He should be able to sense where creativeness ends and where pressure begins. He should be able to analyze any
given work into its component parts, to see what is real and what is
commercial, what is free to function as art and what is bound into
various constricting patterns.

The more the times do not back him up, the more the young writer
should apply himself, with patience, to learning. The time is coming
when it will be an accepted fact that writing cannot function either in a
vacuum (without touching the human history of which it is a part) or in
any kind of ideological strait jacket. The time has already come when we
must read literature with a full knowledge of its reasons, both historical
and psychological—of the backgrounds with which literature is inter-
penetrated. We can no longer run back and forth on the surface, from
book to book, picking up a pretty little anecdote here or a piece of period
costume there. So little has been done since inquiry into modern literature began, so much remains to do. Profoundly interesting linkages have
been made between literature and the life literature must express, en-
noble, and interpret. But how many remain to be made.

The young writer should be versed in the literature of the other arts.
I have, many times, found ideas more to my purpose and hints as to the
cause and direction of things, in the history of painting and engraving, or
in the history of music, than in histories of literature. The new attitude
toward literature as an indicator of life, the new revaluation of writers

with the use of new critical tools, are still fragmentary. One must look for clues, find ways from one piece of evidence to another. But the material is endless. It is waiting for the sincerity and enthusiasm of the writers and the scholars of the future.

Above all, the young writer must not become hardened and cynical, or sophisticated to the point of insensitiveness and glibness. He must remember that the notion that anyone, given a little good will and effort, can become an earth-shaking author is a rather unenlightened idea. And a culture should not be only *artist-deep;* it must be deep with thousands of appreciators, with a sincere and unaffected and wakeful audience. Therefore, if one has sensitiveness and still cannot manage to turn out a book that the world will not willingly let die, remember that there is a great need for sensitiveness—for steadfast sensitiveness. An unchanging, a non-venal, a detached, and anonymous group of appreciators; not showy, stocked with learning; humane, yet with a good set of arguments lined up to meet the most dogged and pretentious adversary—that is the audience I should like to see in America; ready to back up any glimmering-through of a new awakening of formal art.

Remember that our culture may not develop along the lines of former cultures; there is no reason why it should. We are a romantic people. Shall we be forced into that alternation of restraint and exuberance—classicism and romanticism—that for certain basic historic reasons marks most European cultures? Perhaps it will turn out that we shall resemble some culture where nothing of this sort happens; where, instead, a sparkling and vivid popular art bubbles up through art and life and literature, from source to summit. And our formal art—that tends toward sharpest satire, yet has a line of mysticism and transcendentalism that can be traced from Emerson and Thoreau to T. S. Eliot, that tends toward profound insight allied with elaborate form, as in our master of prose, Henry James—perhaps our formal art, too, will resemble the art of certain cultures somewhat outside the European pattern. Perhaps our ability to wisecrack will ripen into our ability to make profound *aperçus;* and, as Justice Holmes wrote to his friend Pollock: "The systems disappear, but the *aperçus* remain."

Remember, if you are a young poet, that you are endowed with emotion, that makes your work reverberate; with intellect, that gives your work form; and that you have another endowment as well: a spiritual ingredient that has not yet been isolated. It is this spiritual ingredient in which you must put your trust in barren times. It is the ingredient of your talent that the materialists will try to laugh off; but if you are really endowed, you will know that it is there and that it links you with whatever creative stream there is in nature. Stick to it; let it write *you;* allow its crotchets full play. If you hate the ocean, or can't abide the eighteenth century, write with these crotchets fully visible to your readers. Be yourself, to the top of your bent, as André Gide has counseled. "It takes great boldness to dare to be oneself," says Delacroix in his *Journal.* "In fact, the boldest of all things is to escape from the accepted and from habits." Remember that there have been innumerable barren periods in history, when the spirit and heart alike seemed dead. And remember that when the change-over into a creative time occurs, it begins, often, with something so small and simple and unpretentious that no one realizes that the new thing is there. Just one small cry, just one small hand-produced book called *Songs of Innocence and of Experience,* and the whole stiff facade of bad formal writing begins to show alarming fissures.

In conclusion two passages may be quoted that have, it might seem, nothing to do with literature. The first is from an essay by the modern English painter, Walter Sickert. He said:

How is it that you do not know that a work of art is the extraction from natural objects of line, and light, and shade and colour, in themselves beautiful and delicate and precious? And the objects themselves may be *any* object. While the snobs of the brush labor to render the most expensive women and the richest fabrics cheap, the master-draughtsman shows us the wealth of beauty and consolation there is, in perceiving and following out the form of anything. *Anything!* That is the subject matter of modern art. There is the quarry, inexhaustible forever, from which draughtsmen and painters of the future will draw the endless line of masterpieces still to come. Of course there is an understood proviso to this *anything,* as important as the principle itself: namely, that the objects, whether men and women or still-life and landscape, shall be about their business in the world. Not the forms only, but the life within them, must be "significant." In other words, the mind must be drawn to sympathy with a life that is familiar, a life that never stands still, but which may sometimes hover trembling for a space, just long enough for the draughtsman to pin his game.

The second passage is a parable by Tolstoy, used at the end of Bruno Walter's reverent biography of his friend, the musician Gustav Mahler. It is a parable that would puzzle Bouvard and Pécuchet, and, I think, would send certain critics and writers of our day into fits of raucous laughter:

And that he [Mahler] kept on asking questions and wanted, ever again, to "learn" reminds one of Tolstoi's beautiful legend of the three devout old men whom the bishop visited on their island. They made him teach them the Lord's Prayer over and over again because they were unable to retain it. When he finally had succeeded [in his task] and his ship had long since left the island, they came to him one night, running over the waves, because, once more, they had forgotten it. But he said, deeply moved: "Why, you are walking on the waves—what further need is there for you to learn?"

And so it was with Mahler: he possessed and knew so much more than he asked, for in him was Music, in him was Love. And I think that, at the last, he will have found out that in the very fact of his faithful seeking lay the answer . . . .

The Responsibilities of the Critic

F. O. Matthiessen

My deliberately grave title is in the tradition from Matthew Arnold, my
first critical enthusiasm as an undergraduate thirty years ago. But at that
very time a new critical movement was rising, the critical movement in
which we are living today. T. S. Eliot's first important essay, *Tradition
and the Individual Talent,* was written in 1917, when he was twenty-nine;
and I. A. Richards's first independent and most influential book, *The
Principles of Literary Criticism,* came out in 1924, when he was in his early
thirties. The talents and principles of those two then young men have
been the most pervasive forces upon the criticism of the past quarter
century.

We know now what a revolution they instigated, if one may use
such a violent word as *revolution* in the field of the arts, where all victories
fortunately are bloodless, and where what was overthrown remains un-
destroyed and capable of being rediscovered at the next turn of the wheel
of taste. When Eliot was growing up, the tastes and standards of Arnold
were still prevailing; and Eliot found himself wholly dissatisfied with
Arnold's preoccupation with the spirit of poetry rather than with its
form. The form of Eliot's own first poems was deceptively radical, since
he was really rejecting the easily flowing forms of the romantics and the
Elizabethans for the more intricately weighted forms of the symbolists
and the metaphysicals.

When Richards, as a psychologist who believed in the basic importance of the words with which men try to fathom their meanings, began
to read Eliot's poems, he encountered the kind of language that proved
most compelling to readers just after the First World War. The immense
loosening of speech that had accompanied the rapid expansions in mass
education and mass communication had reached the point where, if the
artist was again to communicate the richness and denseness of real experience, he must use a language that compelled the reader to slow down,
to be concerned once more with the trip rather than with the arrival. As
the young English critic T. E. Hulme had been arguing, before he was

killed in battle in 1917, poetry must always endeavor thus "to arrest you . . . to make you continuously see a physical thing, to prevent you gliding through an abstract process."

What resulted from the joint influence of Eliot and Richards was a criticism that aimed to give the closest possible attention to the text at hand, to both the structure and texture of the language. You are all familiar with the names of its practitioners, who, if we confine ourselves to America alone, have already produced a more serious and exacting body of work than we had previously witnessed in this country. To be sure, Richards's most gifted follower was one of his own students at Cambridge, England. William Empson, in his precocious *Seven Types of Ambiguity* (1929), begun when he was still an undergraduate, pushed to its subtle extreme Richards's kind of linguistic analysis. Empson in turn has had a particular vogue here among the critics whom we now associate with the newly founded Kenyon School of Criticism, most notably with John Crowe Ransom, Robert Penn Warren, and Cleanth Brooks. Others whose names are linked with that school, Kenneth Burke, R. P. Blackmur, Allen Tate, Austin Warren, and Yvor Winters, however divergent their methods and emphases, reveal throughout their work how they have had to reckon with Eliot and Richards, whether in concord or belligerence.

The effect of this new movement upon the study of literature in our universities has been by now considerable. Although opposed by both the old guards of philologists and literary historians, most of the critics I have mentioned now hold academic appointments, which may or may not have been good for their work. But their work has thereby become instrumental in the revolt against concentrating exclusively on the past, and against concentrating on literary history instead of on literature. As a result both teachers and students are more capable of close analysis and lively appreciation than they were a generation ago.

But by now we have reached the stage where revolt has begotten its own set of conventions, to use the terms of one of Harvard's great former teachers, John Livingston Lowes. As we watch our own generation producing whole anthologies of criticism devoted to single contemporary authors and more and more detailed books of criticism of criticism, we should realize that we have come to the unnatural point where textual analysis seems to be an end in itself. The so-called little magazines have been essential and valiant outposts of revolt in our time when the magazines of wide circulation, in decline from their standards in the nineteenth century, have abandoned serious discussion of literature almost entirely.

But the little magazines seem now to be giving rise to the conventions and vocabulary of a new scholasticism and to be not always distinguishable from the philological journals which they abhor. The names of the authors may be modern, but the smell is old. The trouble is that the terms of the new criticism, its devices and strategies and semantic exercises, can become as pedantic as any other set of terms if they are handled not as the means to fresh discoveries but as counters in a stale game. In too many recent articles literature seems to be regarded merely as a puzzle to be solved.

This is not to underestimate the great and continuing service performed by the few quarterlies devoted to criticism, or by those even littler magazines that often last only long enough to introduce one or two new talents in poetry or fiction. The important experimental work of our time has again and again been able to secure its first publication only through their pages. This is one of the consequences of what F. R. Leavis, the editor of *Scrutiny,* has called the split between "mass civilization" and "minority culture." But to recognize that phenomenon in our democracy should only be to combat it.

There is potentially a much greater audience in America for the art of literature than the blurb writers, who often pass for reviewers in the Sunday supplements, would seem to suspect. The effectiveness of the critics in the little magazines in having by now prepared a wider public for, say, Joyce or Kafka or Eliot, amply testifies to that. But the dilemma for the serious critic in our dangerously split society is that, feeling isolated, he will become serious in the wrong sense, aloof and finally taking an inverted superiority in his isolation. At that point criticism becomes a kind of closed garden.

My views are based on the conviction that the land beyond the garden's walls is more fertile, and that the responsibilities of the critic lie in making renewed contact with that soil. William James used to insist that the first duty of any thinker is to know as much as possible about life in his own time. Such an exhortation may seem too general to be of much use, but it can be grasped more concretely if we envisage the particular responsibilities of the critic in a whole series of awarenesses. These awarenesses may encompass some of the breadth and comprehensiveness which James assumed to be the thinker's goal, and some of the feeling of being drenched with actual life, which he believed to be the thinker's best reward. Much of the ground that we will traverse was also implied to be within the critic's scope by the early work of Eliot and Richards, though some of it has been lost sight of by their followers.

The first awareness for the critic should be of the works of art of our own time. This applies even if he is not primarily a critic of modern literature. One of Eliot's observations which has proved most salutary is that of the inescapable interplay between past and present: that the past is not what is dead, but what is already living; and that the present is continually modifying the past as the past conditions the present. If one avails himself of the full resources latent in that perception, one is aware that it is not possible to be a good critic of Goethe today without knowing Mann, or of Stendhal or Balzac without knowing Proust, or of Donne or Dryden without knowing Eliot.

The converse is equally true, if less necessary to be argued in the academy. But once outside, particularly in the rapid and rootless life of our cities, the tendency even for practitioners in the arts is to be immersed wholly in the immediate. This is not what James foresaw, since he took for granted the constant meeting point between what was already known and what was still to be known. But today we can take no tradition for granted, we must keep repossessing the past for ourselves if we are not to lose it altogether. The value in this urgency is that what we manage to retain will really belong to us, and not on authority at second hand. The proper balance, even for the critic who considers his field to be the present, is to bring to the elucidation of that field as much of the art of the past as he can command.

A recently dead critic, Paul Rosenfeld, was a heartening example of this balance. Prolonging in this country the rich cultural life of his German-Jewish forebears, he moved naturally among the arts, and it would never have occurred to him that a critic of contemporary music would try to speak without having all the great composers of the past at his finger tips. But he regarded the work of the present, especially in America, as his particular province, and often said that if our younger composers were to have a sense of possessing any audience, someone must make it his function to listen to them all. In complete modesty and selflessness he took that task upon himself. As his friends knew, Paul Rosenfeld gave himself away to his generation, a very unusual act in our fiercely competitive world, where even our intellectual life seems so often to become poisoned by the habits of our business civilization.

I have cited Rosenfeld because his generous openness to all the arts and his devoted impressions of what he found now seem so foreign to the grimly thin-lipped disciples of a more rigorous analysis. Indeed, one of them, writing currently in the *Hudson Review,* has declared that the recent volume of tribute by Rosenfeld's contemporaries from the twenties and thirties praised him for a "thoroughly degraded function." Such total lack of comprehension is a devastating illustration of what Auden meant by saying that one of the worst symptoms of sterility in our present culture is that of "intellectuals without love."

No incapacity could be less fruitful in the presence of the arts. Its recent frequency may be another unhappy by-product of the sort of specialization that leaves the student knowing only his own field. Such self-enclosed knowledge may often mean that he really knows nothing at all. At least it is hard to conceive of a good critic of literature who does not have an alert curiosity about other fields and techniques. Anyone understands his own subject and discipline better if he is aware of some other subject and discipline. To what extent this awareness should lead to mastery will vary greatly with individual aptitude. It does not seem profitable to insist that any given critic should also be expert in linguistic theory or mathematical logic or Marx or Freud, but I can hardly think of a critic today being indifferent to the access of power his mind could gain from a close study of one or more of these.

This does not mean that the misapplication of theory from one field to another is not as big a pitfall as it always was, or that fads don't often outrun facts. But as one instance of valuable cross-fertilization between fields there is cultural anthropology. Utilizing the disciplines of history and sociology, it has proved a particularly stimulating ally to the study of literature in a period when literature itself, in the hands of Joyce and Mann, has been rediscovering the vitality of primitive myth. Through our renewed awareness of folk patterns we now realize that the fertility rites which solemnize the death and rebirth of the year are equally germane to our understanding of *The Waste Land* or *The Winter's Tale* or *The Peace* of Aristophanes or the *Bacchae* of Euripides.

Another awareness which our split society makes it hard for us to keep in the right proportion is that of the popular arts of our technological age. The consequences for all our lives of the mass media of communication become ever more insistent, so that we must either channel them to socially valuable ends or be engulfed by them. The first results of our new discoveries are often as discouraging as when Thoreau scorned the transatlantic cable on the grounds that the initial news that would "leak through into the broad, flapping American ear" would be that the Princess Adelaide had the whooping cough. The first results of television would appear to be that it has made conversation impossible in one of its few remaining American strongholds, the barroom, and is debauching the customers with entertainment that is a long throwback to the juvenile days of the penny arcade. But then one recalls how the radio, despite its intolerable deal of soap, has during the past twenty-five years built up a taste for the best symphony music among millions of listeners who would not otherwise have ever heard it. The chief art form of our age, the moving picture, is the compelling reminder of our immense potentialities and continual corruptions. Even now when, in its postwar doldrums, Hollywood seems again to have forgotten that standardization through mass production is more suitable for soup than for art, the great new Italian films are demonstrating the important access of social truth that the art of the film can gain by utilizing some of the solid techniques of the documentary.

I have mentioned these disparate examples of good and bad as a way of enforcing my conviction that we in the universities cannot afford to turn our backs upon them or upon the world from which they come. The proper place for the thinker, as William James conceived it, was at the central point where a battle is being fought. It is impossible for us to take that metaphor with the lightness that he could. Everywhere we turn in these few fateful years since the first atom bomb dropped on Hiroshima we seem menaced by such vast forces that we may well feel that we advance at our peril. But even greater peril would threaten us if those whose prime responsibility as critics is to keep open the life-giving communications between art and society should waver in their obligations to provide ever fresh thought for our own society.

In using metaphors of battle here and now, I am not thinking in an academic void. If we believe that freedom of thought and of speech are the distinguishing features of the culture of a true democracy, we must realize by what a thin margin they now survive in this country. Within the past year there have been the most serious violations of academic freedom, caused, ironically, by officials who are determined to prove that the United States is so much better than any other country that it is above criticism. We must recognize the full gravity of these casualties of the cold war, for they are a product of the very kind of blind suppression that their instigators declare exists only behind what they denounce as "the iron curtain."

The most flagrant recent case of national importance has nothing to do with the issue of communism, and thus furnishes a concrete demonstration of how, once official opinion embarks on the course of stamping out dangerous views, every shade of dissent becomes dangerous. Olivet College, as you all here know, was founded in the great pioneering period of our education, when Americans were expanding the frontiers of their thought as well as of their territory. Its recent career, particularly in the period between two world wars, added a notable chapter to our experiments with education by tutorial work and group discussion. When members of its faculty of such national distinction as a Pulitzer Prize winner for biography and the candidate for vice-president on the Socialist ticket are dismissed, none of us can stand aloof or feel that we are not implicated.

If what I have just been saying seems an unwarranted digression from the responsibilities of the critic of the arts, I want to correct that impression. The series of awarenesses which I believe the critic must possess lead ineluctably from literature to life, and I do not see how the responsible intellectual in our time can avoid being concerned with politics. It is at this point that my divergence becomes most complete from the formalists who have followed in the wake of Eliot, as well as from Eliot himself, whose reverence for the institutions of monarchy and aristocracy seems virtually meaningless for life in America.

I would like to recall the atmosphere of the early 1930s, of the first years of the last depression, when the critical pendulum had swung to the opposite pole, from the formalists to the Marxists. I am not a Marxist myself but a Christian, and I have no desire to repeat the absurdities of the moment when literary men, quite oblivious theretofore of economics, were finding sudden salvation in a dogma that became more rigid the less they had assimilated it. But I believe the instinct of that moment was right, as our greatest recent cultural historian, Vernon Parrington's instinct was right, in insisting upon the primacy of economic factors in society. Most artists and students of literature remain amateurs in the field of economics, but that does not prevent them from utilizing some of the basic and elementary truths which economists have made available for our culture.

Emerson held that a principle is an eye to see with, and despite all the excesses and exaggerated claims of the Marxists of the thirties, I still believe that the principles of Marxism—so much under fire now—can have an immense value in helping us to see and comprehend our literature. Marx and Engels were revolutionary in many senses of that word. They were pioneers in grasping the fact that the industrial revolution had brought about—and would continue to bring about—revolutionary changes in the whole structure of society. By cutting through political assumptions to economic realities, they revolutionized the way in which thinking men regarded the modern state. By their rigorous insistence upon the economic foundations underlying any cultural superstructure, they drove, and still drive, home the fact that unless the problems rising from the economic inequalities in our own modern industrialized society are better solved, we cannot continue to build democracy. Thus the principles of Marxism remain at the base of much of the best social and cultural thought of our century. No educated American can afford to be ignorant of them, or to be delinquent in realizing that there is much common ground between these principles and any healthily dynamic America.

This is not to say that Marxism gives what I consider an adequate view of the nature of man, or that it or any other economic theory can provide a substitute for the critic's essential painstaking discipline in the interplay between form and content in concrete works of art. But a concern with economics can surely quicken and enlarge the questions that a critic asks about the content of any new work of art with which he is faced, about the fullness to which it measures and reveals the forces that have produced both it and its author. Walt Whitman might have said, in *Democratic Vistas:* "Man becomes free, not by realizing himself in opposition to society, but by realizing himself through society." That sentence was actually written by Christopher Caudwell, a young English Marxist who was killed fighting for the Loyalists in Spain. His book *Illusion and Reality,* published in 1937, has recently been reissued, and is having a renewed vogue now with younger writers and students. Their enthusiasm for it, I gather, springs from the fact that Caudwell, despite the sweeping immaturity of many of his judgments, keeps asking the big questions about man in society that the school of close textual analysis has tended to ignore.

I do not mean for a moment to underestimate the value of that school. It has taught us in particular how to read poetry with an alertness and resilience of attention that were in danger of being altogether lost through the habits set up by an age of quick journalism. All I would suggest is that analysis itself can run to seed unless the analyzing mind is also absorbed in a wider context than the text before it.

Mention of Caudwell's name has brought me to the last of the awarenesses that I would urge upon the critic: that of the wide gap which still exists between America and Europe. Henry James discovered long ago his leading theme in the contrast between American innocence and European experience. Although the world that he contemplated has been altered beyond recognition, that theme is still peculiarly urgent when we are faced with the difference between a Europe which has undergone fascism and destructive war at first hand and an America which has come out of the war richer and more powerful than ever before. Stephen Spender has noticed the difference in reading Randall Jarrell's book of poems called *Losses*. For the American, as Spender observes, even when the losses are those of our own fliers, they are something that happens far away on distant continents, they are not yet immediately overhead and inescapable. Allen Tate has described the kind of false superiority that can be engendered by such special isolation:

> The American people fully armed
> With assurance policies, righteous and harmed,
> Battle the world of which they're not at all.

How do Americans become part of that greater world? Not by pretending to be something they are not, nor by being either proud or ashamed of their vast special fortune. It does no good, for example, to adopt the vocabulary of the Paris existentialists in order to emulate the crisis of occupation which we have not passed through. The ironic lines of Tate's *Sonnet at Christmas* suggest a more mature way of meeting experience. None of us can escape what we are, but by recognizing our limitations, and comprehending them, we can transcend them by the span of that knowledge.

Here is the area where breadth of concern becomes most rewarding for the critic. By perceiving what his country is and is not in comparison with other countries, he can help contribute, in this time of fierce national tensions, to the international understanding without which civilization will not survive. He will also find that he has come to know his own country better.

The art of a country always becomes richer by being open to stimulus from outside, and criticism can find a particularly fertile field in observing the results of that interchange. For one fascinating instance, how much we can learn about both Europe and America from the high estimation that French writers are now giving to the novels of Faulkner.

At a period when the French have felt a debilitation in their own tradition, they have turned to the new world for an access of vitality. But what has seemed to them most real in America is not our surface of optimism, but the terrible underlying violence that has possessed the imaginations of nearly all our naturalistic novelists. It may seem a strange paradox that America, spared so far the worst violences of fascism and war, has imagined violence in a way that impresses men who have experienced the savage brutality of both.

But as we look back at America through French eyes, we become more conscious of what the preponderantly genteel reviewers for our organs of mass circulation have done their best to obscure: that Faulkner is not a writer of meaningless sensationalism, but one who has seized upon basic forces in our history, particularly upon the tensions resulting from our initial injustice to the Negro. Faulkner may often overwrite and use some of the cheap devices of melodrama, but we should not allow these to deflect us from the truth of his record. If we prefer a more smiling version of ourselves, we are liable to the peculiarly American dilemma of passing from innocence to corruption without ever having grasped maturity. By which I mean the maturity that comes from the knowledge of both good and evil.

In proposing an ever widening range of interests for the ideal critic, I have moved from his central responsibility to the text before him out to an awareness of some of the world-wide struggles of our age. We must come back to where we started, to the critic's primary function. He must judge the work of art as work of art. But knowing form and content to be inseparable, he will recognize his duty to both. Judgment of art is unavoidably both an aesthetic and a social act, and the critic's sense of social responsibility gives him a deeper thirst for meaning.

This is not a narrow question of the wrong right or right left politics. The *locus classicus* on this matter was furnished by Marx's judgment of Balzac, who as a monarchist and Catholic reactionary supported the very forces to which Marx was most opposed. Yet Marx could perceive that, no matter what this novelist's views, his vision of the deep corruption of French society by money made him the most searching historian of his time. Engels proceeded to evolve the principle inherent in this judgment: "The father of tragedy, Aeschylus, and the father of comedy, Aristophanes, were both very clearly poets with a thesis. . . . But I believe that the thesis must inhere in the situation and the action, without being explicitly formulated; and it is not the poet's duty to supply the reader in advance with the future historical solution of the conflict he describes."

A poet describes many other things besides conflict, yet without some sense of conflict there is no drama to engage us. The way in which the artist implies social judgments and entices the critic to meditate upon them may be elucidated by a pair of examples. Wallace Stevens's second book, *Ideas of Order,* appeared in 1935. Until then he had been known by his richly musical *Harmonium,* by what he himself had called "the essential gaudiness of poetry." The besetting weakness of criticism, when faced with a new writer, is to define his work too narrowly, and then to keep applying that definition like a label. Stevens had been bracketed as "a dandy of poetry," as an epicurean relisher of "sea surfaces full of clouds," as one who had found his role in discovering "thirteen ways of looking at a blackbird," as identical with his own Crispin in his relish of "good, fat, guzzly fruit."

He was, to be sure, all these enchanting things. But no one seemed to have been prepared for the fact that his imagination was so fecund and robust that it would compel him to launch forth, in his mid-fifties, upon the new territory indicated by his explicitly philosophical title. He was also making his own response to the vast disequilibrium that every sensitive mind had to feel at the pit of the depression. He had come to recognize that "a violent order is disorder." Or, as Horace Gregory put it more explicitly, Stevens's new poems were demonstrating that he was not merely a connoisseur of nuances, but—not unlike Henry James—a shrewdly trained observer of "the decadence that follows upon the rapid acquisition of wealth and power."

Stevens's kind of symbolist poetry never makes the explicit approach. So far as he has any political or social views, they would appear to be conservative. Yet in *Sad Strains of a Gay Waltz,* the second poem in *Ideas of Order,* he gave to a then young radical like myself a sudden clarification of the clouded time in which we are living. It is this kind of "momentary stay against confusion," as Robert Frost has said, that a poem is designed to give, and that becomes one of the measures of its authenticity.

In listening to almost any poem by Stevens, the first thing that strikes you is his past-masterly command of rhetoric, a reminder that, unlike the poets of the imagist movement, he is still rooted in the older tradition that leads from Bridges back to Milton. In this poem his rhetoric is formed into three-lined unrhymed stanzas of a basically iambic pentameter pattern, but with many irregular line lengths which quicken but do not break that pattern. The conflict that constitutes his theme is between an age that is dying and a hazardous potential new birth. He adumbrates this by offsetting a character whom he calls Hoon, a lover of solitude like Thoreau, against the rising masses of men in a still form-less society. But his controlling symbols are more oblique, they are "waltzes" and "shadows." Music that has become played out seems to its listeners to be "empty of shadows," and by a very effective repeti-tion of the phrase, "Too many waltzes have ended," Stevens sets up his counterpoise for a new, more dynamic music that will again be full of shadows:

> The truth is that there comes a time
> When we can mourn no more over music
> That is so much motionless sound.
>
> There comes a time when the waltz
> Is no longer a mode of desire, a mode
> Of revealing desire and is empty of shadows.
>
> Too many waltzes have ended. And then
> There's that mountain-minded Hoon,
> For whom desire was never that of the waltz,
>
> Who found all form and order in solitude,
> For whom the shapes were never the figures of men.
> Now, for him, his forms have vanished.
>
> There is order in neither sea nor sun.
> The shapes have lost their glistening.
> There are these sudden mobs of men,
>
> These sudden clouds of faces and arms,
> An immense suppression, freed,
> These voices crying without knowing for what,
>
> Except to be happy, without knowing how,
> Imposing forms they cannot describe,
> Requiring order beyond their speech.
>
> Too many waltzes have ended. Yet the shapes
> For which the voices cry, these, too, may be
> Modes of desire, modes of revealing desire.
>
> Too many waltzes—The epic of disbelief
> Blares oftener and soon, will soon be constant.
> Some harmonious skeptic soon in a skeptical music

Will unite these figures of men and their shapes
Will glisten again with motion, the music
Will be motion and full of shadows.

The extension of our sense of living by compelling us to contemplate a broader world is the chief gift that literature holds out to us. This sense is never limited to our own place or time. What makes the art of the past still so full of undiscovered wealth is that each age inevitably turns to the past for what it most wants, and thereby tends to remake the past in its own image. The cardinal example is Shakespeare. What the nineteenth century saw in Hamlet was what Coleridge saw, the figure of a transcendental philosopher absorbed in himself. What we see is a man inextricably involved with his own society, as may be suggested in brief by one of the scenes which nineteenth century producers usually cut. This is the scene in the fourth act where Hamlet, on his way to England, encounters a Captain from Fortinbras's army. The Captain is bitter at what his orders are compelling him to do:

Truly to speak, and with no addition,
We go to gain a little patch of ground
That hath in it no profit but the name.
To pay five ducats, five, I would not farm it.

The effect of this speech upon Hamlet is to heighten his awareness of the difference between the Captain's situation and his own, of how he, Hamlet, has every reason for action and yet cannot bring himself to act:

Examples gross as earth exhort me;
Witness this army of such mass and charge
Led by a delicate and tender prince,
Whose spirit with divine ambition puff'd
Makes mouths at the invisible event,
Exposing what is mortal and unsure
To all that fortune, death, and danger dare,
Even for an egg-shell. Rightly to be great
Is not to stir without great argument,
But greatly to find quarrel in a straw
When honour's at the stake. How stand I then,
That have a father kill'd, a mother stain'd,
Excitements of my reason and my blood,
And let all sleep, while to my shame I see
The imminent death of twenty thousand men,
That for a fantasy and trick of fame

Go to their graves like beds, fight for a plot
Whereon the numbers cannot try the cause,
Which is not tomb enough and continent
To hide the slain?

As John Gielgud speaks these lines, we feel what Shakespeare meant his audience to feel, the necessity for Hamlet's revenge. But we also bring to the passage our own sense of vast insecurity, our need of being engaged in the public issues of our menaced time, and yet the need of making sure that the seeming issues are the true issues, that we are not betrayed into engagements that are merely "th'imposthume of much wealth and peace."

There is a basic distinction between bringing everything in your life to what you read and reading into a play of the past issues that are not there. All I am suggesting is the extent to which our awareness of ourselves as social beings is summoned by the greatest art. That is the root of my reason for believing that the good critic becomes fully equipped for his task by as wide a range of interests as he can master. The great temptation for the young writer at the present moment is to think that because the age is bad, the artist should escape from it and, as a superior being, become a law simply to himself. Some memorable romantic poetry has been written on that assumption, but not the great forms of drama or epic, nor the comparable great forms in prose. However, the critic should freely grant that the artist writes as he must. But for his own work the critic has to be both involved in his age and detached from it. This double quality of experiencing our own time to the full and yet being able to weigh it in relation to other times is what the critic must strive for, if he is to be able to discern and demand the works of art that we need most. The most mature function of the critic lies finally in that demand.

In Defense of a Writing Career

Norman Cousins

A few weeks ago a journalism senior at Columbia University visited the offices of the *Saturday Review* in New York. He was looking for an editorial job. He was hardly seated when he began to express serious doubts about the career he had selected and for which he had invested so many years of study.

"I like to write," he said. "My idea of heaven is a big back porch in the country overlooking a green valley, where I can squat in front of a typewriter and poke away till the end of time. Next to that I'd like a job on a magazine or in a book-publishing house. But it's no use. Either as a writer or editor the chance of breaking in is so slight that there's hardly any point trying. And I haven't got enough of that folding green paper to endow myself with my own back porch and let the rest of the world go hang."

This was a new twist. Generally, the journalism seniors stride into the *Saturday Review of Literature*'s offices in the spring with more bounce and spirit than the second act of *La Bohème*. They may be rebuffed, they may be detoured, they may be diverted, but they won't be discouraged and they won't be dismayed. They know exactly what they want to do and where they want to go. They may not have the foggiest idea how they're going to get there, but trying to hold them back is as futile as putting your hand over the spouting nozzle of a fire hose. Yet here was a young man with a brand new script, saying he was sorry he had ever persuaded himself to make writing a career. He meant it, too. His face couldn't have been more liberated from enthusiasm than if he had been dreaming of flying to Paris in a Constellation only to wake up and discover that all the time he was in a subway car stalled under the Hudson River in the tubes to Hoboken.

I was anxious to find out more about both the dream and the awakening. Why did he decide to take up journalism in the first place, and what suddenly soured him? Why so great a gap between the original vision and the present disillusion?

In the next forty minutes he answered those questions fully and frankly. I'd like to summarize what he said because I suspect that his viewpoint and the experience on which it was based may be of some interest to new writers. For almost two months he had devoted nearly every hour of his spare time to visiting magazine and publishing offices, canvassing the possibilities of employment. He had also spoken to a number of prominent writers, soliciting their advice about the glories and perils of free-lance writing. He was especially anxious to find out from these successful writers how he ought to go about persuading a book publisher to give him a juicy advance to sustain him while he wrote the great American novel—no doubt on that big back porch overlooking the green valley.

First of all, he said, the only job opening in a magazine or publishing house he had been able to detect was as assistant to the associate editor of a master-plumber's trade journal. None of the national magazines wanted him, though he was quite sure that at least a few of them really needed him. And, judging from what he observed, even if he could crack open a spot for himself at *Life* or *Time* or *Newsweek* or *Collier's* or the *Atlantic* or *Harper's,* he wasn't sure that it would be a wise thing to do. No possibility for advancement. The good jobs were all sewed up and would be for years to come. Most of the magazines were edited by a few men, who, despite the ulcers and anxiety neuroses of their calling, would probably live forever. Men like Mr. Luce, Mr. Hibbs, Mr. Weeks, and Mr. Allen quite obviously weren't going to step down—at least not during the second half of the twentieth century, and those on the next echelon were all braced to resist any replacements or reinforcements for perhaps even longer.

On the news magazines, he said, the most you could hope for was perhaps breaking out of the open arena of the researchers, where men engage facts like toreadors do bulls, into the well-populated pen of the assistant editors. Here the facts are digested—sometimes passing into the blood stream of the magazine without leaving a trace. Salaries of the assistant editors are adequate though not spectacular. Above everyone, however, is the iron ceiling of anonymity. In such a job one's writing is as shorn of individuality and personality as toothpicks being processed out of a plank of wood. When the mountain labored, it at least brought forth a live mouse; here you labor over your typewriter for a week and produce half of a dead, overset galley—unsigned, of course.

Newspapers were out of the question, my young friend continued. All right, perhaps, as an opening gambit, just to get it out of your system so you could say you were a newspaperman once. A nice thing to have in your past, but not in your future. True, you meet such interesting people, or so they say, but there's not much creative inspiration in the written material or the weekly pay check. Of course, my friend said, it is a different proposition if you are lucky enough to become a syndicated columnist, conjuring up your own assignments in various corners of the world. But it's obvious, he said, that heavy-pay jobs such as this are all filled.

What my friend wanted most of all to do, of course, was to write a novel. He had spoken to a number of prominent writers and had made something of a survey of the creative-writing field—all of which had convinced him that the way was practically barred to all but a few fortunate newcomers. He said he was certain that the unsolicited-manuscript department of the average publishing house was actually the uninvited-manuscript department. He proceeded to give me the results of his investigation, which showed that Norman Mailer's *The Naked and the Dead,* for example, had been rejected by almost a dozen publishers. And Betty Smith's *A Tree Grows in Brooklyn* turned down by about ten. Or Gertrude Diament's *Days of Ophelia* spurned by six. Or Mildred Jordan's *One Red Rose Forever* thumbed-down by twenty-two. Or Mike Woltari's *The Egyptian* ignored by eleven.

Let us suppose, he said, that a young author sending in his first manuscript relied on a single publisher's judgment. Suppose he received a rejection slip the first time out. Wouldn't he be justified in thinking that the publisher knew more about writing than he did, and in deciding to give up his writing career right then and there? And even if he preserved his confidence in his own work, submitting his book to publisher after publisher, what was he to do if he received rejection slips from them all? Does anyone know how many Norman Mailers or Betty Smiths there might be whose manuscripts were spurned by all the publishers?

No, said my young friend, shaking his head sadly, he didn't believe that even if he did write the great American novel, there was any chance that it could get by the unsolicited-manuscript department. The publishers didn't want to risk either their judgment or their capital on untried talent, and most of them string along with the big names. Some of them even dangled bait before the roving eyes of famous authors who belonged to competitors.

Putting all this together, the journalism senior concluded that he had made a serious error six years earlier when he had decided on the basis of his editorship of the high-school paper, that he had a natural talent for a professional career as writer.

It was a bleak picture, but, I am afraid, an incomplete one. There are some facts worth considering—facts, I contend, which would justify the choice of writing or editing as a career for anyone with a reasonable amount of talent in that direction. I agree it's a difficult field to break into, but then again, what profession isn't? Anyone who has applied for admission to a medical school recently might have some underscoring he'd like to do on that point. Or, to underscore the underscoring, talk to a graduate of a medical school looking for an internship. Or a law-school graduate looking for an apprenticeship. Or a young artist trying to get his works exhibited, to say nothing of the business of finding a cash customer. Sisyphus rolling a stone up-hill was on a cakewalk compared to this.

Another conspicuous omission in my young friend's jeremiad concerned his own faulty approach to the problem of finding a job. In talking to him about the magazine and publishing offices he had canvassed, for example, it became apparent that he had failed to apply any imagination to the problem before him. All he had done was to write for an appointment with a key person, and then go in to present his credentials.

"What else was there to do?" he asked.

One thing he might have done, I replied, was to recognize that he had arranged a dead-end tour for himself. What reason was there to believe that his own cold application for employment would stand out in bold relief above the hundreds upon hundreds of other applications— most of them from qualified young people? A job applicant should familiarize himself with each magazine or publishing house the way a surgeon examines the X rays before going into the operating room. Anyone who marches into a publishing office looking for a job ought to know the history of that publication; he ought to know a great deal about its format and editorial content; about the particular audience it is trying to reach and what the problems seem to be in reaching it; about editorial features tried and discarded; about the people who work on the staff, their fields of special interest, and their functions on the magazine.

This is pay-dirt knowledge. It's not easy to come by, but it's worth trying to get, for it can give an applicant a toe hold on an interview. It's axiomatic in human relations that if you expect someone to be interested in your problems, you ought to know something about his. Don't wait for a job opening. Most good jobs don't open up; they are created. You create a job by presenting not only yourself but an idea that can fit into an editorial formula; an idea that reveals your own knowledge of the publication and your understanding of its audience and its needs. My friend had failed to recognize that the best way to sell himself into a publishing job was to sell his ideas. And these should not have been merely random ideas, but ideas carefully tailored to fit the particular needs of a particular periodical or publishing house.

The same theory operates with respect to advancement. Naturally, it's somewhat difficult to offer every young man who goes into publishing a money back guarantee that he can have the boss's job within five years, but ideas plus the ability to carry them out go a long way. If this sounds like a cross between Horatio Alger and Dale Carnegie, I'd be glad to quote names, places, and dates.

Next, for the newspaper business. First of all, let's modify the Hollywood stereotype somewhat. It isn't true that every newspaper man is comprehensively slouched—slouched hat, slouched shoulders, slouched smile, and a slouched psyche. My recollections of my own newspaper experience and my impressions in traveling around America and meeting many newspapermen in many cities are that most American newspapermen are far ahead of their papers. I've met some hard-bitten cynics, to be sure, but I've also met them in politics or teaching, for that matter. The pay doesn't begin to compare with that, say, of the corporation lawyer, but I've known a number of newspapermen who did fairly well by their families by using their spare time to good advantage in free-lance writing. Offhand, I know of at least six newspapermen now writing novels and perhaps three more writing nonfiction books, and, despite the high mortality of the average unsolicited manuscript, I'd be willing to bet that the majority of them will have their works accepted and published. Yes, the newspaper field is a tough one—tough to get into, in some cases even tougher to get out of. But it's excellent proving grounds for disciplined writing. After a while, of course, the discipline can be replaced by routine, and the routine by rote. But, so far as I know there's no law preventing anyone from moving on to more fertile pastures if he finds he's been squatting too long near a dry well.

This brings us to the final problem surveyed by my journalism senior friend—in particular, writing a new book and getting it published. I can agree with him readily that the orphan of the publishing industry is the unsolicited-manuscript department. I believe it to be a fact that no branch of a publisher's organization is as understaffed— qualitatively as well as quantitatively—as the unsolicited-manuscript department. The pay for first readers in many houses isn't much higher than for bookkeeper assistants or even for shipping clerks. Many publishers, on those infrequent occasions when they take their hair down, will confess that they have virtually written off their unsolicited-manuscript department as expendable, returning submitted works on the basis of a cursory examination by a forty-dollar-a-week reader.

A publisher will spend thousands of dollars in sending one of his editors on a tour around America, beating the brush for concealed literary talent, but seems reluctant to spend more than a few dollars to appraise fully and competently such talent as may be found in his own mailbag. It has occasionally happened that an editor on tour will make the discovery of an exciting new manuscript which only the week before had been routinely shipped back with a form letter by his own firm. Apparently, there is no shame in the matter. Indeed, one publisher, on the occasion of his firm's twentieth anniversary, blandly announced in an advertisement that with only a single exception, he had never accepted an unsolicited manuscript. It would have been interesting to get a box score on some of the important books that he happened to miss because they were apparently not worth a careful reading.

My friend was quite right when he listed the names of outstanding books turned down in the unsolicited manuscript departments of many publishing houses. It's even worse than he supposed. Copies of the two opening chapters of *War and Peace,* and an outline covering the rest of the book, by general consent a fairly acceptable novel, were recently sent to ten publishers in order to test the competence of the unsolicited manuscript departments. Only four of them spotted the material for what it was. The others sent back routine rejection slips.

It may be asked, Where then do most of the accepted books come from? They represent books written to order or on contract—books by name writers for whom space is regularly reserved on a publisher's list.

I am not completely unaware of the publisher's problem. When hundreds of book-length manuscripts are received each week—many of them looking more like tied up bundles of leftover leaves from last fall—it would put a publisher out of business if he had to maintain a highly qualified staff of readers who gave thorough consideration to every single manuscript. What has happened is that a sort of literary Gresham's law has been in operation for many years, the bad manuscripts driving out the good.

At one time not so long ago in the history of book publishing, the chief business of the publisher when he arrived at his office in the morning was to inspect personally all the manuscripts in the morning mail. In the memoirs of the publishers of forty or sixty years ago, it is not uncommon to find reference to this daily stint as the most delightful aspect of publishing. The biggest joy in a publisher's life was represented by the thrill of discovery in chancing across an unsolicited manuscript that heralded a new talent. But that was back in the days when a publisher's mail could fit on top of his own desk instead of requiring something on the order of a coal bin, as happens today. And that was before so much of the publisher's time was taken up with arrangements for reprint rights, motion picture negotiations, contests for bookstores, and the care and spoonfeeding of authors.

A few publishers have recognized this problem and their own responsibility in meeting it. Their experience is worth citing. These publishers have worked out a triple-platoon system whereby the first shock wave of manuscripts is absorbed by a corps of readers who have authority to reject only the blatantly inadequate. All the others are passed along to somewhat more specialized readers, who make no final decisions themselves but who winnow out the worth-while books for the editors, who constitute the third platoon. It is an expensive system, if done by competent and well-paid people all along the line, but it does succeed in filtering out in many cases the really deserving books, which, so far as the general public is concerned, would seem to be the main function of book publishing.

Meanwhile, the new novelist would do well to stay out of the bottomless pit that is the unsolicited-manuscript department. That is, to stay out if he can. At the very least, no manuscript ought to be submitted without the benefit of an advance letter to the publisher attempting to establish some contact on a responsible level and seeking some genuine expression of interest. The reply to such a letter is not, of course, conclusive, but its tone and responsiveness may offer some encouragement. It is sound policy, moreover, to write to firms whose lists over the years reveal no prejudice against beginners.

It would be even better, of course, if the young novelist were able to obtain the enthusiastic backing of a recognized third party—perhaps a book reviewer or a teacher or another author who might be sufficiently interested to write to a publisher, expressing his high opinion of a particular manuscript. Strategically, this puts the young author in the happy position—if the plan works—of being courted by a publisher. Of all the consummations in a writer's heaven most devoutly to be wished, none can quite compare with the postal ecstasy of opening a letter from an established publisher which begins: "Dear Mr. Smith: It has come to my attention that you have just written a book . . . " etc., etc.

Perhaps the most meaningful and fruitful way of all to fashion a key to the literary kingdom is through such writing and study units as exist at the University of Michigan—though I doubt that there are more than a dozen really first-rate writing courses at the university level in the country. The men and women who head these workshops are known and respected in the publishing offices and are constantly pursued by publishers for promising names. These magistrates of writing talent have built up over the years a position of respect among publishers and editors.

Finally, there are the various literary awards, of which the Avery Hopwood Awards in creative writing occupy such an important place. There are fifty-three local, regional, and national writing prizes and distinctions of one sort or another—many of which lead to publication. The value of these contests, however, is represented not only by the prizes themselves, but by the fact that a manuscript generally receives a much more careful and competent reading than in the ordinary course of submission through the unsolicited-manuscript channels. Leading national publishers, such as Harpers, or Dodd, Mead, or Houghton Mifflin, or Farrar, Straus, accept many manuscripts for publication out of their prize contest hoppers in addition to the ones that receive the top awards.

All in all, I told my young friend that anyone with ability who selects writing as a career today—whatever the particular branch may be—need not fear that all the doors are shut or that once inside there is no place to go. The difficulties are real, but they are not insuperable, so long as there is a reasonable degree of familiarity with what not to do, a fair amount of ingenuity in mapping and pursuing alternatives, and, most important, patience of the order usually associated only with camel drivers.

Writing as a career offers a good life and a rewarding one. It represents a continuing challenge. Each writing project is like a difficult battle, requiring a skilled combination of strategy and tactics to accomplish a specific objective. It demands a mobilization of concentration—and concentration is or should be one of the higher gifts of human mental activity. It is agonizingly difficult work at times, and you almost feel in need of a drip pan to catch the droplets of cerebral sweat, but, as John Mason Brown recently said about creative writing, it is the sweetest agony known to man. This is the one fatigue that produces inspiration, an exhaustion that exhilarates. Double-teaming the faculties of imagination and reasoning and keeping them coordinated and balanced is a tiring process, but you've got something to show for your efforts if you succeed. I suppose that was why Socrates liked to refer to himself as a literary midwife—someone who helped to bring ideas to birth out of laboring minds. As a master of cerebral obstetrics, Socrates also knew and respected the conditions necessary for the conception of ideas and recognized the need for a proper period of germinating reflection.

With all these delights of the creative process it may seem extraneous and crass to mention the tangible inducements, but it may be said for the record that most people in the writing profession eat very well. Some authors even make as much money as their publishers, and a few of them a great deal more. True, there is what you might call the law of the dominant fraction these days by which the government can obtain the larger part of an author's royalties, but retention of capital has always been the prime problem of authors anyway, with or without respect to taxes. A not inconsiderable advantage is also afforded by the fact that this is one profession in which you can take a trip to Paris or Switzerland or the Riviera or the Antarctic, for that matter, for the purpose of obtaining material and vital repose for your next book, and be able to charge all the costs of this soul-stretching safari up to deductible business expenses.

Apart from all these reasons—biological, philosophical, materialistic—in favor of a writing career, there is yet another reason as significant as it is compelling. That prime reason is that there is great need in America today for new writers. I am not thinking here of a technical shortage of supply, for production is still several light years ahead of consumption. The need for new writers I am thinking of has to do with the type of book and voice America is hungering for today. That type of book will not be afraid to deal with great themes and great ideas. It will not be afraid to concern itself with the larger visions of which man in general and America in particular are capable, for America today is living far under its moral capacity as a nation. It will not be afraid to break away from the so-called hard-boiled school of writing which has made a counterfeit of realism by ignoring the deeper and more meaningful aspects of human existence.

This need of which I speak has come about because too many writers have been writing out of their egos instead of their consciences; because too many of them have been preoccupied with human neuroses to the virtual exclusion of human nobility; because too many of them, in their desire to avoid sentimentality, have divorced themselves from honest sentiment and honest emotion. Indeed, we have been passing through what later historians may regard as the Dry-Eyed Period of American literature. Beneath the hard and shiny surface of the school of the super-sophisticates there is no blood or bones, merely a slice of life too thin to have meaning. Instead of reaching for the grand themes that can give literature the epic quality it deserves, too many writers have been trying to cut the novel down to the size of psychiatric case histories.

Beyond this there is need for writers who can restore to writing its powerful tradition of leadership in crisis. Most of the great tests in human history have produced great writers who acknowledged a special responsibility to the community at large. They have defined the issues, recognized the values at stake, and dramatized the nature of the challenge. Today, in the absence of vital moral leadership on the official world level, it is more important than ever that writers see themselves as representatives of humanity at large. For the central issue facing the world today is not the state of this nation or that nation, but the condition of man. That higher level needs champions as it never did before. There is no more essential and nobler task for writers—established writers, new writers, aspiring writers—than to regard themselves as spokesmen for human destiny.

The Possible Importance of Poetry

Mark Van Doren

Poetry desires to be interesting; or it should. By tradition it has a great right to this desire, for there have been times when nothing was more interesting than poetry. If this is not such a time, the reason may be simply that we have lost our desire; or if not so, that we have lost touch with tradition. The present fact would seem to be that people do not consider poetry either interesting or important—two words for the same thing; and the people are the judge. So have they always been, in spite of every appeal to something beyond or above or beneath them. There is no appeal. It is to people that poetry must be interesting.

When they do not find it so, the fault conceivably is theirs: they have forgotten how to read. It is they, and not the poets, who have lost touch with tradition. But it is dangerous for poets at any time to make such a charge. In our time it is a plausible charge, for we can suspect, and indeed we are often told, that universal literacy has depressed literature. When the only aim is that everybody should be able to read something, no matter what, and when mass production of printed words has become the business of cynics who despise the very audience by which they profit, the outlook for distinguished thoughts and feelings would appear on the face of it to be poor. The contemporary poet, however, cannot afford to rest here. His job is what the job of poets has always been: to think and feel as deeply as he can, and to assume the existence of persons who will be glad that he has done so. And he had better assume that these are more than a few—ideally, he had better assume that they are all of us. He had better not count the number, at least beforehand; for if he does, he will end by limiting himself. "I am always made uneasy," Emerson wrote in his Journal, "when the conversation turns in my presence upon popular ignorance and the duty of adapting our public harangues and writings to the mind of the people. 'Tis all pedantry and ignorance. The people know as much and reason as well as we do. None so quick as they to discern brilliant genius or solid parts. And I observe that all those who use this cant most, are such as do not rise above mediocrity of under-

standing. . . . Remember that the hunger of people for truth is immense.
The reason why they yawn is because you have it not."

If Emerson sounds optimistic, one should remember his reputation
in his time. It was a popular reputation, not incompatible with the fact
that Matthew Arnold and other young aristocrats of the mind in Oxford
of the 1840s thought they heard nowhere else so high and fine a voice as
this of the American prophet who assumed that everybody could understand him. It was a remarkable time, that generation before our Civil
War. Lewis Mumford has called it the Golden Day, and F. O. Matthiessen called it a Renaissance. It was full of writers who said great
things and sang great songs, and they wanted multitudes to hear them.
Walt Whitman, who had no illusions about the average American, addressed himself nevertheless to the normal American for whom no subject was too noble. The subject, for instance, of death. A great people, he
decided, would have great poems of death; and he proceeded to write
some—proceeded, and all of his life continued, so that his two masterpieces, *Out of the Cradle Endlessly Rocking* and *When Lilacs Last in the
Dooryard Bloom'd,* have that for their subject without which life cannot be
comprehended to its depth. I have never heard that Whitman believed he
would not be understood by more than a few friends and fellow poets.
His faith was simpler and broader than that; and it has been vindicated.

Whenever poetry has been good, it has had good subject matter—
good for anybody, and it has not agonized about numbers. Today, I
think, we do not hear enough about the subject matter of poetry. Criticism tends to ignore the question altogether. Poets are damned or
praised for their way with language, as if language were the aim and end
of all their art. Language is a lovely thing, and only human beings have
it; but they have it, presumably, for something better still, and the greatest poets are those who have best understood this. There is no lord of
language like Shakespeare; he could and did do everything with it; but
what finally moves us as we read him or watch his plays is the knowledge he has of us, on a level deeper than words. We adore Shakespeare
because he is wise, and because the world of men is given its right value
in his works. It was for the same reason that the Greeks all but worshiped
Homer, whom they knew by heart even though they knew nothing
about the world of which he had written. The truth was, of course, that
they did know his most important world, for it was the human world,
and as such it was not different from theirs. Again they had in him a lord
of language, but they noticed this less than they noticed how well he

understood the passions, the ideas, and the absurdities of men. They watched Achilles learning what honor means; they watched Odysseus coming home; and they saw the soul of Hector reflected in the love of those around him—his family, his comrades, and his friends among the gods. By the same token, what is it that in modern times convinces a true reader of Dante that his reputation is deserved? His verbal cunning, and the peculiar fitness of his rhymes, his syntax? These of course; but at last it is the knowledge of the man, and the pity; the power of his feelings, the unwearied work of his thought, and the deep lake of his heart. Without these he would merely be ingenious, as without them Homer would be sound and fury, and Shakespeare nothing but incessant bustling in the scenery.

But those three are the greatest poets, one of you may say—the very greatest; and what can we learn from them? They are too far removed, they are monsters of perfection, they are studied more than they are read, they are statues whose pedestals only may be approached. I do not doubt at all that one at least of you is saying these things now. And nothing could be more mistaken. Yet it is the custom of our time. We do not believe that we can learn from the greatest things. They are not for us. Which is why so few discussions of poetry today, even among those who ought to know better, even mention the names of Shakespeare, Homer, and Dante; and why the poet is defined in terms that exclude those masters; and why the impression is abroad that it is somehow bad taste for poetry to be interesting to people. Subject matter is itself an embarrassing subject, from which quick refuge is sought in the techniques of rhythm and image, of caesura and ambiguity. Those things all have their fascination, but it is secondary to the further fascination of the art when ultimate demands are made upon it. The ultimate demand is that it be faithful to its ancient trust; that it treat of human truth, and more wisely and movingly than most men treat it even when they know, as ideally all men know, the content of such truth.

Poetry today means lyric poetry; it means the short poem; and that too can be a great thing, but it is not the greatest. It is as great as it can be when its author has wisdom and passion, and when it is clear that if there were an occasion he could convey his understanding in the more complex forms of narrative and drama. The Greeks never forgot that lyric poetry is but a third of poetry itself, and perhaps the least third. The big things are done in narrative and drama, for poetry's chief business is the business of story—of mankind in motion. Philosophy and science give us knowledge of men in the aggregate, or in essence; poetry commits individuals to action, and follows them through careers. It conceives beginnings, middles, and ends, and is perhaps the only thing that can conceive them. Nature does not, and neither may philosophy or science; but poetry must. And it is the test of any poet—that is, of any story-teller—whether or not he can finish the story he has started. The beginning is fairly easy, as any young writer knows; even the middle sometimes charts its own course; but the end—for that, alas, experience and penetration are required. And in addition to those, a familiarity with the forms in which all human conduct finally manifests itself, the two forms of tragedy and comedy.

Tragedy and comedy are forms, not statements; or it may be that they are forms of statement. But any statement which they make is as far from platitude as the most sophisticated poet could desire. Poetry today despises platitude, and it is right in that. The pompous homilies, the "affirmations" and hymns of self-praise that pass in times like these as the sort of thing we ought to love in preference to the dim poetry we do on the whole have—I for one will take the dim poetry, since at least it is not hollow. But it must be clear that I would rather have something better than either of these. I would rather have story, and I would like to see it well grounded in the tragic and the comic visions which embrace all the knowledge we have yet accumulated concerning the significance of man's life.

Man's life is never good enough, and only men can know what this means. It means more than that the world of any given moment is a poor thing for even the best persons in it. Contemporary literature spends too much time, perhaps, and certainly too much effort in proving by documentation that the twentieth century is not what some people thought it was going to be. What did they think it was going to be? An earthly paradise? Heaven itself? But if they thought this they were children, and poetry is not for children. Neither can it be written by children. It is the product of long seasoning and of bittersweet experience, neither of which things we have any right to expect in the very young. We do not think of Homer as very young; or Dante, or Shakespeare, or Sophocles, or Milton, or Hardy, or Yeats. Or Chaucer—who sounds in every verse he wrote as if he had been born with quizzical old eyes, and perhaps the small beard we cannot think of him without. The great poet knows the world, and how to live in it—also, how not to live in it. He is not surprised because it has failed at being heaven, or because most people in it fall grotesquely short of being angels. He seems to have expected this, and to have been prepared. The current notion of the poet as young, ignorant, helpless, and complaining is more recent than many of us think. Through most of human time the poet has been thought of in terms that suggest the old man of the tribe—the one who has lived longest and seen most, and whose voice nevertheless has retained its original sweetness. Even in our day we have been witness to examples of this: Thomas Hardy, beginning to write poetry at fifty-five and ceasing only with his death at eighty-eight; William Butler Yeats, turning at middle age into the great poet he was at last to be; Robert Frost, unheard of by the world until he was nearing forty, and proceeding after that to become better with every advancing decade. We have these examples, and still we go on thinking of the poet as knowing less than we do—less, not more, which immemorially has been the assumption.

The poet knows how to live in the world and how not to live in it. That is to say, he locates the good life where it actually is—in the mind that can imagine and believe it. The mind of man not only sees worlds but creates them; and the worlds it creates are not here. This does not mean that they are illusory worlds, made up for solace and thin comfort. They are more substantial than the one we move through every day; but they are not here, and they cannot be verified by those who think this is the only world there is. Those who think that are either deceived or disillusioned, and chronically so. The poet is not deceived, for he has sharp eyes. But neither is he disillusioned, for in one very important sense he has never suffered from illusion. He has not thought that heaven was in cities—or in the country, either, if that is what you think I mean. It is where it is, and only the mind can travel there. Shakespeare must have known contemporary England very well, but his mind traveled elsewhere in search of persons, stories, tragedies, comedies. It traveled to that region where all men's minds are at home, and it brought back news that made this world seem somehow a foreign place, as indeed it must always seem to the uncompromising imagination. It is the only place where we have addresses, but it is not where we chiefly live. Nor need we hate it because this is true. Dante, traveling also into heaven and hell, took his memories with him and used them there. Homer, dropping back several centuries in time, found heroes—which was what he wanted, and he knew he should not look for them in his next-door neighbors; whom nevertheless he did not despise. They had not disappointed him, because he had never counted on them for more than they could deliver.

Poetry, in other words, takes it for granted that the world is not good enough for its best men. But all it can do with these men is to make them tragic or comic heroes—to show them as defeated by the very world to which they are superior. What if they succeeded? Poetry asks this question; asks it again and again; and at last decides that the answer is for no man to give. The poet is a man, too, laughing and crying with other men. He certainly is not God. So he does not know the answer. But he knows the question, which he asks over and over in such a way as to suggest the extreme distinction of man's predicament. Man wants to change the world and cannot do so. The world will punish him if he tries, just as gravity will operate upon his body no matter how light he thinks it is. Hamlet is inconceivably brilliant, but he must die like any other man, and for the commonest reason—he has not survived his crisis. Don Quixote is the greatest gentleman we know, but the world cannot tolerate one who tries to teach it to be other than it is. The world is indeed a tough place. But what man could make it tender? No man, says poetry, no man at all; and sacrifices King Lear on the altar of the unchangeable. He learned, but learned too late. There is no appeal from the ways of the world, which must continue on its own terms or take us all down with it into chaos and confusion. Which does not mean that we should think it a nice thing. It is a terrible thing; or if not terrible, absurd. So tragedy and comedy say; and salvage out of the wreck the best ideas we have, the ideas that certain men could become heroes by expressing, even though they failed.

What if they had succeeded? The question is meaningless; or rather, we cannot imagine what it means, nor does the poet try. What if Socrates had succeeded in making all Athenians think well? What if Jesus had succeeded in making all Jerusalem over into the image of his Father? What if Don Quixote had persuaded all of Spain that knights were more real than merchants and monks? What if Hamlet had cleansed Denmark of its sin? What if Oedipus's finding of the truth had made him free? For one thing we should not now have the books of which these persons are the heroes. Or if we did have them, we could not believe them. We believe them as it is because they falsify nothing in their report of the world. Their report of the human spirit—well, that is another matter. Neither do they falsify that by minimizing the dangers it must undergo, or by denying the supreme courage it inspires in those who properly possess it. The world is what it is, and the human spirit is what it is. And somehow they live together: ill-sorted companions, but the only companions there are for poetry to watch disappearing down the long perspective of life. The final distinction of the author of *Don Quixote* is that he both put them in perspective and personified them as two men.

The possible importance of poetry is immense at any time. And why not now? I would make no exception of our time, though there are those who do. They are the ones who persist in identifying poetry with short poems, and who even then do not remember how great a short poem can be—for it can be dramatic, too, and somehow narrative; it can imply careers, for ideas and for men. The short poem is better in those ages when the long poem is better; or, at the minimum, when it exists. The forms of literature reinforce one another, as tragedy and comedy do, which are the forms of thought. When fiction is good, then poetry can be good; and vice versa. Fiction indeed is poetry; or as I have put it here, poetry is story. This is not my idea, as you very well know; it is at least as old as Aristotle, and it has prevailed whenever poetry has been important to people.

But when I say fiction do I mean merely narratives or dramas in verse? Not necessarily. The ancient categories of lyric, epic, and dramatic poetry were not conceived in terms of verse alone, and it is fatal for us to suppose so. What we call prose fiction today is in fact the most interesting poetry we have; Aristotle would think so if he were alive, and he would be justified by the interest we show. Our movies, our westerns, our detective tales—he would wonder, perhaps, why so many of us failed to recognize those things too as contributions, however bad or good, to the poetry of this age. I have already spoken of Cervantes as if I thought he was the great poet of his age, along with Shakespeare his contemporary. That is exactly how I regard him, and I am not prevented from doing so by the fact that he wrote his greatest work in prose. He was a versifier too, but as such he does not interest us; whereas his vast poem called *Don Quixote* is among the glories of the world. Shakespeare wrote both verse and prose—sometimes, it would seem, indifferently, as if convenience alone dictated his choice; and his prose, unlike the verse of Cervantes, was itself a great thing, there being no better prose I think in English. But the question does not greatly matter. The vision was the thing in either case: the vision, and the knowledge that backed it up. The wisdom of these men is what makes them poets, as it is the wisdom of Tolstoy and Dostoyevski and Chekhov that makes us think of them, when we are serious, as Russia's poets. Is Dickens not a poet? Consider his passion and his joy as he contemplates humanity and sets it moving.

He is among the very great, and we are missing more than we know if we think of him merely as one of six hundred English novelists. The possible importance of poetry includes the chance that such men as these should continue to appear, and that we should have the generosity to recognize them as belonging to the highest class.

That we do not do so is perhaps the fault of our education, which keeps first things separate from one another. We study literature as if it were a thing by itself, and not only literature but English literature— even American literature, God save the mark. When American literature is good it is *literature,* as English or Greek literature is. And when *literature* is good it is a part of all we know. Not the only part, or even the best part, but certainly a part; and it is well that we should remember this. It is more likely to excel when the society that produces it considers neither it, nor science, nor mathematics, nor philosophy, nor theology, nor medicine, nor law, nor mechanics, nor politics, nor economics, nor history as the central subject matter of its thought. The central subject matter for any great age is life and truth; or perhaps it is justice and mercy. At any rate it is something that all arts and studies serve, and serve, we may suppose, equally. The Greeks were at one and the same time supreme in poetry, in philosophy, in science, and in mathematics. But this was not a coincidence, I suspect. They were great in each of these things because they were great in all the others, and because they thought that each of them but testified to a vision which itself was the central thing. Their education, that is to say, was not specialized. All arts for them were finally one art, and the name of it was living well. Nor did they set the fine arts of poetry, painting, music, and sculpture above the practical arts and the intellectual (we should say liberal) arts. There was no hierarchy of importance among them, because there was none of them with which serious men could dispense. The carpenter made a house, the logician made a syllogism, and the poet made a poem. Each was doing what he could and therefore should, and nobody doubted the benefit.

We specialize, with the paradoxical result that no one knows for sure what it is that he is doing. Where there is no connection there can be no comparison. What is the difference, for instance, between the poet and the philosopher, or between the poet and the scientist? We do not state it well, because we do not think of all three men as artists. If they had that much resemblance in our minds, then they might have differences, too, and we could measure these. We tend to assume that the differences are absolute; but this means in the end that they are absolutely small; or that the men themselves are. We often talk, as I have said, as if the poet were very small. He might grow larger if he knew, or if we knew, what sphere he works in as distinguished from any other man; and if we thought of him as working in that sphere for our benefit; and if we thought of all men in their spheres as working in them for our good— our knowledge, our happiness, and our wisdom.

The poet has his subject matter as well as his skill; and his skill increases as he realizes what his subject matter is. If poetry has made any advances in our time—in, that is to say, the twentieth century—we should wonder what new subject matter it has found. I for one think it has made advances; but I am not in sympathy with those who say that these are merely technical. The concern, the conscious concern, has often been with devices of language and principles of diction. So was it in 1798, when Wordsworth called for poetry to adopt the language that men use. But Wordsworth had something to say in his new language; he needed the language, in fact, so that he *could* say what he thought and felt. The situation is no different now. With the new style of 1912—if that is the year from which we date a certain renaissance—there came new stuff; and I think the stuff explains the style. Wherever we look in that time we discover poets who themselves have discovered, or re-discovered, something worth saying in human speech. Irony returned, and the sense of tragedy; the sense of comedy, too, and even the sense of sin. Edgar Lee Masters dug up the Greek Anthology; Ezra Pound ransacked the older poetries of Europe and Asia; and E. A. Robinson attempted again the difficult art of story. T. S. Eliot experimented, to be sure, with stanzas and free verse; it is quite important that he did so; but it is still more important that he restored to poetry the stuff of theology, long absent and all but lost. What explains the peculiar interest of his verse plays? Their verse? I do not think so. I think it is rather the serious concern he has been able to manifest with some of the oldest and deepest ideas that men have had—ideas of martyrdom and salvation. What he has done with these ideas is another question, not especially relevant here. The relevant point is that he deals with them at all, and thereby makes poetry once more interesting to people. They may say that they do not know what his poems mean, but they do not talk as if they were about nothing. They are about something indeed, as poetry at any time had better be.

Robert Frost, if he has done nothing else, has rediscovered Job, whose wife says in *A Masque of Reason:*

Job says there's no such things as Earth's becoming
An easier place for man to save his soul in.
Except as a hard place to save his soul in,
A trial ground where he can try himself
And find out whether he is any good,
It would be meaningless. It might as well
Be Heaven at once and have it over with.

There we have the accent of great poetry, and it is inseparable from the subject Frost has found. He found it where it waited for him, as the world waits for any man to recognize it. For any man, and for any poet. For there is nothing more important about a poet than that he is a man. He may not know more at last than all men do, but what he does know he knows well, and perfects himself in the art of expressing. What he knows, and what we know, is that the world is a hard place to live in at any cost, but that the cost is prohibitive only for those who make the mistake of thinking it is heaven—or should have been.

The Young Writer,
Present, Past, and Future

Stephen Spender

On this, the occasion of giving the annual Hopwood Awards, a few of you must be thinking about the first step in your career signified by receiving an award. In a rather varied life, one of the things I have never done is to win a literary prize. My first duty is to congratulate you on an achievement that fills me with admiration. But I must add a word of warning, which you can attribute to sour grapes if you wish. You only have to look at lists of Nobel Prizes, Pulitzer Prizes, and the rest to realize how changeable—if not fallible—is the judgment of literary juries.

In a way of course, this is rather consoling. To those of us—who are always in a democratic majority—who have not won prizes, it shows that we may be better than you who have. There is even more solid consolation to be derived from reflecting that those of us who do not deserve prizes may well win them, since the example of many who have won them shows that in the past there has not always been an absolutely necessary connection between prize-winning and dessert.

Now that I'm on this aspect of the literary career—of which you are today tasting the first fruits—I may as well tell you that, economically speaking, being a writer is very like being a gambler. The story or article that earns you $10 might equally well earn you $1,000. Sometimes you are paid a few pennies for a review, sometimes enough to keep you for a month. And what is true of the economics of the thing is also true of reputation. Many writers living today who have great reputations were hardly known during the long years when they were doing their best work. Anyone who has lived as a writer for twenty years or more knows too that one's stock goes up and down in what is a fluctuating market of critical opinions.

I mention these things in order to get them out of the way. The point really is that, although writers have to get started in one way or another with earning money and getting work published, these things are irrelevant. When I say irrelevant, I don't mean just that they don't matter; I mean that part of the struggle of being a writer is to watch and to be on guard that they don't have relevance. To be a failure can be discouraging. To be a success may mean something much worse: that you feel surrounded by people who want you to go on being one. Your publisher has sold fifty thousand copies of your last book, and is appalled when you bring in a manuscript of what may be a better book, but of which he knows he can sell only two thousand copies. The more you are known the more you discover that you are in some mysterious way arousing expectations in all sorts of individuals and groups of people who, since they read your work, feel that you have a certain responsibility towards them.

Shortly before he died, the English novelist Sir Hugh Walpole outlined to me the idea of a novel he wanted to write. It was on a subject very close to his heart, which he felt he understood better than others. From the way he spoke it was clear that this unwritten book was the one work in which he could portray his realest experience of life. However, it would describe people and behavior very different from those expected by the readers of his best-selling novels. I became excited at his idea and pressed him to start writing this book which I felt sure would be his masterpiece. "No," he said, "I shall never write it." "Why not?" "Because I could not write it in a way which would please my best-selling public. It would have to be produced in a small edition, for not more than two thousand readers. And after selling one hundred thousand copies of each of my novels, I could not endure that."

We can assume, I think, that anyone who simply wants to sell a lot of copies of his books will—if he knows this already—plan his career accordingly. He will not be a writer, but a businessman who is dealing with words as other people deal with any other mass-produced commodity. He will have no illusions, so he will not suffer at the end of his life from the kind of heartbreak which makes Sir Hugh Walpole—if a failure in his own art—the subject of a great biography by Rupert Hart-Davis, which has recently been published.

Now that the decks have been cleared of success and failure, what are the legitimate needs of the young writer? It's better, I think, to put the question in a form in which it can be examined by examples. What did the young writer of the past need, as the pre-conditions necessary to his gift?

Let us consider for instance, John Keats and Ernest Hemingway, two young men; one in London at the beginning of the nineteenth and the other in Paris at the beginning of this century.

What of Keats? Well, first of all, he wanted to write poetry for no reason except that he wanted to write poetry. His concept of poetry was formed from reading Spenser, Shakespeare, and, later, Milton. To him, poetry was the means of entering the world of other poets and then creating his own poems. Besides being a poet, he was a medical student, he was devoted to his brother Tom (whom he nursed through the consumption that he himself was very soon to die of), to his sister, Fanny Keats, and in the last months of his life, to Fanny Brawne, with whom he fell so hopelessly in love.

Poetry was for him a separate world from the real world of his medical studies, his brothers and sisters, even his love. Thus, in one of his letters he describes an occasion when the classroom or laboratory where he was studying suddenly disappeared, and he found himself in another world, even more real to him, of Shakespeare's *A Midsummer Night's Dream*. In another letter, written when he was nursing his brother, he complains that the identity of Tom Keats presses on him unendurably, a pressure he resents not out of selfishness but because he felt responsible to his world of poetry more even than to his brother. There was also something about his love for Fanny which seemed to him the surrender of his poetic world to a human one.

The next thing we note about the young Keats is that he wanted convivial friends who shared his love of poetry, provided that they did not press on him too much with their personalities. When he was twenty or so, he allowed himself to think that with Reynolds, Benjamin Robert Haydon, Cowden Clarke, Leigh Hunt and the rest, he had found a circle of enlightened people who recognized the same poetic values as he did. He wanted to belong to a group of friends who correspond very much to the group of French writers who will frequent the same Parisian cafe. Perhaps, in America today, this function of literary companionship is being fulfilled rather self-consciously, and with not enough frivolity to accompany the seriousness, by the creative writing courses. Brandy and coffee ought to be compulsory at all the creative writing seminars.

The next thing Keats wanted was to chart his course among the currents of literature and thought in his time. He disliked Pope's poetry, which he regarded as mere versification. He had very clearly developed ideas of his own about the world of pure imagination which poetry should create. He found precedents for his concept of poetry in Shakespeare. He was critical, though admiring, of Wordsworth. He was a not very generous rival of Shelley. He came to sneer at Leigh Hunt, and he grew out of the circle of his Hampstead friends into the isolation of genius.

Although he wrote that he had never allowed a shadow of public thought to enter his work, Keats was not without opinions. He was what we would call a liberal. He loved freedom (by which he meant Liberal Freedom) and hated Napoleon and the British government of his day.

Now let us turn to the young Hemingway in Paris a hundred years later. His attitudes are less literary than those of Keats. He would deny, I think, having read much of anything, though he would admit to a great admiration for Stendhal. But don't let us be put off by his anti-literary pose without examining it more closely. He is not bookish, but he cares immensely about writing well, and takes a conscious pride in his use of words. Despite his pride, he goes humbly to Gertrude Stein and learns all he can from her about adding word to word with as much thought as if one were making a mosaic, and each word a separate stone.

Thus, the difference between the literary conscience of Hemingway and that of Keats may be the difference between romantic poet and modern novelist rather than that between man of literature and hairy-chested philistine. Hemingway knows that the roots of the novel are not in literature but in life. Although he can learn how to make sentences from Miss Stein and how to write about a battle from the description of Fabrice on the battlefield of Waterloo with which *The Charterhouse of Parma* opens—he sees that beyond learning how to write his own novels from other writers such a novelist must avoid literature like the plague. His source-books are the conversations of soldiers and drunks, the lonely thoughts of fishermen and hunters.

Just as much as Keats, Hemingway had then his special vision of a world of his imagination, a world in which love and drinks and fights and scenery were more real than, say, intellectual conversation, journalism, money, and stuffed shirts. In a drawing room his picture of prize fights, hunting in Africa, and war in Spain would doubtless drive out the china and chippendale, just as much as the world of *A Midsummer Night's Dream* came dancing down on a beam of sunlight into the room where Keats was learning medicine and made him forget the lecture.

Given the fact that he was trying to make novels out of life and not out of other novels, Hemingway also had his circle. Just as Keats, without

very much success, looked in Hampstead for friends who shared his
passion for the arts, Hemingway was looking for people who shared his
passion for the real—which was the quality he wanted to put into his
novels. They turned out to be bull-fighters, soldiers at Caporetto and in
the front line at Madrid, and Americans in Paris. But the real Hemingway no more belongs to his tough circle than Keats to his Hampstead
literati. The ultimate image we have of Hemingway is of the old man left
fighting the fish of his art alone.

This is, indeed always, the situation of the artist with his vocation,
pursuing his vision. All the same, he probably needs to start off from the
fertilizing group of his friends who—perhaps only because they are generous and young, and do not themselves know as yet what they really
want—form a magic circle round his youth.

Hemingway, like Keats, fought his battle among the ideas of his
time. When he was lion-hunting in Africa he was also carrying on a
polemic against Aldous Huxley, who had reproached him with being
anti-intellectual. He showed pretty well, I think, that the intellect is a
matter of passion and not of books. A few asides in his work about Goya
and El Greco are impressive enough to make the reader realize that a
writer with an understanding of painting does not need to show it all the
time. Then, just as Keats without ever being what is called "political"
wrote his sonnet to salute Leigh Hunt when he had been imprisoned for
defamation by the British Government of that time, Hemingway took
up the attitudes of an unpolitical man who loved freedom to the politics
of the 1930s. *For Whom the Bell Tolls* corresponds in his work to Keats's
sonnet celebrating Leigh Hunt when he was sent to prison. And all
through his work there is a preoccupation with the relationship of those
characters who are felt to be real because they have done real things—or
because they have lived close to the values of nature—with the unreality
of the politicians who direct the soldiers, the businessmen who have
more power than the artists and the fishermen. For him freedom is the
struggle of real life to assert itself against meddling and self-interested
authority.

I could go on multiplying examples to illustrate that the young
writer is someone with a mysterious sense of his own vocation, and a
vision of reality which he wishes to communicate: to show, too, that in
his youth he can benefit by the magic circle of those who are touched to
sympathy by him, perhaps more for what he is than for what he does.
His friends believe in him and they take his work on trust. Later on they

become interested in other things—they cannot share his vocation—and he learns to be alone. But his youth has been watered by their sympathy.

He must certainly care for his craft as a writer. He must choose other writers who are guardian angels from the past whose works seem to be fighting on the side of his unborn poems or novels. What I very much doubt, though, is whether he should know more than this. One of the things that many modern writers perhaps suffer from is intellectual indigestion. We are told that Shakespeare had small Latin and less Greek, and the number of works he is supposed by scholars to have read would certainly not have filled even a small library. What he knew is so perfectly absorbed within his own genius that we are scarcely aware of his knowing it.

Shakespeare probably understood just so much of what he read as he required for the purpose of his writing. This is all a writer needs and it may be very little or it may be a great deal. With Dante and Milton it was a lot. A writer should think of every experience (and this includes the books he reads and the paintings he sees) in terms of the life which he is going to put into his work. He should be as much on guard against the corruption which comes from excessive sophistication and a too great load of learning as he is against any debasement of his gifts. Rimbaud advised writers to throw away dictionaries and reinvent words, and Blake thought that the forms in which past poets wrote became the shackles of new poetry. D. H. Lawrence, who was probably the most profound critic of modern values in this century, was utterly opposed to all the intellectual tendencies of our time, read little of his esteemed contemporaries, and not very selectively from the past.

None of these writers was an ignoramus, but all saw the necessity of approaching knowledge and theories about literature with the same lively precaution as you would enter a forest full of poison ivy and snares. They saw that intellectual life is not a passive process like hypnosis which you submit to, hoping that you will be entranced into doing something beyond your natural powers. You have to meet the intellectual work of others with your own powers, according to your capacity to cope with it, and not be overpowered by it. Intellectual life for a writer should be a struggle of all the forces of his life with other minds which he can meet on equal terms.

So here we have that timeless creature, the young writer, with his vocation, his vision of what is real to him, his magic circle of friends, the struggle of his whole existence within the ideas, the movements and the history of his time. He is timeless, and yet he is a kind of animal who tries to find the place within his time where he can best fulfill his gifts. He struggles to be received into the court of Queen Elizabeth or Louis XIV, or to be patronized by some great aristocrat of the eighteenth century, or to achieve the independence of a bourgeois living and working for himself in the nineteenth. He is a parasite, and often rather an ungrateful one. In her novel *Orlando,* Virginia Woolf describes the poet who comes to stay at Orlando's residence, where he charms everyone, and then goes away to write a perfidious lampoon on Orlando and his friends. When he claims his right to middle-class independence, as poets did in the nineteenth century, it is in order to spit on the bourgeois. He arrives as Rimbaud arrived in Paris in 1870, puts his feet up on the table of Madame Verlaine's clean dining room, takes out his pipe, smoking it upside down so that the hot ash falls onto her tablecloth, and shoos away her lap dog, with the expletive comment: "Les chiens sont les liberaux."

But the position of the young writer differs according to the time in which he lives. His impossible behavior takes different forms according to whether he emerges from the cocoon of his family in 1450, 1550, 1650, 1750, 1850, or 1950, or whatever day of whatever year between these dates. In 1800 he is a revolutionary patriot, wild-eyed, unshaven, and influenced by the self-dramatizing self-pity and passion for freedom of Byron's *Prisoner of Chillon.* In 1900 he holds a lily in his hand, is languid, tired, dissipated, and infinitely superior to the universe. In 1914 he marches onto the battlefields of Europe and with a song on his lips proclaims that the world is about to be purified of ignoble qualities. In 1916 he is the voice of the youthful dead of both sides which hold no hatred for one another. By 1920 he has taken to alcohol and various other excesses, and he represents the naked, almost brutal assertion of his survival against a background of recently past death. He swears that whatever else happens, he will never be responsible towards anyone or anything again and he spits into the faces of the older generation. Under all these attitudes, he maintains the sense of his vocation. What in our time can the writer do, is the question he is asking, but by "doing" he means, how can he write his novels or poems. The answers are always changing, and as the time-process of our civilization speeds up they change from year to year with ever-increasing rapidity.

So the differences are less confusing when we recollect that the writer adopts attitudes for the sake of his writing. An attitude—or, for that matter, a literary movement—is the simplified statement of the

relationship to his time which he adopts in order that he may best write
his best work. Thus the young writers at the beginning of the French
Revolution had to relate themselves to two things in contemporary history, which became one thing within their work. One was the changed
attitude towards values which had been brought about by the French
Revolution, the other was the fact that their immediate predecessors
were writing in a style which could not possibly be the vehicle for the
altered sensibility resulting from the change from aristocratic values to
democratic ones. These two things became one imaginative life within
the colloquial manner of writing of Wordsworth, the romanticism of
Keats.

What is the writer's vision, though? With the poet it is his significant
experience expressed in a poetic idiom which responds or is sensitive to
the circumstances of his time. The poet's ideas of what is most valuable,
because most living is experience, confront the world with his idiom of
the contemporary human situation. The novelist illustrates, in his depiction of character, the struggle of individual human existence within the
circumstances of a particular historic period. The young man Tolstoy
shows us a whole panorama of the circumstances of individuals living
through the Napoleonic wars. Although *War and Peace* is all, in a sense, a
depiction of life, the values of living are only realized at their most
intense in moments of the lives of particular characters. Moments of
Natasha's vivid childhood, of Pierre Bezukhov's changes of heart—most
of all perhaps the moment when Prince Andrew lies wounded on the
battlefield. The novel portrays the struggle for the realization of life
within the circumstances of living. If the conditioning circumstances are
not truly imagined and portrayed within the work, then the life in the
novel seems false; and if the circumstances are realized, then the work
becomes a depressing exercise in what is called realism.

There is no way in which a writer can cheat himself into having a
greater awareness of life than his genius has given him. There are, however, circumstances and conditions which can cheat him out of the possibility of realizing his gifts. It is more difficult to be a young writer at
some periods than at others. There are some decades when the mood of
the time seems to permit of a much wider realization of the values of
living than others. In England the Elizabethan age was certainly such a
time. There are others when a great many writers work under circumstances where life itself seems weighed down and oppressed, and yet the

material development of society is so expansive and confident that masterpieces are written. The Victorian Age was such a period. But although nineteenth-century England was ebullient and expansive, yet it is really the literature of France in this period which tells us more of what was happening to the spirit of man.

"What is the position of the young writer today?" That is the question at the back of my mind all the time that I have been talking. For it seems to me that in certain ways this question is more difficult to answer than it has been for a great many years.

The reason it is difficult to answer is that the one thing that previously was clear about the position of the writer has suddenly become amorphous. What has been clear for so long was his extreme individuality. The writer has for a hundred and fifty years regarded himself and been regarded as an independent creator or critic within society who brought to it his own vision or who attacked it from the point of view of a detached observer. For instance, we think of Keats and the other romantics as being outside the materialism of the industrial revolution. Perhaps they opposed the materialism of the nineteenth century, or perhaps they added something to life which made circumstances tolerable and even justified modern civilization. Whichever it was they did, rightly or wrongly, we think of them as *outside* their society. The French poets, like Baudelaire, Verlaine, and Rimbaud, we think of as still more savagely isolated individualists, who were antagonistic to all contemporary values. We think, too, of the novelists either as being critics of Victorianism who judged their age from a disinterested point of view or as truthful observers of character, who were able to indicate the points at which life acquires the greatest significance. Flaubert's *The Sentimental Education,* for example, is a scrupulous and exact study of the lives of a group of individuals against a background of history, and at the end we are able to measure the extent to which Frederic Moreau and the other characters have lived their lives, attained happiness, suffered to some purpose, created beauty, or loved.

Today we suddenly find ourselves living in a world where it is very difficult to think of the poet creating a unique vision like that of Keats, which will so enormously enhance the value of living for his readers that his poetry will seem a system of the imagination where "beauty is truth, truth beauty," and nothing else need be added to life. It is equally difficult to think of the novelist being an independent, detached critic of society. We suddenly find that the individual visions, which right up to the time of the aesthetic movement could add something so significant within art to the value of life that ordinary life itself seemed scarcely worth living, have shrunk into private fantasies, childhood memories, squibs like Truman Capote's novel about some people who decide to go and live in a tree—or like Henry Miller's books in which all his characters indulge themselves to the utmost in physical sensation and have no philosophy or purpose beyond such indulgence.

What has happened is that the idea that there are writers and other artists and sensitive individuals who in some way can preserve an integrity and create beauty outside the materialism of society, has suddenly been completely shattered. We may not live in a totalitarian world, but a kind of totalitarianization of the spirit has overtaken all of us. In a world where within a matter of hours or days the whole of our civilization may be destroyed, or where if this does not happen we may find our minds the passive objects of political dictatorship, using psychological propaganda, everyone shares with everyone else such enormous secrets of fear and anxiety that the idea of being outside what is happening—as Keats in his way, and Dickens in his quite different way, were outside it—seems impossible. Indeed a writer, like T. S. Eliot, who does retain a certain outsideness, only manages to do so by describing a religious experience which is outside time and history altogether.

We cannot imagine that the young writer of genius will today believe himself to be a unique person in a unique position bringing to other people a picture of living values which will change the lives of those who have eyes to see and ears to hear. Instead now of an art which will add another world of the imagination to the material world, we have literature of young novelists which, however eccentric or fantastic it may seem, is really documentary. Someone who lives in the deep South had some very extraordinary and crazy relatives whom he is going to tell us about. Someone else had a very odd relationship with one of the masters at his preparatory school or at the military academy. A woman who was frustrated in her desire to become cultured never got to the Museum of Modern Art, so she became a nymphomaniac, upset her family badly and was finally taken away in a van. All these experiences can be original and it is possible to write about them well, but they do not enhance the life of the reader, and they do not criticize the world in which we are living. No amount of odd experience and good writing and all the characters going mad can really get away from the fact that they are really just embroidered documentary material.

In these circumstances, the young writer is tempted to abandon his artistic responsibility—that is, his responsibility to do what he knows he alone can do in the way he alone can do it. On every side, there are voices which say: "Don't be responsible to yourself. It is no longer any use. Be responsible to us." In England he is invited to become an agent for disseminating culture through the British Broadcasting Corporation, or the British Council. In the United States he is invited to join a university to become a teacher of creative writing, with a certain real though vaguely defined responsibility to the academic world. Meanwhile a tremendous critical apparatus based on a study of the past works of writers, most of whom hated the very idea of critics and criticism, grows up, and rules about technique, influences, myths, and so on are extracted from past works, which get very near to supplying the young with objective formulae for creating new ones. There is a great deal of talk about Freud and Jung and the unconscious, but the fact that writing should be a process of whose development the writer himself should be largely unconscious is forgotten. At this point it may be well to remind ourselves that Goethe observed to Eckermann that it would be impossible in the future for any poet to attain the stature of Shakespeare. The reason he gave for this conclusion was that the result of contemporary criticism would make it impossible for any poet to develop, as Shakespeare did, without being self-conscious about his own development. The true development of a poet like Shakespeare—Goethe thought—was like that of a man who walks in his sleep.

The temptation of the writer of yesterday—W. H. Auden has said— was to be too individualistic, too proud, too isolated. But the temptation of the writer today—he went on—is to prostitute himself, to make slight concessions all the way round: to the academies, to the cultural agencies, to the glossy magazines which have decided that they want to publish something "better" than they have done before, but not too good.

In the present situation it is extremely difficult to say what is the right course for the young writer. You can't, as you would perhaps do in the past, advise "Find the right patron who will give you the freedom to do your best work which will glorify his name," nor yet "Create in your work the vision of an inner life of aesthetic values which will enable your readers to escape the vulgarity and banality of modern living"; nor "Take sides with the cause which represents greater human freedom and draw strength from the life and future of the just cause you support." It is not as easy as that. Nor do I accept the despairing view of George Orwell in his very interesting essay on Henry Miller, entitled *Inside the Whale*. Orwell says in words which I paraphrase: "Accept the fact that you can do absolutely nothing to alter the condition of the world today. Make a virtue of necessity, and like Jonah, use your art to get inside the whale. Don't object, don't rebel, just accept everything and then make the best of the circumstances of a life of private sensations and experience which is still possible to you." His own book, *Nineteen Eighty-Four*, like Camus's novel, *The Plague*, refutes him. It is still possible, by trying to see the largest truth about the time in which we live, and by simply stating it, to get outside the whale.

Meanwhile, one can also say that there are certain things which are wrong, and even a few which are right. It may be necessary to accept the situation of working in a more official capacity—as a teacher, or a cultural agent—than before, but it is still not necessary to sell your soul. By selling your soul I mean not cherishing the distinction between work which one does to satisfy one's own standards and that done to satisfy other people's standards. One's own standards are simply to write about the truth as one experiences it, in the way in which one can write about it. To discover these two things is already the task of a lifetime, and by simply devoting oneself to them one may solve the problems which I have stated here.

Another positive thing which I can say is that the young should be an audience for one another. In this the creative writing courses, of which I feel critical in some ways, offer a tremendous opportunity to young writers. It may not be that all of you are going to be writers, but there is every reason why all of you should be interested in the writing of each one of you. The interest that you can give to the writer who is going to be outstanding among you is the equivalent, at this stage of his development, to a blood transfusion. And it is blood which only the young can give to others who are young, because later on in life everyone is too preoccupied with his own affairs to give so generously. No one ever receives in all his life any praise which is comparable to that which one receives when one has sent one's first work to a friend who feels it to be a new and exciting experience in his own life.

The most important thing of all, though, is to have an absolutely sacred sense of the vocation of being a writer. A writer is a person who experiences with part of himself the life around him and with some other part of himself the life of those past writers whose works have filled him with the desire to be a writer. In his own work he relates his sense of that past with his awareness of this present. In doing so he creates something entirely new, and this new thing, if it is worthy, is to write the words which the past master would write about contemporary life if he were now living. Through the contemporary writer's hand flows the blood of past writers, and to the degree that the present writers fulfill their vocation they are extending into the future the life of the old. There remains the problem of relating oneself to the present situation. But the true writer lives in a past and a future situation for which the present is only a bridge. This reduces the contemporary problem to its true proportions. It means that although you must be aware of the present situation you must see it in the light of the past and future, pursue your vocation, write as well as you can and not better than you can, provide an audience for your contemporaries, and judge life from the center of your artistic conscience, to which you are alone responsible.

"Why Can't They Say What They Mean?"

Archibald MacLeish

They being, of course, the poets. Or rather, the contemporary poets—those who are now around. "Why can't they put it in so many words?" "Why can't they just come out with it?" There are various forms of the question and various tones of voice to ask it in—the indignant tone of the letter to the editor of the literary review, the contemptuous tone of the full-page institutional ad in the *New York Times* which bellows (lie quiet, ghosts of Avon and Weimar and Florence!) that the prime characteristic of a great work of art is to be easily understood, the earnest tone of the manifesto of the local poetry society, the outraged tone of the student who can't sit there silent any longer. But whatever the form and whatever the tone the intention is the same: "Why can't they say what they *mean?*" "Doesn't a poet need to be read?" demanded a student of mine in the blazing first paragraph of a paper on Pound's *Hugh Selwyn Mauberley*. "If not, what is the purpose of poetry? Art must be amazed at what some people do to attain her!"

No humane man can be indifferent to such a cry as that even when it leaves him with a lecture to write over. At least I cannot be indifferent, for its anguish takes me where I live. Not only am I a practitioner of the art of poetry and contemporary to the extent of being still alive: I am also, in a sense, a teacher of the art. That is to say that I spend a considerable part of my time attempting to teach young men and young women, not how to write poetry—no one, I think, would seriously undertake to do that—but how to read it. The angrily held conviction, therefore, that one of the most characteristic of contemporary poems is not only unreadable but not seriously to be read is, to me, a matter of concern. When I reflect, as I must, that this conviction is not peculiar to one student in one college but may be held by many students in many institutions, including, conceivably, the University of Michigan itself, the concern becomes an active anxiety.

And an anxiety of a rather disturbing kind. I am not anxious only for the intelligence of the rebellious student—he happened, as a matter of fact, to be one of the most intelligent members of his class. Neither am I fearful for the reputations of my contemporaries among American and English poets. They have done quite well in spite of the revolt and it is at least arguable that some of them have flourished because of it. What disturbs me is the relation of all this to what can only be called the health of our civilization. A civilization without a poetry of its own is a contradiction in terms, and a civilization which rejects a poetry it has itself produced is sick: it is an Oedipus civilization stabbing at its own eyes. We may not like the kind of poetry we have produced in the West in this century. We may wish it were some other kind of poetry. But the fact is that this poetry exists and that it is ours. And the further fact is that if we lose contact with it we shall lose an essential contact with ourselves. Only *this* poetry can give us to see that aspect of our lives which poetry in any generation makes visible. When the poetry produced by a particular kind of sensibility is obscure to those to whom the sensibility belongs, the sensibility is obscure also—and the life out of which that sensibility has developed.

If this seems to imply that obscurity in poetry is, at bottom, a reader's problem rather than a writer's, I should have to agree that it means just that. Where the obscurity complained of is obscurity in an achieved work it is the reader, not the writer, who must deal with it. Gide's observation that "obscurity is something the true poet should neither seek nor fear" carries the necessary corollary that obscurity is something the true reader must neither evade nor avoid: he cannot reject the poem merely because he finds it obscure without failing in his reader's duty to the art.

This does not mean, of course, that there are not forms of obscurity which justify the rejection of a poem. Gide makes it plain that his remark applies to "true poets" only. The poet who is obscure because he is incapable of accomplishing understanding, or who is obscure because he is afraid of being understood, is not a true poet and should be judged accordingly. If a man *cannot* write clean English, or if he affects, by calculated dubieties, meanings of which his intelligence is incapable, he deserves no one's serious consideration. There is, however, all the difference in the world between the writer who deliberately contrives ambiguities in the hope of hoisting himself into significance, not by his own petard but by the chances of the dictionary, and the true poet who is obscure, or seems so, because of the controlled and achieved and intended implications of his work. With the true poet, obscurity, where it exists, is the condition of the poem and must be accepted by the reader in that sense. If the accomplished poem of the true poet is worth reading— we would agree, I suppose, that it must be—it is worth reading with its density upon it, for its density is part of what it is.

But to say so much is not, of course, to dispose of the problem. The obscurity, if there is obscurity, remains—and all the darker because the reader must stand before it alone. What is he to do about it? The answer depends, of course, on what his difficulty is and only he himself can tell us that. Let us therefore put the question to ourselves. What is this contemporary obscurity of which we so persistently complain when we speak of our own poets? Is it something more than mere difficulty of interpretation? If so, what? When the student rages or the respectable lady in the correspondence column spits, is it merely because the reading of this poetry is hard, or is it something else the protestants have in mind? Take Yeats for example. Is Yeats "obscure" within our contemporary usage of that word? Certainly "Byzantium" is as difficult as it is great, which means very difficult indeed. I have spent months over its reading in the past and I have no doubt I shall spend further months before I die. But is "Byzantium" *obscure?* Are any of Yeats's greatest poems *obscure?*

Not, I think, if one means by the word an obduracy which will not yield to ordinary intelligence and perceptiveness. One of Yeats's less important poems, a lyric from *Words for Music Perhaps* which has discouraged many readers, may serve us here:

His Confidence

Undying love to buy
I wrote upon
The corners of this eye
All wrongs done.
What payment were enough
For undying love?

I broke my heart in two
So hard I struck.
What matter? for I know
That out of rock,
Out of a desolate source
Love leaps upon its course.

There is not a single word here which is not readily readable nor is the syntax in any way complicated. What troubles those readers who experience trouble is apparently the images and the implications. Writing "all wrongs done" upon "the corners of this eye" strikes them as meaningless. But the meaning, however dark it may be to the intellect, is perfectly available to the image-reading imagination, is it not? The imagination knows that it is in the corner of the eye that the wrinkles of suffering are written. Once that is perceived the first stanza reads itself. I suffered wrongs willingly to buy what I hoped would be undying love for which no payment would be too great.

What then of the second stanza? Here again the only problem is that of the image and here again the image presents itself to the eye that can see. The heart is struck so hard that it breaks as one might strike and break a rock—as Moses struck the rock from which water gushed forth in that wilderness. Only here what gushes forth from the rock of the heart—from that desolate source—is love: love that leaps upon its course.

How then does the second stanza relate to the first? There is no syntactical connection, but the connection of emotional relationship is obvious enough. I had hoped to buy love *for* myself—undying love—by suffering: I did not succeed but by this suffering I broke my heart, and from my broken heart—that desolate source—poured forth my love. It is a small poem but a poem profoundly and unforgettably true, not only of Yeats and his unhappy love, out of which came so much else that leaped upon its course—poetry—insight, but of many, many others also: indeed, in some measure, of all of us.

The difficulty in reading "His Confidence," in other words, is in no way to be distinguished from the difficulty of reading a sonnet by Shakespeare or one of the odes of John Keats. And the same thing is true of Yeats's greatest poems also. Indeed Yeats differs from his comparable predecessors in two ways only: in his use of particular symbols and metaphors provided by his personal philosophic system, and in the special character of the critical apparatus which has grown up around his poems. The symbols and metaphors, however, create philosophical rather than poetic problems: they are *poetically* comprehensible in their own right and the philosophic significances can usually be ignored for reading purposes. As for the critical apparatus, it need not interfere unduly with the pleasure of reading Yeats. It is true of Yeats's work as of the work of many of his contemporaries that interpreters have sometimes increased the poetic difficulties in order to increase the academic triumphs, but the general reader is under no obligation to accept professional estimates of the hardships and adversities. Yeats's poems are poems, not puzzles, and the academic tendency to make riddles of them should not delude nor discourage the reader who comes to them as works of art. He should remember that "difficult" poets, or poets who can be made to seem so, are godsends to the unpoetical instructor—which is why so many courses, miscalled courses in modern poetry, are devoted to their work: the instructor can teach the difficulties, not the poems—a far easier task. With Yeats, as with all true artists, it is the poems which matter.

And Yeats's poems are, to an unusual degree, whole and complete within themselves, requiring nothing of their readers—if we may call it nothing—but the power to see and hear and feel and smell and taste and, above all, think. Misinterpretation comes when it does come, not from ignorance of the glosses but from a failure to understand the syntax (which, in Yeats, is as powerful as it is subtle), or from a failure to be *present* sensuously and imaginatively at the scene, or from a failure to exercise the full power of the intelligence in relating the experience of the poem to one's own experience of the world. None of these things are easy to do in a poem like "Byzantium" or "Vacillation" or "Among School Children" or "The Statues," but the difficulties in the way are not difficulties which anyone, I think, could properly call obscurities. A work of art is not *obscure*, as I understand the usage of the word, if it demands of its readers or listeners or observers that they come to it fully awake and in the possession of all their faculties. It is obscure only if it demands of them what their faculties at their best and liveliest cannot provide.

No, what the assailants of contemporary poetry have in mind is not the difficulty of inward meaning one finds in Yeats. At least it is not Yeats they mention. Their principal target is and has been for many years Ezra Pound, and if there is one thing more than another which is patently true of Ezra Pound it is the fact that the meanings of *his* meanings are not in doubt. His diagnosis of his time and of all previous times in his *Cantos* comes down to the simplest of propositions—that usury is the mother of all ill. His ideas about literature—and they are numerous—are as definite and precise, and as fruitful, as ideas could well be. And his emotions, at least the emotions his poetry expresses, are as plain as they are few:

Tard, trés tard, je t'ai connue, la Tristesse,
I have been hard as youth sixty years.

J'ai eu pitié des autres
probablement pas assez, and at moments that
suited my convenience.

It is accurately said. Love of dead men and women you will find in Pound, but for the living—including, at the last, himself—little but exasperation or contempt or rage. It is not, therefore, because his intentions are dark that Pound can be charged with obscurity. It is for another and a wholly different reason—a reason which may go some way to elucidate the nature of the whole complaint about contemporary poetry.

What brings the charge of obscurity down upon Ezra Pound is the *character of the references* to persons and to events out of which he constructs the fabric of his more important work. The beginning of the Sixth Canto will serve as an example:

What you have done, Odysseus,
We know what you have done . . .
And that Guillaume sold out his ground rents
(Seventh of Poitiers, Ninth of Aquitain).
 'Tant las fotei com auzirets
 'Cen e quatre vingt et veit vetz . . . '
The stone is alive in my hand, the crops
will be thick in my death-year . . .

Who, says the indignant reader, is this William? And what was seventh of Poitiers and ninth of Aquitaine? And why ground rents? And what is this Provençal couplet about making love to somebody a hundred and eighty-four times? And in whose hand is the stone alive? And what stone? And what is the relation between the live stone and the thick crops and the death year? And who am "I" who suddenly appears at the end? And why—a thousand times why—go at it in this way anyhow?

Well, the answers to the first seven questions can be quite accurately supplied if anyone is willing to take the trouble. A Mr. Carne-Ross was, with the following results: William is William IX of Aquitaine (d. 1127), crusader and troubadour, who sold his lands to tenants instead of hiring them out and thus living by "usury," and the couplet is from one of William's poems in which he boasts of having spent eight days incognito with two noble ladies who believed he was dumb and wouldn't be able to tell anybody (with the frequent consequences aforesaid), and the thick crops refer to the fruitful results throughout the kingdom of so much royal potency, and the stone alive in the hand, orchidaceous pun aside, refers to the fact that the arts of the stonecutter and the builder, like all the rest of the arts, flourish under a potent father-king as distinguished from an impotent usurer-king. All of which, of course, makes complete sense as well as establishing the fundamental truth in view: that everything does well, including, presumably, the two noble ladies, where wealth isn't hired. The last question however still remains. Why go at it this way? Why not say it in so many words? Why, in any event, not put it all down so that it can be understood without the assistance of such scholars and interpreters as the ingenious Mr. Carne-Ross?

But here again our guide has gone before us. The fault, says Mr. Carne-Ross, is in ourselves, not in Mr. Pound. Mr. Pound should not be denounced because we can't take his broad hints and reconstruct an entire corner of history out of a man's name and a tag of Provençal verse. The trouble is that we have lost the common heritage of myth and legend to which earlier and more fortunate writers could appeal and have become incompetent readers. No one is to blame but the generations which broke the tradition and the only remedy, if we wish to read again, is to shore up the shattered columns and rebuild the city.

It is not, I think you will agree, a very comforting or a very persuasive answer. It is quite true that Milton made copious use of curious names and events which his readers were able to identify only because they and he had read the same books and studied the same languages. It is true also that all those elder poets who constructed their poetic world out of classic mythology or ancient history or the tales of Boccaccio found ready readers only because their generation knew Boccaccio and the myths as well as they. But are Guillaume and his couplet really of that order? Was there ever a time when an English poet could expect to be generally understood in such terms? And Pound—let there be no mistake about that—does wish to be understood: ". . . in discourse," he says in his Seventy-ninth Canto, "what matters is / to get it across e poi basta." Indeed the aim of writing, as his Eightieth Canto sees it, is "to bring your g.r. to the nutriment / gentle reader to the gist of the discourse."

No, the problem is considerably more complicated and more interesting than Mr. Carne-Ross makes it seem. Pound's references in his *Cantos* are drawn from the poetry and art and politics of a dozen languages and countries and there has never been a "common heritage of myth and legend" in English, or, I think, in any other tongue, which contained anything like that body of public knowledge. Nor has any "common heritage of myth and legend" in any country ever contained the *kind* of recondite or purely personal or purely scholarly allusion to which Pound is prone. Take, for example, the First Canto with its magnificently cadenced account of the voyage of Odysseus from Circe's island to that beach in Hell: the strong pull of the rhythm when the wind takes hold of the ship and the leveling off after, like the leveling off of the vibrations of a climbing plane, when the sail truly fills and the ship runs in the open sea. Towards the end of this Canto, after an extended passage which would be wholly intelligible to anyone who knew Homer, and readable enough whether one knew Homer or not, there suddenly appears a character named Divus (patently no Greek) who is commanded to lie quiet, and, beside him, a "Cretan" of whom nothing is said but that an unspecified "phrase" is his. Their position in the Canto indicates that they are persons of importance but nothing in the Canto itself identifies them, nor is there anything in the common heritage of the English-speaking peoples either now or at any previous time which would enable a reader to discover who they are or why they are there. As a matter of fact, only Pound himself, or a sedulous student who had read Pound's other writings, or, conceivably, a specialist in late Latin texts, should such a man take to reading contemporary poetry, could very well know the necessary answer. For Andreas Divus was a scholar who lived early in the sixteenth century and wrote a Latin translation of the Odyssey, "little more than a trot or a pony," which Pound, as he tells us in an essay of 1918, had picked up in a Paris bookstall about 1908 or 1910 in an edition of the early 1800s which contained also the *Hymni Deorum* of a certain Cretan named Georgius Dartona, the second of which (to Aphrodite) contained, in turn, the phrase here suggested. And why is Divus to lie quiet? Because the preceding matter is largely a translation, or rather a magnificent transubstantiation, of his text.

Now this, you may very well think, is a special and understandable case: an ingenious method of at once confessing and concealing plagiarism. It is, I assure you, no such thing. To begin with, Divus, not Pound, is the beneficiary of this traffic as the great translator—for Pound is surely one of the greatest in the history of our tongue—very well knew. Again, and more important, Divus and the Cretan are not isolated instances. They are two among multitudes in the *Cantos* and elsewhere. The Second Canto, the most lyrical of the lot, contains, for example, in the midst of such a Mediterranean scene as no other modern poet has accomplished, "the voice of Schoeney's daughters." You find there Sordello, whom even an age which has forgotten Browning remembers; you find Eleanor of Aquitaine—no problem surely; you find Homer— "Ear, ear for the sea-surge, murmur of old men's voices"; you find Helen; you find Tyro whom any classical dictionary will identify as the beautiful daughter of the King of Elis who was seduced by Neptune as she walked by the river bank

> And the blue-grey glass of the wave tents them,
> Glare azure of water, cold-welter, close cover . . . ;

you have the Mediterranean full of light and dazzle with (Pound's phrases) the quiet sun-tawny sand-stretch and the gulls broading out their wings in the sun and the snipe coming for their bath, spreading wet wings to the sun film; you have evening and that tower like a one-eyed great goose craning up out of the olives "And the frogs singing against the fauns / in the half light"—you have all this, and in the middle of it you have the voice of Schoeney's daughters. And who are Schoeney's daughters? How can a man discover them? Only by reading Golding's translation of Ovid, which few have read and none can now buy, where it is written:

> Atlant, a goodlie lady, one
> of Schoeney's daughters.

Atlanta and her sisters stand alone in their private darkness amidst all that light, but not so the rest of the masked figures of Pound's poems. As you read on into the later *Cantos* the masks crowd around you until, in the Pisan group, the naked face is the exception. Only a reader who was himself present in the Disciplinary Barracks of the American Army at Pisa during the months of Pound's incarceration there could possibly identify the greater part of the shadowy figures of that Inferno: could possibly know, for example, that the roster of Presidents of the United States refers to a list of Negro prisoners, or that the Steele of "Steele that is one awful name" identifies the officer in command of the stockade. The references here are not only outside any common cultural heritage: they are outside the possibilities of common knowledge of any kind. Only with the aid of commentators and interpreters—very special commentators and interpreters—can they be read at all and some references have thus far mystified even the most devoted of the glossarists. The world still waits, I believe, for the identification of a certain nobleman with dirty lace cuffs who pops up out of nowhere in the Café Dante in Verona.

Now, the cumulative effect of all this is, without doubt, infuriating. Even so wise and gentle a man as that fine Greek poet, George Seferis, betrays irritation when he thinks back over his experience of the *Cantos:* "The reader turning the pages becomes dizzy noting the successive insertions of foreign texts; of incidents or of conversations, very often in a foreign language; of persons known from history or entirely unknown, whose unexpected presence he cannot explain . . . ." The irritation is understandable. But is irritation or even rage an adequate answer to the puzzle? Is it really enough to say, as a very considerable number of our contemporaries do say, that you "can't read" Pound—or "can't read" contemporary poetry in general because of Pound; that its obscurities are unnecessary; that they could easily be dispensed with; that the whole thing is a fraud? Here is a man whose position as "true poet" is not open to question: Eliot gave it as his opinion some years ago that Pound was then the most important poet writing in English. Here, furthermore, is a man whose declared purpose as a poet is to communicate: a man to whom the first law of discourse is to communicate *e poi basta*. Is it possible to dismiss the work of such a man as deliberately dark or intentionally obscure or merely incompetent? Is it conceivable that a writer of this stature and these beliefs would devote his life and his art to frustration or could, without adequate reason, construct so curious a monument to himself?

And yet what reason can there be for the use by any writer, no matter what his position or his convictions, of a vocabulary of reference which no one but himself or his coterie or some desperate candidate for the Ph.D. can ever be expected to unravel? How can Pound feel obliged to represent essential parts of what he has to say not by common but by proper nouns, unknown as well as known; by fragments of quotations in numerous tongues, including tongues neither the writer nor his readers speak; by fragments of history as it was or as it might have been, either in his own country or in some other; by bits of conversation between unrecognized conversationalists; by the dry feathers and old tags of the gossip of the art studios? Why doesn't he come straight out with it in comprehensive and comprehensible words? Why, in brief, doesn't he say what he means?

The question with which we started has, you see, somewhat altered its character. What began as an irritable complaint about the habits and practices of contemporary poets as a group has become a disturbed and rather disturbing inquiry into the reasons for the behavior of one of them. Unless we are prepared to assert, as no intelligent man could, that Pound's principal poems are a vast and foolish hoax, we must consider that their method has a purpose. But what purpose?

A specific example, taken from Pound's finest poem, *Hugh Selwyn Mauberley,* may perhaps make the question more precise. In the first section of *Mauberley,* the Ode, which sums up the dilemma of the literary young man whose literary fate is to be the subject of the sequence, there occurs the line

His true Penelope was Flaubert.

Here, of five words, two are proper nouns, but proper nouns in this case with which any intelligent reader will be familiar. Penelope is of course the beloved to whom through thick or thin a wanderer returns. Flaubert is a novelist whose theories of style and whose handling of experience altered the course not only of the novel but of the art of letters generally. What is being said, then, to the reader who understands these references, is that a certain literary style and attitude were the end and object of someone's searchings—in this case Hugh Selwyn Mauberley's. But this is being said not in several dozen words but in five, and with a gain, not a loss, of allusiveness and precision. Pound's line is far more meaningful than my paraphrase, as well as being briefer, handsomer, and more memorable. And the same thing is true, it will be found, throughout this remarkable poem. Very little of *Mauberley* is *about* its subject: the greater part of it is its subject. The poem is less a poem, in the ordinary sense, than a detailed tapestry made up of proper names and the figures they evoke; made up of moments of past time, of gods, of mottoes, of land-scapes. Where a literary generalization would have been possible, there is Flaubert *tout court*. Where Mauberley's frenzied pride is in issue there, instead of the appropriate epithet, is Capaneus on the walls of Thebes. Where it is Mauberley's gullibility which is to be exposed there is no adjective, there is only the image of the trout and its factitious bait. The figure takes the place of the abstraction.

But what then is this figured writing? How, except in its own terms, is it to be described? In an age in which every other book is a book about symbolism, are we to call these figures symbols? Not certainly in any sense but Suzanne Langer's, to whom everything that means is so defined. These are rather *signs* than symbols. They stand, not, as Yeats's symbols do, for the invisible essence which only this particular visible form can express, but for general ideas or conceptions which general terms could also have communicated. The particular is chosen *instead* of the general: the figure *in place* of the abstraction.

What we have, in other words, as a number of recent writers on Pound have helpfully pointed out, is a kind of picture writing. The common coinage of familiar discursive writing in which the same word may serve a multitude of different uses, designating now one particular event and now another, is rejected wherever possible in favor of a series of unique and specific words designating unique and specific situations. As in the case of picture writing, the number of signs is limitlessly increased, but each sign belongs much more nearly to its thing than in the case of signs made out of the interchangeable terms of the generalizing dictionary. One critic of Pound's work has referred to his figures as pictograms or ideograms, but they are much more specific than that. Ideograms have also, in their way and within their limits, exchangeable meanings: Pound's figures have not. The figure of the line "His true Penelope was Flaubert" is not pictogram Flaubert set down beside pictogram Penelope in associated conjunction. The figure is Flaubert *and* Penelope; Flaubert *in the context* of Penelope; Flaubert, if you will, in Penelope's dress.

We could multiply instances throughout *Mauberley* and the *Cantos,* but the situation is, I think, clear. *The obscurity of which complaint is made in Pound is an obscurity of the specific.* His meanings are dark because he composes in pictures and because his pictures are sometimes, like private photographs, too peculiarly unique; because the particular figure does not signify to all, or, in extreme cases, to any, of Pound's readers. Here is somebody in *Mauberley* whom an expert on the generals of the Franco-German War might recognize as one of them—though even he might well be wrong. Here in the *Cantos* is what may be a Chinese god or a Chinese girl or even a Chinese philosopher: only a Taoist would know, and not many Taoists read Pound. Here is "Poor Jenny" whom no one but the Pre-Raphaelites would recall—and the Pre-Raphaelites are dead. The figures are meaningful enough—specifically and wonderfully meaningful—when they are identified, but until we can place these ambiguous figures they are so many faces in a heap of faces signifying nothing, and our question repeats itself with point and passion: Why not *say* it in general and generally comprehensible terms? Why hand us the private photographs to figure out if we can?

Pound, if we asked him—if we looked back through his theories and his theorizing—would tell us something by way of answer but not enough. For years in his younger days he went about London attacking English poets of renown as fabricators of a mere "vehicle for transmitting thoughts" and demanding the substitution of what he called "specific rendering." Now *rendering* is a Symbolist word of the nineties and we may look to Symbolist doctrine to define its meaning. To the Symbolists the poet's business was with his experience, and particularly with the experience of his consciousness, and every moment of that experience was unique. It was therefore the poet's task to invent a particular language appropriate to his particular life. What was basic to Symbolist doctrine, in other words, was the diversity of experience, and what Pound was doing in his early days in London was to carry Symbolist doctrine to its logical conclusion: the conclusion that diversity of experience must be expressed in diversity of terms. If you can't generalize experience neither can you generalize *about* experience. All you can do is "render" it "explicitly" in its inherent explicitness, placing your reader where you yourself have been—naked among the minute particulars. Literature to Pound, as every fortunate school boy has now been taught, is language "charged with meaning" to the greatest possible extent, and the greatest possible extent is the extent made possible by "explicit rendering."

That is the theory. But face to face with a poem we cannot read because the explicitness of the rendering is explicit in terms of someone or something we can't identify, the theory does not help us very much. It does not resolve the obscurity. If anything the obscurity resolves it. The poem stands there meaningless for all the talk, and we are suddenly given to see that the theory is merely what literary theories so often are—an excuse and a self-justification. Pound has made a virtue, as the Symbolists before him made a virtue, of rejecting the generalization, the least common denominator, and presenting the unique and diverse and fragmented experience in equivalents of itself. But in so doing he has quite obviously been driven, as the virtue-makers commonly are, by something other than literary choice—by an unnamed literary necessity. "Explicit rendering" is not inevitably and always a good thing in itself. It may produce marvelously precise and moving effects when its explicit equivalents are legible, but when they are not legible it may produce no effects at all. And it is quite obvious that they must often be illegible. There are simply not enough publicly recognizable photographs in any man's bureau drawer to enable him to present an extensive or complicated experience by this means.

The theory therefore fails to justify the obscurity of which we complain: we must go beyond the choice to the necessity. We must go to the reasons which produced the theory. We must ask why, granted that "explicit rendering" is not always and under all circumstances a better way of writing poetry, Pound was obliged to persuade himself and others that it was? Why was it impossible for him to employ those readier means of communication which had been open to poets, including the greatest poets, in the past? When anything happened to Goethe, as Gide once remarked, he turned it into a generality. Why could not Pound?

The answer—and it is an answer which has much to say about the whole question of obscurity of reference in contemporary poetry—is, I think, this: *Neither Pound nor his contemporaries have been able to turn the particular into the general as Goethe did because the general is not available to them as it was a hundred years before.* Goethe's was a time in which the particular found its place in the general naturally and easily and was best observed in that context. Ours is a time of a very different character. The "general order," if there is one, is no longer open to serious writers in prose or verse, and the particular is so overwhelming in its particularity that it can only be understood, when it can be understood at all, in its character as itself. The consequence is that our literature has of necessity become a literature of particularity. In prose we have been forced toward that particularity of the external world which we call "realism," or toward that other inward particularity which attempts to present the moments of the individual consciousness in their ungeneralized and ungeneralizable diversities. Poetry, moved by the same influences, has been driven in the same direction. But because the end and purpose of poetry is not merely to represent or to comprehend experience but to possess it, "realism" of whichever kind has not served as the poetic means. Poetry has been driven not merely to *designate* the particulars but, in some way, to *contain* them. The labor is not new in kind. Thousands of years before our epoch it was practiced by Chinese poets in their attempts to possess isolated moments of experience. What is new with us is the application of the method. Ours are the first poets in the history of the art to attempt to use the poetry of specific equivalents for such extended renderings of public experience as Eliot's vision of the modern world in *The Waste Land* or Pound's view of universal history in *The Cantos*.

The essential point, however, so far as their obscurity goes, is not that our poets have made the attempt. The essential point is that the attempt has been forced upon them. Lacking a "general order" to contain the great sequences of time and space and to provide metaphors for their expression, our contemporaries have had no alternative, if they wished to handle those sequences, but to represent them in their specific equivalents. The obscurity of reference in contemporary poetry, in other words, is truly an obscurity of necessity rather than of choice. If it is not, for that reason, less obscure, it is, or should be, less offensive. A reader who feels that difficulties have been deliberately thrown in his way in accordance with some aesthetic doctrine or other, has occasion to feel indignant: a reader who understands that the difficulties he faces are difficulties inherent in the approach to the experience he is attempting to possess, has none. If labor is demanded of him it is labor imposed not by the whim of the poet but by the necessities of the poet's task.

This is not to argue that all the difficulties of reference in modern poetry are inescapable. The greatest of modern poets, Yeats, succeeded in forcing the most characteristic of all contemporary experiences to express itself in terms and images which any reader with the least awareness of himself and of his world can comprehend. There can hardly be a student in any American college worthy of the name to whom *The Second Coming* is not a meaningful statement. But the fact that other contemporary poets have not achieved Yeats's mastery of the experience of the age does not mean that their work is not essential to an understanding of the sensibility of our time, or, what is perhaps more important, to its expression. Those readers who have come to see that poetry is an instrument of knowledge, and that the knowledge it can convey is a knowledge of their own lives, and that their own lives must be lived in the age into which they have been born, will not willingly be excluded from the poetry of their own time by those difficulties of communication which are a characteristic of the time and a condition of its experience.

The Swaying Form:
A Problem In Poetry

Howard Nemerov

I

The present essay is not an attempt to solve a problem so much as an attempt to make certain that a problem of some sort exists, and, if it does, to put it clearly before you. No matter how many problems really exist—and now, as at all times, there must be plenty of them—the world is always full of people inventing problems simply as make-works for their prefabricated solutions. As a friend of mine wrote in a prize-winning poem at college, "We know the answers, but shall we be asked the questions?" He has since become a novelist.

The problem I want to try to elucidate is most often discussed as one of belief, or of value, which is prior to poetry, and the great instance of Dante's *Comedy* stands at the gate of the discussion. It is usually argued on this basis that an explicit and systematized belief is (a) intrinsically of value to the poet in his composition and (b) a means for improving his communication with the mass of mankind.

Now I shall be taking up this theme by what many people will consider to be the wrong end, and talking from the point of view of the poet. My reflections are very far from being impartial and objective, and positively invite objections, or even cries of protest. I shall be suggesting, roughly, that the poet, if he has not attained to a belief in the existence of God, has at any rate got so far as to believe in the existence of the world; and that this, sadly but truly, puts him, in the art of believing, well out in front of many of his fellow citizens, who sometimes look as if they believed the experience when they read a copy of *Time*. (These, by the way, are the people who, adapting a metaphor of Aristotle's, think of poetry as a gentle laxative for the emotions.)

So when I hear discussions, or see symptoms, of some *rapprochement* between religion and the arts—A has written a passion play in modern dress, B has composed an atonal oratorio, C has done murals for the little church in the hometown which he left thirty years ago to become a not quite first-rate cubist with a world reputation—my response is not one of unmixed happiness, and I incline to see, in the characteristic imagery of this period, religion and the arts as two great corporations, each composed of many subsidiary companies but both in roughly the same line of business, circling each other warily in the contemplation of a merger, wondering meanwhile where the ultimate advantage will lie, and utterly unable to find out. To unfold a little this metaphor, I should say that in my view the persons seated around the conference table on this occasion are not the inventors of the product—not the prophets, saints, teachers, and great masters of art—but the usual vice-presidents, accountants, and lawyers on either side; the bishops and grand inquisitors, the critics and epimethean pedagogues who arbitrate these matters.

In other words, between ourselves and any clear view of the problematic area lies the Plain of Shinar, where the usual construction work is going forward vigorously, and the serious planners exchange their watchwords: "culture," "responsibility," "values," and "communication." In this Babel, the word *religion* may mean "weekly attendance at the church of your choice," or it may mean the sort of thing that happened to Job—impossible to say. Similarly, the word *art* may be applied equally to the forty-eight preludes and fugues and to advertisements for whisky. That these things are so says nothing against either whisky or church attendance, but may be seriously damaging to art and religion.

Somewhere toward the beginning of things the two have a connection; as our somewhat frequently employed word *creative* will suggest. "Non merita il nome di creatore," said Tasso, "si non Iddio od il poeta." Clear enough: God and the poet alone deserve to be called creative, because they both create things. The recent history of this word is revealing: one reads, e.g., of "creative advertising," "creative packaging," and the possibility of becoming "a creative consumer." A dialect usage may be equally revealing: the mother says of her infant, "he is creating again," meaning either that the child is kicking up an awful fuss, or that he has soiled his diaper.

The relation of religion to more worldly activities is frequently characterized by extreme positions. To show what I hope I am not talking

about, I shall give an example of each. Here is the extreme whereby
religion, in seeking a connection with the world, becomes worldly itself:

SEES BOOM IN RELIGION, TOO

Atlantic City, June 23 (1957) AP.—President Eisenhower's pastor
said tonight that Americans are living in a period of "unprecedented
religious activity" caused partially by paid vacations, the eight-hour
day, and modern conveniences.

"These fruits of material progress," said the Rev. Edward L. R.
Elson of the National Presbyterian Church, Washington, "have provided the leisure, the energy, and the means for a level of human and
spiritual values never before reached."

Despite an air of farcical silliness which will accompany any display
of *hubris* which is at the same time unheroic, this statement—a kind of
cartoonist's exaggeration of what one suspects is the real belief of many
right-thinking persons—does fix the attention on a real question:
whether it is possible for a religious attitude to exist in the acceptance of
prosperity, and with its face set against suffering; a question near the
heart of Christianity, and a question asked over and over, always to be
answered negatively, in the Old Testament, where any statement that
"the land had rest for so and so many years" is certain to be followed by
the refrain, "And the children of Israel did evil *again* in the sight of the
Lord, and served Baalim and Ashtaroth . . . ."

The opposed extreme, wherein religion purifies itself quite out of
the world, may likewise be identified by anecdote. At a conference on
Elizabethan and seventeenth-century poetry, where a number of college
students presented papers for discussion, the first three or four essays
dealt with the lyrics of such poets as Campion and Herrick; after which a
most serious young man arose, frowning, to say that his topic was
George Herbert. He completed his impromptu introduction by saying,
"We have heard a good deal this morning on the subject of *Love;* well,
now we must turn our attention to an entirely different and more serious
topic: *Religion.*" This inadvertence, I am sorry to say, seemed to me the
revelation of something sad and true in attitudes bearing the official
institutional name of religious attitudes. We might compare a remark of
Yeats, that only two subjects are of interest to a serious intelligence: sex
and the dead.

II

But our problem may be as easily obscured from the other side, the side which professes to be that of art, as from the side of religion. If we look to that great arena of the war of words where there are no poems but only Poetry, no paintings but only Art, we find statements of similar monolithic simplicity, which affect to find nothing problematic in the matter at all.

In that arena, for example, a well-known literary journalist has recently written (*New York Times Book Review,* May 3, 1959): "What the arts, literature included, need more than anything else just now, is a declaration of faith—faith in man's potentialities, faith in God, however you may conceive Him."

As a citizen, I may incline to accept the vague benevolence of all this. But as a practitioner of the art of writing, I am bored and disturbed by this sort of loose talk; just as I should probably be, were I a member of some religious community, by the pseudo-liberality of that casual rider to the idea of God—"however you may conceive Him." Again we might compare the view of an artist, in the saying of Joseph Conrad that it is the object of art to render the highest kind of justice to the *visible world:* "It is above all, in the first place, to make you see."

By such exclusions I come to some definition of my theme: the elucidation of what things may be called religious in poetical works and in the professional attitude of the artist to the making of such works.

Even in this somewhat narrower definition, the problem is not easy to focus. I shall be trying to say that the artist's relation to spiritual and eternal things is comprised rather in the form of his work than in its message or its content; but that form is itself somewhat elusive, as I have indicated in titling these reflections "The Swaying Form" after the following passage in Florio's translation of Montaigne: "There is no man (if he listen to himselfe) that doth not discover in himselfe a peculiar forme of his, a swaying forme, which wrestleth against the art and the institution, and against the tempest of passions, which are contrary unto him."*

Florio's somewhat dreamlike English duplicates nicely the possibilities of Montaigne's phrase, "une forme maistresse." The form, that

---

*The phrase about "the art" is not included in all editions.

is, is simultaneously ruling and very variable, or fickle; shifting and protean as the form of water in a stream, where it is difficult or impossible to divide what remains from what runs away. The passage, read in this way, speaks of something in us which is double in nature, on both sides of things at once or by turns. And I would identify this "forme" with the impulse to art, the energy or libido which makes works of art. It is no paradox to say that the artistic impulse fights against "the art," for anyone who persists in this business knows that a part of his struggle is precisely against "the art," that is, against the accepted and settled standards of art in his time.

So this "forme" has the following characteristics. It is (1) allied with religion, for it is against "the tempest of passions" and thus in favor of control, discipline, *askesis,* renunciation. But it is (2) opposed to religion, for it is also against "the institution," that is, against church, state, dogma, or any fixed habit of the mind. Finally, it is (3) against something in its own nature, called "the art," against, perhaps, the idea of form itself.

For a curious tension exists between poetry and belief, idea, principle, or reason. That is, while we hear a good deal about poetry's need to be based upon an explicit view of the meaning of existence, we are very often bored and exasperated by the poetry which testifies to such a view, and incline to say that it is bad poetry precisely in the degree that the poet has insisted on referring the natural world to prior religious or philosophic valuations.

Perhaps it will be illuminating now if I try to sum up the swaying form, this complicated condition of the mind, by imagining a poet at his table in the morning. He faces the blank page, the page faces his mind— which, if it is not also a blank, is a palimpsest on which fractions of world, which he receives chiefly through language, are continually being recorded and erased and coming into strange, dissolving relations to one another; these are, for the most part, not the consequential relations of thought, but rather insanely atomic instead.

To be piously in keeping with the values of the age, I imagine this poet as asking himself, "What can I afford this morning?" And going on to consider the possibilities, or impossibilities: A little *saeva indignatio?* Something smart and severe in a toga? A romantic pathos, or pathology, with wild glances *de chez* Hölderlin? The dewy freshness of an early lyricism, say about the period of Skelton and really, after all, noncommittal? And so on, since the alternatives are very numerous.

There is only one, however, which now arises to give him trouble: "How about me? Shall I be me? And who is that?" He looks doubtfully at his tweeds, his grey flannels, stares at his alert (but modern, but rootless) face in the mirror, and tries to view that crew-cut in quick succession as a Franciscan tonsure, an Augustan wig, a Romantic disorder. No good. He would like to be himself, but acknowledges that himself is poetically not what most interests him, nor what is likely to interest others very much. Sighing, he wonders if poetry, if all great effort in the world, does not involve a necessary hypocrisy (even if one calls it, more politely, not hypocrisy but drama or metaphor, a necessary approach by analogy), and now he gratefully recalls having read somewhere (it was in Castiglione, but he likes the elegant indolence of "somewhere") that Julius Caesar wore a laurel crown to disguise the fact that he was bald. Encouraged a little, he jots down a note reducing to iambic pentameter mighty Caesar—

Who hid his baldness in a laurel crown

—and adds, in prose, "Poets do this, too." Comforted, he occupies the rest of the morning contemplating the publication of a small volume of epigrams on this theme. But come lunchtime, his wife having uncanned a can of alphabet soup which seems to him the image of his condition, the problem remains: Hypocrisy. Seeming, Angelo, seeming. The truest poetry is the most feigning. But is it, really? And how shall we edify the common reader this afternoon? By being Plato? Moody and Sankey? The Pope? Alexander Pope? How shall we solve the problems of society? Affirm the eternal verities? Become rich and famous and sought-after for our opinions (the filing cabinet is full of them) on all sorts of important themes?

No, this will never do. Hypocrisy merges with cynicism. Where is that portrait of Keats?

And so the weary circle begins again. Only once in a while it opens, as something comes into his head and he suddenly commits a poem. At that time, curiously, he does not worry in the least about whether this poem faithfully represents himself, his beliefs, values, tensions, or the absence of all these. He simply writes the poem.

By this ordinary anguish, occasionally relieved in action, a great deal of literature, both good and bad, gets itself produced.

The troubles of this hypothetical or generalized poet will perhaps strike some of you as very literary, over-educated, or even positively neurasthenic, and you may be inclined to say impatiently to him, "Fool, look in thy heart and write," not caring to consider that when Sir Philip Sidney made this excellent recommendation, he was speaking, just like our poet, to himself. And, too, such is the confusion over these things, instructions to look in one's heart and write may turn out translated for practical purposes in weird ways, e.g.: "Look in thy heart and be big, free and sloppy, like Whitman, who is now becoming fashionable again." There is no end, except for that poem once in a while, to the poet's ability at perverting sound doctrine.

If the foregoing description is even partly applicable to the poetic process, it will be plain that the world will wait a long time for "a declaration of faith" in the poems of this poet. It may also be a consequence of his problem with his identity that a good deal of modern poetry is poetry about the problem, poetry which reveals to interpretation one reflective dimension having to do with the process of composition itself. This development, where the mind curves back upon itself, may be always a limit, not only for poetry but for every kind of thought, for that "speculation" which Shakespeare says "turns not to itself till it hath travel'd and is mirror'd there where it may see itself," adding that "this is not strange at all." But perhaps it has become more strange in the present age, that palace of mirrors where, says Valéry, the lonely lamp is multiplied, or where, as Eliot says, we multiply variety in a wilderness of mirrors, and where the "breakthrough," so pathetically and often discussed in relation to all contemporary arts, is most faithfully imagined in Alice's adventure through the looking-glass, the last consequence of narcissism and "incest of spirit" (Allen Tate, "Last Days of Alice") being the explosion into absurdity, very frequently followed by silence.

Silence, alas, may be preferable to the demand of "educators" that the poet should affirm something (anything?) or the often iterated instruction of certain literary persons that he should *communicate* (what?). But silence, for anyone who has set out to be a poet, is an unlovely alternative, containing in itself some religious (that is, some sinful) implication of being too good for this world, so that many poets accept the disabilities of their elected condition by making many small refusals to prevent one great one. The vanities of publication, these seem to say, are better than the silences of pride. And so, for them, the weary round begins again after every poem, as they seek over and over an image of their being: hermit crabs, crawling unprotected from one deserted shell to the next, finding each time a temporary home which, though by no means a perfect fit, is better at any rate than their nakedness.

It is gratuitous, or even impertinent after all this, and surely offers no defense, to say that they sometimes write good poems in their planetary course from house to house. What can we possibly mean, now, by a *good poem?* Let that be another circle, in another hell. While the present purpose is to say something about the process itself, the kind of relation with the world which results in poetic writings and is an attempt to fix for a moment the swaying form.

III

When people are impatient with a work of art they assert their feeling in this way: "What does it mean?" Their tone of voice indicates that this is the most natural question in the world, the demand which they have the most immediate and God-given right to make. So their absolute condemnation and dismissal of a work of art is given in this way: "It doesn't mean anything. It doesn't mean anything *to me*." Only in those plaintive last words does there appear a tiny and scarcely acknowledged doubt of the all-sufficiency of this idea of meaning—that there may actually be meanings, which one does not personally possess.

Now we are all forced to believe about large areas of the world's work that this is so: that all around us physicists, financiers, and pharmacists are conducting complex operations which do have meaning though we do not know what it is. While we may occasionally wonder if those emperors are in fact wearing any clothes, we more usually allow that our bewilderment belongs to ourselves and does not say anything destructive about those disciplines in themselves, even where they do not produce any overwhelmingly obvious practical result such as an atomic explosion. But about works of art we continue to ask that question, "what do they mean?" and regard the answer to it as somehow crucial.

In a realm of contemplation, the question about meaning could, though it generally does not, begin a chain reaction involving the whole universe, since the answer can be given only in terms to which the same question is again applicable. But because we are well-mannered people, or because we haven't the time, or really don't care, or because we are in fact reassured and consoled by receiving an answer—any answer—we know where to stop. So that a large part of our intellectual operations takes inevitably the following form:

A. Why is the grass green?

B. Because of the chlorophyll.

A. Oh.

So, in a realm of contemplation, meaning would itself be inexplicable. The typewriters rattle, the telephones ring, the moving finger keeps writing one triviality after another, the great gabble of the world goes incessantly on as people translate, encipher, decipher, as one set of words is transformed more or less symmetrically into another set of words—whereupon someone says, "Oh, now I understand. . . ."

But the question about meaning attests, wherever it is asked, the presence of civilization with all its possibilities, all its limitations; attests the presence of *language,* that vast echoing rattle and sibilance, buzzing between ourselves and whatever it is we presume we are looking at, experiencing, being in, and which sometimes appears to have an independent value, if any at all, like the machine someone built a few years back, which had thousands of moving parts and no function. The semanticist to the contrary, words are things, though not always the things they say they are. The painter Delacroix expressed it by saying that Nature is a dictionary. Everything is there, but not in the order one needs. The universe itself, so far as we relate ourselves to it by the mind, may be not so much a meaning as a rhythm, a continuous articulation of question and answer, question and answer, a musical dialectic precipitating out moments of meaning which become distinct only as one wave does in a sea of waves. "You think you live under universal principles," said Montaigne, "but in fact they are municipal bylaws."

Language, then, is the marvelous mirror of the human condition, a mirror so miraculous that it can see what is invisible, that is, the relations between things. At the same time, the mirror is a limit, and as such it is sorrowful; one wants to break it and look beyond. But unless we have the singular talent for mystical experience we do not really break the mirror, and even the mystic's experience is available to us only as reflected, inadequately, in the mirror. Most often man deals with reality by its reflection. That is the sense of Perseus' victory over the Gorgon by consenting to see her only in the mirror of his shield, and it is the sense of the saying in Corinthians that we see now as through a glass darkly—a phrase rendered by modern translators as "now we see as in a little mirror."

Civilization, mirrored in language, is the garden where relations grow; outside the garden is the wild abyss. Poetry, an art of fictions, illusions, even lies—"Homer," said Aristotle, "first taught us the art of framing lies in the right way"—poetry is the art of contemplating this situation in the mirror of language.

"Only connect . . . " is the civilized and civilizing motto of a book by E. M. Forster, where he speaks eloquently of meaning, art and order in "the world of telegrams and anger," and of what exists outside that world: "panic and emptiness, panic and emptiness." W. H. Auden, also very eloquently, writes of the limiting extremes within which meaning means, between "the ocean flats where no subscription concerts are given" and "the desert plain where there is nothing for lunch."

But meaning, like religion, seeks of its own nature to monopolize experience. For example, in children's playbooks there are numbered dots to be followed in sequence by the pencil; the line so produced finally becomes recognizable as a shape. So the lines produced among stars (which can scarcely all be in the same plane) become the geometrical abstractions of a Bear, a Wagon, Orion the Hunter, and by softening or humanizing the outlines, recognizable images are produced, but in the process the stars themselves have to be omitted. So does meaning at first simplify and afterward supersede the world. Poetry, I would say, is, in its highest ranges, no mere playing with the counters of meaning, but a perpetual rederiving of the possibility of meaning from matter, of the intelligible world from the brute recalcitrance of things. Poetry differs from thought in this respect, that thought eats up the language in which it thinks. Thought is proud, and always wants to forget its humble origin in things. In doing so, it begins to speak by means of very elevated abstractions which quickly become emptied and impoverished. The business of poetry is to bring thought back into relation with the five wits, the five senses which Blake calls "the chief inlets of soul in this age," to show how our discontents, as Shakespeare finely says of Timon's, "are unremovably coupled to nature." So the ivory tower must always be cut from the horn of Behemoth.

The relation of poetry to religion is both intimate and antithetical, for poetry exists only by a continuing revelation in a world always incarnate of word and flesh indissolubly, a world simultaneously solid and transpicuous. At the same time, religion can never really dissociate itself from poetry and the continuing revelation, and its attempts to do so turn it into a form of literary criticism, as the scriptures and sacred books of the world, in comparison with their interminable commentaries, will sufficiently show. Poetry and institutionalized religion are in a sense the flowing and the static forms of the same substance, liquid and solid states of the same elemental energy.

This is a simple thing; it has been said many times and forgotten many times plus one. William Blake says it this way:

> The ancient Poets animated all sensible objects with Gods or Geniuses, calling them by the names and adorning them with the properties of woods, rivers, mountains, lakes, cities, nations, and whatever their enlarged and numerous senses could perceive.
> And particularly they studied the Genius of each city and country, placing it under its Mental Deity;
> Till a system was formed, which some took advantage of, and enslav'd the vulgar by attempting to realise or abstract the Mental Deities from their objects—thus began Priesthood;
> Choosing forms of worship from poetic tales.
> And at length they pronounc'd that the Gods had order'd such things.
> Thus men forgot that All Deities reside in the Human Breast.

The poet's business, I would say, is to name as accurately as possible a situation, but a situation which he himself is in. The name he gives ought to be so close a fit with the actuality it summons into being that there remains no room between inside and outside; the thought must be "like a beast moving in its skin" (Dante). If he does his work properly, there won't be any other name for the situation (and for his being in it) than the one he invents, or, rather, his name will swallow up all the others as Aaron's rod swallowed up the rods of Pharaoh's wizards.

Sometimes the name so given is a relatively simple one, as when Alexander Pope gave the Prince of Wales a dog, and had inscribed on its collar:

I am his Highness' dog at Kew.
Pray tell me, sir, whose dog are you?

And sometimes the name so given, the situation thus identified and brought into being, is immensely complex, so that one has to refer to it by a tag, an abbreviation, e.g., "King Lear."

A poem, whether of two lines or ten thousand, is therefore the name of something, and in its ideal realm of fiction or illusion it corresponds to what is said of the Divine Name in several significant respects:

> *It is unique.*
> *It can never be repeated.*
> *It brings into being the situation it names, and is therefore truly a creation.*
> *It is secret, even while being perfectly open and public, for it defines a thing which could not have been known without it.*

As to the poet himself, one might add this. Writing is a species of *askesis,* a persevering devotion to the energy passing between self and world. It is a way of living, a way of being, and, though it does produce results in the form of "works," these may come to seem of secondary importance to the person so engaged.

The young writer is always told (he was, anyhow, when I was young) that writing means first and last "having something to say." I cherish as a souvenir of boyhood that honorable and aged platitude, but would like to modify it by this addition: writing means trying to find out what the nature of things has to say about what you think you have to say. And the process is reflective or cyclical, a matter of feedback between oneself and "it," an "it" which can gain its identity only in the course of being brought into being, come into being only in the course of finding its identity. This is a matter, as Lu Chi says, of how to hold the axe while you are cutting its handle.

I say that writing is a species of *askesis.* But as it works in an ideal or fictional, rather than in a practical, realm, so it purifies not the character but the style. There is, however, a connection between the two, at least in the hope that a charity of the imagination shall be not quite the same thing as an imaginary charity.

IV

That, then, is what I have tried to characterize as "the swaying form," a process of becoming related to nature and the nature of things (*natura naturata and natura naturans*). The view here taken suggests that art has some evident affinities with both religion and science on the very simple basis that all three exist in the presumption that the truth is possible to be told about existence; but these affinities themselves also define differences, distances, and intrinsic antagonisms.

As to art's relation with science. The experimental method was
defined, by Galileo, I believe, as putting nature to the question, where
"the question" meant the judicial process of torture. The definition seems
to imply a faith that nature, so treated, will reveal the secret name for a
situation; when once that situation has been isolated, treated as a situation
in itself and considered for a moment apart from the flux of all things,
nature will, as it were, confess her presumably guilty secret.

Well, the artist, it seems to me, works on a not so different principle, leading from hypothesis—"what will happen to this noble nature if
it can be led to believe Desdemona unfaithful?"—through experiment—
the question as put by Iago—to result, to "the tragic loading of this bed."
In this sense, and not in the fashionable popular sense, art is "experimental," and its methods to a certain extent resemble those of the laboratory; art, too, produces its process under controlled and limiting conditions, cutting away irrelevancies, speeding up or slowing down the
reaction under study, so that the results, whatever they may be, will
stand forth with a singular purity and distinction. The instruments of
science, of course, have as their aim the creation of an objectivity as
nearly as possible universal in character; the poet's aim might be thought
of as the same and reversed, a mirror image—to represent in the world
the movement of a subjectivity as nearly as possible universal in character.

And art is akin to religion, if we will be non-denominational about
it, in that the work (though not, perhaps, the artist, oddly enough) is
driven by its own composition to the implication of invisible things
inherent in visible ones. The subject, the content, of the art work is
sorrowful, because life is sorrowful; but the work itself, by the nature of
its form, dances. A beautiful passage from Proust's novel will be relevant
here. Marcel is thinking of the writer Bergotte, who died of a stroke
while contemplating a detail, a piece of yellow wall, in a painting by
Vermeer:

> He was dead. Forever? Who can say? After all, occult experiences
> demonstrate no more than the dogmas of religion do about the
> soul's continuance. But what can be said is this, that we live our life
> as though we had entered it under the burden of obligations already
> assumed in another; there is, in the conditions of our life here, no

reason which should make us believe ourselves obliged to do good, to be fastidious or even polite, nor which should make the godless painter believe himself obliged to start over twenty times a detail the praise of which will matter very little to his body eaten by worms— a detail such as the section of yellow wall painted with such skill and taste by an artist forever unknown and scarce identified under the name of Vermeer. All such obligations, which have no sanction in our present life, seem to belong to a different world based on good- ness, consideration and sacrifice, a world altogether different from this one, and from which we emerge to be born on this earth, before perhaps returning there to live under the rule of those unknown laws which we have obeyed because we carry their teaching within us though unaware who traced it there—those laws to which every profound work of the intelligence tends to reconcile us, and which are invisible only—and forever!—to fools.

So the work of art is religious in nature, not because it beautifies an ugly world or pretends that a naughty world is a nice one—for these things especially art does not do—but because it shows of its own nature that things drawn within the sacred circle of its forms are transfigured, illuminated by an inward radiance which amounts to goodness because it amounts to being itself. In the life conferred by art, Iago and Des- demona, Edmund and Cordelia, the damned and the blessed, equally achieve immortality by their relation with the creating intelligence which sustains them. The art work is not responsible for saying that things in reality are so, but rather for revealing what this world says to candid vision. It is thus that we delight in tragedies whose actions in life would merely appall us. And it is thus that art, by its illusions, achieves a human analogy to the resolution of that famous question of theodicy—the rela- tion of an Omnipotent Benevolence to evil—which the theologians, bound to the fixed forms of things, have for centuries struggled with, intemperately and in vain. And it is thus that art, by vision and not by dogma, patiently and repeatedly offers the substance of things hoped for, the evidence of things unseen.

Where Do We Go from Here:
The Future of Fiction

Saul Bellow

We know that science has a future, we hope that government will have one. But it is not altogether agreed that the novel has anything but a past. There are some who say that the great novelists of the twentieth century—Proust, Joyce, Mann, and Kafka—have created sterile masterpieces, and that with them we have come to the end of the line. No further progress is possible.

It does sometimes seem that the narrative art itself has dissolved. The person, the character as we knew him in the plays of Sophocles or Shakespeare, in Cervantes, Fielding, and Balzac, has gone from us. Instead of a unitary character with his unitary personality, his ambitions, his passions, his soul, his fate, we find in modern literature an oddly dispersed, ragged, mingled, broken, amorphous creature whose outlines are everywhere, whose being is bathed in mind as the tissues are bathed in blood, and who is impossible to circumscribe in any scheme of time. A cubistic, Bergsonian, uncertain, eternal, mortal someone who shuts and opens like a concertina and makes a strange music. And what has struck artists in this century as the most amusing part of all, is that the descriptions of self that still have hold of us are made up of the old unitary foursquare traits noted according to the ancient conventions. What we insist on seeing is not a quaintly organized chaos of instinct and spirit, but what we choose to call "the personality"—a presentably combed and dressed someone who is decent, courageous, handsome, or not so handsome, but strong, or not so strong, but certainly generous, or not so generous, but anyway reliable. So it goes.

Of all modern writers, it is D. H. Lawrence who is most implacably hostile toward this convention of unitary character. For him this character of a civilized man does not really exist. What the modern civilized person calls his personality is to Lawrence figmentary: a product of civilized education, dress, manners, style, and "culture." The head of this modern personality is, he says, a wastepaper basket filled with ready-made notions. Sometimes he compares the civilized conception of character to a millstone—a painted millstone about our necks is the metaphor he makes of it. The real self, unknown, is hidden, a sunken power in us; the true identity lies deep—very deep. But we do not deal much in true identity, goes his argument. The modern character on the street, or in a conventional story or film, is what a sociologist has recently described as the "presentation" self. The attack on this presentation self or persona by modern art is a part of the war that literature, in its concern with the individual, has fought with civilization. The civilized individual is proud of his painted millstone, the burden which he believes gives him distinction. In an artist's eyes his persona is only a rude, impoverished, mass-produced figure brought into being by a civilization in need of a working force, a reservoir of personnel, a docile public that will accept suggestion and control.

The old unitary personality which still appears in popular magazine stories, in conventional best-sellers, in newspaper cartoons, and in the movies, is a figure descended from well-worn patterns, and popular art forms (like the mystery novel or the western) continue to exploit endlessly the badly faded ideas of motives and drama or love and hate. The old figures move ritualistically through the paces, finding, now and then, variations in setting and costume, but they are increasingly remote from real reality. The functions performed by these venerable literary types should be fascinating to the clinical psychologist who may be able to recognize in these stories an obsessional neurosis here, a paranoid fantasy there, or to the sociologist who sees resemblances to the organization of government bureaus or hears echoes of the modern industrial corporations. But the writer brought up in a great literary tradition not only sees these conventional stories as narcotic or brain-washing entertainments, at worst breeding strange vices, at best performing a therapeutic function. He also fears that the narrative art, which we call the novel, may have come to an end, its conception of the self exhausted and with this conception our interest in the fate of that self so conceived.

It is because of this that Gertrude Stein tells us in one of her lectures that we cannot read the great novels of the twentieth century, among which she includes her own *The Making of Americans,* for what happens next. And in fact *Ulysses, Remembrance of Things Past, The Magic Mountain,* and *The Making of Americans* do not absorb us in what happens next. They interest us in a scene, in a dialogue, a mood, an insight, in language, in character, in the revelation of a design, but they are not narratives. *Ulysses* avoids anything resembling the customary story. It is in some sense a book about literature, and offers us a history of English prose style and of the novel. It is a museum containing all the quaint armour, halberds, crossbows, and artillery pieces of literature. It exhibits them with a kind of amused irony and parodies and transcends them all. These are the things that once entranced us. Old sublimities, old dodges, old weapons, all useless now; pieces of iron once heroic, lovers' embraces once romantic, all debased by cheap exploitation, all unfit.

Language too is unfit. Erich Heller in a recent book quotes a typical observation by Hofmannsthal on the inadequacy of old forms of expression. Hofmannsthal writes, "Elements once bound together to make a world now present themselves to the poet in monstrous separateness. To speak of them coherently at all would be to speak untruthfully. The commonplace phrases of the daily round of observations seem all of a sudden insoluble riddles. The sheriff is a wicked man, the vicar is a good fellow, our neighbor must be pitied, his sons are wastrels. The baker is to be envied, his daughters are virtuous." In Hofmannsthal's *A Letter* these formulas are presented as "utterly lacking in the quality of truth." He is unable, he explains, "to see what people say and do with the simplifying eye of habit and custom. Everything falls to pieces, the pieces to pieces again, and nothing can be comprehended any more with the help of customary notions."

Character, action, and language then have been put in doubt and the Spanish philosopher Ortega y Gasset, summing up views widely held, says the novel requires a local setting with limited horizons and familiar features, traditions, occupations, classes. But as everyone knows, these old-fashioned local worlds no longer exist. Or perhaps that is inaccurate. They do exist but fail to interest the novelist. They are no longer local societies as we see them in Jane Austen or George Eliot. Our contemporary local societies have been overtaken by the world. The great cities have devoured them and now the universe itself imposes itself upon us, space with its stars comes upon us in our cities. So now we have the universe itself to face, without the comforts of community, without metaphysical certainty, without the power to distinguish the virtuous from the wicked man, surrounded by dubious realities and discovering dubious selves.

Things have collapsed about us, says D. H. Lawrence on the first page of *Lady Chatterley's Lover,* and we must each of us try to put together some sort of life. He offers us a sort of nature mysticism, love but without false romanticism, an acceptance of true desire as the first principle of recovery. Other writers have come forward with aesthetic or political or religious first principles. All the modern novelists worth mentioning aim at a point beyond customary notions, customary dramas, and customary conceptions of character. The old notion of a customary self, of the fate of an all-important Me displeases the best of them. We have lived now through innumerable successes and failures of these old selves. In American literature we have watched their progress and decline in scores of books since the Civil War, from buoyancy to depression. The Lambert Strethers, the Hurstwoods and Cowperwoods, the Gatsbys may still impress or please us as readers, but as writers, no. Their mental range is no longer adequate to these new circumstances. Those characters suit us better who stand outside society and, unlike Gatsby, have no wish to be sentimentally reconciled to it, unlike Dreiser's millionaires have no more desire for its wealth, unlike Strether are not attracted by the power of an old and knowing civilization.

This is why so many of us prefer the American novels of the nineteenth century, whose characters are very nearly removed from the civil state—*Moby-Dick* and *Huckleberry Finn.* We feel in our own time that what is called the civilized condition often swings close to what Hobbes calls the state of nature, a condition of warfare in which the life of the individual is nasty, brutish, dull, and short. But we must be careful not to be swept away by the analogy. We have seen to our grief in recent European and especially German history the results of trying to bolt from all civilized and legal tradition. It is in our minds that the natural and the civil, that autarchy and discipline are most explosively mixed.

But for us here in America discipline is represented largely by the enforced repressions. We do not know much of the delights of discipline. Almost nothing of a spiritual, ennobling character is brought into the internal life of a modern American by his social institutions. He must discover it in his own experience, by his own luck as an explorer, or not at all. Society feeds him, clothes him, to an extent protects him, and he is its infant. If he accepts the state of infancy, contentment can be his. But if the idea of higher functions comes to him, he is profoundly unsettled. The hungry world is rushing on all continents toward such a contentment, and with passions and desires, frustrated since primitive times, and with the demand for justice never so loudly expressed. The danger is great that it will be satisfied with the bottles and toys of infancy. But the artist, the philosopher, the priest, the statesman are concerned with the full development of humanity—its manhood, occasionally glimpsed in our history, occasionally felt by individuals.

With all this in mind, people here and there still continue to write the sort of book we call a novel. When I am feeling blue, I can almost persuade myself that the novel, like Indian basketry, or harness-making, is a vestigial art and has no future. But we must be careful about prophecy. Even prophecy based on good historical study is a risky business, and pessimism, no less than optimism, can be made into a racket. All industrial societies have a thing about obsolescence. Classes, nations, races, and cultures have in our time been declared obsolete, with results that have made ours one of the most horrible of all centuries. We must, therefore, be careful about deciding that any art is dead.

This is not a decision for a coroner's jury of critics and historians. The fact is that a great many novelists, even those who have concentrated on hate, like Céline, or on despair, like Kafka, have continued to perform a most important function. Their books have attempted, in not a few cases successfully, to create scale, to order experience, to give value, to make perspective, and to carry us toward sources of life, toward life-giving things. The true believer in disorder does not like novels. He follows another calling. He is an accident lawyer, or a promoter, not a novelist. It always makes me sit up, therefore, to read yet another scolding of the modern novelist written by highly paid executives of multimillion-dollar magazines. They call upon American writers to represent the country fairly, to affirm its values, to increase its prestige in this dangerous period. Perhaps, though, novelists have a different view of what to affirm. Perhaps they are running their own sort of survey of affirmable things. They may come out against nationalism, or against the dollar, for they are an odd and unreliable lot. I have already indicated that it is the instinct of the novelist, however, to pull toward order. Now this is a pious thing to say, but I do not intend it merely to sound good. It should be understood only as the beginning of another difficulty.

What ideas of order does the novelist have and where does he get them and what good are they in art? I have spoken of Lawrence's belief that we must put together a life for ourselves, singly, in pairs, in groups, out of the wreckage. Shipwreck and solitude are not, in his opinion, unmixed evils. They are also liberating, and if we have the strength to use our freedom we may yet stand in a true relation to nature and to other men. But how are we to reach this end? Lawrence proposes a sort of answer in *Lady Chatterley's Lover,* showing us two people alone together in the midst of a waste. I sometimes feel that *Lady Chatterley's Lover* is a sort of *Robinson Crusoe* for two, exploring man's sexual resources rather than his technical ingenuity. It is every bit as moral a novel as *Crusoe.* Connie and Mellors work at it as hard and as conscientiously as Robinson, and there are as many sermons in the one as in the other. The difference is that Lawrence aimed with all his powers at the writing of this one sort of book. To this end he shaped his life, the testing ground of his ideas. For what is the point of recommending a course of life that one has not tried oneself?

This is one way to assess the careers and achievements of many modern artists. Men like Rimbaud, Strindberg, Lawrence, Malraux, even Tolstoy, can be approached from this direction. They experiment with themselves and in some cases an artistic conclusion can come only out of the experimental results. Lawrence had no material other than what his life, that savage pilgrimage, as he called it, gave him. The ideas he tested, and tested not always by an acceptable standard, were ideas of the vital, the erotic, the instinctive. They involved us in a species of nature-mysticism which gave as a basis for morality, sexual gratification. But I am not concerned here with all the particulars of Lawrence's thesis. I am interested mainly in the connection between the understanding and the imagination, and the future place of the intelligence in imaginative literature.

At this point in a lecture this is a rather large subject to announce, but what I have in mind is relatively simple. It is necessary to admit, first, that ideas in the novel can be very dull. There is much in modern literature, and the other arts as well, to justify our prejudice against the didactic. Opinion, said Schopenhauer, is not as valid as imagination in a work of art. One can quarrel with an opinion or judgment in a novel, but actions are beyond argument and the imagination simply accepts them. I think that many modern novels, perhaps the majority, are the result of some didactic purpose. The attempt of writers to make perspective, to make scale and to carry us toward the sources of life is, of course, the didactic intention. It involves the novelist in programs, in slogans, in political theories, religious theories, and so on. Many modern novelists seem to say to themselves, "what if," or "suppose that such and such were the case," and the results often show that the book was conceived in thought, in didactic purpose, rather than in the imagination. That is rather normal, given the state of things, the prevalence of the calculating principle in modern life, the need for conscious rules of procedure, and the generally felt need for answers. Not only books, paintings, and musical compositions, but love affairs, marriages, and even religious convictions often originate in an idea. So that the *idea* of love is more common than love, and the *idea* of belief is more often met with than faith. Some of our most respected novels have a purely mental inspiration. The results are sometimes very pleasing because they can so easily be discussed, but the ideas in them generally have more substance than the characters who hold them.

American literature in the nineteenth century was highly didactic. Emerson, Thoreau, Whitman, and even Melville were didactic writers. They wished to instruct a young and raw nation. American literature in the twentieth century has remained didactic, but it has also been unintellectual. This is not to say that thought is lacking in the twentieth-century American novel, but it exists under strange handicaps and is much disguised. In *A Farewell to Arms* Hemingway makes a list of subjects we must no longer speak about—a catalogue of polluted words, words which have been ruined by the rhetoric of criminal politicians and misleaders. Then Hemingway, and we must respect him for it, attempts to represent these betrayed qualities without using the words themselves. Thus we have courage without the word, honor without the word, and in *The Old Man and the Sea* we are offered a sort of Christian endurance, also without specific terms. Carried to this length, the attempt to represent ideas while sternly forbidding thought begins to look like a curious and highly sophisticated game. It shows a great skepticism of the strength of art. It makes it appear as though ideas openly expressed would be too much for art to bear.

We have developed in American fiction a strange combination of extreme naïveté in the characters and of profundity implicit in the writing, in the techniques themselves and in the language, but the language of thought itself is banned, it is considered dangerous and destructive. American writers appear to have a strong loyalty to the people, to the common man; perhaps in some cases the word for this is not loyalty, perhaps it might better be described as *fear*. But a writer should aim to reach all levels of society and as many levels of thought as possible, avoiding democratic prejudice as much as intellectual snobbery. Why should he be ashamed of thinking? I do not claim that all writers can think, or should think. Some are peculiarly inept at ideas and we would harm them by insisting that they philosophize. But the records show that most artists are intellectually active, and it is only now in a world increasingly intellectualized, more and more dominated by the productions of scientific thought, that they seem strangely reluctant to use their brains or to give any sign that they have brains to use.

All through the nineteenth century the conviction increases in novelists as different as Goncharov in Russia and Thomas Hardy in England that thought is linked with passivity and is devitalizing. And in the masterpieces of the twentieth century the thinker usually has a weak grip on life. But by now an alternative, passionate activity without ideas, has also been well explored in novels of adventure, hunting, combat, and eroticism. Meanwhile, miracles, born of thought, have been largely ignored by modern literature. If narration is neglected by novelists like Proust and Joyce, the reasons are that for a time the drama has passed from external action to internal movement. In Proust and Joyce we are enclosed by and held within a single consciousness. In this inner realm the writer's art dominates everything. The drama has left external action because the old ways of describing interests, of describing the fate of the individual, have lost their power. Is the sheriff a good fellow? Is our neighbor to be pitied? Are the baker's daughters virtuous? We see such questions now as belonging to a dead system, mere formulas. It is possible that our hearts would open again to the baker's daughters if we understood them differently.

A clue may be offered by Pascal, who said there are no dull people, only dull points of view. Maybe that is going a little far. (A religious philosophy is bound to maintain that every soul is infinitely precious and, therefore, infinitely interesting.) But it begins perhaps to be evident what my position is. Imagination, binding itself to dull viewpoints, puts an end to stories. The imagination is looking for new ways to express virtue. American society just now is in the grip of certain common falsehoods about virtue—not that anyone really believes them. And these cheerful falsehoods beget their opposites in fiction, a dark literature, a literature of victimization, of old people sitting in ash cans waiting for the breath of life to depart. This is the way things stand; only this remains to be added, that we have barely begun to comprehend what a human being is, and that the baker's daughters may have revelations and miracles to offer to keep fascinated novelists busy until the end of time.

I would like to add this also, in conclusion, about good thought and bad thought in the novel. In a way it doesn't matter what sort of line the novelist is pushing, what he is affirming. If he has nothing to offer but his didactic purpose he is a bad writer. His ideas have ruined him. He could not afford the expense of maintaining them. It is not the didactic purpose itself which is a bad thing, and the modern novelist drawing back from the dangers of didacticism has often become strangely unreal, and the purity of his belief in art for art in some cases has been peculiarly unattractive. Among modern novelists the bravest have taken the risk of teaching and have not been afraid of using the terms of religion, science, philosophy, and politics. Only they have been prepared to admit the strongest possible arguments against their own positions.

Here we see the difference between a didactic novelist like D. H. Lawrence and one like Dostoyevski. When he was writing *The Brothers Karamazov* and had just ended the famous conversation between Ivan and Alyosha, in which Ivan, despairing of justice, offers to return his ticket to God, Dostoyevski wrote to one of his correspondents that he must now attempt, through Father Zossima, to answer Ivan's arguments. But he has in advance all but devastated his own position. This, I think, is the greatest achievement possible in a novel of ideas. It becomes art when the views most opposite to the author's own are allowed to exist in full strength. Without this a novel of ideas is mere self-indulgence, and didacticism is simply axe-grinding. The opposites must be free to range themselves against each other, and they must be passionately expressed on both sides. It is for this reason that I say it doesn't matter much what the writer's personal position is, what he wishes to affirm. He may affirm principles we all approve of and write very bad novels.

The novel, to recover and to flourish, requires new ideas about humankind. These ideas in turn cannot live in themselves. Merely asserted, they show nothing but the good will of the author. They must therefore be discovered and not invented. We must see them in flesh and blood. There would be no point in continuing at all if many writers did not feel the existence of these unrecognized qualities. They are present and they demand release and expression.

On Recognition

Arthur Miller

I accepted the Hopwood Committee's invitation to speak today with misgivings. In fact, many years ago I swore that if I were ever asked to, I would never speak on the occasion of the award ceremonies. This, because I recalled too vividly how I sat where you are sitting now, listening to I think it was Christopher Morley droning on and on in what was probably a fascinating way, while on the table were the envelopes with the winners' names inside. If there was ever a captive audience, this is it. You have to listen to me or you don't get your money, and who knows, I could go on for an hour. It is even worse when I know that the very people I am most interested in reaching—namely the best writers among you and presumably the ones who are going to win today—are least likely to be paying me any attention.

So in the hope of flagging down your greedily racing thoughts, I am going to speak today on a subject which, along with money, must surely be on your minds. On Recognition. It may not sound like a particularly literary subject, but you would be amazed at how powerful a force it is in literary affairs. Offhand, I should say that if everybody who expressed a desire to be a writer were automatically recognized and were given a lapel button saying "Writer," approximately eighty percent of those who devote their lives to some form of writing or another would not have bothered. I can even imagine a society in which practically everybody is born a writer, and there is a contest each year in some university where prizes are given for the most persuasive *business proposition*. I can imagine the winners' parents going around boasting, "Imagine, my son won a prize for not writing!" I can imagine the genius business man in such a society surrounded after his lecture by envious people all asking the same questions—"How did you start? What is it like not to be stuck at home every day, having to write a poem or a play like everybody else, but to go off by yourself into a nice busy office where all you've got to deal with are other people?"

It's hard, but I can imagine it. Distinction, after all, is relative. More precisely, distinction abhors relatives. In some cases it despises just about everybody. The other day I got a pamphlet containing three speeches by writers delivered at the Library of Congress under some grant or other, and one of them, McKinlay Kantor's, I may as well say, was almost wholly taken up with an attack on other historical novelists who fail to do enough research to justify the honor of being called an historical novelist. It turns out that Lincoln did not have a deep baritone, as some writer had written in a recent best-seller, but a high nasal twang, and that the belt-buckle worn by Union soldiers did not say U.S.A. on it but U.S. He was also mad at Stephen Crane because the *Red Badge of Courage* could have been about any war and was not specifically what it claimed, a book about the Civil War. In short, distinction in itself is no guarantee of anything in particular.

The trouble is that the writer has to win recognition almost before he is recognizable. Before, that is, he is distinct. He needs recognition in order to win it. He therefore has to invent it first in the hope that his invention will be pronounced a fact by the outside world. The effort to first invent one's own distinction, and then to get others to agree to it, is so strenuous that in a great many cases the man is exhausted just when he ought to be starting. But having won his own reality, so to speak, having won his public license to practice his recognition, he faces the danger—possibly the greatest danger writers face in this particular time of enormous publicity and big money—the danger of placing himself in the service of his continuing recognition. In that service he is tempted to repeat with greater polish, perhaps, or louder stridency, what he has done before, in which case his trade-mark burns a little deeper into his soul. To the need for recognition, as to the making of books, there is no end. It is finally not enough even to be distinct from others; the time comes when you have to be distinct from yourself, too. That is, it must not be too apparent that you are always writing the same book or play, but on the other hand it is also bad if your work appears to be written by three, four, or six different people. That way you may distinguish yourself as a wonderfully varied writer, but the danger is that you may vary your style out of recognition.

Now this is hardly the time in your lives to be warning you to beware of a mindless pursuit of recognition. In any case, a man who somewhere in his soul does not feel, however shyly, a burning desire to put himself forward, has no business trying to become a writer. I speak on this subject only because of the times in which we live. They are extraordinarily treacherous for a writer. Never was publicity so remorselessly in search of the least signal of a successful author; never was money more plentiful for a successful book or play. The writer motivated by the wish to shine, by that mainly, can very quickly mistake himself for a finished product when in fact he has only begun his rightful and ordained struggle to perfect his art. The pressures of exploitation of literature, the photographic reporter, the television interview, the newspaper and magazine columnists—all these forces tend to press the writer closer to the position of performer. What comes to matter is less his work than the cult which comes to surround his personality.

Obviously, this is hardly the first time or place in history that has sought to celebrate writers, but the quality of celebration has taken on a new tone, not only among us but in a different way in Europe too. The writer, as far as the mass publications and media are concerned, is of interest in much the same way as an actor is, or God save the mark, a politician. He has made himself known and that is all.

Now we have had Hemingway, and Samuel Clemens, and Charles Dickens, and Bernard Shaw, and a long line of writers who were or could easily have been actors had they not been too embarrassed too early in life. Sinclair Lewis actually made the jump and acted in his own plays toward the end of his career, and even so careful a workman and so jealous a man of his own privacy as James Thurber made the eight-thirty curtain night after night in the year or two before he died. Shakespeare was an actor too, but it is important to note that he started as an actor, he did not end as one. I am a pretty good actor myself, despite the impression I may be giving today, and I would probably have become one except that I could never remember lines, and worse yet, have a tendency to change everything I hear. You can't revise with an audience watching, so I act alone in a room, perform all the parts, and come away with the lion's share of the glory.

There is nothing wrong in recognition providing it is not permitted to devaluate, finally, what it is supposed to elevate. Nor is this an entirely esoteric problem. I think it true that fewer American writers have won the mature growth of their art and talent than writers anywhere in the world. As with everyone else, the writer in America is in a country that fits him only when he is young and starting out; as he grows to maturity, or what should be maturity, he is much more likely to have lost his way than to have more securely discovered it. I think one reason for this is the quality of the recognition we give to writers. We recognize him as a success rather than as a writer. It is hard to earn success, but much harder to keep it; evidently it is nearly impossible to forget all about it and keep on calling oneself a writer, but I think it is the only way to earn that much abused title, that much abused recognition—it is, for one thing, to never turn pro. In short, to remain a failure, forever unrecognized in one's heart.

This may sound easy, but it is immeasurably more difficult to really admit failure while still accepting the rewards of success—harder than to believe that those rewards truly have a connection with oneself as a writer. To come directly to the point, of how many writers can it be said that their later work was wiser, deeper, more beautiful than what came earlier? Extraordinarily few. As a class, especially in America the writer is a great beginner and a very bad finisher.

I do not propose to solve this problem today, but some totally ignored fundamentals of what I can only call the fact of the writer seem to me to need repeating. To start at the end of my thought and work backwards, I believe that so many fine and truly talented writers fail of their promise because they adopt the perspective of their society toward themselves. Before I mention an alternative perspective, let me tell you what I think the American perspective—and gradually the European perspective—is toward the writer.

To begin at the absurd extreme, we cannot believe that a writer who is not known is really a writer. Ergo, the more known he is the more writer he is.

There are various proofs that he is known, which is to say that he is a writer. He has published a book with his name on it, a play has been produced on the stage. He is more of a writer, however, if he has another attribute—if he has made money with his book or play. He is most writer if he has made a fortune. And this will become truer and truer as time passes because it has dawned on publishers now, just as it did on the patent medicine industry in the eighties of the past century, that the more the product is publicized the more reliable it will come to appear.

The distortions forced upon writers by baths of publicity are not all the same. A Salinger reacts by evidently refusing to see or speak to anyone at all. Other writers are busy speaking to everyone on radio, television, and over expensive restaurant tables. You can be driven mad in many different directions by the same cause.

The worst of this distortion is that it undermines the only recognition worth the name: a recognition that a book or a play or a poem has delivered up a genuine insight into the nature of man and the human condition. That you or I happen to have been the author of it is extremely pleasant, but it is not the point. I try to read a work or see a play as though I did not know who the author was. I try to see and read not in order to lay praise on a person or to blame him, but to receive into myself whatever that work is purporting to say to me. The uses of publicity are such that this kind of seeing and reading has become impossible; in fact it is unimaginable to ninety-nine percent not only of the public but of the critics as well. At the risk of immodesty, warranted I think by the proof it can give, I will say that I try to write in the same mood. To ask of myself, either at the beginning of a work or in the middle, and certainly by the end—what will this add, if anything, to what is known?

Admittedly, this is an old man's question. When I was much younger it would never have occurred to me. I was too eager to find the proof in others' eyes that I in fact was a playwright, and this indeed ought to be so. As I said at the beginning, we must first invent a recognition before it can be recognized, and it matters less what its contribution might be to what has gone before than to what we were before we wrote it. But the time does come, or should, I think, when one admits that one has learned one's job and that it is not enough merely to prove it once again. There are and have been writers who have done more through middle and old age and up to the end, and Faulkner is perhaps the most noteworthy, and I say this without being one of his fans. For the most part, however, it seems to me that by far the majority of writers have done and are doing perhaps a little better, perhaps a little worse, what they did before. A writer ought to have the right to shut up when he has nothing he feels he must say; to shut up and still be considered a writer. To consider and still be a writer; to nose about as long as it takes until he can once again enslave himself to some voice that has entered him. I wonder if the destruction of many writers is in part the fear of silence E. M. Forster found; the clarity of aim which can turn back the whorish demand that at all costs he say something, even something not worth the saying, rather than face a deeper suffering, the suffering of silence, a suffering, however, which may honestly open out into wisdom and a new art.

The perspective of society, of the world, is the perspective of competition. Again, this is invaluable for the young who always live in a world of comparisons. It is a way of dying however, for those no longer young. Hemingway was forever comparing; one year he had "taken on" Dostoyevski; then he was about to "take on" Tolstoy. I strongly doubt that Dostoyevski "took on" any writer, and I know Tolstoy could not have kept such an idea in his head for more than ten minutes. And yet both these men were pursued by a sense of their own failure but in the correct, if one may use such a word, the proper way. They had failed, as certainly Tolstoy's diaries make clear, and knew they were doomed forever to fail to hear with absolute clarity the voice of their people's suffering. Not the voice of *Time* Magazine, or the voice of the latest fashionable critic or the voice of the salon, but the only voice whose expression literature was invented for. Which is to say that a writer is a writer not because he is known, and not by how much he is known, but by how truly he hears and sees the essentials of the human situation in his time.

Now it will be objected that there is no contradiction between excellence and the wish to excel, and certainly if proof is needed it is supplied by the competitions among the Greek dramatists at the festival performances of their plays. Nor is King of the Hill a game confined to this age; battles of the books have been fought in many places and in many different times. But there are battles which enliven literature and battles which are nonbattles, such as we have today, in which nothing is at stake, neither a literary viewpoint, a social ideal, or any other question of value but who stands on top of the heap. This was finally institutionalized, as it were, in a long article in the *New York Times Book Review* a few months ago. Who, it was asked, will be the new Hemingway and the new Faulkner? Whereupon some ten or so young and middle-aged writers were presented as contenders for the title. The conclusion, as one must expect in the *Times Book Review,* was of course a loud shrug of the shoulders. But even if there could be a conclusion where there cannot be an argument, who should care? And supposing, unbelievable as it sounds, supposing neither Hemingway nor Faulkner twenty years from now, or fifty or ten, turn out to be the best writers of their time? Then truly the crown would not exist at all and the vacuousness of the whole competitive concept would be laughably obvious.

But if the printed consensus and the word-of-mouth augmentation of that opinion is not to guide a young man toward his models and finally toward an evaluation of himself and his work, where can he look? The only answer I know to be unassailable is also unacceptable; it is *nowhere*. Nor am I lamenting this; we live in an age bankrupt of a truly independent public criticism. In one sense it is a fine opportunity, for the new writer today has no critical institution to overthrow. In writing there is no ruling idea to buck or go with, there is no particular style or form either frowned on or overwhelmingly fashionable. The simple truth is that a terribly small number of Americans read books or see plays; I will not even speak of poetry. If fifty thousand copies of a new book are sold it is regarded as a triumph in a country of over a hundred and eighty million. If half a million people see a play it is a monstrous hit and probably a masterpiece, at least that year. So that these readers and playgoers are really tight little islands in a sea of real Americans who don't know they are there and couldn't care less. The pond, as big as it seems, is really quite small, which need not mean that its quality is bad but that the victory it can offer is not the victory it appears to offer. The American people do not play a part in the art works of our time. The working class is all but illiterate, the middle class is mostly sheep frightened of not liking what it should and liking what it shouldn't. As a consequence, I think, of the narrowness of the audience, there is no body of peers worthy of your creative respect. Nobody writing public criticism today represents anybody, at least not anybody with a real crown to give you. I don't like bandying about the names of other writers so I'll use my own work and give you an example.

The Crucible opened in New York in 1954, at the height of the McCarthy hysteria. It got respectful notices, the kind that bury you decently. It ran a few months and closed. In 1960, I believe it was, an off-Broadway production of the play was put on. The same critics reviewed it again, this time with what are called hit notices, which is to say they were fairly swept away, the drama was as real to them as it had seemed cold and undramatic before. Reasons were given for the new impression; the main one was that the script had been improved.

This rather astonished me, since the scripts were exactly the same in both productions. Worse yet, the cast of the original was all in all far superior to the second production. The answer is quite simple; when McCarthy was around the critics, reflecting the feeling in the audience, were quite simply in fear of the theme of the play, which was witch hunting. In 1960 they were not afraid of it and they began to look at the play. It is perfectly natural and not even particularly reprehensible. My only point is that had I been a new playwright in 1954, and *The Crucible* my first professional production, and had I looked outside myself for recognition, I would not have found it.

But let us not get too romantic; it is all very well to tell you to look within yourself for your values. The lonely genius ahead of his time is a hallowed image which probably infects more writers with monomania than inspiration. The truth, I think, is that at its best and at its highest, literature is not the monologue the age has made it out to be but a personal conversation between a people and its artists. Whether it be our educational system, our Puritan tradition suspicious of art, or simply the mechanization of man and his dehumanized nervous system, it cannot be said that a dialogue exists today between the American people and the American artist, excepting the kind who decorate packages.

Nor is this news, of course. Everybody knows about the lonely Melville trudging back and forth to his customs house, unrecognized by anyone around him, even he the author of America's great epic. Everybody knows about Hart Crane, and Sherwood Anderson, and God knows how many others who tried to speak to America and got no answer. Some people even know about Samuel Clemens trying to hoist some flag of spirit over an America he saw turning to iron and iron values. There is one word traditional for the American writer—*alone*. Alone as a failure, alone as a success. But what does it mean? What, you may ask, is the opposite of being alone? Well, the average answer is, together. Like perhaps a movie star is together with his fans, or a ball player, or some other species of entertainer. In other words, the usual response is some kind of recognition. Like wouldn't it be more cultured if a good novelist were mobbed in the street instead of somebody who needs a haircut and plays a guitar? And to be sure, on a much more austere level, the present administration has sought now and then to supply a new recognition. A lot of us have been to the White House. Well then, maybe the solution is to have us all to the White House every other Wednesday or something like that. We might even have a National Writers' Day.

Obviously, recognition of the writer, of his person, is not the issue. Recognition of writing is. Recognition of what writing is for, of why it has a mission, of what its mission is, this kind of recognition is unknown among the people and, for the most part, among those whose business it is to criticize. What is that mission?

Now, I am not going to wax poetic about, let's say, the writer as the conscience of mankind or the voice of the nation's spirit. No one can set out to be a conscience or a voice for anyone but himself, and if he succeeds in even that he is going a long way already. But we are faced with a curious situation; I think it is probably true to say that there are more young writers today than there used to be who have a command of the forms they write in, but are at a loss for something to say. I am sure of this in the theater, and I judge it to be little different in fiction. From my painter friends I get the same sense of bafflement. There is no longer a battle to establish a new form, at least not west of the Russian border. Certainly on the stage you can now do anything from the point of view of form, anything you can possibly imagine. The shape of realism has been shattered; like all the fixed social ideas of the past our art lies in pieces, and some of them are quite beautiful.

Now part of the work of art is to say something to art; Hemingway's early stylistic discoveries spoke not only to the reader but to all the books that had been written before. Joyce spoke to all of literature, Pound to all of poetry. The speech one can make to art itself has been made.

What has not been made, and can never be completed, is the speech one can make to mankind. It seems to me that possibly because most of America does not hear us we have ceased to try to engage a vast attention and have been backed up into the invisible salon of art. There opinions are made, discoveries are registered, the imprimatur is given or with-held, but it is not the source of something to say. The source is in the way men live. But since the mass of men cannot hear us or will not, how can one address the multitude? There is no answer excepting to say that one can imagine doing it. One can write as though the many were in fact listening. Or, if not actually listening, as though the fate of all were at stake on one's pages even as they do not know and cannot know. For the time being the dialogue can only go on from the artist's side; but it is better than to let it die.

All of which is said in face of a certain number of books which in fact have attempted to carry on that dialogue. The underlying scheme of *Lolita* is a painting of American adolescence as it appears in the middle-aged man; *Catch–22* is a frontal attack on the idiocies not only of modern warfare but of society itself; the work of Saul Bellow has reached out beyond the preoccupation with salable sexuality into the investigation of what man might become, which is what *Henderson the Rain King* is especially about. It would be easy to list twenty books, at least, in the past few years, which are in the tradition of the dialogue with mankind, with his general condition; I am not, in other words, attacking writers. It is simply that if we even had National Writers' Week, and open house at the Kennedys' every Thursday, the other half of the dialogue would not have begun. The people, in short, do not read books, do not answer books, and consequently are not in a position to answer for the truth or validity of books. A National Book Award has about the same importance among us as the Grand Prize for the Best Table Setting. I say this in face of the much greater number of paperbacks sold as compared to former years; I say this, moreover, with no assurance whatever that if everybody read two books a week the country would be a better place in which to live. The Germans, for example, have always read an immense number of books, and the Russians too.

So I am concerned not with the sociology of book reading or publishing, or even with improving the country in this context, but with the weight and the maturity of our literature. To make the statement as unvarnished, as clear as I can, I believe the mission of writing is tragedy. I think that in the works in which man is most human, in addition to being the works that last, and reflect most deeply and most truthfully the situation of man on this earth, tragedy must confront the work itself, the artist himself, and the country itself. I believe at bottom, that the word has not yet entered the blood stream of America because it is a country which as yet has no tragic sense of itself. Without that sense, without that longing, a people does not, strictly speaking, need the answers and the formulations which art was made to give. If a people conceives that death is a kind of accident or, worse yet, an inconvenience to be remedied by insurance policies; if its religion is designed to ameliorate suffering rather than to make it meaningful; if its soul-searching is self-blame and psychoanalysis, it is not yet ready to ask the questions a tragic literature can give.

I am not going to launch into what tragedy is or what I think it is beyond saying that when Christ hung on the cross it was not tragic until He spoke and asked why God had forsaken Him, and having spoken that shattering doubt, nevertheless did not ask to be taken down, nor wish He had His life to live over again, nor express remorse or a resolution to do differently. Above all, He did not say that He felt nothing, that He was not really on the cross, that His faith had vanquished pain, and that He was sure He had done what He was fated to do.

It is not tragic, which is to say it lacks humanity, which is to say it lacks human meaning, when a people presumes to possess the final answer for all mankind as to what life is for and how to live it. It lacks human meaning, equally, when a people, and a literature, seizes only on doubt and will not accept the torture of trying to believe in the midst of doubt. It lacks human meaning if a literature merely exemplifies what dies and what shows the signs of death, quite as meaninglessly although less obviously than when life and what gives life is all that vision can see. The literature I am talking about engages the tension between an event and the human experience of it; between the meaningless particular career and the situation of the race.

The battle of the writer today is not primarily a battle to break through old forms but against a world-wide conspiracy to call things by their wrong names; it is a battle against human presumption whose end will be, for one thing, the destruction of the planet under the banner of saving mankind. I think that so few American writers have matured because only in the tragic confrontation is there the possibility of escaping from the themes and attitudes and controlling visions of adolescence, that time in a writer's life when his usable sources of wonder and originality are richest, newest, and most deeply imbedded in his heart. Our literature, its deepest stamp and line, is the adventure of the young, the young man, the young spirit, the voyage begun, the first arrival. Two authors come to mind, three perhaps, who went beyond: Faulkner, Melville, and O'Neill. But is it not worth noting that Faulkner had to create, literally, a world in which tragedy was possible, a world manifestly his own and not industrial America? And Melville and O'Neill had to cut loose to the sea for an arena of tragic action? Only there, I think, did O'Neill feel at home with his sense of life. Whatever is mawkish, contrived, learned, and unworthy in his work comes to the high surface whenever he is on land, where social institutions rule, where Americans really live, and where the landscape is always inhuman.

I shudder at the thought of giving advice to anyone, let alone young writers. To paraphrase an old Army poster, your country needs you, but it doesn't know it. But you have a way around that, you can pretend it does. You can pretend you are not at all alone but in a community, a community of mutes, and you the only one around with the gift of speech. In this dream you alone have the responsibility for proving to your people what they are doing, and perhaps what they ought to do in order to be glorious and true to their nature. Remember, the writer has one gift from life which nothing can take from him—he is describing a species that has to die. So when the mutes signal to you that this world or this country is bound for glory and you are nothing but a pest, you can always ask if that's enough to die with, and if not, is it enough to live with? And if they signal that man is worthless, you, standing at the lip of the grave, you, with time pouring through your fingers, meaningless without your shaping hand, you can reply similarly, that if we are indeed worthless how is it possible that we can know it when the very concept requires a concept of worth. You are writers because you have inherited the ageless tension between despair and faith, the two arms of the tragic cross. The situation never changes; but man does. How and why is what you have to say.

Now, forgive me this delay before your moment of recognition. I have kept you in tension between your own self-doubts and the faith which others may give you in these prizes. Permit me to say that I have won Hopwoods and also lost them, and I know the power that winning gives and the way the soul shakes when, all ears, you hear silence instead of your name. Either way it matters very much and always will, but not as much as knowing that it is not one another we must finally vanquish, but life's brute fist clamped around the reason for our being. To bend back one finger and glimpse what it conceals, and harder yet, to dare remember what one has seen inside that hand—this is the power you have a right to seek and the only recognition worth the work.

Autobiography as Narrative

Alfred Kazin

Before he died, Ernest Hemingway left a memoir of Paris in the 1920s, *A Moveable Feast,* that is just now published. Anyone who grew up with Hemingway's writing, as I did, and who has always valued his early short stories in particular for the breathtaking clarity and beauty with which he could develop his effects in this miniature and subtle form, cannot help reading Hemingway's memoir with amazement. For line by line and stroke by stroke, in the color of the prose and the shaping of the episodes, Hemingway's autobiography is as beautiful in composition as Hemingway's best stories, it is in subject and tone indistinguishable from much of Hemingway's fiction, and it is full of dialogue as maliciously clever as Hemingway's fiction.

He begins here, as his stories so often do, with the weather, the color of the weather, the tone and weight of the weather in Paris. There was the bad weather that would come in one day when the fall was over—"We would have to shut the windows in the night against the rain and the cold wind would strip the leaves from the trees in the Place Contrescarpe. The leaves lay sodden in the rain and the wind drove the rain against the big green autobus at the terminal and the Café des Amateurs was crowded and the windows misted over from the heat and the smoke inside." Anyone who knows his Hemingway will recognize in these artful repetitions, these simple flat words shaped like the design in a painting by Braque and gray as a Paris street by Utrillo, Hemingway's most familiar touch. And most astonishing, in what is after all presented as a memoir, there are conversations with Gertrude Stein, Ford Madox Ford, Scott Fitzgerald, that are as witty and destructive as those dialogues in *Men Without Women* or *The Sun Also Rises* that Hemingway used, in exactly the same way, to get the better of the other speaker in a dialogue with the hero who in Hemingway's fiction is called Nick Adams or Jake Barnes or Frederic Henry. Ford Madox Ford comes on the young Hemingway quietly sitting in a café, sagely observing life in Paris, but Ford is described as "breathing heavily through a heavy, stained mustache and holding himself as upright as an ambulatory, well clothed, up-ended hogshead." Ford is shown as a heavy, wheezing, distrustful, and confused presence; he scolds waiters for his own mistakes and, as if he were a fat actor playing Colonel Blimp and not the almost over-subtle writer that Ford Madox Ford actually was, he pronounces that "a gentleman will always cut a cad." Hemingway plays it cool. "I took a quick drink of brandy. 'Would he cut a bounder?' I asked. 'It would be impossible for a gentleman to know a bounder.' 'Then you can only cut someone you have known on terms of equality?' I pursued. 'Naturally.' 'How would one ever meet a cad?' 'You might not know it, or the fellow could have become a cad.' 'What is a cad?' I asked. 'Isn't he someone that one has to thrash within an inch of his life?' 'Not necessarily,' Ford said. 'Is Ezra a gentleman?' I asked. 'Of course not,' said Ford. 'He's an American.'"

This is of course standard Hemingway dialogue—it is literary in itself, and it is a burlesque of the pretentious or false civilization that Hemingway always portrayed as the enemy. Yet this artful mixture is presented as autobiography, and it must be taken in some measure as a truthful account of Hemingway's relations with Ford. To suppose—and who can help it—that Hemingway was reshaping the facts many years after the encounter in that café, is to miss the point of what makes Hemingway's book so remarkable a piece of writing. For Hemingway uses the convention of autobiography—real names, dates, places— entirely for his imaginative purpose as a creative artist exactly as a statesman will use autobiography in the interest of his historic reputation. General Eisenhower's memoirs of his first term, *Mandate for Change,* probably contain as many retouchings of the original facts, whatever these may have been (and Eisenhower was probably the last to know), as do Hemingway's. But Eisenhower's intention in writing autobiography is to present a public image of himself for the history books. And while Hemingway's aim is psychologically no doubt the same, Hemingway cannot think of Paris in 1921 without making a picture of the city and a narrative about his friends; Eisenhower, by contrast, stuffs his memoirs with documents of the period in order to persuade the reader that his decisions were made on the basis of the information recorded in these documents. The artfulness of this does not make Eisenhower's autobiography a work of art.

Autobiography, like other literary forms, is what a gifted writer makes of it. There is great autobiography that is also intellectual history,

like *The Education of Henry Adams;* great autobiography that is equally
theology, like the *Confessions* of St. Augustine; autobiography that is
desperately intended for understanding of self, like Rousseau's *Confessions;* autobiography that is actually a program for living, like Thoreau's
Walden. These are all classics of autobiography, and the stories they tell
are among the greatest narratives in world literature. But the kind of
autobiography I am discussing here is autobiography as fiction—that is,
as narrative which has no purpose other than to tell a story, to create the
effect of a story, which above all asks (as the books by St. Augustine,
Rousseau, Thoreau, and Henry Adams do not) to be read for its value as
narrative. Of course it is ironic to find that some of the greatest narratives
in autobiography have actually been written by people like Benjamin
Franklin, who thought that he was setting himself up as a model for
emulation. James Baldwin, in his powerful book of essays, *Notes of a
Native Son*, writes as if his only aim were to shame the white middle class
and to arouse it to the plight of the Negroes. But his book is most felt as
autobiography, and succeeds as a kind that only a practiced fiction writer
could have created. There is in fact a kind of autobiography, very characteristic of our period and usually written by novelists or poets, that has
no other aim, whatever the writer may think he is doing, than to be
enjoyed as narrative. And books like Hemingway's *A Moveable Feast*,
Vladimir Nabokov's *Speak, Memory*, Edward Dahlberg's *Because I Was
Flesh*, Colette's *My Mother's House* and *The Blue Lantern*, Robert Lowell's
Life Studies, Denton Welch's *Maiden Voyage*, are so characteristic of the
use that an imaginative writer can make of the *appearance* of fact in
autobiography that they make us think of how cleverly the imaginative
writer exploits "real facts" in novels like *Sons and Lovers, A Portrait of the
Artist as a Young Man, Ulysses, Remembrance of Things Past, Journey to the
End of the Night, Goodbye to Berlin, Tropic of Cancer.* Even to mention
Henry Miller among such novelists and storytellers is to recognize that
there is a kind of narrative in our day which is fiction that uses facts, that
deliberately retains the facts behind the story in order to show the imaginative possibilities inherent in fact, and yet which is designed, even
when the author does not say so, to make a fable of his life, to tell a story,
to create a pattern of incident, to make a dramatic point.

Hemingway begins with the weather; Dahlberg opens the naturalistic poem that he makes of his life by intoning that "Kansas City is a vast
inland city, and its marvelous river, the Missouri, heats the senses; the
maple, alder, elm and cherry trees with which the town abounds are

songs of desire, and only the almonds of ancient Palestine can awaken the hungry pores more deeply." Robert Lowell says that "in 1924 people still lived in cities," Colette in *My Mother's House* invokes her mother's cry, "Where Are The Children?" Edmund Wilson begins his memoir of Talcottville, in upper New York State, with a sentence that more immediately recalls the spirit of fiction in our day than does the flat account of the hero's beginnings in eighteenth-century novels like *Gulliver's Travels* and *Robinson Crusoe*. Here is Wilson—"As I go north for the first time in years, in the slow, the constantly stopping, milk train—which carries passengers only in the back part of the hind car and has an old stove to heat it in winter—I look out through the dirt-yellowed double pane and remember how once, as a child, I used to feel thwarted in summer till I had got the windows open and there was nothing between me and the widening pastures, the great boulders, the black and white cattle, the rivers, stony and thin, the lone elms like featherdusters, the high air which sharpens all outlines, makes all colors so breathtakingly vivid, in the clear light of late afternoon." Robinson Crusoe is more prosaic: "I was born in the year 1632, in the city of York, of a good family, though not of that country, my father being a foreigner of Bremen, who settled first at Hull." Obviously the creation of mood in Wilson's opening is more in accordance with what we think of as the concentration of effect essential to fiction, and Defoe's opening is in the leisurely chronicle style suitable to a time when novelists wrote masterpieces without being self-conscious artists in the style of Flaubert. This self-consciousness is by no means a proof of talent or the style of genius; Defoe and Fielding did not have to try so hard as Flaubert to create masterpieces, and they were actually more successful. But art is no longer easy, in the sense of being comfortable, and autobiography as narrative is as artful as the contemporary short story or short novel, which usually obeys canons of poetic form rather than of the realistic novel. There is a correct and self-limited kind of fiction that Eliot and Pound have made an aesthetic standard in our time, and the kind of art in autobiography that I am discussing usually has the tension and manipulated tone that we associate with such modish fiction as Salinger's stories.

Autobiography as narrative obviously seeks the effect of fiction, and cannot use basic resources of fiction, like dialogue, without becoming fiction. Yet if Hemingway had wanted to write the story of *A Moveable Feast* as fiction he would have done so; indeed, several incidents and characters in this memoir were used by him as fiction. And Dahlberg's

Because I Was Flesh actually relates as autobiography material that he had presented in his novels *Bottom Dogs* and *From Flushing to Calvary*. When a good novelist relates as fact what he has already used as fiction, it is obvious that he turns to autobiography out of some creative longing that fiction has not satisfied. One can hardly reproach Hemingway, Nabokov, Colette with lacking imagination. On the contrary, it would seem that far from being stuck with their own raw material and lacking the invention to disguise or use it, they have found in the form of autobiography some particular closeness and intensity of effect that they value. The "creative" stamp, the distinguishing imaginative organization of experience, is in autobiography supplied not by intention, but by the felt relation to the life data themselves. The aesthetic effect that gifted autobiographers instinctively if not always consciously seek would seem to be the poetry of remembered happenings, the intensity of the individual's strivings, the feel of life in its materiality. Henry James expressed it perfectly when he said in tribute to Whitman's letters to his friend Peter Doyle that "the absolute natural," when the writer is interesting, is "the supreme merit of letters." In Whitman's material, James recognized "the beauty of the natural is, here, the beauty of the particular nature, the man's own overflow in the deadly dry setting, the personal passion, the love of life plucked like a flower in a desert of innocent, unconscious ugliness. . . . A thousand images of patient, homely American life, else undistinguishable, are what its queerness—however startling—happened to express."

Of course, autobiographical writing, even when it assumes the mask of sincerity and pretends to be the absolute truth, can be as fictional as the wildest fantasy. Obviously, autobiography does not appeal to us as readers because it is more true to the facts than is fiction; it is just another way of telling a story, it tells another kind of story, and it uses fact as a strategy. When Nabokov in *Lolita* writes a formal fiction with made-up incidents and farcical episodes that dip into surrealism, what he is in effect saying to the reader is: This *could* have happened, and my effort is to persuade you, through the concentrated illusion of my fiction, that it is happening. But when Nabokov describes his younger self hunting butterflies in the Crimea, in that other Russia that vanished after 1917, his whole effort is to communicate to the reader the passion and tone of the young man's happiness in nature. That young man alone is the story, and a summer day long ago is all the setting and all the plot. "On a summer morning, in the legendary Russia of my boyhood, my first glance upon awakening was for the chink between the shutters. If it disclosed a watery pallor, one had better not open the shutters at all, and so be spared the sight of a sullen day sitting for its picture in a puddle. From the age of six, everything I felt in connection with a rectangle of framed sunlight was dominated by a single passion. If my first glance of the morning was for the sun, my first thought was for the butterflies it would engender. . . ."

The difference between formal fiction and autobiography-as-narrative is not the difference between invention and truth, between the imaginative and the factual; the imagination is in everything that is well conceived and written. But autobiography is centered on a single person, who may be related to the world of nature more profoundly than he is to other human beings—which is the story of Nabokov's *Speak, Memory,* as it is of Thoreau's *Walden.* Fiction cannot limit itself to one individual's sensations, feelings, and hopes, except for reasons of satire, or as an experiment in surrealism. And it can be shown, I think, that the creative indecisiveness that is so marked in fiction today can be traced to the fact that power is now felt to lie everywhere but in the individual's own judgment. He gets to feeling smaller, more self-conscious, more uncertain of what he thinks and believes; it is then that the novel turns into a document of the thwarted individual will. But this is not a natural subject for the novel, which takes its very energy from the life of society.

Autobiography is properly a history of a self, and it is this concern with a self as a character, as an organism, that makes autobiography the queerly moving, tangible, vibratory kind of narrative that it can be. Everyone knows that the emergence of the self as a central subject in modern thinking and modern art is no proof of individual power or freedom. Shakespeare, of whom we know so little as a person, left a fuller record of the effect of human experience on a single mind than we get from the most tenderly self-cherishing passages in Proust or Nabokov or Hemingway; we know very little about Shakespeare's *self,* and Keats's statement sums up profoundly the creative inferiority of all modern writing that turns on the self as hero when he compares Wordsworth with Shakespeare's bewildering lack of self. Keats says that as distinguished from the Wordsworthian, or "egotistical sublime, which is a thing per se, and stands alone," the "poetical character is not itself—it has no self—It is everything and nothing—It has no character. . . . A poet is the most unpoetical of anything in existence, because he has no Identity—he is continually in for and filling some other body. . . . It is a wretched thing to confess; but it is a very fact, that not one word I ever utter can be taken for granted as an opinion growing out of my identical Nature—how can I, when I have no Nature?"

This is magnificent in its truth about Shakespeare. But it is less true of Keats than it is of Shakespeare, and it does not easily apply to such self-haunted writers of narrative as Proust, Céline, Joyce, Nabokov, and Hemingway. We cannot reflect on such key talents of our time without recognizing the immense role that the self now plays in fiction. The "egotistical sublime," Keats's keen phrase, suggests the sublimity that the ego finds in itself, in its own strivings, as well as the sublimity that it confers upon the world as the object of the self's consciousness. And we all understandably disparage the egotistical, whether sublime or not, especially when we compare it with Shakespeare's ability to enter into so many characters.

But remember that Keats, who understood this lack of egotism in Shakespeare, could not himself write a good play, and that neither could any of the English romantic poets. In our day the contemporary theater, at least in English, does not use poets well, does not depend on poetry for dramatic expression though it may occasionally exploit and impersonate poetic rhythms in its rhetoric. Shakespeare's lack of personal identity is now a mystery, and first-rate dramatic narrative is found only in prose fiction, and prose fiction of the kind, as one can see in Joyce, Faulkner, Lawrence, Hemingway, that has grown out of the egotism of romantic poetry. Faulkner once told an interviewer—"I'm a failed poet. Maybe every novelist wants to write poetry first, finds he can't, and then tries the short story, which is the most demanding form after poetry. And, failing at that, only then does he take up novel writing." Hemingway, whose first book was called *Three Stories and Ten Poems,* learned to write prose in rhythms learned from poetry. From Melville to Joyce and Faulkner, the novelists in English who have come to mean most to us have been those associated with just the kind of self-insisting and self-exploring romanticism that Keats deprecated. And in the most interesting novelists who have come up since the Second World War, like Malcolm Lowry and Saul Bellow, one feels that the egotistical sublime has been their key to the chaos of the contemporary world. Perhaps it is when the world becomes a screen for the self's own discoveries and imaginings, when the self becomes a passage to some mysterious collective truth that waits upon the self to be revealed, that gifted writers turn to autobiography as artistic strategy. And of course the ideal subject for such purposes is childhood—a subject that has become successively more interesting from age to age, and that has never interested any age so much as it does ours.

One reason for this is of course the solicitousness for one's self that is a mark of our culture; but the main literary reason is the belief, which the Romantics first propounded, that knowledge is attached to ourselves as children which later we lose. And it is only when a subject or interest or form is associated with an advance in his creative thinking—which is his power—that it is valued by a writer. No good writer chooses a form for psychological needs alone, since it is not *himself* he is interested in as an artist; he chooses a mask, an imagined self, for the control it gives him over disconnected, sterile, often meaningless facts. There is an artistic shrewdness to the exploitation of autobiographical devices that derives from the fact that since the writer tends to be more engaged with his self than he used to be, he is also more demanding of what the self can make of the world, and that he finds a power in this engagement and demand. There is an imaginative space that every true writer seeks to enlarge by means of his consciousness. The writer seeks to press his consciousness into being—to convert his material openly and dramatically into a new human experience.

The fascination with childhood as a subject in contemporary narrative derives, I think, from the aesthetic pleasure that the writer finds in substituting the language of mature consciousness for the unformulated consciousness of the child. Joyce in the beginning of *A Portrait of the Artist as a Young Man* tries to express the smells, sounds, textures, and pleasures of the cradle. Lawrence in *Sons and Lovers* tries to recreate Oedipal experiences with his mother. Proust, in the "Overture" to *Remembrance of Things Past*—and this opening section is the classic expression of this use of childhood in modern fiction—describes his earliest impressions in sentences that affect us as if no one before him had ever found the words for these intense experiences. The creative rapture of Proust's own slowly discovering genius becomes the theme of the salvation through art; language can shape and recreate the dead memories that weigh us down, language can raise us from our bondage to self and to the past.

In this power over his past is the writer's key to such immortality as we can ever achieve. Proust's rapture has little to do with psychology itself, for it is not a condition that Proust is writing about but the *recapture* of life and of true meaning. The rapture celebrates the artist's present consciousness, his creative power. In all these great autobiographical narratives of modern literature, from Wordsworth's *Prelude* through Whitman's great songs of himself to the implanting of the romantic consciousness as a metaphor and technique of twentieth-century fiction, the only hero is the writer; the epic he writes is the growth of the writer's mind, his rejoicing in his conscious gift. Of such classic modern books as *A Portrait of the Artist as a Young Man, Remembrance of Things Past, Journey to the End of the Night, Sons and Lovers,* as of *Moby-Dick, Walden,* and *Song of Myself,* one can say that the subject is the triumph of the creative consciousness in the hero. Creativity has indeed become a prime virtue in our culture—and it is this pride in consciousness for itself and of itself that has marked the literature we most admire.

Consciousness, in this literary sense, is not so much consciousness that powerfully dramatizes an object as it is an awareness of oneself being conscious. One sees on every hand today an idea of consciousness that is self-representative. One art critic has admiringly said of action painting that the painter deliberately engages in a struggle with the painting in order to release the fullest possible consciousness in himself, that the painting is the occasion of his self-discovery as an imagination. And perhaps this trait, this growing celebration of one's own powers, can be found among pure scientists as well; Heisenberg has said that to the farthest limits of outer space man carries only the image of himself. The more one studies the mind of contemporary literature, the more one sees what Poe, who fancied himself a universal savant, meant when he said that this is emphatically the thinking age; that it may be doubted whether anyone can properly be said to have thought before. What interests the contemporary critic is usually not literature as a guide to belief, or conduct, or action, but the forms or myths or rituals that he can uncover in works of literature as universally recurring traits of the imagination itself. No one turns now to novels for a key to the society in which we live; we expect that of the sociologists. The only novelists who seem truly creative to us now are those who command the language to interest us; more and more in the last few years the stimulating new novelists have been those, like J. P. Donleavy and William Burroughs, who start from the stream of consciousness and stay inside this world. Such writers protest that the outside world is simply insane, but what they really mean is that it is boring compared with the farce that is played inside the mind. A book like *Naked Lunch* is an experiment in consciousness, like taking drugs.

It is to this pride in consciousness as creativity that I attribute much of the idolatry of art in our time—the idea of art now means more than the concrete works of art. The self is inevitably the prime guest at this party of celebration. And in the high value that we put now on artistic consciousness I see a key to the character of literature in our day. When we look back at Hemingway's *A Moveable Feast,* we can see why Hemingway, for all the radiant and unforgettable pages he created out of his struggles to become an original artist, never became a mature novelist or a novelist of mature life—we can see why fascination with the tone and color of his own growth actually replaced many other interests for him. When we look back at Nabokov's *Speak, Memory,* we can see why this writer, who is so gifted as a fantasist and inventor, nevertheless makes us feel that his is the only active voice in his novels. Nabokov has even written a book on this theme called *The Gift;* whenever I read even his best work, I seem to hear Nabokov saying to the reader—"How talented I am!" Proust is the only writer of his time I can think of who used autobiography to create a classic novel. Proust was a child of the great French literary tradition, deeply rooted in and concerned with French aristocracy, French politics, French manners; Proust wrote his novel out of a profound intellectual faith that the past is not merely recovered but to be redeemed as a key to immortality. The imagination, thought Proust, makes all things immortal in the kingdom of time—and it was this immortality that Proust celebrated, not himself. When the writer affirms that his resources of consciousness alone save him from the abyss of non-being, which is what writers mean when they say that the outside world now is crazy, autobiography reduces the world to ourselves and the form has reached the limit of its usefulness.

Still, autobiography as narrative is usually of intense interest—intensity is indeed its mode, for nothing is more intense to a person than his own experience. This is also its aesthetic dilemma, on which contemporary fiction is often hung up; for autobiography deals with a case history, not with plot; with portraits, not with characters; it fixes the relation between the artist and the world, and so fixes our idea of the world instead of representing it to us as a moving, transforming power. It may be that the great social epics of the past are impossible to duplicate today because the plot in such books really hung on an argument about how society functions; today the novelist has no such argument of his own, or is not convinced that such argument is the final truth. But it is also clear that the exploration and celebration of individual consciousness represented an effort to find a new intellectual faith through psychology, and this faith has not been forthcoming. The stream-of-consciousness novel is as outmoded as the old realistic novel of society, for it has become a way of performing and repeating the discoveries that Proust and Joyce made half a century ago. The story of the artist as a young man has become tiresome, for all such artists tend to be the same. But this is by no means the only story that autobiography has to tell. Sartre said that during the occupation of France, Proust made him think of a lady on a chaise lounge putting one bonbon after another into her mouth. One can easily sympathize with this impatient radical feeling that Proust is not for an age in which we all feel that we are being overrun by politics. Society is no longer a backdrop to anybody's sensitivity. It is ferocious in its claim on our attention, and so complex as at times to seem a bad dream. We have all suffered too much from society, we are now too aware of what it may do to us, to be able to dispose of it as literature. But correspondingly, the new novels of society may come from those who can demonstrate just how much the individual is under fire everywhere in today's world. Autobiography as narrative can serve to create the effect of a world that in the city jungle, in the concentration camps, in the barracks, is the form that we must learn to express even when we have no hope of mastering it. We are all, as Camus showed with such exemplary clarity in his first and best novel, strangers in our present-day world—and as strangers, we have things to say about our experience that no one else can say for us. In a society where so many values have been overturned without our admitting it, where there is an obvious gap between the culture we profess and the dangers among which we really live, the autobiographical mode can be an authentic way of establishing the truth of our experience. The individual is real even when the culture around him is not.

Sincerity and Poetry

Donald Davie

Kenneth Rexroth declares, introducing *Selected Poems of D. H. Lawrence* (Viking, 1959):

> Hardy could say to himself: "Today I am going to be a Wiltshire yeoman, sitting on a fallen rock at Stonehenge, writing a poem to my girl on a piece of wrapping paper with the gnawed stub of a pencil," and he could make it very convincing. But Lawrence really was the educated son of a coal miner, sitting under a tree that had once been part of Sherwood Forest, in a village that was rapidly becoming part of a world-wide disemboweled hell, writing hard, painful poems, to girls who carefully had been taught the art of unlove. It was all real. Love really was a mystery at the navel of the earth, like Stonehenge. The miner really was in contact with a monstrous, seething mystery, the black sun in the earth.

And again:

> Hardy was a major poet. Lawrence was a minor prophet. Like Blake and Yeats, his is the greater tradition. If Hardy ever had a girl in the hay, tipsy on cider, on the night of Boxing Day, he kept quiet about it. He may have thought that it had something to do with "the stream of his life in the darkness deathward set," but he never let on, except indirectly.

This is outrageous, of course. In part, at least, it is meant to be. It is outrageously unfair to Thomas Hardy. But then, fairness is what we never find from anyone who at any time speaks up for what Rexroth is speaking for here. Are prophets fairminded? Can we expect Jeremiah or Amos or Isaiah to be *judicious*? D. H. Lawrence was monstrously unfair; so were nineteenth-century prophets like Carlyle and Ruskin, so was William Blake unfair to Reynolds and to Wordsworth. And some of them, some of the time—perhaps all of them, most of the time—know that they are being unfair, as I think Kenneth Rexroth knows it. Fair-mindedness, Lawrence seems to say, is not his business; if judiciousness is necessary to society, it is the business of someone in society other than the prophet or the poet.

"The prophet *or* the poet"—for, although I've gone along with Rexroth for the last few minutes in accepting this distinction, I am not really convinced by it. For what is the distinction which Rexroth has drawn, between Hardy and Lawrence? As he presents it to us, it has nothing to do with prophecy, though he seems to think it has. The distinction is quite simply that when "I" appears in a poem by Lawrence, the person meant is directly and immediately D. H. Lawrence, the person as historically recorded, born in such and such a place on such and such a date; whereas when "I" appears in a poem by Hardy, the person meant need not be the historically recorded Thomas Hardy, any more than when King Lear in Shakespeare's play says, "I," the person meant is William Shakespeare.

When Rexroth introduces the notion of a tradition of *prophecy*, above all when he puts in that tradition the most histrionic of modern poets (W. B. Yeats), he is shifting his ground abruptly and very confusingly. What he is saying to start with is simply and bluntly that Lawrence is always sincere, whereas Hardy often isn't; and Lawrence is sincere by virtue of the fact that the "I" in his poems is always directly and immediately himself. In other words, the poetry we are asked to see as greater than Hardy's kind of poetry, though it is called "prophetic" poetry, is more accurately described as *confessional poetry*. Confessional poetry, of its nature and necessarily, is superior to dramatic or histrionic poetry; a poem in which the "I" stands immediately and unequivocally for the author is essentially and necessarily superior to a poem in which the "I" stands not for the author but for a persona of the author's—this is what Rexroth asks us to believe.

In asking us for this he is asking us, as he well knows, to fly in the face of what seemed, until a few years ago, the solidly achieved consensus of opinion about poetry and the criticism of poetry. That consensus of opinion seemed to have formed itself on the basis of insights delivered to us by the revolutionary poets of two or three generations ago. It had taken the idea of the persona from Ezra Pound, and the closely related idea of the mask from W. B. Yeats, and it had taken from T. S. Eliot the ideas that the structure of a poem was inherently a dramatic structure, and that the effect of poetry was an impersonal effect. It had elaborated on these hints to formulate a rule, the rule that the "I" in a poem is *never* immediately and directly the poet; that the-poet-in-his-poem is always distinct from, and must never be confounded with, the-poet-outside-his-poem, the poet as historically recorded between birth-date and date of death. To this rule there was a necessary and invaluable corollary: that the question, "Is the poet sincere?"—though it would continue to be asked by naive readers—was always an impertinent and illegitimate question. This was the view of poetry associated with the so-called New Criticism, and (although it has been challenged from other directions than the one we are concerned with) it is still the view of poetry taught in our university classrooms. Must we now abandon it?

I think we must—or rather, that we may and must hold by it for the sake of the poetry which it illuminates, but that we can no longer hold by it as an account which does justice to *all* poetry. It illuminates nearly all the poetry that we want to remember written in England between 1550 and about 1780; but it illuminates little of the poetry in English written since 1780. For my own part, much of the time I bitterly regret having to give it up as regards the poetry of our own time. I see too clearly the grievous consequences of doing so, of having the question of "sincerity," which we thought to be safely scotched, once again rearing its head as a central question. Anyone can see these consequences—see them, not *foresee* them, because they are with us already. For the question has been settled already, off campus; and it is only in the university classrooms that anyone any longer supposes that "Is he sincere?" is a question not to be asked of poets.

Confessional poetry has come back with a vengeance; for many years now it is the poetry that has been written by the most serious and talented poets, alike in this country and in Britain. Consider only the case of Robert Lowell, probably the most influential poet of his generation. It is a very telling case indeed: trained in the very heart of New Criticism by Allen Tate, Lowell made his reputation by poems which are characteristically dramatic monologues, in which the "I" of the poet was hardly ever to be identified with the historical Robert Lowell. Then in the mid-fifties came his collection called *Life Studies* in which the "I" of the poems nearly always asks to be taken, quite unequivocally, as Robert Lowell himself. At about the same time, from under the shadow of Rexroth himself, came Allen Ginsberg's prophetic-confessional poem, "Howl!" And ever since, confessional poems have been the order of the day, with

the predictable consequences—the poem has lost all its hard-won auton-
omy, its independence in its own right, and has once again become
merely the vehicle by which the writer acts out before his public the
agony or the discomfort (American poets go for agony, British ones for
discomfort) of being a writer, or of being alive in the twentieth century.
Now we have once again poems in which the public life of the author as
author, and his private life, are messily compounded, so that one needs
the adventitious information of the gossip columnist to take the force or
even the literal meaning of what, since it is a work of literary art, is
supposedly offered as public utterance. And woe betide that poet whose
life, when the gossip columnist-reviewer goes to work on it, does not
reveal fornications and adulteries, drug addictions, alcoholism, and spells
in mental homes. "What?" the reviewer exclaims, "When it appears that
your poems have cost you so little, when the writing of them has apparently disorganized your life hardly at all, can you expect me to give them
as much attention as the poems of Miss X here, whose vocation drove
her last week to suicide?"

If this is what can happen when the question of sincerity once again
becomes central to the judgment of poetry, how much we must wish
that we could hold firm to those precepts of the New Criticism which
ruled that question out of order. Why not? If the universities are the
bulwarks of that more decorous view of poetry, what more proper than
that the universities should resist with disdain the disheveled sensationalism of the literary worlds of London and New York? And after all, aren't
most of these new confessional poets very bad poets? Yes, they are; as
most poets of any kind, at any given moment, are bad poets. But Robert
Lowell isn't. And in fact, it won't wash: the question of sincerity can
never again be out of order. For, as we see now, even in the heyday of
the persona and of impersonality in poetry there were poets writing who
would not fit the doctrine and who came off badly in consequence. Ezra
Pound, the very man who introduced the concept of persona, was one of
those who came off badly. His *Pisan Cantos,* written late in his career, are
confessional poems, and they have been esteemed by many who find all
or most of the rest of Pound unreadable. Who shall say those readers are
wrong? William Carlos Williams wrote confessional poems which a criticism evolved to do justice to T. S. Eliot could get no purchase on.
Thomas Hardy, for all that Kenneth Rexroth herds him in with the poets
of the persona in fact came off badly at the hands of a criticism which
based itself on the persona. And there is, indeed there is, D. H.

Lawrence. Was Lawrence a poet at all? The New Criticism, true to its lights, decided for the most part that he wasn't. But he wrote, along with too much that is messy and strident "River Roses" and "Gloire de Dijon" and "Snake," poems which any candid and unperverted taste must applaud, poems which do indeed (and this is the strength of Kenneth Rexroth's case) make us exclaim at finding the business of poetry once again so simple, so straightforward, so direct.

To be sure, Lawrence is not a confessional poet as Lowell and Ginsberg are confessional poets. For the confessional poet comes in two sizes: there are the Wordsworthian poets who confess to virtue (like Pasternak), as well as the Byronic poets who confess to vice (like Baudelaire). Lawrence in this respect is of the Wordsworthian sort, and in fact he was very hard and contemptuous toward writers such as Rozanov who confessed to meannesses and perversities. For myself, I find it easier today to sympathize with the Wordsworthians than the Baudelaireans. For our leaders of literary fashion long ago fell over backward in their determination not to treat the Baudelaires of our day as the pundits of Paris in the 1860s treated Baudelaire. In other words, those who demand most insistently that our poetry be confessional, demand also that its confessions be Baudelairean; they are so determined that the poetic vocation be agonized and disheveled that they are never so affronted as by the Wordsworthian or Pasternakian poetry which confesses, on the contrary, to having found the poetic vocation stabilizing and composing and refreshing. Robert Bly is one contemporary poet who makes this Wordsworthian claim to have gained access through his vocation to sources of refreshment and composure; and however we might differ as to the intrinsic quality of Bly's poems, we can see that it is this pretension which has provoked some of his reviewers to fury.

But there is more than this to be said. *Byronic* is a term we may use lightly; *Wordsworthian* is not, or not in my usage. If it is true, as I am suggesting, that with those of our poets who confess to virtue we have a recovery of the note of Wordsworth, we need to understand just what this means. What is involved is the assumption or the contention (with Wordsworth it was a contention) that the living of a poetic life is more important than the writing of poems; that the poems indeed have their value less in themselves than as pointing back to the life that they have come out of, which they witness to. (It may be indeed that "poetry of witness" would be a better name for what I have called "confessional poetry." "Witness," for instance, fits Williams's poems better than "confession." And "witness," as we hear it used from the pulpit ["a Christian witness"], explains better than "confession" why such poetry is often "prophetic" into the bargain.) This view of poetry is horribly dangerous, especially in our age when publicity is an industry with a fearsome range of techniques for exploiting the personality, distorting it, and destroying its privacy. This view of poetry opens the door to the exhibitionists; to the deceivers and self-deceivers (the conscious and unconscious hypocrites); to the man who will plume himself on his status as a poet, and demand special privileges on the strength of it, without ever submitting to having his qualifications examined. All this is true. These are indeed the lamentable consequences of once again admitting the Romantic pretension that the poetic life is more important than any of the poems which come out of it. Nevertheless these consequences must be accepted, and even gladly accepted. For I want to say now that at those infrequent moments when, as readers or writers, we think really earnestly about what poetry is and means, we cannot regret that the question of sincerity has once again become central. On the contrary we must welcome it; we must welcome the change from poetry seen as the extant body of achieved poems, to poetry seen as a way of behaving, a habit of feeling deeply and truly and responsibly. If poetry is once again making Wordsworthian pretensions, we must be glad of this, whatever the untidy and embarrassing and disconcerting consequences.

In the first place we must be glad to be compelled to recognize that we are all, like it or not, post-Romantic people; that the historical developments which we label "Romanticism" were not a series of aberrations we can and should disown, but rather a sort of landslide that permanently transformed the mental landscape which in the twentieth century we inhabit, however reluctantly. It seems to me now that this was a recognition which I came to absurdly late in life; that my teachers when I was young encouraged me to think that I could expunge Romanticism from my historical past by a mere act of will or stroke of the pen, and that by doing this I could climb back into the lost garden of the seventeenth century. It is not a question of what we want or like; it is what we are stuck with—post-Romantic is what we are.

But there is a more urgent reason why we should welcome *sincerity* back into our vocabulary. And it's for this reason that I have coupled (I think justly) the name of Pasternak with that of Wordsworth. For who of us can doubt, examining the spectacle of Pasternak, that here is a case in which the witness of a poet's life lived through matters more than any of the poems which that poet wrote—poems which most of us can't judge in any case, for lack of adequate translations? It was poets, it was at all events writers, who brought the Hungarians into the streets of Budapest in 1956, as it was a poet, Petöfi, who in 1848 incited the Hungarians into revolt against the Austrian Empire. This is what it means to be a poet, or what it can mean, in societies less fortunate than yours or mine. What these extreme situations put to the test is not a poem but a poet; or (more precisely) it is poetry embodied in persons who have dedicated themselves to a life of sincere feeling, not poetry embodied in poems which resist all the guns of the critical seminar. And isn't this indeed what Pasternak spells out for us in his *Doctor Zhivago,* that narrative of a poetic life, a life which, simply by being lived through, challenges and criticizes and condemns the society about it?

To be sure, it is easier to applaud in this way the Wordsworthian poetry which witnesses to virtue, than the Byronic or Baudelairean poetry which confesses to vice. The name of Baudelaire is there to show (and in some measure the name of Ginsberg shows it also) that the latter sort of poetry can challenge and condemn the society it is written from. But over this Byronic sort of poetry there necessarily falls the shadow of a divided purpose: the poet confesses to discreditable sentiments or behavior, but in doing so he demands credit for having the courage or the honesty of his shamelessness. By contrast the Wordsworthian poet is asking for credit quite unequivocally. He may be deceiving himself, he may not have earned the credit which he asks for, and we may withhold it. But at least he knows, and we know, what he is up to; he is not wooing us, coquetting with us, glancing at us sidelong.

If the question "Is he sincere?" is reinstated as a legitimate question to be asked of a poet, what is the consequence of this for those of us who read and write poetry specifically in the universities? The most revolutionary consequence is one that is really counterrevolutionary: the biographer, who a generation ago was excluded from literary criticism, or at least demoted, must now be reinstalled as a highly respectable figure. In itself this does not matter much, for in fact we've all continued drawing on the biographies of dead poets, though it's been important for some of us to pretend that we weren't doing so. In the case of our living contemporaries, however, the case is different; for until the biography of a poet is written, his place has to be taken by the retailer of gossip. Or so it may seem. In fact, however, in the case of a living contemporary poet, we rely not on biography but autobiography; the confessional poet is his own biographer, and his poems are his autobiography. Like any other autobiographer, he selects what he will reveal and suppresses much more. And insofar as the confessional poet thus presents only a trimmed and slanted image of himself, he may still be thought to be revealing to us not a personality but a persona. This is to use the term *persona* in an extended but thoroughly legitimate sense. Yet it seems to me unhelpful, and even a sort of evasion. The poets we are speaking of are trying to break out of the world of rhetoric; and although we can spread the nets of rhetoric wide enough to catch them despite their struggles, in doing so we are being ungenerous and we are even being dishonest, because we are refusing to acknowledge what is so patently the impetus behind their writing. Moreover, as critics we need to ask ourselves why we should so much want to do this. Why is it so important to us as critics to seal off the world of literature from the adjacent worlds of biography and history and geography? What are we afraid of?

In any event, however, we are not required to dismantle the whole body of our current assumptions. In part at least, the measure of a poet's sincerity is, it must be, *inside his poem*. This is to say that confessional or prophetic pretensions in the poet do not absolve him from producing poems that are well written. This seems too obvious to be worth saying. But alas! among the hoary fallacies which the new confessional poetry has brought to life among us is the notion that we know sincerity by its dishevelment; that to be elegant is to be insincere. To be sure, we must beware of supposing that the marks of good writing are few and obvi-ous. Confessional poetry, when it is good, is characteristically limpid, thinly textured semantically. And so for instance ambiguity, a high inci-dence of words with double meanings—this, which we have thought of as a feature of all good writing, we must not recognize as a feature of only *one kind* of good writing. For rather different reasons, irony and paradox are features which we must learn to set less store by. We must learn, I dare say, to give more weight to other features, notably to the *tone* in which the poet addresses us, and to the fall and pause and run of spoken American or spoken English as the poet plays it off against his stanza-breaks and line-division. In short, a poet can control his poem in many more ways, or his control of it manifests itself in more ways, than until lately we were aware of. Nevertheless we were right all along to think that a poem is valuable according as the poet has control of it; now we must learn to call that control "sincerity." For after all, what is the alternative? Are we to collect gossip about his private life? Are we to believe the poet sincere because he tells us so? Or because he shouts at us? Or (worst of all) because he writes a disheveled poetry, because the poem and the experience behind the poem are so manifestly out of his control?

To be sure, *control* is a word that may easily be misunderstood. Yet I think we need it in order to acknowledge how much of the poetic activity in the act of composition can be summed up in words like *judgment* and *prudence*. For I should maintain, in the teeth of Kenneth Rexroth, that, as for prophetic poetry (which may be, but need not be, confessional poetry also), it is necessarily an inferior poetry. My reasons I have given already. The prophet is above being fair-minded—judiciousness he leaves to someone else. But the poet will absolve himself from none of the responsibilities of being human, he will leave none of those responsibilities to "someone else." And being human involves the responsibility of being judicious and fair-minded. In this way the poet supports the intellectual venture of humankind, taking his place along with (though *above,* yet also along with) the scholar and the statesman and the learned divine. His poetry supports and nourishes and helps to shape culture; the prophet, however, is outside culture and (really) at war with it. The prophet exists on sufferance, he is on society's expense account, part of what society can sometimes afford. Not so the poet; he is what society cannot dispense with.

Origins of a Poem

Denise Levertov

Some time in 1960, I wrote "The Necessity," a poem which has remained, for me, a kind of testament, or a point of both moral and technical reference; but which has seemed obscure to some readers. Since I don't think its diction or its syntax really are obscure, it seems to me their difficulties with it must arise from their unawareness of the ground it stands on, or is rooted in; or to put it another way, the poem—any poem, but especially a poem having for the poet that character of testament—is fruit, flower, or twig of a tree, and is not to be fully comprehended without some knowledge of the tree's nature and structure, even though its claim to *be* a poem must depend on internal evidence alone. What I propose to do here is not to paraphrase or explicate "The Necessity," which I assume to be a poem, but to provide and explore some of the attitudes and realizations to which it is related.

I keep two kinds of notebooks: one is a kind of anthology of brief essential texts, the other a journal that includes meditations or ruminations on such texts. In drawing from these sources, as I propose to do here, I am not implying that all of them are literally antecedents, in my consciousness, of this particular poem. In fact, although most or all of the sources— the quotations I shall be making from other writers—were probably familiar to me by 1960, and in many instances long before, and had been copied out by then into my private anthology, the reflections on them written in my journals are of later date. I am therefore not speaking of simple sequence but of habitual preoccupations, which accrue and which periodically emerge in different forms.

One such preoccupation forms itself as a question. What is the task of the poet? What is the essential nature of his work? Are these not questions we too often fail to ask ourselves, as we blindly pursue some form of poetic activity? In the confusion of our relativistic age and our eroding, or at least rapidly changing, culture, the very phrase, *the task of the poet,* may seem to have a nineteenth-century ring, both highfalutin and irrelevant. Our fear of the highfalutin is related to the salutary dislike of hypocrisy; but I believe we undercut ourselves, deprive ourselves of certain profound and necessary understandings, if we dismiss the question as irrelevant, and refuse, out of what is really only a kind of embarrassment, to consider as a task, and a lofty one, the engagement with language into which we are led by whatever talent we may have. And precisely this lack of an underlying conception of what the poet is doing accounts for the subject-seeking of some young poets—and maybe some old ones too—and for the emptiness, flippancy, or total subjectivity of a certain amount of writing that goes under the name of poetry.

Years ago, I copied out this statement by Ibsen in a letter.

The task of the poet is to make clear to himself, and thereby to others, the temporal and eternal questions. . . .

In 1959 or 1960, I used these words as the subject of one of "Three Meditations." The three formed one poem, so that in referring to this one alone certain allusions are lost; but it makes a certain amount of sense on its own:

Barbarians
throng the straight roads of
my empire, converging on black Rome.
There is darkness in me.
Silver sunrays
sternly, in tenuous joy
cut through its folds:
mountains
arise from cloud.
Who was it yelled, cracking
the glass of delight?
Who sent the child
sobbing to bed, and woke it
later to comfort it?
I, I, I, I.
I multitude, I tyrant,
I angel, I you, you
world, battlefield, stirring
with unheard litanies, sounds of piercing
green half-smothered by
strewn bones.

My emphasis was on asking oneself the questions, internalizing them, on coming to realize how much the apparently external problems have their parallels within us. (Parenthetically, I would suggest that man has to recognize not only that he tends to project his personal problems on the external world but also that he is a microcosm within which indeed the same problems, the same tyrannies, injustices, hopes, and mercies act and react and demand resolution.) This internalization still seems to me what is essential in Ibsen's dictum: what the poet is called on to clarify is not answers but the existence and nature of questions; and his likelihood of so clarifying them for others is made possible only through dialogue with himself. Inner colloquy as a means of communication with others was something I assumed in the poem but had not been at that time overtly concerned with, though in fact I had already translated a Toltec poem that includes the line, "The true artist / maintains dialogue with his heart."

What duality does *dialogue with himself, dialogue with his heart,* imply? "Every art needs two—one who makes it, and one who needs it," wrote Ernst Barlach, the German sculptor and playwright. If this is taken to mean *someone out there* who needs it—an audience—the working artist is in immediate danger of externalizing his activity, of distorting his vision to accommodate it to what he knows, or supposes he knows, his audience requires, or to what he thinks it ought to hear. Writing to a student in 1965, I put it this way:

> . . . you will find yourself not saying all you have to say—you will limit yourself according to your sense of his, or her, or their, capacity. In order to do *all that one can* in any given instance (and nothing less than all is good enough, though the artist, not being of a complacent nature, will never feel sure he *has* done all) one must develop objectivity: at some stage in the writing of a poem you must dismiss from your mind all special knowledge (of what you were *intending* to say, of private allusions, etc.) and read it with the innocence you bring to a poem by someone unknown to you. If you satisfy yourself as *reader* (not just as "self-expressive" writer) you have a reasonable expectation of reaching others too.

This "reader within one" is identical with Barlach's "one who needs" the work of art. To become aware of him safeguards the artist both from the superficialities resulting from overadaptation to the external, and from miasmic subjectivities. My reference to "self-expression" is closely related to what I believe Ibsen must have meant by "to make clear to himself." A self-expressive act is one which makes the doer feel liberated, "clear" in the act itself. A scream, a shout, a leaping into the air, a clapping of hands—or an effusion of words associated for their writer at that moment with an emotion—all these are self-expressive. They satisfy their performer momentarily. But they are not art. And the poet's "making clear," which Ibsen was talking about, *is* art: it goes beyond (though it includes) the self-expressive verbal effusion, as it goes beyond the ephemeral gesture: it is a construct of words that *remains* clear even after the writer has ceased to be aware of the associations that initially impelled it. This kind of "making clear" engages both the subjective and objective in him. The difference is between the satisfaction of exercising the power of utterance as such, of *saying,* of the clarity of action; and of the autonomous clarity of *the thing said,* the enduring clarity of the right words. Cid Corman once said in a broadcast that poetry gives us "not experience thrown as a personal problem on others but experience as an order that will sing to others."

The poet—when he is writing—is a priest; the poem is a temple; epiphanies and communion take place within it. The communion is triple: between the maker and the needer within the poet; between the maker and the needers outside him—those who need but can't make their own poems (or who do make their own but need this one too); and between the human and the divine in both poet and reader. By divine I mean something beyond both the making and the needing elements, vast, irreducible, a spirit summoned by the exercise of needing and making. When the poet converses with this god he has summoned into manifestation, he reveals to others the possibility of their own dialogue with the god in themselves. Writing the poem is the poet's means of summoning the divine; the reader's may be through reading the poem, or through what the experience of the poem leads him to.

Rilke wrote in a letter:

art does not ultimately tend to produce more artists. It does not mean to call anyone over to it, indeed, it has always been my guess that it is not concerned at all with any effect. But while its creations having issued irresistibly from an inexhaustible source, stand there strangely quiet and surpassable among things, it may be that involuntarily they become somehow exemplary for *every* human activity by reason of their innate disinterestedness, freedom, and intensity.

It is when making and needing have a single point of origin that this "disinterestedness" occurs. And only when it does occur are the "freedom and intensity" generated which "involuntarily become exemplary"—which do, that is, communicate to others outside the artist's self. That is the logic of Ibsen's word *thereby* ("to make clear to himself and *thereby* to others").

I'd like to take a closer look at this word *need*. The need I am talking about is specific (and it is the same, I think, that Rilke meant when in the famous first letter to the Young Poet he told him he should ask himself, "*Must* I write?"). This need is the need for a *poem;* when this fact is not recognized, other needs—such as an undifferentiated need for self-expression, which could just as well find satisfaction in a gesture or an action, or the need to reassure the ego by writing something that will impress others—are apt to be mistaken for specific poem-need. Talent will not save a poem written under these misapprehensions from being weak and ephemeral.

For years, I understood the related testimony of Jean Hélion, the contemporary French painter, only as it concerned "integrity" and as an affirmation of the existence of an "other" within oneself, when he wrote:

> Art degenerates if not kept essentially the language of the mysterious being hidden in each man, behind his eyes. I act as if this hidden being got life only through the manipulation of plastic quantities, as if they were his only body, as if their growth were his only future. I identify him with his language. Instead of a description, an expression, or a comment, art becomes a realization with which the urge to live collaborates as a mason.

But when I reconsidered this passage in relation to how the transition from the inner world, inner dialogue, of the artist, to communication with any external other, is effected, I came to realize that Hélion is also implying that it is through the sensuous substance of the art, and only through that, that the transition is made.

The act of realizing inner experience in material substance is in itself an action *toward others,* even when the conscious intention has not gone beyond the desire for self-expression. Just as the activity of the artist gives body and future to "the mysterious being hidden behind his eyes," so the very fact of concrete manifestation, of paint, of words, reaches over beyond the world of inner dialogue. When Hélion says that then art becomes a realization, he clearly means not "awareness" but quite literally "real-ization," making real, substantiation. Instead of description, expression, comment—all of which only refer to an absent subject—art becomes substance, entity.

Heidegger, interpreting Hölderlin, says that to be human is to *be a conversation*—a strange and striking way of saying that communion is the very basis of human living, of *living humanly*. The poet develops the basic human need for dialogue in concretions that are audible to others; in listening, others are stimulated into awareness of their own needs and capacities, stirred into taking up their own dialogues, which are so often neglected (as are the poet's own, too often, when he is not actively *being* a poet). Yet this effect, or result, of his work, though he cannot but be aware of it, cannot be the *intention* of the poet, for such outward, effect-directed intention is self-defeating.

Man's vital need for communion, his humanity's being rooted in "conversation," is due to the fact that since living things, and parts of living things, atrophy if not exercised in their proper functions, and since man does contain, among his living parts, the complementary dualities of needer and maker, he must engage them if they are not to deteriorate. That is why Hélion speaks of "the urge to live collaborating as a mason" in the realization of art. The two beings are one being, mutually dependent. The life of both depends not merely on mutual recognition but on the manifestation of that recognition in substantial terms—whether as "plastic quantities" or as words (or in the means of whatever art is in question). The substance, the means, of an art, is an incarnation—not reference but phenomenon. A poem is an indivisibility of "spirit and matter" much more absolute than what most people seem to understand by "synthesis of form and content." That phrase is often taken to imply a process of will, craft, taste, and understanding by which the form of a work may painstakingly be molded to a perfect expression of, or vehicle for, its content. But artists know this is *not* the case—or only as a recourse, a substitute in thin times for the real thing. It is without doubt the proper process for certain forms of writing—for exposition of ideas, for critical studies. But in the primary work of art it exists, at best, as a stepping-stone to activity less laborious, less linked to effort and will. Just as the "other being" of Hélion's metaphor is *identified*, in process, with his language, which is his "only body, his only future," so *content*, which is the dialogue between him and the "maker," *becomes* form. Emerson says, "insight which expresses itself by what is called Imagination *does not come by study,* but by the intellect being *where and what it sees,* by sharing the path or circuit of things through forms, and so making them translucid to others" (emphasis added). Goethe says, "moralists think of the ulterior effect, about which the true artist troubles himself as little as Nature does when she makes a lion or a hummingbird." And Heidegger, in "Hölderlin and the Essence of Poetry" writes:

> Poetry looks like a game and is not. A game does indeed bring men together, but in such a way that each forgets himself in the process. In poetry, on the other hand, man is reunited on the foundation of his existence. There he comes to rest; not indeed to the seeming rest of inactivity and emptiness of thought, but to that infinite state of rest in which all powers and relations are active.

"Disinterested intensity," of which Rilke wrote, then, is truly exemplary and affective intensity. What Charles Olson has called a man's "filling of his given space," what John Donne said of the presence of God in a straw—"God is a straw in a straw"—point toward that disinterest. The strawness of straw, the humanness of the human, is their divinity; in that intensity of the "divine spark" Hasidic lore tells us dwells in all created things. "Who then is man?" Heidegger asks. "He who must affirm what he is. To affirm means to declare; but at the same time it means: to give in the declaration a guarantee of what is declared. Man is *he* who he *is,* precisely in the affirmation of his own existence."

Olson's words about filling our given space occur in a passage that further parallels Heidegger:

> . . . a man, carved
> out of himself, so wrought he
> fills his given space, makes
> traceries sufficient to
> others' needs. . .
> here is
> social action, for the poet
> anyway, his
> politics, his
> needs . . .

Olson is saying, as Heidegger is saying, that it is *by* being what he is capable of being, *by* living his life so that his identity is "carved," is "wrought," *by* filling his given space, that a man, and in particular a poet as a representative of an activity peculiarly human, *does* make "traceries sufficient to others' needs" (which is, in the most profound sense, a "social" or "political" action). Poems bear witness to the manness of man, which, like the strawness of straw, is an exiled spark. Only by the light and heat of these divine sparks can we see, can we feel, the extent of the human range. They bear witness to the *possibility* of "disinterest, freedom, and intensity."

"Therefore dive deep," wrote Edward Young, author of the once so popular, later despised, "Night Thoughts,"

> dive deep into thy bosom; learn the depths, extent, bias, and full fort of thy mind; contract full intimacy with the stranger within thee; excite and cherish every spark of intellectual light and heat, however smothered under former negligence, or scattered through the dull, dark mass of common thoughts; and collecting them into a body, let thy genius rise (if genius thou hast) as the sun from chaos; and if I then should say, like an Indian, Worship it (though too bold) yet should I say little more than my second rule enjoins, *viz.,* Reverence thyself.

What I have up to now been suggesting as the task of the poet may seem of an Emersonian idealism (though perhaps Emerson has been misread on this point) that refuses to look man's capacity for evil square in the eyes. Now as perhaps never before, when we are so acutely conscious of being ruled by evil men, and that in our time man's inhumanity to man has swollen to proportions of perhaps unexampled monstrosity, such a refusal would be no less than idiotic. Or I may seem to have been advocating a Nietzschean acceptance of man's power for evil, simply on the grounds that it is among his possibilities. But Young's final injunction, in the passage just quoted, is what, for me, holds the clue to what must make the poet's humanity *humane. Reverence thyself* is necessarily an aspect of Schweitzer's doctrine of Reverence for Life, the recognition of oneself as *life that wants to live* among other *forms of life that want to live.* This recognition is indissoluble, reciprocal, and dual. There can be no self-respect without respect for others, no love and reverence for others without love and reverence for oneself; and no recognition of others is possible without the imagination. The imagination of what it is to *be* those other forms of life that want to live is the only way to recognition; and it is that imaginative recognition that brings compassion to birth.

Man's capacity for evil, then, is less a positive capacity, for all its horrendous activity, than a failure to develop man's most human function, the imagination, to its fullness, and consequently a failure to develop compassion.

But how is this relevant to the practice of the arts, and of poetry in particular? Reverence for life, if it is a necessary relationship to the world, must be so for all people, not only for poets. Yes; but it is the poet who has language in his care; the poet who more than others recognizes language also as a *form of life* and a common resource to be cherished and served as we should serve and cherish earth and its waters, animal and vegetable life, and each other. The would-be poet who looks on language merely as something to be used, as the bad farmer or the rapacious industrialist look on the soil or on rivers merely as things to be used, will not discover a deep poetry; he will only, according to the degree of his skill, construct a counterfeit more or less acceptable—a subpoetry, at best efficiently representative of his thought or feeling—a reference, not an incarnation. And he will be contributing, even if not in any immediately apparent way, to the erosion of language, just as the irresponsible, irreverent farmer and industrialist erode the land and pollute the rivers. All of our common resources, tangible or intangible, need to be given to, not exclusively taken from. They require the care that arises from intellectual love—from an understanding of their perfections.

Moreover, the poet's love of language must, if language is to reward him with unlooked-for miracles, that is, with poetry, amount to a passion. The passion for the things of the world and the passion for naming them must be in him indistinguishable. I think that Wordsworth's intensity of feeling lay as much in his naming of the waterfall as in his physical apprehension of it, when he wrote:

> . . . The sounding cataract
> Haunted me like a passion. . . .

The poet's task is to hold in trust the knowledge that language, as Robert Duncan has declared, is not a set of counters to be manipulated, but a Power. And only in this knowledge does he arrive at music, at that quality of song within speech which is not the result of manipulations of euphonious parts but of an attention, at once to the organic relationships of experienced phenomena, and to the latent harmony and counterpoint of language itself as it is identified with those phenomena. Writing poetry is a process of discovery, revealing *inherent* music, the music of correspondences, the music of inscape. It parallels what, in a person's life, is called individuation: the evolution of consciousness toward wholeness, not an isolation of intellectual awareness but an awareness involving the whole self, a *knowing* (as man and woman "know" one another), a touching, a "being in touch."

All the thinking I do about poetry leads me back, always, to Reverence for Life as the ground for poetic activity; because it seems the ground for Attention. This is not to put the cart before the horse: some sense of identity, at which we wonder; an innocent self-regard, which we see in infants and in the humblest forms of life; these come first, a center out of which Attention reaches. Without Attention—to the world outside us, to the voices within us—what poems could possibly come into existence? Attention is the *exercise* of Reverence for the "other forms of life that want to live." The progression seems clear to me: from Reverence for Life to Attention to Life, from Attention to Life to a highly developed Seeing and Hearing, from Seeing and Hearing (faculties almost indistinguishable for the poet) to the Discovery and Revelation of Form, from Form to Song.

There are links in this chain of which I have not spoken, except to name them—the heightened Seeing and Hearing that result from Attention to anything, their relation to the discovery and revelation of Form. To speak intelligibly of them would take more time and space than I have. But I hope that I have conveyed some idea of the true background of a poem, that I have helped to define for others much that they have already intuited in and for their own labors, perhaps without knowing that they knew it:

The Necessity

From love one takes
petal to *rock* and *blesséd*
away towards
descend,

one took thought
for frail tint and spectral
glisten, trusted
from way back that stillness,

one knew
that heart of fire, rose
at the core of gold glow,
could go down undiminished,

for love and
or if in fear knowing
the risk, knowing
what one is touching, one does it,

each part
of speech a spark
awaiting redemption, each
a virtue, a power

in abeyance unless we
give it care
our need designs in us. Then
all we have led away returns to us.

Exploring Inner Space

Peter De Vries

There is more than a faint element of imposture in my standing before you in the role of lecturer, since to discharge that function creditably is to play the critic, which is not at all my speed—or bag, as one should perhaps say today. I suppose it's hard to know what to say about my books. Some think of them as caricatures of the white race. Others assign them to their classes as suggested or required reading, and even approve them as subjects for dissertations. All of which I think vindicates me by bearing out what I've been saying in those books all along—that everything is going to hell in a handbucket.

At least some of you out there are scholars, full-blown or in embryo, and I'm sure you're thinking to yourselves, possibly even murmuring to one another, "This character will talk for half an hour about the creative process, or some such, without telling us a damned thing." I shall not disappoint you. You may return to your classrooms and studies confirmed in the knowledge that what goes on in an artist's head is something about which he hasn't the slightest personal comprehension, but is the proper concern of scholars, and after I have returned home you can write crisp notes to the Hopwood Committee saying, "Why do you invite cows to analyze milk?"

Nevertheless, I can ask intelligent questions, furnishing answers of whatever caliber. Simply as readers we periodically wonder, by way of taking inventory, what the literature of the hour is up to. We know what our scientists are up to: one mechanistic triumph after another. By contrast, our artists grow more determinedly humanistic, private, and, as the cries of lay protest occasionally have it, obscure. That the twain will never meet, that the gulf grows ever wider, is a concern of course formally expressed by C. P. Snow, articulating for all of us with his idea of the two cultures, the scientific and the intellectual running full speed away from each other, or at best in irreconcilable parallels. Still, it's important to remember that over the long haul men do work together whether they work together or apart, as Robert Frost reminds us in the

229

poem "The Tuft of Flowers." In the distant future, or even now in some larger perspective, there may be somewhere an ultimate fusion of the two seemingly hopelessly divergent elements. For the time being, I have at least mentioned Frost and Snow in the same breath, which will have to suffice us as a token unity.

The rickety spirits and demoted egos whose inner space our best novelists navigate in the name of characterization are very good counterparts of our own, and whether we shall be vicariously enlarged by our astronauts' exploration of outer space, or merely shrunk into punier earthlings by contrast, depends on our individual makeup. There will certainly, in any case, be further feats to leave us magnified or dwindled, for make no mistake about it: our arrival on the moon and our departure for points more distant will without a doubt be counted among the scientific miracles of this century of the common cold. The humanistic scruple remains, "Should we spend all that money on trips to other astral bodies when there's such a heap still to be done on this one?" Should man go to the moon? The romantic instinctively replies, "Yes. He must have been put on this earth for a purpose."

In any event—to get this so-called lecture in orbit—it's fair to say that literature has found the exploration of private consciousness and even unconsciousness, which I am calling inner space, enough of a challenge. It is perhaps just as well that our poets and novelists—and you can name them for yourselves—concern themselves principally with the microscopic half of the full human reality, leaving the telescopic to science. It would take a combined Homer, Milton, and Shakespeare to dream our cosmological dream in an epic commensurate with the commonplaces of the front page. But to think of the "two cultures" as absolutely polarized is too neat, too slipshod, as I tried to say a moment ago. That men do work together whether they work together or apart, that there are points of similarity between such seemingly irreconcilable endeavors as the artistic and the scientific, is suggested by our very attempts to understand the one in terms of the other. Some of you may remember how, in the first blush of Virginia Woolf's vogue, terms like "rain of atoms" and "atomic dance" were applied to the minute and seemingly random thoughts, associations, and particles of memory out of which she constructed, particular by particular, the evocations of individual consciousness that in turn collectively made up, for her, a novel. Rereading her now, as I recently did, one would be lured a step farther into the metaphor and say that she was bent on a kind of psychic fission, which releases the energy of the association.

Edmund Wilson first elucidated Proust to us as the literary counterpart of Einsteinian relativity, with time so clearly a fourth dimension as to make *Swann's Way* end: "remembrance of a particular form is but regret for a particular moment; and houses, roads, avenues are fugitive, alas, as the year." If Joyce's stream of consciousness is no stream at all but precisely the sequence of disconnected droplets it appears on paper, it may suggest to us that psychic energy flows as quantum physics tells us physical energy does, not continuously but in individual packets. A Joycean association—a Planckian erg-second? Why not? And as though this were not enough, even as a humble humorist scurrying back to his proper depth, I might define the self-disparagement in which modern humor almost exclusively consists as the human counterpart of what is known in atomic physics as the loss of unstable carbon isotopes—and if *that* doesn't hold the boys on the academic quarterlies, I don't know what will. If from here on in I talk about myself a lot, you will understand that I do so out of insecurity. There goes an unstable carbon isotope already!

I thought that in the remaining minutes I might perform a kind of public exercise aimed at showing how the writer can only explore the inner space of his characters by perceptively navigating his own, and that this, and this alone, results in anything worth calling characterization. To say that literature illuminates life is platitudinous enough, and I haven't come nine hundred miles to sock that apocalypse to you; but it may be instructive to suggest how the sheer *practice* of fiction as such can sometimes help the practitioner understand what he is writing about, that is to say living with, and to conduct the experiment by recalling an incident that recently befell me—or rather, to focus the point down to where I want it, a character I ran foul of, and he me, and whom I misjudged completely at first and did not comprehend until I had spent some time trying to put him down on paper, though he may have had my number from the beginning on a somewhat more primitive level.

The purpose of fiction is still, as it was to Joseph Conrad, to make the reader see. That is our quarrel with television, is it not? That it is not visual enough? It cannot make us *see* Jeeves the butler, entering the room, "a procession of one." It cannot make us see the woman in *Dorian Gray* whose dresses always looked as though they had been designed in a rage and put on in a tempest. It cannot make us see the character in Ring

Lardner who served what he thought was good Scotch though he may have been deceived by some flavor lurking in his beard. Least of all can it ever hope to begin to make us see anything like the young girl in Elizabeth Bowen's *The Death of the Heart,* who "walked about with the rather fated expression you see in photographs of girls who have subsequently been murdered, but nothing so far had happened to her." Such wild rich subtleties require transmission from one mind to another via the written word upon the printed page, and remain beyond the power of the boob tube to convey.

The task I recently set myself was to make the reader see—and now for the next few minutes to make you see—a character who was nothing if not flamboyantly vivid on the merely visual plane in real life. I was prepared for him by my wife, whom I saw, as I came home one evening, waiting for me at the front door, not with a smile of greeting but somewhat grimly, her arms folded on her chest, holding in one hand a magazine that she had rolled into a truncheon.

"Wait till you see this one," was her first remark after my bestowal of the greeting kiss, and something in her tone made me know exactly what she meant, and made me hurry on past her into the house and head straight upstairs for my predinner bath. Scars left by hospitalities recently extended to my fourteen-year-old son's friends were an aid to the instinctive understanding that this elliptical opening referred to the latest specimen he had brought home, in the way of an overnight guest. "Remember the last one?" my wife pressed on, close at my heels.

I did indeed. This was a thirteen-year-old character who excoriated the false values my generation had given his, and who expressed his disapproval of bourgeois criteria by keeping his chewing gum in his navel. He believed in the abolition of money. Not that he conclusively infected my son with any of those iconoclastic notions. I still keep missing dollar bills and an occasional fin from my wallet just the same. "So cheer up," I said to my wife, summarizing the episode briefly in those terms as I hurried down the passage to the bedroom. "Things aren't always as bad as they seem."

"And the one before that?"

Him I remembered too, him indeed. Lad who brought a gerbil. Lad who also believed in the primacy of instincts, and who pursuant thereto got up some time during the night and ate all the breakfast Danish, and who in his freedom from the tyranny of material possessions inadvertently walked off with one of my derby hats.

"Well, when you get a load of *this* one," said my wife, "you'll wish you had either of *them* back, *if not both*."

"I love the way you talk in italics," I said, throwing a fond smile over my shoulder as we sped down the passage toward the bedroom.

There I had a moment to catch my breath and get my bearings, the dinner my wife was preparing requiring, presently, her attention in the kitchen. But it was only a moment. I was pulling off my clothes and flinging them in every direction in my haste to get into the tub before hearing anything else that might qualify the peace in which I planned to luxuriate there, for a bit, when the door I had shut behind me opened and she reappeared, again nursing the cudgel. She tapped it mysteriously in a palm as she sat down on the bed to resume the interrupted dossier. (What such a cylindrical elongation might mean to a housewife I have no idea, having lost my taste for symbolism with the two steel balls the crazy captain in *The Caine Mutiny* kept rolling in his palm.)

"We're used to kids who live with one or the other of their parents, right? Well, *this* one doesn't live with *either* of his. Oh, he's with the mother technically, because she has custody of him, but he only goes there to sleep because he can't *stand* her, while his *father* can't stand *him*. So he likes to farm himself out to *other* people."

"Abrogation-of-the-family-pattern bit, eh? And must you speak in italics all the time, dear? It gives a man such a sense of stress.

"The father," she continued, crossing her legs, "says the mother lost the toss, so let her see to him. That's how he puts the custody decision. Apparently this one likes to sleep with the phonograph going—he's brought along an album of some group called The Burning Bananas that'll make you hanker after the gerbil days—and is said to make passes at his school teachers." I cleared my throat, kicked my shoes about, and in general made as much noise as possible in order to hear as little of this information as I could before gaining the safe haven of the bathroom. "Now, as to the father, *he's* currently shacked up with some cookie half his age in a cottage by the beach. She's about twenty, and models for—"

I sprang into the bathroom, clapped the door shut and turned the tub faucets up full blast, instantly cutting off all further data. I lolled as best I could in the promised warmth, for five minutes, perhaps ten. She was waiting for me when I emerged.

"—and models for these."

She opened the magazine and exhibited a picture of the baggage he was knit up with. I pored over it as she held it out for my inspection, nodding as I dried my shoulders with the towel. It showed a girl of the age specified, posing at the water's edge in a polka-dot diaper and nothing more—half a bikini. I set her up in a small waffle shop in the east Fifties, read aloud to her evenings from my favorite authors, and in general exposed her to something better than was intimated by the evidence in hand.

"A face that could launch a thousand ships, all right," I murmured, dropping the towel on a chair. "To say nothing of the topless towers of Ilium."

"You don't ask how I got this magazine. Aren't you curious? Well, Mike—that's your guest's name, Mike Hackett—carried it around with him to show people. *As though it's something about his father to be proud of.*"

"*Stop talking in italics.*"

A knack for dramatic construction will have been discerned in my narrator. Nothing more displayed this gift than the manner in which she now inserted the keystone in her expository arch. Setting the magazine down on a table, she waited until I had finished extracting a clean pair of shorts from my bureau drawer, then yet a moment while I drew them on. Then she said:

"So that is what the father is lollygagging around with, leaving it to other people to raise—*that.*" She pulled aside a corner of the curtain and pointed down into the yard. I stepped to the window to look out.

I saw an Old Testament prophet dressed in loose-fitting vestments of muslin, or perhaps hopsacking, haranguing my attentive son. A lighted cigarette hung in one corner of his mouth, flapping briskly as he spoke. He talked with apparent authority, judging from the rapt, nodding concentration he received. He seemed to be denouncing something, possibly the garage against which he slouched, because once or twice he poked a thumb at it over his shoulder, as though he opposed it on some ground or other, possibly as symbolic of something he must deny his personal approval—such as the two cars it normally houses. Presently, and rather abruptly, the diatribe ceased, and the two gazed about them at the waning day. The prophet drummed the side of the garage with the palms of his hands. Then he took a last drag on the cigarette and snapped it into the shrubbery.

"Well," I said, turning from the window, "we can't judge all our young people by the behavior of most of them. But what's with the long hair? I thought that was on the way out."

"Huh!"

I swam into a pullover shirt of bleeding Madras, paused at the glass to brush my displaced hair, and then from the closet selected a pair of mulberry slacks. Leaning against a wall with folded arms, much in the manner of the prophet against the side of the garage, my wife coldly watched these sartorial preparations. My feet I slipped into a pair of white calfskin Belgian casuals.

"So you say his father won't have him around. It's probably his way of atoning for his adultery. Denying himself the pleasure of his children."

"Oh, will you stop being perfect!" my wife snapped with unaccustomed zest. "Nothing is more irritating than that. And all that I-would-never-sit-in-judgment cool is really a form of holier-than-thou, you know." Then she began slowly to pace the room. "But how to handle the boy is the problem now. The thing is, he doesn't let on his old man won't have any part of him. His story is that he's there with him all the time, that they're real pals, go for rides together in the father's Porsche roadster and what not. Skippy told me the real dope on the side—that the old man hauls off on him whenever he shows up. So we play dumb about that."

"All in all then, what the boy seems to need is some good normal family life. Let's give him a little of that, shall we?" I said, signaling that I was ready to go down.

"All right, but one thing. Don't go being incomparable at table. Nothing confuses children more than that. It upsets them. They don't understand it, and so they resent it. So lay off the savoir faire for tonight, shall we?—the style?"

Hardly. Standards must be upheld, a tone set at all costs, that setting, in turn, an example. That was especially important for those hailing from environments so lamentably lacking in it as that of which I had just been vouchsafed a glimpse. One must put one's best foot forward at all times.

Proof of how the grossest origins may be transcended lay allegorically in wait for us in the very soup to which we sat down—four cups of that vichyssoise whose genesis in the lowly potato of peasant France may be forgotten in the elegant restaurants (and fine homes) in which we sip it. I opened the table talk on just that point, in a properly oblique and subtle fashion of course. We were disposed round a circle of gleaming marble set with showy napery and hereditary plate, the prophet on my right, Skippy on my left, and my wife visible across from

me above a floral centerpiece. Her lips delicately puckered to a spoonful
of her soup, she watched the boys drink theirs, not to say listened
to them, for they made hydraulic noises as they fed. "You may pick
up your cups if you wish," she said, addressing to both boys an assurance aimed principally at the prophet, whose hair was hanging in his
soup.

"You like this?" Skippy asked him.

"Yar's like groovy. But whassat like bee-bees?"

"We like to float a few grains of caviar in it, " I said. "Gives it a
certain zing, don't you think? Tell me," I continued in a pleasantly
rambling fashion, "has anybody here been to that new diner on the Post
Road yet? Teddy's. I dropped in there for a hamburger the other day and
noticed something on the menu that struck me as funny. Among the
desserts was listed a Jello du Jour. I thought that rather amusing."

"Kina flavor's that, man?"

I opened my mouth to explain, but a terse headshake from my wife
persuaded me to shove along to other matters. The subject of mothers
somehow came up, and I noticed a play of pained grimaces cross the
prophet's face. A reference to his father, however, brought a broad smile
to it. "He's got this cool place on the water," he related. "Man, you
get up mornings and jump right in. Then he takes me for rides in his
Porsche. He's got a Porsche that's like really where it's at."

No one taking as sacred the obligation to evolve—the progressive
refinement of sensibility of which Henry James was so exquisitely a
stage, now restated as Pierre Teilhard de Chardin's principle of "com-
plexification"—will ever unrealistically blind himself to the impediments
everywhere awaiting this long and uphill climb. The struggle to elevate
our guest's temper was beset at every turn by a commensurate threat: I
mean the decline of our host's. For the next quarter-hour we heard little
but paeans of praise to the prophet's father, deluded as we know. He told
of waterside sport (with or without Miss Twin Peaks was never said), of
camaraderie in the open Porsche and convivial hands of rummy.
Throughout the encomium, the prophet sat hunched over his plate with
his hands around it, as though it were itself the steering wheel of a motor
car in which he and, indeed, we all were traveling at high speed, his hair
streaming behind him like a witch's instead of depending like a beagle's
ears into his food.

The conversation at some point turned to hippies, and their ironical
migration to Boston.

"You think they're really like the early Christians, Pop?" Skippy asked. "You buy that?"

"I do indeed," I said. "And I would like to see the parallel completed by having them thrown to the lions. If not the Kiwanians. Fix both sides."

"The idea is to live as though every day is Christmas right?"

"Right. And dress as though every day is Halloween. Where did you get that chiropractor's tunic and those bare feet?" He had been given dispensation to come to the evening board unshod, in deference to his guest status.

"Timothy Leary's got charisma," said the prophet contentiously.

"Aw, I'm sorry to hear that," says I. "He certainly doesn't look well. I hope he's taking something for it."

The prophet shot a look into the kitchen over his shoulder. "Like I have some beer? My father lets me have it."

"Mine doesn't let me. But there are plenty of soft drinks out there," I said, seeing he hadn't touched his milk. "Coke, Seven Up, Like. Ever had Like? You might like like Like."

My wife was noting that he had also, in all this time, scarcely touched his food, since the soup. "Don't you like lamb chops?"

"Well, no. I don't seem to care much for chops of any kind."

"Maybe he'd like a karate chop," I said, looking into my wine glass.

There was no doubt I was being worn thin. The odds seemed too great at least so far. We had by midnight not discernibly evolved. Indeed, the backslidden state apprehended above increasingly marked the scene. The hour found me hammering my pillow and hissing the name of the Nazarene into it at the sound, issuing faintly but remorselessly from the boys' bedroom, of the Burning Bananas. The struggle for men's minds was not going at all well. Perhaps a battle must be granted as lost while bearing the war in mind. I tossed onto my back with a fresh oath as the vocalist, apparently pursuing a technique of singing the "words" of a song other than that being performed by the instrumentalists, belted out: "Atsa mah wah dig muh baby, lemme rock ya frunks!" or some such.

I sprang out of bed and thudded down the passage to the other bedroom. I snapped off the light, switched off the machine, and barked, "OK, that's it. That wraps it up, know what I mean? No more playing, talking, nothing. Good night!"

This night's sleep was a sequence of snoozes from the next of which I awoke to the murmur of voices below my chamber window. Leaning out of which I saw them sitting on the doorstep leading to the flagstone terrace. They were both smoking cigarettes, and the prophet was sucking on a bottle of Löwenbräu.

I suppose my manner, as I thundered down the stairs again in the Belgian casuals, resembled that of the movie actor Franklin Pangborn, whose thirty years of apoplectic fits still checker the Late Late Show. No later than this one, this was the Late Late Show too. They parted to let me storm down the stoop between them. I marched out to the terrace and wheeled to face them.

"Now then. You will go back in there—right in that house," I said pointing to it so there would be no mistake about which house was meant, "you will go back in there and get to bed. And if I hear one more peep out of either of you it'll be the razor strap. Now git!"

My kid skedaddled. The prophet, however, hung back a moment, gesturing with his free hand. "But like we couldn't sleep, so we just—"

I snatched the bottle from his grasp and flung it into the bushes, dealing a generous spray of foam about, and flecking us both with it. "Goddamn you, get in there!" With that, I drew my right foot back and let fly with all my might.

We use the term *good swift kick* with an everyday familiarity, as though delivering one were a regular occurrence, whereas in fact most of us go to our graves without experiencing the solid satisfaction of doing so. This one was well planted. But in planting it, I lost my balance and sat down on the terrace with an impact at least equal to that felt in the prophet's case. Also, in finding its target my foot lost its slipper, one of the white Belgian casuals, which sailed an inch past his head, through the open doorway, and straight at my wife, who had by now been awakened by the ruckus and come down herself to see what was going on. She ducked just in time, the slipper spinning end over end into the room giving onto the terrace, which is the library, where it struck a far row of bookshelves with a flat *splat* and dropped to the floor behind an easy chair. "Son of a *bitch*!" I said, closing the generation gap.

That did it. That turned the trick. The prophet from then on was nice as pie. I set to work the very next day on a story about the incident, about how young people really do want a firm hand (if that's the mot juste); discipline; a sense of authority. But when I reached the turning point of the narrative, the crisis I've just described, something about it didn't ring right. Some sneaking doubt about my grasp of the prophet's motivation nagged me. It was his grin as he bade me goodbye, thanking me for my hospitality, that hung me up. Each time I reread my interpretation of the prophet's sudden shift of attitude, as exhibiting the masculine adolescent's need for the authority principle, it rang hollow. The grin became a laugh, remote but unnerving. The principle was true enough, but not in this case. Something told me it was not relevant to this story. The author himself did not quite dig what he was illuminating.

I put it aside, and, as one often does, let the unconscious get in its licks. The badgering question on which the conscious agenda remained stuck was: why had my central character become nice as pie if not for the reason so far stated? Why had he come to like like me? The firm-hand theory didn't seem right in the exposition, any more than the best-foot-forward hypothesis.

The key to his sudden change lay, of course, in his relationship with his own father, so obviously that it is still a matter of embarrassment to me that light didn't break over me sooner. It broke, at any rate, in the form of an incident involving my own son and me, of no significance in itself; a minor traffic altercation between me and another motorist, in which he got decidedly the best of me. He had made what I thought a dumb move, for which I undertook to rebuke him with what I regarded as a rather neat thrust while we were both waiting for a green light. His riposte still makes me think of the cartoon of the prizefight manager saying to his battered boxer between rounds, "The next time you think you see an opening, duck." Having sent his repartee home, he shot away through the intersection and disappeared—leaving my son, who was sitting in the front seat beside me, blushing a brick red. I was startled to find how my humiliation stung him, until I remembered from my own boyhood how keenly a father's shame can become the son's. In the twinkling of a split second I had orbited all those memory-miles of inner space, and in that splinter of time my literary problem was illuminated. I understood what had made the prophet so happy.

His boasts of companionship with his father were only a cover-up, a shell carefully concealing an inner hurt, a wound that throbbed anew with every fresh evidence of parental decency and familial integrity elsewhere, stilled only by any proof, again at last, that his own old man wasn't so bad after all, relatively speaking. The last thing he needed was the civilized domestic environment I had egotistically striven to supply. Confronted with such another hazard to his self-esteem, he had spent that whole damned evening, and then half the night as well, reducing it to the shambles his own private life had become; in particular, reducing me to a clod at least as bad as his old man, if not worse. He had proved—or I had proved—the truth of Mark Twain's remark, that there are few things in life harder to bear than the irritation of a good example. That example liquidated, he could get on with the business of behaving toward me with comparative decency.

He still does, though it is now I who find the example hard to bear. I catch glimpses of him about town, always nodding politely to me and with a grin behind which lurks the gleam of cunning, the secret knowledge that I know what he knows.

That is the story of how I restored one boy's faith in his father. Little wonder it remains unwritten! I had sat down to write it without the faintest idea that was what it was about. I had surmised it to be about something else altogether. Thus it was the practice of my craft that, ultimately, enabled me to understand the reality the craft was intended to illuminate. Light did not break as I sat at the typewriter. That's not what I mean. I simply mean that my struggle with the literary problem kept my mind and spirit open to the revelation when it came, in the shape of real persons, places, and things.

To say that the story remains unwritten is to ignore its unexpected culmination in lecture form. It is in that form that I may now analytically equate my loss of heart for the narrative with the loss of my role in it as the hero. For the flash of illumination entailed, of course, my sudden switch to that of villain. In real life, the story with its transferred function remains unresolved, since I keep seeing the putative villain, now its martyr. Indeed, I saw him only last week when he was once more an overnight guest, and this time I had to steel myself for the confrontation in quite another manner than in the original instance when my wife's exposition had set up the drama to follow. Perhaps it is thus not a story after all, much less a novel, or a play, but the subject of a poem, and that, indeed, already written, put down not by a latter-day exponent of the suburban mores, or an interpreter of corroded metropolitan egos, but by the white-clad recluse of Amherst, Emily Dickinson, who a hundred years ago said:

> What fortitude the soul contains
> That it can so endure
> The accent of a coming foot,
> The opening of a door.

Modern African Writing

Nadine Gordimer

There are two kinds of writers in Africa: the testifiers and those who are actually creating a modern African literature. But perhaps I ought first to explain a little more fully on what criteria I base the distinction between the testifiers and the creative writers. The testifiers supply some fascinating folklore and a lot of useful information about the organization of traditional African life, and the facts of social change in Africa. Like their counterparts, lesser writers all over the world, they take stock-in-trade abstractions of human behavior and look about for a dummy to dress in them, a dummy put together out of prototypes in other people's books rather than from observation of living people. They set these dummies in action, and you watch till they run down; there is no attempt to uncover human motivation, whether of temperament, from within, or social situation, from without. Such writers do not understand the forces which lie behind the human phenomena they observe and are moved to write about.

In passing, there is one difference between these writers in Africa and their European counterparts which is interesting because it relates so closely to Africa in its present state of transition. Elsewhere, people who are ill equipped creatively write out of vanity or because there is a profitable reading public for the third-rate. In Africa, a literature is still seen largely as a function of the benefits of education, automatically conferred upon a society which has a quota of western-educated people. The West African Pidgin English concept "to know book" goes further than it may appear; many school teachers, clerks, and other white-collar workers seem to write a novel almost as a matter of duty. The principle is strongly reinforced, of course, by the fact that the shortage of western-educated people means that Africa's real writers all, I think, without exception, have to perform some other function in addition to their vocation—from Africa's greatest poet, Leopold Sedar Senghor, who is also the president of Senegal, to T. M. Aluko, a fine Nigerian novelist, who is director of public works.

But this is by the way. Let me give some examples of the work of writers whose factual material is interesting but whose ability falls short of that material. The would-be writer says to himself, "All over Africa village boys have become prime ministers and presidents: Kenyatta, Obote, Toure, Banda, Launda. I will write a book about a village boy who, like them, leaves home, struggles for an education, forms a political party, resists the colonial authorities, wins over the people, and moves into Government House." Another would-be writer, aware of the move to reestablish the validity of the African way of life, says to herself, "It is one of the customs of my country for the husband of a childless woman to take another wife; I will write about a childless woman whose husband takes another wife." The result is, at best, something like the Sierra Leonian William Conton's *The African,* and the Nigerian Flora Nwapa's *Efuru.* While Conton's hero, Kisimi Kamara, progresses from village bright boy through the care of gin-tippling missionary ladies to Cambridge certificate, England, lodgings, urban poverty, and midnight oil, enlivened by boyish plans for African liberation, he has a certain autobiographical veracity behind him. When he returns to his country and becomes a public, less subjective figure, his author, lacking the creative insight into the complex motivation—psychological, political, and historical—needed to give his hero substance in this situation, resorts to sudden bald statements to be taken on trust by the reader—"Six months later I was Prime Minister"—and finally turns in desperation (and wild defiance of the political facts of life) to having Kamara resign office, buy an airline ticket, and land in South Africa to organize a boycott to bring down apartheid.

Flora Nwapa's *Efuru* is a childless woman whose bewilderment and frustration are stated and left unexplored. Again, not knowing enough about her own creation, the author has to resort to something to fill the vacuum. She uses rambling details of daily life, mildly interesting but largely irrelevant. Among them the key to the objective reality of *Efuru* lies half buried and less than half understood. Efuru is presented as beautiful, clever, a successful trader, and she performs all the rites and neighborly duties without which these attributes would not be valid in a tribal society, but she has had two unsuccessful marriages and seen her only child die. In a somewhat offstage incident, a sage diagnosis that a river goddess has chosen Efuru as her honored worshiper, it seems that other women chosen by the river goddess have been childless, too. Are we then being shown, through the life of an individual, how sublimation of frustrated natural instincts takes place in a woman of a particular type, and how an African society invents or employs religious or mystical conventions to reconcile her to her lot and give her a place within the society despite the fact that she cannot fulfill the conventional one? Is this novel really about an interesting form of compensation, not merely personal, but also social? The answer is yes, but Flora Nwapa, the author, only dimly senses the theme of her novel; all she has seen is the somewhat disparate series of events in the life of Efuru. Perhaps you remember E. M. Forster's famous definition of the difference between story and plot. "The king died and then the queen died"—that is a story, a series of events arranged in their time sequence. "The king dies and then the queen died of grief"—that is a plot; the time sequence is preserved but the emphasis is on causality. If I carry the definition one step further and suppose the author sets out to explore the questions, "What sort of woman is it who dies of grief and what sort of social and historical context shaped her?" we reach a definition of theme, the third dimension of the novel, and the one where it fulfills art's function of eternally pushing back the barriers of understanding in order to apprehend and make sense of life.

Flora Nwapa is one among the many African writers who are not able to do this for African life because she is not capable of dealing with theme. But she is a countrywoman of one of the few African writers whose name already belongs to world literature—Chinua Achebe. He handles the dominant themes of African writing, commanding all the resources of a brilliant creative imagination, from a classical sense of tragedy to ironic wit. In his first novel, *Things Fall Apart,* he shows at once a comprehensive insight into his characters. Their psychological makeup is never seen in isolation, as a neurotic phenomenon; his historical sense sets them at the axis of their time and place. He knows who they are, and why they are as they are; he shows them as stemming from the past, engaged with the forces of the present, and relevant to a future. He chooses as his hero what Hegel calls a world-historical figure, a man who, though not obscure, is not a king, not a history maker in the obvious sense, but someone through whose individual life the forces of his time can be seen to interact.

Okonkwo is a person of authority and achievement in his eastern Nigerian village. He was born the son of a failure and is self-made; by his own efforts he has a reputation as a fine wrestler, has distinguished himself in tribal wars, has an excellent yam crop, two tribal titles, and can afford three wives. A hostage of a tribal skirmish, a young boy, Ikemefuna, is given into his care until the council of tribal elders decides the boy's fate. Ikemefuna becomes so much a member of Okonkwo's family that he often has the honor of carrying Okonkwo's stool; yet when the elders decide Ikemefuna must die, Okonkwo is expected to be present when the deed is done, and, indeed, to dispatch him in his final agony. Okonkwo tries to put the dead boy out of his mind. Then later, at the funeral rites for an old man, the gun with which Okonkwo is to fire a salute explodes and fatally wounds another young boy. It is a crime to kill a clansman, and so Okonkwo is exiled from the village for seven years.

These are the disparate facts of the narrative; in Achebe's hands they grow out of one another with the surging inevitability of a Greek tragedy. Okonkwo's own son, Nwoye, was a disappointment; Ikemefuna had come to stand in his place. Yet when Ikemefuna received his deathblow and turned to Okonkwo, calling out "My father, they have killed me!" Okonkwo, afraid of being thought weak, drew his machete and cut him down. The curse of Okonkwo's guilt over Ikemefuna hangs over subsequent events; the man at whose funeral Okonkwo inadvertently killed a young clansman was Ezuedu, the same old man who had said to Okonkwo at the time of Ikemefuna's killing, "That boy calls you father. Bear no hand in his death." So ends the first part of the novel. In it we have seen the personal psychological makeup of Okonkwo stemming from his private situation and background: the forces of the past which have combined to make him the man he is.

The second half brings the man into engagement with the specific politico-historical situation of his time. The seven years of Okonkwo's exile coincide with the infiltration of white missionaries and the colonial administration that follows, the flag close behind the cross. When Okonkwo returns to his village, his crime against the clan expiated, he finds that the white man's religion has come and "led many of the people astray"; the white man's government has built a court where he judges cases "in ignorance" of African law, and a store has been opened where for the first time palm oil and kernel have become "things of great price." Okonkwo's son, Nwoye, has become a Christian convert, and disowns his father. Okonkwo, whose exile has cost him his position of authority in the clan—"The clan was like a lizard; if it lost its tail it soon grew another"—regains authority when, on his advice, the church is burned down because an *egwugwu* (an ancestral spirit impersonated by a clansman) has been unmasked and desecrated by a Christian convert. As a result, Okonkwo and five other leaders are summoned by the district commissioner for a discussion and are then arrested and held hostage for a fine to be paid by the villagers. Lashed and humiliated by underlings of his own race while he was in prison, Okonkwo decides that if the clan will not fight to drive the white man away, he will avenge himself alone. At a meeting of the clan, he kills a government messenger who comes to declare the meeting illegal. Before the district commissioner arrives with soldiers to arrest him, he hangs himself.

Again, the train of events falls into a more profoundly meaningful arrangement than that of causality when Achebe's deep understanding of the nature of the white man's impact on Africa is brought to bear on them. Okonkwo kills himself because the authority he takes up again is already a broken thing; there can be no real return to the clan, for him, because the African ethos that held it together has faltered before the attraction-repulsion of the white man's ethos. When Okonkwo kills the government messenger,

> The waiting backcloth jumped into tumultuous life and the meeting was stopped. Okonkwo stood looking at the dead man. He knew that Umofia would not go to war. He knew because they had let the other messengers escape. They had broken into tumult instead of action.

The white man's gods more than the white man's guns—Achebe shows how, above all, these were what no one was armed against, at this stage in Africa's history.

Tumult instead of action: *No Longer at Ease,* the title of Achebe's second novel, at once takes up the theme of the era for which the scene was set at the close of *Things Fall Apart. No Longer at Ease* begins in a courtroom in Lagos where Obi Okonkwo (I don't know whether the suggestion is that he is a later generation of the dead Okonkwo's family) is on trial for taking bribes. The time is still pre–Nigerian independence. Obi is a been-to, a civil servant educated in England, personable, with a taste for poetry and Scotch, and a car. Friends, white administrators—all discuss his downfall: "Everyone wondered why." The book explores the irony of the statement, working back to it through the conflict of social pressures that have made this courtroom almost a predestination for young Obi. When he returned from England, full of enthusiasm for the new Africa his generation is going to build, and determined to set an example of dedication, honesty, and disinterest in the Africanized civil service, he was at once burdened with two incompatible sets of obligations: on the one hand, to pay back to his village the money advanced for his overseas education and the necessity to assist his family; on the other, to live in a European style befitting his position as a civil servant. With a terse ironic touch, Achebe places him not between some sweeping abstraction of "natural" forces of past and future, but between social stresses, as he extends himself docilely on the rack of the bourgeois values his society has taken over from the white man, values totally unreal in the economic and social conditions of that society. It is not that Obi cannot do his work efficiently, but that he accepts the necessity for the trappings of a European bourgeois life that, during a European administration, went along with it. Even the obligation to support his family is not measured in accordance with their actual needs, but with what is thought to befit the family of a man who lives according to European white-collar values.

In his third novel, *Arrow of God,* Achebe turns back to the early colonial era, predating that of *Things Fall Apart.* There are similarities between the first and the third; but, in the first, the conflict between the white man and Africa is overt, whereas in the third, African confidence is still unshaken and the African ethos intact, a positive value not yet brought into question by others. It is significant that whereas Okonkwo loses his son as a convert to Christianity, Ezeulu in *Arrow of God* sends *his* son to the mission school in cold calculation that it is useful and necessary to acquire the white man's magic—his skills. Although the threat of the white man's presence hangs over these people, they have not yet realized that they could ever be anything but masters of their own destiny. In *Things Fall Apart,* Achebe's purpose was to show traditional life disintegrating; in *Arrow of God* his purpose is above all to reinstate the validity of life *without the white man.* He examines, through the ordinary devices of the psychological novel, the stresses and emotional problems of that life and the social order created to contain them. They are presented in themselves, in the tension of their own order, rather than in conflict with another. Although the actions of colonial administrators precipitate events in the novel, it is the events themselves and the Africans who deal with them who take up the foreground—the white men, prominent in Achebe's other books, this time remain curiously unimportant and remote.

The scene is a complex of villages in eastern Nigeria and the people are Ibo. Ezeulu, chief priest of Ulu, local deity of the Umuaro people, is the protagonist. The central narrative is his double struggle: against rivalry among his own tribesmen, and the incomprehensible demands (scarcely recognized as authority, yet) of the district officers and missionaries. This story line is so richly overlaid with the intrigues, counter-intrigues, ceremonies, customs, feasts, and legends of the Umuaro, not to mention character studies of Ezeulu's wives, children, in-laws, and friends, and the brilliantly observed relations among them all, that it comes as something of a shock, in the last chapter or two, to realize that while this abundance of life has been occupying one's mind, Ezeulu has been moving toward one of those Lear-like destinies of defeat before social change that Achebe understands so well. This novel attempts the complete evocation of African life—not an exoticist exploitation of local color and strange customs, but the total logic of a particular way of life. Only *The Dark Child,* an autobiographical novel by the French African writer Camara Laye, can compare with it, and then only as an exquisite detail can be compared with the superbly realized complete canvas. For Achebe has succeeded superbly, even though he has perhaps not solved all the technical problems of fitting this particular theme into the form of the conventional modern novel.

In his latest novel, *A Man of the People,* he turns to comic irony as the best approach to the theme of political corruption in an independent African state—and he is almost the only English-writing African able to use it. Again, so far, one has to look to French African writers for comparison—the rather clumsy satire of Mongo Beti's attack on the Catholic Church in *King Lazarus,* and the immensely stylish, sophisticated bite of Ferdinand Oyono's *Houseboy,* written in the form of a diary which records the servant's-eye view of the private life and loves of the white master race.

James Ngugi of Kenya is another novelist who attempts important African themes on a scale of complexity and depth, although he does not always manage to bring them off with the skill of an Achebe. He attempts to relate the African past—not just historical but also mythological—to the present-day life of the Gikuyu people. The period of his novel, *The River Between,* is immediately pre-Mau-Mau—or pre-Kiama, to give the movement its proper name. The approach is that of an exploration of the background of social and historical forces that led to the formation of a liberation movement. The novel begins with a scene setting in which the mythological origin of the Gikuyu—their Adam and Eve story—is invoked, and the prophecy of an ancient Tikuyu seer is recalled: "There shall come a people with clothes like butterflies." Now they have come; the familiar struggle is on between the clanspeople who remain within tribal disciplines and the white missionaries and their black converts. The young boy Waiyuki, like Ezeulu's son in *Arrow of God,* goes to the mission school to learn the secrets of the white man; but for Waiyuki this is seen as part of the fulfillment of a political destiny. His father is a descendant of the seer and believes that his son is the chosen one whom it was also predicted would come from the hills to save the Gikuyu. The feud between the mission and the clan finds its martyr in Muthoni, daughter of the convert pastor, Joshua. The issue is, not surprisingly, her circumcision—white condemnation of female circumcision coming second only to the settler appropriation of the White Highlands in the canon of Gikuyu resentment of colonial rule. Muthoni is a devout Christian, but she cannot accept the Christian edict against a rite without which she will not belong, in the true sense, to her people. She says "I want to be a woman made beautiful in the manner of the tribe." Waiyuki realizes that Muthoni "had the courage to attempt a reconciliation of the many forces that wanted to control her" from the tribal past and the westernized future. She dies of the operation: to the tribe, a saint; to the mission, a pagan punished for her sins. Waiyuki, while he follows his father's admonition to remain true to his people and the ancient rites, becomes a teacher and believes that the salvation of the people before the threat of annihilation by the white man's ethos lies in western education, the organization of the Tikuyu independent schools movement. He joins the Kiama at its inception, when it is chiefly a society to keep Gikuyu cultural traditions alive, but resigns when it takes on a more militant character, putting off the political mission that he sees is necessary: to unite the people, both Christian and tribal, in a common purpose of liberation from white rule. Later he rejoins the Kiama but fails to commit himself fully to leadership. Finally, he is expelled when he goes to warn the mission of an impending attack by the Kiama. The conflict is now between Waiyuki and the tribe; like other saviors before him he is threatened with crucifixion at the hands of those he has come to save. He understands at last that no evasion is possible—"the new awareness of the people wanted expression at a political level," and no other would do.

This overlong and clumsy novel does analyze with considerable insight the spiritual conflict between the values of tribal life and those imposed by white conquest. Ngugi creates a world-historical figure. The man who seeks to go beyond the either-or and believes that a new synthesis is necessary if Africa is to take her place in the modern world becomes a victim of the force of nationalism. Waiyuki is seen as a failure because he cannot fulfill the demands of his time; Ngugi understands the forces of that time and places him squarely in it.

A Grain of Wheat, James Ngugi's latest novel, is an extremely interesting piece of work because it brings a new theme to African literature—the effects on a people of the changes brought about in themselves by the demands of a bloody and bitter struggle for independence. How fit is one for peace, when one has made revolution one's life? Set in the immediate post-Mau-Mau period, the novel looks back to the personal tragedies of a number of people who were active in Mau-Mau, and examines how the experience now shapes their lives. In the uneasy peace, they have to come to terms with one another, but their relationships are determined by the experience that has put all human relationships through the test of fire—the guerilla revolution itself. Here are the wild-looking bearded men who lived in the Aberdares for years, emerging after the revolution with almost all their instincts for normal life lost; brave men half-broken by the experience; and men accepted as brave men who must live the rest of their lives with the secret knowledge that they were traitors. Mugo, a local small farmer, is such a man. He has betrayed a fellow Gikuyu to the British; as a result of various events which enmesh him in the sense of his own guilt, he brings his own world crashing down around his head by confession, and the words of one of the Mau-Mau veterans who are his judges at a private trial sum up the light in which Ngugi presents him: "Your deeds alone will condemn you. No one will ever escape from his own actions." It is the measure of James Ngugi's development as a writer that none of the protagonists in this novel is marred by the pseudo nobility of some of the characters in his earlier work, and yet he succeeds in placing the so-called Mau-Mau movement in the historical, political, and sociological context of the African continental revolution. What the white world perhaps still thinks of as a reversion to primitive savagery (as opposed, no doubt, to civilized savagery in Nazi Germany) is shown to be a guerilla war in which freedom was won, and which brought with its accomplishment a high price for the people who waged it.

Wole Soyinka, another Nigerian, made his name as a poet and Africa's finest playwright. He deals with a postindependence Africa in an

extraordinary first novel, *The Interpreters*. Sagoe the journalist, Sekoni
the engineer, Lasunwon the lawyer, Egbo the aristocrat working in the
Foreign Office, Bandele the academic—these are the friends that the
painter Kola is using as models for the pantheon of Nigerian gods in
an ambitious canvas. These contemporary Africans are interpreting,
through their lives, modern Africa, and the painter is interpreting the old
godhead anew, through them. These men are western-educated, but
they are certainly not been-tos—far from being precariously extended
between two worlds (African life and the cities of Europe), they have
reached the synthesis of both which many Africans writing before
Soyinka have seen as the ideal solution to the problem of modern African
identity. But it is a critical synthesis: it turns out that the spiritual inade-
quacies of both worlds become clear to those who, at long last, have
come into the heritage of the two as one. The journalist Sagoe's
scatological philosophy of Voidancy ("the most individual function of
man")—a lavatory philosophy with the smallest room in the house as its
temple of meditation—is a send-up of negritude along with the hairsplit-
ting of orthodoxy and revisionism in the fad philosophies of East and
West. Sekoni, the engineer, has a nervous breakdown (the first one I've
come across in African writing) when a power station he has built is
never used because of some piece of political finaglery. Dr. Faseyi has
problems with his English wife, not because she is not acceptable to his
family, but because she forgets her white gloves and asks for palm wine
instead of a cocktail at an embassy reception, behaving, he says, "like a
bush-Cockney." Egbo, taking his friends on a visit to his ancestral home,
where his family is still a great one, casts a cold eye on both his grandfather's feudal dignity and his own sycophantic life at the Foreign Office:
"What is my grandfather but a glorified bandit? Only that doesn't help
either. Sooner a glorified bandit than a loudmouthed slave." And Sagoe,
watching a Lagos crowd in pursuit of a wretched young pickpocket, says
to himself, "Run, you little thief, or the bigger thieves will pass a law
against your existence as a menace to society. . . . run from the same
crowd which will reform tomorrow and cheer the larger thief returning
from his twentieth Economic Mission, and pluck his train from the mud,
dogwise, in its teeth."

Nothing is what it seemed—what it seemed it would be before
African emancipation; even the prophet of a new Christian sect in Lagos,
a Lazarus claiming to have risen from the dead, turns out to have as his
disciples a gang of thieves. Does Soyinka see him as the symbol of the

new African society? Perhaps. But this magnificent novel, with its poet's command of the torrents of language, its wit both fiery and laconic, is not defeatist. One cannot do justice to its complexity in a brief summary and discussion; but it is significant that episodes most meaningful—whether as fulfillment or disillusion—to the protagonists are often those rooted in Africanness, in the subsoil of the new society.

It is interesting to compare for a moment the total involvement—in both Europe and Africa—of Wole Soyinka's people with the almost total disengagement of Doumbe in a novel called *A Few Nights and Days,* by the Cameroonian Mbella Sonne Dipoko. Doumbe is just another one of the deracinated young everywhere, moving through the cafés, dance halls, and beds of Paris. To him, the moment, privately tangible, is all that matters; so that one might take him as an example of the African depersonalized by the West. In traditional African societies, the welfare of the tribe is the concept of ultimate concern, and the constant presence of the spirits of the ancestors, influencing daily life, makes the western division of life into secular and spiritual a meaningless concept. Soyinka's sophisticated protagonists are fully engaged in attempting to interpret this concept in modern terms.

Ezekiel Mphahlele, the South African writer, maintains that the cultured elite of black Africa is becoming middle-class because the diplomas of its members give them access to positions of responsibility, whereas in South Africa the Negro intellectual is still a member of the proletariat because racial segregation prevents his obtaining white-collar jobs and privileges reserved for whites. This applies to African literature and writers, too, of course; he implies that there is no proletarian literature in black Africa, only in South Africa. If he has in mind an urban proletariat, what he says is true; apart from Cyprian Ekwensi's *Jagua Nana,* the story of a Nigerian prostitute, and perhaps one or two others, the literature of black Africa, where it deals with urban life, deals with the African middle class. But consider novels dealing with rural life, such as John Munonye's *The Only Son,* Ekwensi's *Burning Grass,* Ghanaian S. A. Konadu's *A Woman in Her Prime,* and James Ngugi's novels as well as Achebe's *Things Fall Apart* and *Arrow of God*—if subject and theme, and not the manner of life of the author, are the criteria, then surely this is the literature of an agrarian proletariat?

Apart from a very few notable exceptions (Mofolo's *Chaka,* Abrahams's historical novel, *Wild Conquest)* imaginative African writing in South Africa is overwhelmingly a proletarian literature in a society where color and class are identified. It ranges from Peter Abrahams's countryman-comes-to-town story, *Mine Boy,* with its view of the violent baptism of a mineworker into city life seen through the saving grace of individuals and individual racial attitudes, to Alex La Guma's *A Walk in the Night,* in which the debasement of life on the wrong side of the color bar hangs a pall of degradation over every human activity, so that every relationship is demeaned in the generalization of an overwhelming inhumanity: the color bar itself. Alex La Guma's protagonists in District Six do not talk about inequality; they bear its weals. In this novel, Michael Adonis is a colored boy who has just lost his job in a society where his ambitions are limited by job reservations and his security as a worker is not ensured by a trade union. He wanders the streets around his Cape Town tenement room, and in an atmosphere of cheap wine, sex, and the meaningless aggression of frustrated human beings, unintentionally kills a decrepit old white man who has sunk too low for acceptance among whites. Adonis's moral dissolution culminates when he lets his friend, Willieboy, be blamed for the crime, while Adonis himself joins a gang of thugs. In his short stories, Alex La Guma shows the same ability to convey the sight, sound, and smell of poverty and misery, so that the flesh-and-blood meaning of the color bar becomes a shocking, sensuous impact. His stories are set in prisons, cheap cafés, backyards, yet eschew the cliché situations of apartheid—the confrontations of black and white in the context of the immorality act or liquor raids, which are done to death by lesser writers. He is able to make a subtle piece of social comment, in his slight story "Nocturne," out of a colored delinquent attracted upstairs into a white house by the sound of music he has never heard before. James Matthews, in the same story collection, *Quartet,* shows the other face of deprivation in a brilliantly observed story, "The Portable Radio," in which the black man's desire for material possessions, cynically fostered across the color bar by the white man, becomes yet another fake foisted upon the black man in place of the self-respect discrimination denies him. Both these stories convey more about the particular social situation in which they occur than the too obvious allegory of a story like Richard Rive's version of the nativity in color bar dress, with a white village hotel owner, and Mary and Joseph as black laborers. When James Matthews deals with political action, as in his bus boycott story "Azikwela" ("We Will Not Ride"), he shows not generalized heroic or saintly figures, but ordinary, frightened men, driven to find themselves through experiences they half shrink from, tempted to prefer deprived life to the danger of risking what little they have in the hope of attaining something better, coming slowly to the discovery that it is the intangibles, a sense of one's innate dignity and an identification with the hopes of one's fellows, which become both means and end, and give one the courage to act. Throughout South African black literature— in the autobiographical writings of Mphahlele and Lewis Nkosi, Bloke Modisane, and others, as well as in fiction—it is these protagonists and these qualities that are taken to represent the only true values for a dispossessed proletariat.

What are the most striking features of the way Africa sees itself and its relation to the rest of the world, emerging from African literature in English? Well, to begin with, some attitudes that are likely to be surprising to the white world. The way Africa sees the role of Christianity in Africa's history, for example. The general view of Christianity is as intrinsically alien and destructive. Whether Christian values did or did not offer any spiritual advance on those of African religions is not seen as the issue; the church is evil because it lures the people away from their own gods. When the missionaries brought the gospel to Africa, so far as traditional African society was concerned they were the devil's disciples: to be a convert was to be damned, not saved—an attitude that sets on its head the traditional white view of Christianity, leading the dark continent into the light. Well, one's own god is always the true one; the other man's is the pagan idol. Of course, one also sees how the African view of Christianity was conditioned first by the slave trade, when certain bishops were zealous in baptizing slaves before they were shipped off, and then later—when missionaries like Livingstone had influenced the white world to outlaw slavery, and had brought white administrators in their train instead—by resentment against the interlopers for whom the white man's religion had opened the way. On the other hand, where Islam enters African literature it is not presented as a foreign religion at all, so easily, it seems, it was assimilated. And the fact that Arabs bought and sold Africans both before the whites began and after the whites had ceased to do so brings no trace of resentment into acceptance of the Arab's Mohammedanism. What is striking is the religious fatalism that pervades the protagonists in novels about arabized Africans—Ekwensi's *Burning Grass,* for example—and the submissiveness of the woman portrayed, in contrast with the vigor and initiative of those remarkable women who often dominate fiction about societies which still worship their ancestors.

The African view of white colonial administrators—apart from the missionaries, Africa's entire experience of the white world for several decades—is seen to change, from the monstrous bad-man figures of some African writers, through the figures of fun drawn by others, to the picture being presented in postindependence literature of the white administrator as a man who, although he may have had a genuine wish to be useful in Africa, an integrity of purpose fully granted, is completely unable to make real contact with African life. It is as if the man who for so long claimed to "know the African" can now never hope to get to know him in any meaningful way. As for the white liberal, in the main he or she appears in African fiction in the role summed up by the South African political thinker, Majeke, as "conciliator between the oppressor and the oppressed" (Nosipho Majeke, "The Role of the Missionaries in Conquest"). A notable exception is Lois, the Englishwoman in Peter Abrahams's *Wreath for Udomo;* he makes a heroine of her.

But then writing from black South Africa is different from that of any other part of the continent. As Wole Soyinka said recently, "the experience of the South African writer is approached by that of other Africans only remotely by the experience of colonial repression." The difference in experience is reflected in the picture of the African that emerges from South African black literature, compared with that of the rest of the English-writing continent. It is as a dispossessed proletariat that the Africans emerge in black South African literature, a people struggling under the triple burden of industrialization, color, and class discrimination, in a capitalist economy which orders their lives as if they were still living in a feudal age. It is as a people dealing with the problems of power that the rest are shown, exercising the right even to misgovern themselves and struggling not to live an anachronism, but to reestablish the African past as something contiguous with the drastic, profound, and necessary change of the present.

What main trend does African English literature show in its development? George Lukacs, the Hungarian philosopher and one of the two or three important literary critics of our time, discerns three main trends in modern world literature in his *The Meaning of Contemporary Realism:* first, the literature of the avant-garde—experimental modernism from Kafka and Joyce to Beckett and Faulkner, which he condemns for its subjectivism, its static view of the human condition, its dissolution of character, its obsession with pathological states and its lack of a sense of history; and second, socialist realism, which he criticizes for its oversimplification, its failure to see the contradictions in the everyday life of society, and its view of history—"Utopia is already with us" under communism—a view he finds no less static than that of the western avant-garde. He contrasts with these two systems of artistic dogmatism the trend of critical realism—work in which the social changes that characterize our era are most truly reflected, character is not sacrificed to artistic pattern, the human condition is understood dynamically, in a historical context, and the pathological aspects of modern life are placed in a critical perspective. George Lukacs sees the critical realists as the true heirs, through writers such as Thomas Mann and Conrad, of the great realists of the nineteenth century—Balzac, Stendhal, and Tolstoy—and critical realism as not only the link with the great literature of the past, but also the literature that points to the future. There seems to me no doubt that African English literature's best writers are critical realists, and that this is the direction in which African literature is developing.

The Practical Critic:
A Personal View

Theodore Solotaroff

The invitation to give this lecture is the most gratifying one I've ever received, for at this very moment one of my longer-standing fantasies is being fulfilled. The fantasy began during one of the four afternoons I sat in Rackham—my short stories once again having gone down to defeat—and consoled myself with the thought that someday I would show them. Someday, the Hopwood Committee would be saying among themselves, "My God, how could Solotaroff have written those tremendous novels and not have won even a minor award in fiction when he was here?" And so, to make amends, I would be invited to give the Hopwood lecture, and back I would come to Ann Arbor in modest triumph, my suitcase full of crow. Well, it didn't quite work out like that. But here I am anyway. Though I'm about ten years behind the timetable I'd set and have made the journey not along the high road of fiction but the low one of literary journalism, my vanity is well content and advises me not to quibble.

In the Hopwood lecture that I would compose during those years after leaving Ann Arbor and living in Greenwich Village and other lonely places, I would always find time to say a few words in consolation to my fellow losers who would be sitting in the audience. In fact, as those years dragged on and the Hopwood judges were joined by a lengthening line of magazine editors, my fellow losers became exceedingly real to me: more real than I was to myself, since in my fantasy lecture I was transformed into a winner, a state that was very pleasant but not very real. By the same token, my tremendous novels still being unwritten, my only basis for being there in my fantasy as a writer was my growing pile of rejection slips. So my thoughts turned easily to the sweet uses of adversity and to those who most needed to be reminded of them.

All of which, of course, was a bit crazy: a kind of vain (in both senses of the word) and glum effort to rise above the mire of rejection.

"Fame is the spur," as Milton said, but still one needs a horse: otherwise there's not much to kick but yourself. There was lots of future glory for me in writing fiction but not much present substance or energy, for reasons which I've already written about ("Silence, Exile, and Cunning," *New American Review* 8 [January, 1969]: 201–19) and will spare you this evening. Instead, I'd like to talk a bit about why I went into literary journalism, or practical criticism, why it provided me with a horse of sorts, or, to put it less metaphorically, a positive motive for writing. Perhaps you plan to stay away from criticism like the plague, in which case you may want to set your mind for forty-five minutes from now, when I finally get out of the way of the awards, and drift off into composing your own future Hopwood lecture. But perhaps I may say something, sooner or later, that applies to your situation too, for all forms of writing share a certain identity as physical and metaphysical labor: like this lecture, each is a bridge of words being led across an abyss of doubt.

One of the courses I took at Michigan was called "Practical Criticism." I think I was a junior at the time, and know that I was full of newfangled complexities, a kind of New Critic in training, an ingenious reader between the lines, where all of the ironies and paradoxes and symbols were hidden from common view. Reading between the lines also meant between one's actual gut responses, but armed with the magical lamp of ambiguity one forged on into the darkness. I'm not putting down the New Criticism, which has become kind of a mug's game—the standard form of parricide among critics of my generation—I'm merely saying that it was the way I found to be pretentious, of which each generation has its own modes. Ten years before, I would no doubt have come on like a Marxist, twenty years later, perhaps, as a wild and woolly trasher of literature, or a stoned farmer, or a media freak, or all rolled into one. Anyway, I took this course in Practical Criticism because I was getting out of my depth and not a little screwed up. A few months before, I'd been asked to write a review for the *Michigan Daily,* of a collection of stories by William Carlos Williams. I had given it the big treatment, as though Williams was sort of like Borges (he was really like an American Chekhov—all eyes and heart), and the review was rejected. Very put out, I took it to my friend Herbert Barrows, who read it and said he felt like he had been hanging by his suspenders for two minutes. So since he was teaching Practical Criticism I decided to take it.

It was a swell course, or rather, class, or better, group: that is to say, a course that became a kind of little community that assembled three hours a week so that we could all learn from each other. At first, Herbert would read us a story or poem, and we would jot down what struck us as significant. The first few times I was left at the post in a kind of panic. I could barely make out the lines on one reading: how was I supposed to read between them? This, of course, was the point of the exercise, which had to do not with ingenuity but with a kind of primary responsiveness, known as paying attention, and with letting a central impression grow inside you, and with articulating it.

Clearly, I had a lot to learn, beginning with the distinction between having an impression and making one. The pretender critic (same root as pretentious) in myself didn't have impressions: that was to be impressionistic, which was the last thing a New Critic could afford to be in his pursuit of order and complexity. But someone with my name had better begin to have some impressions, I realized, if he was to stop handing in this desperate gibberish.

As I said, I had a lot of help from our group. I remember one student in particular who almost regularly came up with an amazingly sharp and interesting response. He seemed older than most of us, and was very quiet, and wore a hearing aid, which I thought might be really a secret miniature tape recorder by which he would play back to himself what the rest of us had heard only once and were stumbling to remember. But, as I began to see, his secret advantage lay elsewhere. Instead of groping about to describe and judge the poem or story—"This poem is about X; what I liked about it was Y," and so forth—he would find an image which, as he deftly developed it, characterized the work and stated its appeal in such a way that it came back from his mind as freshly and distinctively as it had entered. I remember his speaking of a poem by Frost or Lawrence as being like a patch of ocean where two mighty warships had fought and gone down, leaving a single empty lifeboat floating on the surface. So I began to see that practical criticism was not only trusting your own impressions but also using your imagination to take the measure of a work and to locate it in the world of experience.

All of which, as time went on, was like being let off a leash, one's mind running free among its natural interests and with its natural energy. Or, to put it another way, by making criticism practical, Herbert brought it level with one's taste and experience rather than setting it on a higher, more abstract plane. Or, to put it a third way, he brought literature back to the reasons I'd had for being interested in it in the first place. The course didn't make me into a practical critic or even make me desire to become one, but it did help to straighten me out a bit and planted certain seeds that were to crop up later.

My second encounter with practical criticism came about six years later and also took place in a classroom. By then I had pretty well given up writing fiction, was now a graduate student at the University of Chicago, and had just begun to teach composition and a literature course at a two-year college called Indiana University Calumet Center. It was located in East Chicago, Indiana, which was known as "The Workbench of America," and most of my students worked in local oil refineries and steel mills. The center was one grim brick building just off Route 12, a major trucking route, and as the diesels roared by outside, we talked about comma faults and dangling modifiers and other "gross illiteracies," and about such immediately relevant writers as Homer, Plato, Dante, and Chaucer.

For a time, we were miles apart—I with my sense of being in an academic slum, my Flaubertian notion of style and my Aristotelean approach to structure, which I was learning at Chicago and, faute de mieux, teaching at East Chicago; my students, half-awake after eight hours of tending an open hearth furnace or a catalyst cracker and otherwise puzzled, intimidated, or hunched defensively in their leather jackets, staring at their copy of *The Agamemnon* as though it were still in the original Greek. I struggled and groped, cajoled and bitched; none of it did much good.

In one of my composition courses was a boy named John Dovitch. Dovitch was from Calumet City, another garden spot, whose main industry was vice, and he looked like he had grown up on the street corners there: the DA haircut, the motorcycle boots, the swagger. He was small and tough and smart as a whip. He liked to sit in the front and give me the fish-eye, and every so often he would contribute to the discussion:

"What's the matter with repeating a word?"
"It makes your writing monotonous."
"But that other word was two sentences back."
"Well, it's still not good style."
"Who says so? I mean besides you?"
"It's not a question of who says so. It's a question of varying your word choice, of finding the precise word."

"I read a story by this guy Hemingway and he repeats himself all the time."

"That's different. . . . He does it for an effect."

"Yeah . . . so?"

And so on and so forth. Dovitch's next theme was sure to be full of repetitions, just as it was sure to be full of comma faults and dangling modifiers and misspellings—taunting me. The only problem was that he could write. He wrote a composition on the gang he'd belonged to that could have been written by Nelson Algren. I didn't know what to do, so I gave him an A for content and a D—for mechanics. He came up to see me after class.

"You want to know about your grade," I said, steeling myself.

"It's pretty screwy, but what I want to know is where you're from."

"Chicago."

"Yeah, I know that. You're one of those graduate students. I mean where did you grow up?"

"Elizabeth, New Jersey."

"That's sort of like around here."

"That's right," I said, "lots of refineries."

"Then why do you talk like you grew up at Harvard?"

I took that one home with me. After a good deal of brooding, I decided that he was telling me to wise up. To realize where I was. Why the airs and graces? Mainly because I was so wrapped up in teaching composition and literature as though I were selling Omega watches at Woolworth's that I hadn't realized that I was teaching persons. And meanwhile there was a whole side of me that knew these persons, had gone to high school with them, buddied with them in the Navy, worked with them in restaurants. And clearly the burden of relating to them was on me, and so was the burden of interest. They were rightly interested in their accounting or lab courses, for through them they might someday have jobs that wouldn't break their backs. But what did using precise transition words or understanding the tragic form have to do for them? What had they to do for me when I had started college, only a little less in the dark than they were, and also bent on moving up in the world?

I make this sound like a moment of truth, but the realities of teaching in East Chicago dawned on me in stages, as I settled into the work

and began to see my way, which was to make use of the common
ground between us and to make it pertain. Instead of teaching grammar,
say, as rules and regulations, I tried to teach it as thought, a kind of rock-
bottom logic. We tried to imagine what the dawn of language was like
and how a grammar came into being as a way of sorting out chaos of
phenomena. Instead of teaching the dicta of correct usage, we played
around with etymologies, giving words their weight and color as ar-
tifacts, placing them in the affairs of men. In the literature course, we
compared Odysseus with Davy Crockett, a big pop-cult hero at the
time, to figure out what an epic hero was. We put together a modern
scenario of *Agamemnon* with Douglas MacArthur as the tragic hero. We
tried to imagine why Socrates wasn't just a sucker to stay in prison and
get executed and why even the laws in East Chicago had something to be
said for them. But this puts the experience too pedagogically. Much of
the time, I simply plunged in, letting a line of inquiry develop of its own
course. I free associated and improvised, stimulated mainly by those
faces in front of me that I wanted to amuse and involve, to wipe the film
of dullness away from their eyes. And of course I was stimulated myself
by all that I was learning by going back to the fundamentals and letting
them fill with useful content.

What did all of this have to do with practical criticism? A good deal,
as I was subsequently to find out. For one thing, I had begun to learn
what an audience was: a group of people who were waiting to be interested, which was within their right. I had also begun to learn what the
terms of the appeal were: that one addressed them as a man among men
rather than as a highly literary type who had just parachuted in from
graduate school. I was also learning that the main problem and opportunity was to be clear: to approach the unfamiliar by means of the familiar, the abstract by the concrete, the concept by means of the example. I
was also learning something about tone: the right one coming from the
natural play of individuality, the wrong one from role playing. Finally, I
was beginning to learn that to make matters interesting you had to first
make them interesting to yourself. That was where imagination came in:
seeing something in another way. As a corollary of this, I was beginning
to understand that the truly interesting was likely to have an element of
risk in it.

Obviously, I didn't reach all of these students, and I learned from
that too. I remember one exam in which I asked which was the more
tragic play: *Agamemnon* or *Oedipus*. Back came my definitions, distinc-

tions, and examples in more or less garbled form. One student told me that the play about the general was more tragic because he was like MacArthur getting bumped off during the San Francisco Parade in 1954, which was very unusual, but the other play by Socrates wasn't very tragic because for someone to kill his father and marry his mother, that happens all the time. So there was no common denominator: you tried to keep a vision of the best possibilities in the class—or audience—and address them. This would also come in handy later.

Meanwhile, there was Dovitch, who turned up the next fall in the second half of the literature course, a little less daunting but still up in the front seat, his skepticism still intact. To what did I owe this privilege of teaching him again, I asked. He told me that I fitted into his schedule. So we went round and round again until one day he stayed behind after class.

> "You've gotten a little smarter," he said.
> "Thank you," I said, "maybe I have."
> "Yeah, you said some interesting things now and then."
> "Maybe you're getting smarter too."
> He shrugged, summoning his truculence.
> "It takes two to communicate," I said.

Or something like that. Anyway, from then on the tension between us diminished; we continued to play each other tcugh but there was a rapport that kept each of us from his form of crapping around. By the time we got to the last two novels, *Crime and Punishment* and *Huckleberry Finn,* I was much more interested in discovering how their two renegades established themselves in his mind than in imposing my own analogies and structure. Once I knew what was reaching him, what was charged for him, we could try to figure out the circuits. I had been trained to work the other way around: find the form and you'll find the power. It was a much tidier way of teaching; there is nothing like the word *structure* to cool out a class. But it was more interesting to teach an alert class, beginning with myself.

The next semester I passed Dovitch on to a friend who was teaching the sophomore literature course. By the end of the year, Dovitch had won a scholarship to Illinois and another to Southern Illinois. He decided to go to Carbondale. "I'd be lost with all those fraternity guys at Champaign," he told me. "I mean, I don't have the right clothes, or table manners." I said that Illinois probably wasn't all fraternities. "Nah, I'm better off with the other hunkies."

Meanwhile, I was still a Ph.D. candidate at Chicago, which was a very different thing from teaching at East Chicago. The main task seemed to be to depersonalize your mind, to sound like a scholar, to write prose that was mostly dull factuality and timidity, as reserved as a corpse or, to quote myself: "I have chosen to continue my discussion of Thoreau's theory of poetry to its more practicable aspects: that is, to the ideas and opinions that appear to bear directly upon what Thoreau presumably wanted to achieve when he sat down to write a poem."

One of the last courses I took was in Contemporary Criticism. It was taught by Norman Maclean, the stylist of the Chicago Critics, a man with a passion for Hemingway as well as Aristotle. There was a five-minute quiz each week; the first was on Croce's *Esthetics:* "What does Croce mean by an 'intuition'?"

So, following my practice of giving them what I thought they wanted to hear, and aping Croce as much as possible, I scribbled down something like, "An intuition, in the Crocean view, partakes of the relational aspect of consciousness . . . " and continued on in that vein.

The next class meeting, Maclean read a few of the answers. "'An intuition is a perception,'" he began and stopped. "That's good," he said. "Right to the point. She puts up a clothesline she can hang the washing on. Listen. . . ." and he read it to the end.

"Now, I want to read another. 'An intuition, in the Crocean view . . . . " He read a few more of my sentences and stopped. "I'm sorry," he said. "I love the English language too much to read this kind of hokum." After a despairing pause, he went on. "Why does a young person want to write like a broken-down philosophy professor in a third-rate teacher's college?"

I didn't know whether to be angry or crestfallen. After all, Croce didn't sound so different. I'd even gotten that "partake" expression from him or his translator. As I was leaving class, Maclean caught my eye and I walked over to him.

"You seem pretty bright," he said, "when you talk in class. But if you don't learn to write clearly by the end of this course, I'm going to flunk you."

It hurt but it was what I needed to be told. Under Maclean's goading and encouragement, and especially under the influence of his teaching that went to the center of a subject like an arrow ("Eliot's criticism is that of a lyric poet, the two main issues being a writer's sensibility and style"), I labored to write as accurately and cleanly as possible. I thought of it as "coming clean," and "going straight," expressions that suggested the true nature of my project. How difficult it was to cut out the crap. And what a relief. For the first time in my life, I found myself writing for someone—a good voice in my head that drew out my better nature and gave it backing. So Chicago and East Chicago began to come together, two tasks connected by a common aspiration.

Two years passed. One summer morning I was sitting in the office I used at the University of Chicago where I had been teaching and was now finishing up my thesis and getting ready to move on. A young man strolled into the room. He was wearing a nice suit and a rep tie and smiling broadly, and it took me a few seconds to recognize him. It was Dovitch. We chatted for a while about what we had been doing and then he told me why he had looked me up. "I'm going to graduate school," he said.

"You don't say."

"Yeah. I'm going to be an English teacher."

As it turned out, my own teaching career ended a few weeks later when I was offered a job at *Commentary*. So I went to New York and became an editor and a literary journalist. I still had a lot to learn but thanks to Dovitch and Maclean, I pretty well knew what my purpose was.

The way I still see it, eleven years later, is that a great many Americans are in a peculiar bind. They've grown up in homes, and communities, and schools which provide little intellectual nourishment and go off to college, mainly because that's where one goes if he can. And there with practically no preparation or basis—except possibly in math and science—they study the liberal arts. And if they are bright and fortunate, sooner or later, they are turned on to one another of these arts, and like Plato's slaves, are led from the cave into the light. And like them are led back again. For once they graduate and go off to Middle America, the mass society and the mass culture take over again, and the deprivations resume, all the more sharply for being made conscious. Or to put it another way, education in America tends to be a brief, discontinuous or else solitary activity.

All of which is perhaps a fifties view. There's now the counterculture. But I wonder where most of its members will be five years from now and how much "greening" they will be achieving. And it may be that my view of college education is also from the fifties. But I wonder if the tremendous demands that students make today on the institution aren't generated partly, at least, by the recognition that these four or five years must be made vital to their lives, for there's not much else in the society that has been or will be.

Be that as it may, it's how I see my work as a practical critic: the opportunity to teach literature in the public forum. This is not the way I would have viewed it if I had taken up criticism twenty years ago. I would have dismissed the reading public as hopelessly shallow and vulgar and tried to write for the Happy Few who subscribed to *Partisan Review*. But having followed the road I have, the notion of fostering an avant-garde has come to seem rather precious and beside the point. (If there is an avant-garde. What I tend to see is a lot of writers, in Richard Howard's phrase, "alone in America.")

I have spoken a lot about the transaction that the practical critic makes with an audience and said almost nothing about his transaction with the books and authors he writes about. Obviously, the claims of the audience are general and those of the writer are specific and pressing, and most of the time one is too embattled with the problems of trying to characterize him justly to worry about how all of these uncertainties and approximations of judgment will be taken. A good review, it seems to me, does three things—it describes a book, judges it, and identifies a context, the place it may occupy in contemporary consciousness. I used to think that the last was more crucial than I do now: i.e., gauging the book's relevance to the general reader. Mostly that can be left to him to figure out, once the writer and the book are placed against the ground of one's own interest in them. The rest is often just sniffing the zeitgeist, which grows wearisome to everyone and deflects attention from the task, which hasn't changed since Matthew Arnold defined it, as seeing the object as it truly is.

But if your primary obligation as a practical critic is to the writer and his work, he is not the audience you write for. You aren't there to cheer him up or put him down or set him straight. You're there to listen and respond and to develop your image of the book, the actual impressions it has made on you, into a description and an inquiry; that is to say, a learning process of your own. Unless you're learning something yourself as you write, the chances are that you are merely going through the motions of literary journalism and plodding along one of the ruts in your mind. That is why it is best to risk a line of inquiry that starts in uncertainties rather than assurances, to go off the deep end rather than the shallow. The main thing is to be clear, but an easily won clarity is likely to be superficial.

So you yourself make up the beginning of your audience. But unless you get a great deal of satisfaction out of talking to yourself, you need others—not many, a few good faces and voices will do. By now, the face I see is of no one I know. He belongs to my generation and has come to ideas the hard way and on his own; he is in this society but not quite of it, his face being sensitive as well as practical; he likes books but is not, strictly speaking, literary. He is keenly conscious of the "scrimmage of appetites" in America, and he is stimulated by alternative possibilities. He is fundamentally straight and positive, is put off by posturing, malice, and bad faith. Several people I've mentioned have contributed to this composite, and I've also encountered him as an apple grower, a psychoanalyst, a novelist, and as the head of a steel construction company. He keeps me company as a practical critic and keeps me going.

Moonshine and Sunny Beams: Ruminations on *A Midsummer Night's Dream*

W. D. Snodgrass

"A Midsummer Night's Dream!" exclaims one early editor. "Who is the dreamer? The poet, any of the characters of the drama, or the spectators?"

Well carped, critic! Let's go on from there. Not only who is dreaming; who gets dreamed? Surely a dream, or a play, must be "about" someone. In this dream, we find four separate groups of characters derived from different periods of history, far-flung areas of the world, diverse literary and mythological backgrounds, opposed levels of reality. Can we decide which group is central to the play's concern? Mightn't we even ask for a central character?

And is it really too much to ask what the dream means? What most critics tell us about this play would apply to the dreariest hackwork. No one would perform a play that means so little—neither Peter Brook, the Comédie Française, nor Podunk Junior High. Yet all those troupes have been performing this airy flummery for 350 years and with almost unmitigated success. What has this play been imparting to so many actors, so many audiences, all these years?

Until Jan Kott came along and said some really interesting things about this play, it seemed almost impossible to give a performance lacking in all interest. Should we not question this play's secret workings, lest some well-meaning director snap up our speculations, turn them into overt and conscious motifs for his production, and ruin the thing once and for all?

The Rulers

Scholars tell us that *A Midsummer Night's Dream* was probably first written and produced to celebrate a wedding in the British royal family. If there is little hard evidence for that, it does seem to fit our feeling about the play. Its first scene opens on just such a royal pair, Theseus of Athens and Hippolyta of the Amazons, planning their own marriage. And if marriage implies a joining of opposites, Theseus and Hippolyta have assuredly been opposed:

> Hippolyta, I wooed thee with my sword
> And won thy love doing thee injuries;
> But I will wed thee in another key
> With pomp, with triumph, and with revelling.

Modern practice, of course, has changed all that. To have the fighting all settled before the wedding must have left them little to look forward to; we'd be bored.

And if that seems old-fashioned, it seems downright quaint for Theseus and Hippolyta, each of whom has quite a past, to forgo sex until after the ceremony. We moderns have reversed that, too. If we fail to stay chaste before the wedding, we frequently make up for that afterward.

Still, in most things, Theseus seems old-fashioned. He governs by right of conquest and by ability to rule. No wonder he seems half-mythical! He even obeys the laws he enforces on his subjects. No sooner has he announced his wedding plans and his determination to restrain his lusts until that time, than in rushes Egeus with his daughter Hermia, to accuse her and her two suitors of a willful desire to break Athens's marriage laws. Most of us sympathize with Hermia, yet we see a justice in Theseus's rule. Suppose we thought he and Hippolyta were slipping off now and then to make out on the sly?

All the better then, if Theseus is upright as well as erect; restraint is valuable, especially when it channels great force:

> . . . . but oh, methinks how slow
> This old moon wanes; she lingers my desires
> Like to a step-dame, or a dowager,
> Long withering out a young man's revenue

His desires for Hippolyta, then, are strong; yet his telling of them sounds strangely rancorous. Hippolyta's reply seems almost threatening:

> Four days will quickly steep themselves in night
> Four nights will quickly dream away the time;
> And then the moon, like to a silver bow

New bent in heaven, shall behold the night
Of our solemnities.

Even lusts so high-strung needn't be imaged as weaponry. Both rulers
seem to have slipped back into recollections of that war between them
which we had hoped was finished.

Who are these two we have come together to join? Surely, Theseus
stands for the model ruler and male, the man of conquest as of conquests,
who is yet capable of noble commitment. If his rule is just and central, so
is reason's rule in him. When he later comes to the forest, his hounds
baying musically, he gives an admirable picture of the animal forces
trained and held in harmonious order. The hunter's bow (which elsewhere stood for Diana's chastity or for sexual attack) now is turned to
useful sport. Such controlled sport, such harmony, he must induce in
himself as in the lovers, those who look to him as their authority.

Hippolyta? She is an Amazon. Spenser's Radigund makes her role
clear enough: the warrior woman whose single aim is to defeat and
enslave the male. As the story goes, all Amazons cut off one breast lest it
be injured by the bowstring—that is, partly defeminized themselves to
better fight the male. Still, we imagine Amazons were thoroughly democratic; would as readily subject the male to surgery. So the sexes would
be more equal, yet the woman would rule. Hippolyta, seen here in
defeat, has none of these fiercer qualities. True, she seems to get the last
word in arguments; yet she is both right and uninsistent, an engaging
combination. She carries herself with such grace and dignity that we
wonder if a woman might be as improved by defeat as some men can.

These two, then, have been fierce enemies; it would be a wonder if
no bitterness remained. Their reconciliation, their coming marriage, is
indeed a consummation devoutly to be wished. To them, the present
moon seems a time of drained resources, of grudging tightfistedness.
How shall we reach a new moon of generosity, of free spending and
fulfilled desire—how shall we bring this couple to union? How but by
airing and expiating, owning and healing those age-old grudges, the
wounds of our long war?

Where better to do that than in our dreams—perhaps in just such a
dream as this play? Midsummer Night, after all, was the night when a
girl might dream about her future husband. A Midsummer Night's
dream, then, tells the truth about our love. Dare we ask it not only to
reveal, but also to reconcile us to our love?

The Fairies

OBERON   Ill met by moonlight, proud Titania.

TITANIA   What, jealous Oberon? Fairies, skip hence:
           I have forsworn his bed and company.

OBERON   Tarry, rash wanton; am not I thy lord?

TITANIA   Then I must be thy lady; but I know
           When thou hast stolen away from fairy land,
           And in the shape of Corin sat all day,
           Playing on pipes of corn, and versing love
           To amorous Phillida.

Now *that* has a good modern sound—nothing restrained about the fairies' rage or their lust. Like Theseus and Hippolyta, they are chaste; theirs, however, is that spiteful abstinence many of us have found in marriage. These fairies fully display and act out those passions which compel all the couples—though Theseus tries to control them, though the lovers try to disguise them. The fairies could almost be a negative and all the other couples its various positive prints.

The fairies' war echoes another of the problems plaguing Theseus, not only the struggle for dominance between the sexes but also that between parents and children. He has just heard Egeus's claim that his daughter, Hermia, is his property to give in marriage as he wills. The fairies, too, are struggling for ownership of a child—a "little changeling boy" each wants as a page and follower.

Faced by such problems, Theseus defeated his woman in open conflict; Oberon uses subtlety, magic, stealth. It hardly seems cricket (even among lovers) to win the war by putting your woman to bed with the most bestial creature available:

Be it ounce, or cat, or bear,
Pard, or boar with bristled hair,
In thy eye that shall appear,
When thou wak'st, it is thy dear.
Wake when something vile is near.

Bottom may not be all *that* vile; most wives would scarcely thank their husbands for so asinine a lover. Yet, the very queen of fairies, once her vision has cleared, does almost thank Oberon. How can her humiliation result, not in a deeper rejection of Oberon, but in acceptance? Can he, like Theseus, win his woman's love doing her injuries? Perhaps the ferocity of his strategy flatters her—he must love her very much to fight so fiercely. Or persuades her to surrender quickly before he does *worse*. More likely it shows her something about her own desires and her rejection of her lord—that she would be willingly embowered only with a man who could be made an ass. Or that her love is a love of the ass.

Anyway, Oberon's strategy works; who is to quarrel with success? The fairies' reconciliation is surely no less desirable than is the rulers'—do we imagine any love can be happy while these fairies rage? These are love's divinities, parental figures who have guided both Theseus and Hippolyta through all their past loves and must now assure their permanent union. By their own admission, they have caused the world's present coldness and sterility. The seasons are disordered, disease rampant, the rivers rebellious and uncontained; fields are barren, the folds empty, the flocks dying:

> And this same progeny of evils comes
> From our debate, from our dissension;
> We are their parents and original.

In the normal rounds of his practical business, Theseus encounters most of the other characters of the play. He judges and helps reconcile the lovers; their wedding becomes part of his. The artisans devise their play just to celebrate that same marriage. For all his hard-nosed narrow-mindedness, he seems a splendidly capable ruler; we expect him to be a good husband. Moreover he has had a considerable hand in straightening out the lovers, his subjects. On the one hand, he has made it clear to Hermia that he will maintain the laws of Athens; on the other, he has drawn both Egeus and Demetrius aside for "private schooling" in matters that concern them closely. We have seen that his rule is firm and effective.

Yet Theseus never meets the fairies, those who have guided his past and on whom his future totally depends. How strange that he should not even believe in forces which he has somehow successfully enlisted, and without whose help all his reason and power would be useless.

In act 5, Theseus issues various firm pronouncements on the unreality of love and lovers, plays and players, above all fairies:

. . . I never may believe
These antique fables nor these fairy toys.
Lovers and madmen have such seething brains,
Such shaping fantasies, that apprehend
More than cool reason ever comprehends.

No sooner has he left the stage, though, taking his bride to bed, than those same nonexistent fairies enter to bless his marriage and make that bed fruitful. Had their quarrel gone on, not only his bed but his household, his state, his world had been barren and fruitless.

No more than Theseus do we believe in fairies. Yet we see something that he cannot—you had better have them on your side. There is no Oberon. And Titania is his consort.

The Lovers

If you ask the romantic lovers—Hermia and Lysander, Helena and Demetrius—they don't want to rule each other, only to serve each other. "I am your spaniel." If you ask the lovers, they wouldn't think of hurting each other. (There's a fact—they do it without a thought.) If you ask the lovers, they want only to marry.

But who believes a lover? They are as full of passion as the fairies, as full of reason as the rulers. But they use reason not to channel passion, rather to disguise and license it. So they remain willfully chaste, willfully sexual. Yet, being so ready to fool themselves, they seldom fool anyone else:

LYSANDER   Oh, take the sense, sweet, of my innocence.
            Love takes the meaning in love's conference. . . .
            Then by your side no bed-room me deny,
            For lying so, Hermia, I do not lie.

HERMIA   Lysander riddles very prettily; . . .
            But, gentle friend, for love and courtesy
            Lie further off, in human modesty.

At times their speeches have more truth than they yet recognize:

Love looks not with the eyes, but with the mind,
And therefore is winged Cupid painted blind.
Nor hath Love's mind of any judgement taste;

Wings, and no eyes, figure unheedy haste;
And therefore is Love said to be a child,
Because in choice he is so oft beguiled.

The lovers demand to choose love by their own sight, yet they obviously can't see who they are, what they want, or what they are doing. As the play later shows, they are running around lost in a fog. They think they are trying to get married; to us they seem to be doing the exact opposite.

The law will not let Hermia and Lysander marry, so they plan to run away to the home of his widow aunt. (A very moony aunt she seems, "a dowager of great revenue.") No sooner has Hermia joined him in the woods, eager to marry him, than Lysander becomes curiously unable to find that place where marriage will be so easy; within hours he has fallen desperately in love with someone else. Soon, he is plying Helena with all the frantic endearments he once gave Hermia, meantime treating Hermia as hatefully as Demetrius ever did Helena. Throughout the play the truly hurtful things are always said by someone to the person they most love—Titania to Oberon, Lysander to Hermia, Demetrius to Helena. We are told art imitates life.

Where did all these tangles start, these triangles among our four lovers? Apparently when Demetrius, having won Helena, turned from her to Hermia, obtaining her father's permission to marry her. Why did he suddenly desire the scornful Hermia, abandoning the willing Helena? Perhaps just because Helena was willing? Lysander certainly turned against Hermia precisely at the point he could marry her.

Consider the advantages for Demetrius in this "unhappy" unfulfilled love. Imagine saying to your true love:

Hang off, thou cat, thou burr! Vile thing, let loose
Or I will shake thee from me like a serpent!

and getting this answer:

Why are you grown so rude? What change is this?
Sweet love . . .

Or better yet, to say:

I do not and I cannot love you

and then get this reply:

And even for that do I love you the more . . .
Use me but as your spaniel, spurn me, strike me,
Neglect me, lose me; only give me leave,
Unworthy as I am to follow you.
What worser place can I beg in your love—
And yet a place of high respect with me,—
Than to be used as you use your dog.

What victory has either Oberon or Theseus compared to that? What has marriage compared to that? Suppose Demetrius won either Hermia or Helena—he would have to live with her. He would have to give up self-pity in being deprived of some imagined love, stop rejecting what love is convenient and available. He would have to become an adult; small wonder both he and Lysander postpone it as long as possible. Meantime, each is deeply indulging himself in injuries to the girl he loves:

LYSANDER   What, should I hurt her, strike her, kill her dead?
            Although I hate her, I'll not harm her so.

HERMIA   What can you do me greater harm than hate?
            Hate me? Wherefore? O me, what news, my love?

That is almost motive enough in itself.

But meantime, both girls are just as agile in preserving their "single blessedness." In the first scene, Helena hears that Hermia and Lysander are about to elope—that she will be relieved of her rival. Instead of bidding them a fond good riddance, she tells Demetrius of their plans:

Then to the wood will he tomorrow night
Pursue her; and for this intelligence,
If I have thanks, it is a dear expense.
But herein mean I to enrich my pain,
To have his sight thither, and back again.

If she ever was as available as Demetrius thought, she must since have learned the pleasures of rejection and abandonment.

Earlier in this scene, she wished she might be translated into Hermia, who is pursued by both men. In the woods, she gets her wish; under Puck's enchantments both men turn gaga over her. How does she respond? By refusing both, starting a quarrel with Hermia, then running away. What else can you do if events threaten to impoverish your pain?

As to Hermia, when both men courted her, she chose the one forbidden. Listening to Egeus's long speech, we cannot quite make out whether Hermia wants Lysander because her father insists on Demetrius, or whether her father insists on Demetrius because she wants Lysander. Both may be true. It's worth noting, though, that in the companion play (I cannot think of them separately) Juliet fell in love with Romeo only just after her father gave her to Paris. That, surely, is part of the reason she fell in love with someone else, especially with an enemy of her family. In this play, we feel that one of Pyramus's greatest attractions is precisely that he is a family enemy and so forbidden to Thisby. As to Hermia's choice between Lysander and Demetrius, everyone concedes there is no difference between them. How does she tell them apart?— ideally they would be played by identical twins. Lysander has only two discernible advantages: he is not available to Hermia, and he gives her a way to oppose her father.

Only occasionally do we have glimpses of the girls' disdain for their lovers. Hermia gives only a hint:

Before the time I did Lysander see,
Seemed Athens as a paradise to me.
O then, what graces in my love do dwell
That he hath turned a heaven unto a hell!

Helena's slam against Demetrius is much nearer the surface:

. . . as he errs, doting on Hermia's eyes,
So I, admiring of his qualities.
Things base and vile, holding no quantity,
Love can transpose to form and dignity.

Except for Hermia's opposition to her father, neither girl shows much desire to directly assault the male. (There will be years and years for that.) On the other hand, before the young men are accepted as husbands, each has proved himself inconstant, trifling, and childish. Perhaps the girls need do nothing to humiliate their lovers; Lysander and Demetrius can be counted on to make asses of themselves.

The rulers then have already fought out their war and wish to be married; the fairies are married and fighting harder than ever. The lovers must keep up the pretense of wanting marriage but are actually doing everything to evade it—at least until they have carried their battle to a point where the final outcome is clearly indicated.

The Craftsmen

Like the lovers, the artisans live in Theseus's world and must seek resolution there; like the lovers, they can reach that only by first withdrawing into Oberon's world. The young lovers now must enter a world of adulthood, marriage, business, reason; in their revulsion, they regress even further into fantasy, childhood, magic. The artisans also go there, apparently sensing that's the place to learn a role, to discover one's part. So develops one of the major structures of the play—the general migration from the sunlit city into the moonlit forest, then back again.

Just as Theseus never had contact with the fairies, the world most comparable to his own, so the lovers have no contact with the artisans, the world that most reflects theirs. True, they watch the craftsmen perform "Pyramus and Thisby." But only after they have married—it is questionable whether they *are* lovers then. In any case that's small contact with a world which sheds such light on theirs.

From the first, "Pyramus and Thisby" has been a mockery of lovers:

FLUTE   (as Thisby) My love! thou art my love, I think.

BOTTOM   (as Pyramus) Think what thou wilt, I am thy lover's
                    grace,
                 And like Limander am I trusty still.

FLUTE   (as Thisby) And I like Helen, till the Fates me kill.

Like the lovers whose names they just echoed (Lysander and Helena), Pyramus and Thisby ran away to meet far from the constraints and divisions of society. There, they found much what the lovers found, much what Romeo and Juliet found—that they are certainly not "trusty still," that they are much more likely to kill themselves than to be killed by Fate. All are like the old joke about the spinster and the hen: "Poor dears, they'd rather die!"

That old sexual pun (among a myriad others) is much in evidence here. The artisans not only rehearse "obscenely and courageously," they perform that way as well. Pyramus picks up Thisby's mantle, bloodied by the lion's mouth, and exclaims:

O wherefore, Nature, didst thou lions frame?
Since lion vile hath here deflowered my dear:
Which is—no, no, which was—the fairest Dame

That lived, that loved, that liked, that looked with cheer.
Come tears, confound:
Out sword, and wound
The pap of Pyramus:
Ay, that left pap,
Where heart doth hop
Thus die I, thus, thus, thus.

Now am I dead,
Now am I fled, . . .

Now die, die, die, die, die.

Demetrius sets out to cap the pun:

No die, but an ace for him; for he is but one.

Then Theseus caps the cap:

With the help of a surgeon he might yet recover, and prove an ass.

We are reminded, of course, of Bottom's earlier transformation. Yet, much as the court mocks the craftsmen's acting, this whole playlet remains a mockery of the hammier performances these lovers just gave with the very substance of their lives.

We are never allowed to forget that the playlet is only a way to pass the time till the lovers may and must bed each other for the first time. By the end of the play, even Hippolyta (who earlier had soothed Theseus's impatience) seems anxious to get on to bed:

I am a-weary of this Moon; would he would change!

THESEUS   . . . in courtesy, in all reason, we must stay the
                time.

The play's purpose is, in part, to make us more eager for marriage and for bed; it does this partly by its mockery of romantic love. At the same time, it helps reveal and expiate our fear of marriage, even of sex itself.

Demetrius calls Snug the Joiner (O sweetly fitting name!):

The very best at a beast, my lord, that e'er I saw.

then says of Bottom and Flute:

A mote will turn the balance, which Pyramus, which Thisby is the better, he for a man, God warrant us, she for a woman, God bless us.

Such ready criticism suggests that he is trying to rise to better performance himself but may be none too sure of his abilities. Still we must not be overcritical ourselves—he has had a courage lacking in Pyramus or Romeo, has come back from the world of fantasy and settled down to live with the woman he loves. No mean feat, that.

Yet it is not only in their playlet that the craftsmen provide an ironic view of love and lovers; they do that far more richly in their forest scenes. There, we watch Puck tangling and untangling the lovers; watch him first transform Bottom into an ass, then, with the same herb that charmed the lovers, put him into the cradle of Titania. Bottom went to the forest when the lovers did, was enchanted by the same magical powers, was released when they were. He of all people has known the quintessential love experience, has been embraced by the queen of love, gone to the very bottom of the world of passion and imagination. And he was an ass. And he is an ass. Watching Titania coo and gurgle over him, we see as nowhere else how

Things base and vile, holding no quantity,
Love can transpose to form and dignity.

In some sense, then, all the lovers have proven an ass in the bower of divinity.

Bottom, above all, has had the power (a very passive power it must be) to reenter the world of the child's, even the baby's, sexuality—the world of Mustardseed and Cobweb, of Mother Squash, Father Peascod, and Baby Peaseblossom. There, without the faintest qualm, he replaces the "King of shadows." If he does not actually cuckold that king (we cannot be sure), it is only because he is more interested in eating. The queen has made every amorous advance to him and he has come back safe and sound to tell of it. Well, not perhaps to tell of it:

Man is but an ass if he go about to expound this dream. . . . Methought I was, and methought I had . . . . I will get Peter Quince to write a ballad of this dream; it shall be called "Bottom's Dream," because it hath no bottom and I will sing it in the latter end of the play, before the Duke.

He never does but the clear implication is that it is this experience which is not only the basic love experience but also the material which must be translated into the work of art, the experience which makes "Pyramus and Thisby" possible. In the play's last act, the artisans bring back to the city their forest experience; there they wield (however awkwardly) the powers of transformation which they must have gathered from the fairies who had transformed them in the woods.

All along, we have seen that the artisans making their play to further Athenian royal wedding clearly image Shakespeare and his company making their play to celebrate an English noble wedding. Who knows better than Shakespeare what goes into the making of a play?

The Firmament

You could scarcely imagine, unless you had looked into the Furness *Variorum,* what energy critics have spent arguing for the centrality of some one or another of these four worlds. The lovers, the fairies, the rulers—each has its partisans heatedly arguing that their candidate holds the central place while the others only revolve around it, reflecting and illuminating its meaning.

No critic (excepting Dr. Gui, whose penetrating and eccentric analysis appears in the *American Imago*) sees the artisans as central. Yet actors and directors often make them so. We surely remember their scenes most vividly—the enchanted Bottom in Titania's bower; the hilarious "Pyramus and Thisby"—and those scenes are often extracted to play separately.

I certainly don't intend to take sides here. The mere existence of the dispute lends force to my view—that none of these worlds is central. As I see it, all four worlds exist only in their balanced relationship to one another. Just as four dancers, or four groups of dancers, might all be part of a larger pattern, each maintaining relation with the others, none more important than the others, our four lovers did, in fact, create just such a dance pattern in their shifting and alternating triangulations. Or to return to the astronomical figure, the play's firmament holds four worlds, one of which has created its own moon—the play within the play. These four worlds form a circle, as twinned stars might in *our* universe, holding each other in orbit around a center which no one of them may permanently occupy. Each world has close narrative contact with two of the others; each remains apart from a fourth. Each, as it passes through the center, gives and takes illumination from all the others—often most strongly from that fourth world opposite to and separate from itself.

This play was written, after all, at a time when centrality was being broken down in all areas—I take as my authority here Hiram Haydn's *The Counter-Renaissance*. There, we may trace the rise of individualistic philosophies and religions, of capitalist economies, democratic ideas of government; of the child's rights against his parents, the subject's rights against his sovereign, of relativistic views of the world, of reality, of astronomy. Giordano Bruno, that most daringly relativistic of thinkers, had been in England only about ten years before the writing of this play. Haydn quotes Bruno:

> Since the horizon forms itself anew around every place occupied by the spectator as its central point, every determination of place must be relative. The universe looks different according to whether we conceive it from the earth, the moon, Venus, the sun, etc. . . .
>
> Why, indeed, may not all the stars be themselves suns, and each new sun appear to itself the center of the universe? Where then are its limits? . . . There must be hundreds of thousands of suns, and about them planets rolling, each one, perhaps, inhabited. . . . Throughout, Nature must be the same, everywhere worlds, everywhere the center, everywhere and nowhere.

From this amazingly modern view, Bruno advances directly to relativity of motion, of time, even of weight.

It is Montaigne, however, who can show us a comparable relativity of manners, morals, of levels of reality. First he points out that such relativity of place and judgment makes all agreement between men impossible:

> Men are in agreement about nothing. I mean even the most gifted and ablest scholars, not even that the sky is over our heads.

Yet even if only one man had ever existed, that one could not truly know reality:

> The conception and semblance we form is not the object, but only the impression and the impression and the object are different things. . . .

Now if anyone should want to judge by appearances anyway, to judge by all appearances is impossible, for they clash with one another by their contradictions and discrepancies. . . . Shall some selected appearances rule the others? . . .

Finally, there is no existence that is constant, either of our being or of that of objects. And we, and our judgement and all mortal things go on flowing and rolling ceaselessly. Thus nothing certain can be established about one thing by another, both the judging and the judged being in continual change and motion.

Such men as Bruno and Montaigne had moved into a world of limitless change, of rolling and flowing, boundaries shifting and reforming, realities dissolving and illusions becoming real. Shakespeare was a man of his time; not the man least sensitive to forces which were driving others to create and explore new areas of thought and feeling. Most readers would grant that the play implies that all illusions have their reality, all realities their illusion. It is only a step further (though a dangerous one, as Bruno found at the stake) to suggest that no reality is more important, more real, that no one appearance may be selected to rule the others.

One of the peculiar triumphs of Shakespeare's art is to have taken an artistic convention common to his time—the use of subplot—and let it grow until it quite broke down the whole principle of central plot. What is for lesser writers only a useful device, a way to relieve and vary their central story, is for Shakespeare a way to suggest a whole new view of the world.

Such tendencies must have been very deep in Shakespeare's nature. We see it in every aspect of his work—for instance, his use of imagery. In the sonnet cycle we can watch his technique growing into something that reflects his own psyche, his peculiar vision. In the earlier pieces, imagery tends to be confined to rather low-powered metaphors and similes; we always know what is real and what merely compared to it. As Shakespeare's art grows, the components of an image will be drawn from ever more bafflingly diverse areas of experience, ever more complex structures of reality:

Not marble, nor the gilded monuments
Of princes, shall outlive this powerful rhyme
. . . you shall shine more bright in these contents
Than unswept stone, besmeared with sluttish time.

Not only is metaphor added to metaphor; the vehicle of the first may be snapped up as the tenor of a second, mounted metaphor:

> That time of year thou may'st in me behold
> When yellow leaves, or none, or few, do hang
> Upon those boughs which shake against the cold,
> Bare ruined choirs where late the sweet birds sang.

until we can scarcely say which term is "real" and which only a reflection of it.

In *Rehabilitations,* C. S. Lewis sees a similar urge in Shakespeare's rhetorical practice, contrasting that with Milton's. Milton normally tries to sum up the meaning of his subject in some one description or definitive statement, then lets that stand for better or worse. Shakespeare, on the contrary, tends to come back to his subject again and again—or rather, his characters do. They say things quite as brilliant, as definitive, as anything in Milton. Yet they say them only in the rush and fumble of trying to grasp a reality that seems always elusive, always too broad for summing up. However wonderful their words may be, they never seem to feel them adequate to experience. Again, we find this same drive toward variousness, toward turbulent diversity, in that violent mixing of genres which so disturbed continental critics: realistic scenes collide with highly fanciful stylized scenes; prose rubs shoulders with blank verse or even with tight rhyme; high wit mixes with buffoonery, high tragedy with melodrama. Shakespeare's plays may not, like the artisans', be "tedious and brief"; they are surely "very tragical mirth . . . hot ice, and wondrous strange snow." In their despair of imitating this life, they become downright "tragical-comical-historical-pastoral." All conventions are seized on; none is admitted to yield final truth.

And this, of course, is intimately part of what makes Shakespeare so bafflingly great. Stepping into the universe of his plays, we are surrounded with characters, with situations, with meanings, various and far-flung as stars on a summer night. We can no more locate the center of this universe than we can fathom its edges. We cannot define the creator from within his creation. We cannot sum up Shakespeare; we only set up housekeeping there.

Translations

In the play's first scene, when Hermia is being pursued by both Demetrius and Lysander, Helena says to her:

Sickness is catching; O were favour so,
Yours would I catch, fair Hermia, ere I go. . . . .
Were the world mine, Demetrius being bated,
The rest I'd give to be to you translated.

Soon, she gets her wish: she becomes Hermia; both men pursue her.
That, of course, is even less satisfying.

In that same process, Hermia is translated into Helena and finds
herself abandoned. Weary from wandering in the forest, she and Lysander had lain down to rest. First, however, she has had to persuade him
to lie at a more modest distance. Then, with vows of eternal constancy,
they fell asleep. Suddenly Hermia wakes with a nightmare-vision, a
dream-within-the-*Dream*:

Help me, Lysander, help me! do thy best
To pluck this crawling serpent from my breast!
Aye me, for pity! what a dream was here!
Lysander, look how I do quake with fear.
Methought a serpent eat my heart away,
And you sat smiling at his cruel prey.

Lysander has already abandoned her, chasing after Helena. The dream
has shown her her own plight, both in this abandonment where Lysander enjoys her pain, and also in her fear of being preyed upon—a fear
which Lysander must have activated by his sly and subtle attempt to
seduce her.

Sickness is indeed catching. During the lovers' near-epidemic, Lysander, too, suffers a translation: not into what he wished to be, but into
what Egeus said he already was. In the opening scene, it was ironic that
Egeus should try to take Hermia from the constant Lysander on the
grounds that he was inconstant and feigning, giving her instead to Demetrius, whom we know to be faithless. Yet no sooner have the lovers
fled to the woods than Lysander becomes all Egeus said he was. He even
goes Egeus and the fairies one better: Puck's enchantment may force him
to love Helena; to hate and mistreat Hermia is an improvement supplied
from his own nature.

Puck's final enchantment, the curing of Demetrius's vision, straight-
ens out all the tangles at once—shows Demetrius that he has always loved
Helena and that his pursuit of Hermia was

. . . an idle gaud
which in my childhood I did dote upon;
And all the faith, the virtue of my heart,
The object and the pleasure of mine eye,
Is only Helena . . .
. . . like in sickness did I loathe this food
But, as in health, come to my natural taste,
Now I do wish it, love it, long for it,
And will for evermore be true to it.

This brings the lovers back where they started before the play began. Except that they may be a little more mature after an experience
which reveals so much about themselves. Demetrius is shown who his
love is; Lysander, what. He, once so ready to call others "spotted and
inconstant," is full of inconstancy. Even more, full of hate and venom
which he, like Theseus, must recognize and control. The aim of all these
translations, then, is to change something so we can see how it always
was.

All the lovers are shown lost in a fog where they cannot find, cannot
recognize each other or themselves. They declare a deathless love for
another person, without whom their lives will be desolate; an hour later,
they feel exactly the same thing for someone else. As wild beasts wake
famished and devour the first prey at hand, so the lovers wake enchanted
and fall in love. It is love-in-idleness that enchants them; being of the
leisure class, they can indulge their fantasies, can grieve and blame, can
enrich their pain. Hardworking people like Peter Quince may dabble
with such loves as they dabble in the arts; they haven't the leftover
energy or time to let it control their lives.

I have earlier touched on some of the ways that the enchanted Bottom in Titania's bower reveals the truth about Bottom and about the
rebellious Titania as well. Those same scenes also show much about the
lovers who undergo a similar enchantment in the same time and place.
What happens to Titania and Bottom is obviously related to what happens to the lovers, and not only in the asininity all display.

If the two young men seem almost identical to each other, the two
girls are only slightly more differentiated. They cherish, moreover, a
vision of their union in infancy:

We, Hermia, like two artificial gods,
Have with our needles created both one flower
Both on one sampler, sitting on one cushion,

Both warbling of one song, both in one key;
As if our hands, our sides, voices and minds
Had been incorporate. So we grew together,
Like to a double cherry.

This vision, of which Helena prates so ecstatically, is close kin to that of
Bottom in Titania's bower. It is an imagined bower of bliss where, above
all, the pains of individuality and separateness are turned to ecstasy in a
dream of childish, even babyish, union.

Moving toward maturity and marriage, the lovers must give up the
narcissistic dream of being one with those identical to themselves. As
individuals they must learn not only to accept what is different, but even
what is opposite. They are growing into a world where things are separate and self-willed, yet where union is still possible:

HERMIA	Methinks I see these things with parted eye
	Where everything seems double.
HELENA	So methinks. And I have found Demetrius like a jewel
	Mine own and not mine own. . . .
DEMETRIUS	. . . Do you not think
	The Duke was here, and bid us follow him? . . .
LYSANDER	And he did bid us follow to the temple.
DEMETRIUS	Why then, we are awake.

The lovers, then, are waking from their dream of blissful union (essentially Bottom's dream) and going to the temple and to marriage—a
world of differences, of separations, of walls, yet walls that can be penetrated.

The lovers, making this painful change, have the help of the artisans
who shared their forest experience. In the last act, the artisans take over
from the fairies the power to transform things so they may be truly seen.
Performing "Pyramus and Thisby" they mock their own and the lovers'
flight into moonshine and so help them emerge into the raw and difficult
light of day. Truly, Bottom and his friends do not "stand upon points,"
are poor enough actors. Fearing lest the lion terrorize the ladies, or that
everyone be shocked by Pyramus's suicide, they seem not to discern what
in their art is reality and what illusion. Yet, in effect, they perform very
well indeed. Theseus does well to honor them, not because of their

supposed good will to him (their real aim, of course, is self-advancement), but because their play has a salutary effect on the lovers, helps lead them into reality.

In the play, the lovers leave the world of Bottom's dream to enter the world of marriage. Outside the play, lovers made Bottom's dream the aim of marriage. Alas and alack for us all.

The Fundament

Bottom was translated into an ass. Like all good translators, Puck must have been quick to leap to a pun. And as any good analyst must be quick to hear a pun, Dr. Gui finds Bottom the central character of the play.

Bottom has a strong urge to take over all roles—not just the lover and the lady, but the lion's part as well. He wants to play the tyrant; if there is to be no tyrant, the next best thing is to be the director. While directing the playlet, Peter Quince—whose name echoes Penis Cunt—has continual trouble keeping Bottom in his place.

Bottom himself, almost like a baby, has trouble keeping straight the parts of the body and their proper roles:

> The eye of man hath not heard, the ear of man hath not seen, man's hand is not able to taste, his tongue to conceive, nor his heart to report, what my dream was.

Playing Pyramus, he says:

> I see a voice; now will I to the chink
> To spy an I can hear my Thisby's face.

He does not let many things keep their assigned function:

> Sweet moon, I thank thee for thy sunny beams.

He is not just undiscriminating; he seems determined to break down all distinctions. He dissolves the meaning of words, often saying the exact opposite of what he means:

> You were best to call them generally, man by man.

> There may we rehearse most obscenely and courageously.

I will aggravate my voice so, that I will roar you as gently as any sucking dove.

In our world, doves have voices neither grave nor aggravated; they seldom roar and never suck; in Bottom's world, fish, flesh, and fowl are all one.

There is not a more fearful wild fowl than your lion living.

Bottom so longs to equalize everything that when Quince proposes to write a prologue in eight and six syllable verse (the "fourteeners" then so common), Bottom will not hear of it:

No, make it two more; let it be written in eight and eight.

Loving equality, he tends to break down social distinctions, too. He never hesitates to correct Demetrius or even Theseus. Unlike other characters of the play, he addresses everyone he meets with a complete democracy of courtesy. In Titania's bower, he has no sense that he is out of place, addressing Titania's pages with the absurdly patronizing familiarity of le bourgeois gentilhomme. There, in the bower of the fairy queen, he realizes what must be his dearest dream: the blissful union of the asinine with the sublime, the beastly with the ethereal, the great with the small, the ugly with the beautiful.

This is all thoroughly apt, for in the world of the emotions, anality is the direct counterpart of relativism in philosophy. At bottom, we can scarcely tell male from female; it is the great equalizer which yearns to break down the hierarchies, discredit the phallic or superior. Taking over both male and female roles, it is impatient to assume the world.

Theseus and Bottom, then, stand for diametrically opposed ways of life, not only in their social stance but in the whole bases of their natures. Theseus, the phallic male, always of the elite, holds his position simply because he has more (more anything) than others have. Bottom is the Common Man; he has what we all have.

Theseus takes for granted the artisans' good will toward him. To us, he may seem absurdly complacent. Kaiser Wilhelm, after all, was replaced by a saddlemaker; King Alexander by a mill mechanic. Nowadays, Bottom has not only taken over the throne; Theseus could not even get into the legislature—every chair already has an ass. Theseus is no longer Theseus when he seeks the masses' vote; besides, they wouldn't give it to him.

Not believing in fairies, in the overwhelming powers of the unconscious, Theseus could scarcely suspect what powers Bottom has lain beside. Theseus is very much of the past—a past so ancient it may never have existed.

Yet, as far back as the Bronze Age, perhaps we can see a bit of Theseus after all—a hunting society demands the direct and powerful rule of one man; bronze weapons could only be owned by an aristocracy. Bottom is of a time when artisans, working in a poorer but commoner metal, iron, would give the farmer tools and so a surplus, letting him turn sedentary, anarchic, indulge himself in dreams, would give the masses weapons and so control of the battlefield and ballot box. Bottom directs the present and the future.

One day, I was talking about all this with a dear old friend, Donald Hall. By now, I don't know which ideas came from him and which from me. Suddenly he burst out laughing: "But how predictive! Where did our modern collective and democratic states come from? From the asshole of society; where else?"

Poets and Parents

Romantic love, of course, has no very ancient history; it is open to dispute whether even the Romans were romantic. The first time we can isolate and firmly identify this strange virus in the western world is in the courtly love lyrics of the twelfth-century renaissance in Provence. Oddly enough, there, too, it is involved with a historical movement which helped break down centrality of rule.

We are only now beginning to suspect that neither the troubadour's music nor his sentiments were as "pretty" as we had been told. With some justice, we could say that the troubadour song has only two obsessions: let's go crusading and kill Moors, or let's go seducing and lay the boss's wife.

After many centuries of terrifying upheaval, the twelfth century was a time when men could once again afford unhappy love, self-pity, betrayal, envy of authority. After all, the local strong-arm chief, the feudal equivalent of Theseus, was no longer so desperately needed for protection against invaders, had become in fact a considerable threat himself. It has been seriously argued that one real purpose of the crusades was to keep the turbulent and idle aristocracy out of trouble nearer home. Meantime, the lower orders were beginning to envy their power, their freedom, their women.

The courtly love object is always a married woman, usually the wife of the singer's overlord. Most troubadour songs are much less interested in that lady's excellences (which are praised in habitual, desultory fashion) than in the desire to humiliate, annoy, or deceive her husband. Thus, the singer might satisfy two illicit cravings at once: to get a forbidden woman and, at the same time, exercise a good deal of homosexual fascination. Beyond this were the pleasures of a dual betrayal—offering to the lady that loyalty the singer owed her husband and the Christian deities, then using this false "loyalty" to convince her that she, too, should betray her husband, her feudal lord, her religion. Throughout these songs the husband is known as the jealous one, the thief, the liar. What else can you call a man of whom you are jealous, whose wife you are stealing, to whom you must continually lie?

As prosperity filtered downward during the next two centuries, this tradition spread through the *trouvères* and *minnesänger,* the French *chansons de toile,* and into the folk ballad which apparently began among the French peasantry of the fourteenth century. Throughout this process, the effects of a growing prosperity and security are seen in a growing concern with human wishes and aspirations (not merely actions), with personal psychology, with self-expression, with love.

No doubt the spread of romantic love was hastened by the Albigensian Crusade in which the French obliterated Provence—ostensibly to clean up the vice down there; actually to bring it all back home. One of the chief effects of this crusade, like most earlier ones, was that a little of Arabic high culture rubbed off on the barbarous Franks and Europeans. Likely enough, the Provençals themselves had picked up romantic love (with most of their musical and poetical practices) from brushes with the Moors in earlier crusades. Those who survived the Albigensian Crusade were scattered all across Europe; no doubt this helped disseminate their type of song, their type of love. Yet surely any tradition that offered such lively music, together with so many opportunities for betrayal, was bound to catch on.

By the seventeenth century, the time of *A Midsummer Night's Dream,* the forces of church and state had managed to change romantic love—it had been, in every sense, housebroken. It had moved from the aristocratic warrior classes of the court (which it had helped undermine) into the households of the triumphant middle class. (We should not be surprised that capitalism, value through scarcity, first expressed itself in love.) It remains essential that the lady be unattainable—what's romantic about a woman you can have? But now the lady is single; the obstacle is not her husband, but her father. The aim is not seduction but marriage against opposition. No doubt it must have seemed to the church and state—the initial targets of romantic love—that this was a less dangerous line of attack. Indeed, for a time it probably had a salutary effect: it may be argued that the sudden dramatic rise of western culture over its neighbors was very much furthered and fueled by the tensions romantic love fostered between fathers and sons. When this tension could not be directly expressed, one result would be an increase of competition with other males and so a generally higher level of achievement. You can no more write a great play alone than you can run a great mile. You can only have Shakespeare *with* Marlowe and Jonson; Bannister *with* Landy and Chattaway. Such accomplishment usually demands a kind of admiring competition—and so is often more available to those not entirely comfortable with themselves or their loved ones.

In any case, the art form leading this attack against the father as center of authority was no longer the love lyric, but rather the drama. One often feels that half the surviving Renaissance plays portray the struggle of two young people to marry against their parents' opposition. If they can defeat, trick, or thwart those parents, it is automatically assumed they will settle down to love each other forever, all their dreams fulfilled. The play ends in confident assurance that this may be called "a happy ending."

This is one of the reasons it is so fitting that Bottom be an actor—consider the loss if the craftsmen had decided to form a chorus and sing for Theseus's wedding! Beyond this, to be an actor, a role player, fits in perfectly with the anality, the antisexuality of his nature. The driving aim of an actor has always been to escape his own definition in a borrowed role, above all to escape sexual definition. Theater was greatest when only men played (Renaissance England, ancient Greece); the crowning achievement has always been to play the opposite sex.

This is to say that while actors and dramatists were among the first to demand freedom to control their own sexuality, what they really sought was either the transformation or the obliteration of that sexuality. Thus we can clearly see in them those self-deceptive drives toward freedom which have proved so superbly productive in the hands of the gifted men who could sublimate them into areas such as the creative arts. We can also see the underlying passivity which would make these drives so destructive in the hands of the mob.

Bottom seems to have known all along where fashions in the arts were running, both in our greatest creative geniuses and in our popular travesties of art. The poem did not stop at eight and eight—it finally lost its erect shape altogether, falling into a soft and pliable (at worst, doughy) shape. Music overthrew the phallic hierarchy of the dominant seventh for the artificial communism, the unisex, of the tone row. The same tendencies could be followed out in any of the arts.

No doubt, most of our greatest artistic creations derive a part of their force from profoundly antisexual drives. The phallic artist whom D. H. Lawrence demanded was, after all, only a figment of his fantasies—above all, fantasies of becoming something diametrically opposed to the artist he was. Who can be sure that if he had become as phallic as he wished, he mightn't have stopped all artistic work? Knowing such achievements as Lawrence's or Whitman's, we can only be grateful for those less phallic forces which fostered them. At the same time, we may be horrified at the results of those drives as acted out directly by ordinary men: modern government and modern marriage, glamour and sexlessness, mediocrity and conformity, drugs and television, the paintings everyone can paint, the songs everyone can write.

Who says poetry makes nothing happen? The artist's open rendering of his emotions may have such unpredictable effects on the public that totalitarians from Plato to Stalin have been willing (with some justice) to muzzle or exterminate these unacknowledged and unconscious legislators. Poets and playwrights helped bequeath us a society where we could choose our own mates and settle down to lives of unmatchable wretchedness. A psychoanalyst recently commented that domestic troubles, unhappy love lives, have cost us more misery than all history's wars and famines together. Who can say him nay? It is only one of the ways we are now at the mercy of our pitiless fantasy lives.

Clearly, Egeus is a vengeful old cur, ill-equipped to pick a mate for Hermia. The only person less well equipped is Hermia. No more than anyone else am I willing to give up the right to pick my mate. No more than any other of the freedoms I habitually demand is this likely to make me happy or (unless I am uncommonly lucky) more creative or useful. My personal experience—and I have had too much—has been the exact opposite. To the best of my knowledge, no sensible person has ever tried to show that we westerners have become either happier or more useful since we started picking our own mates.

Neither do I think Renaissance dramatists are responsible for the

wretchedness of our families, the uselessness of our women, the emptiness of our men, the loneliness of our children. The artist's only business,
after all, is to depict his passions honestly; the citizen must decide what to
do about them. Artists, in fact, showed perfectly clearly how self-
deceptive and dangerous those passions were; we preferred not to hear.
We at least need not go on feeding ourselves the old lie that what is good
for the artist is good for the citizen, or that what either one wants (or
thinks he wants) is likely to be good for him. Both might recall what the
Athenians knew: if the gods really hate you, they give you just what
you're asking for.

Weavers and Revolutionaries

If it is strangely apt that Bottom be an actor, how much more so that he
be a weaver. Who can imagine him as anything else—Bottom the
Butcher, Bottom the Greengrocer, Bottom the Hostler?

It's not just the name—that a bottom is the spool or base on which
weavers wound thread. Not only that it is a sedentary trade, demanding
a good deal of *sitzfleisch,* leaving its practitioner time for mooning and
fantasizing (even as the lovers were enchanted by "love-in-idleness"). So,
as Hazlitt commented, it is right that Bottom be "accordingly represented as conceited, serious and fantastical."

It goes far deeper into our past. Weaving is a craft basal to our
history, ingrained to our oldest thinking; it takes us even into our
prehumanity—birds can do it, some with surprising skill. It has come to
image some of life's most fundamental processes. We say a man's life is
spun or woven by the weaving goddesses until his thread is finally cut.
As Pyramus, Bottom rants:

> O Fates! come, come
> Cut thread and thrum,
> Quail, crush, conclude and quell!

In northern mythology, the Norns weave the loom of war, whose threads
are weighted by human skulls. A man and a woman, in marriage and in
sex, are seen as weaving the fabric of our life; Theseus says:

> in the temple, by and by, with us
> These couples shall eternally be knit.

We have long used weaving, or related crafts, to represent the building of the body through digestion, or the building of the mind in its cross-lamination, layer on layer. We image the products of that mind, too, as a woven fabric. The radio announcer who late at night (when no one else would buy the time) read sentimental poems to sentimental music was called, of course, "The Dream Weaver." There is probably no creative art (unless it be weaving) for which we do not use weaving as a habitual metaphor.

If weaving is so involved with our ancient history, it is no less entangled with the building of our peculiar modern society. It was among the artisans, and especially among weavers, that the revolutionary religious ideas of the Albigensi took firmest root. Perhaps no single invention was more crucial in developing our special way of living than was the power loom. In this primeval skill, free craftsmen had to work as only slaves or manual laborers had worked before, not for fulfillment in their work but rather to get the money and free time to buy other enjoyments outside their work. Work became a burden, an imprisonment; the modern itch for fun was born. How much of good and of ill came there into our world! Throughout Europe, the early inventors of power weaving equipment were drowned, hanged, stoned, driven out—as if men knew what a Pandora's box was opening before them. But no use; modern society was not to be escaped.

One of the first plays involved with the revolutionary history of our modern democratic and communistic states is *The Weavers* by Gerhart Hauptmann, a play even more relativistic than is *A Midsummer Night's Dream*. It has no central character, no central group of characters, not even a central theme beyond a never-ending complaint: "It ain't fair!"

The most memorable representation of weavers in modern art, however, is rather to be found in the marvelous early drawings of Vincent van Gogh. In those rough, monumental scribbles I find something oddly bisexual: weaving is an art we always associated with the mother who nourishes, shelters, and comforts, yet it is most often practiced by men—and, in Vincent's drawings, men who are specially square-cut and rough-looking. Watching someone weave, I have always been impressed how satisfying the craft seems to its practitioners. Yet I have to be amused, too: it is as if the weaver had his own built-in sex act where he is both male and female; meantime, he rocks soothingly back and forward not only like the rhythm of sex but like the baby rocked by its mother or calmed by the rhythm of her heartbeat.

In van Gogh's drawings, the weaver sits encased in his enormous loom like a man in the stocks, a child in his pen, the baby in the womb. Meantime, his own creation grows before him like an artificial belly or pregnancy. (It is a creation, too, embodying fundamental patterns, but usually centerless.) Like the fat man Auden mentions in *The Dyer's Hand*, he has a built-in image of the mother he would join once more. (In the play, he rejoins her in the body of Titania. In the playlet he does not; he perishes.) The weaver, then, is symbolically self-sufficient; has taken over all roles. He has rid himself not only of the sex difference but of the size and generation difference—he is not only the contained baby, but also the containing and nourishing mother.

Vincent's weavers seem to me like the devotees of some goddess of fertility and motherhood—say Cybele, whose priests castrated themselves in consecration to her. They sit self-imprisoned in the loom as if in the stocks, totally absorbed in the fabric of their rites. The goddess of their devotion is bodied forth by the almost ever-present lamp hanging over the loom—in his letters, Vincent writes with near ecstasy of finding one of those lamps. We may trace that lamp and its symbolic relatives all through Vincent's work, beginning with the cradle scenes. The lamp (in my mind, it resembles that "lanthorn" Starveling carries into the Duke's chamber as Moon) represents that light which announces to the baby that he will soon be fed and is, ever after, associated in his mind with all that is warm and comforting. It glows over the world of these trapped and shackled weavers just the way the moon glimmers above the world of changeling and Starveling, the enchanted world of *A Midsummer Night's Dream*.

Moonshine

In almost every overt way, the play gives victory to the male, hands the child to its father. The little changeling boy is awarded to Oberon—presumably to be trained and follow in his image. True, Theseus tempers Egeus's vengeful severity against his daughter, even helps her escape a full confrontation with the law by his "private schooling" of Demetrius. Yet he also makes it clear she cannot flout that law: had Demetrius not relented, she apparently would still have to choose between her father's will and chastity or death. Although neither the father's will nor Athenian law, then, are left as immutable or inescapable forces, both remain operant powers which must at least be successfully evaded. That evasion will probably require help from the Duke, a male ordering authority or father-surrogate. Yet the male's victory, like so much else here, may well be illusory. Theseus seems very much in control; he is, in fact, completely dependent on unrecognized forces. Oberon is awarded the child; his triumph never pervades the mind as does the recollection of the imperious Titania, supreme in her bower.

From our vantage in time, it is easy to see that Theseus's and Egeus's days are numbered; Bottom, who has lain beside darker powers, will soon oust both of them. It is astonishing for Shakespeare, so near this culture's first greatness, to render so clearly the drives which first produced that greatness, and now draw us toward decay. He could hardly have imagined that the machine and the bomb would make Theseus, if not obsolete, expendable. He could not imagine a people so luxurious and leisurely they could dispose of Theseus's strength, authority, aggressiveness, ability; that mediocrity could drive out superiority. He did see, only too clearly, the complex of emotions which, once this became possible, would make it inevitable. As a tree or animal contains, in the structures of its growth, the principles of its limits and death, cultures seem to hold, in the very form of their successes, the forces which eventually destroy them. To have attacked so successfully the centers of direct and conscious authority seems to have left us at the mercy of unconscious powers whose despotism may be much more far-reaching.

The play's most powerful image—Bottom in Titania's cradle—holds both the constructive and the decadent side of this complex. On the one hand, we usually think of creative work in strongly phallic terms, and without considerable phallic drive, the creative man can scarcely perform. On the other hand, it must also be noted that most of our truly creative men have had very strong mothers and have been deeply attached to them, even directly imitative of them. We have already noted that the experience of Titania's bower may be quintessential to the creative act; we have also noted what incredible energies we have tapped in the boy's desire to replace his father in that bower, or in the opposing desire to lose his own sexuality in becoming his mother. Yet those desires are only valuable so long as they are frustrated, unfulfilled—so long as the child embodies the unresolved struggle of his parents. Naturally, we all would see that conflict resolved; to resolve it through the evisceration of either power may be to eviscerate the child and perhaps, also, that civilization built partly upon the tensions of that struggle. Detente implies that both opposed powers *remain* powers; for all the dangers of antagonism, we would not lose the enormous energies it has given us.

If the father is successfully castrated or driven out, or if one's own sex is successfully obliterated, then all that tension—the source of energy—is dissipated. How quickly all that phallicism turns anal and passive, all that invention turns sluggish, static, aimless. We fight our way, with what vigor, to the throne, to Titania's bower. Once there, we just can't seem to think of anything to do.

How imperceptibly competition turns to betrayal. Given our special circumstances, the boy's attachment to his mother can be used to enlist him in the general weakening of the male—ultimately, himself. The baby's fear of abandonment has always given the mother immense powers over the imagination. This makes her less subject to our natural compulsion to betray whomever we love. But add to this the industrial revolution which makes the male seem dispensable, romantic love with all its castrative possibilities, individualistic philosophies with all their self-deception; it scarcely bodes well for the male. What can the too successful young man do? He has helped undermine the forces that might have sustained and directed him in this surplus of power. Now there is no one left to betray but himself.

Or he can betray the active ideals he used to reach the seat of power. Why not settle down to be babied, soothed and pampered, lied to, fed, and cajoled?

> Be kind and courteous to this gentleman:
> Hop in his walks and gambol in his eyes;
> Feed him with apricocks and dewberries,
> With purple grapes, green figs, and mulberries;
> The honey-bags steal from the humblebees,
> And for night-tapers crop their waxen thighs,
> And light them at the firey glow-worm's eyes.
> To have my love to bed and to arise; . . .
> Tie up my love's tongue, bring him silently.

Or, better still, feed him on endless beer and potato chips, plant his ever-widening buttocks before an inextinguishable television set, all channels of which play various episodes from an endless soap opera called "Bottom's Dream." We are not ruled by those who have an idea of what the state should do, nor even of what they want from it. We are ruled by any who can contact and control the dream life of the masses. It is not bread and circuses; it is ice cream and revolutions, equal pay and concentration camps. If I speak of Hitler and Stalin, it is only to avoid mentioning anyone closer home.

Nowhere is the mother's dominion over the unconscious world of the play more evident than in the omnipresence of the moon. No doubt Dr. Gui is right to see it as the symbol of the mother's breast, of that nourishment the child must have or die. Titania, her earthly avatar, echoes that breast in her very name; Hippolyta, so closely kin to her, must lack one teat, thus already suggesting the possibility of starvation. Who is it, after all, that carried the moon's lanthorn and thornbush?—none but Starveling. The moon, then, is indeed "governess of floods," the tides of liquid in our world. But the moon is also goddess of virginity and of marriage, of barrenness and of birth, of grudging coldness and of warm affection. She shines on the lovers as on the raging, hate-filled fairies. She is patroness of art, of illusion, of dreaming, of lunacy—of all those forces that control the wide-awake, sunlit, reasonable, paternalistic city of Theseus.

Dr. Gui reminds us that if Theseus's first speech is true, then throughout the whole time of the play there is no moon shining at all. The moon, then, the symbol of illusion, may itself be an illusion. Why talk so much about it, if one were sure that it was really there? Why weave so cunning a web as this play, so circular, so delicately filigreed, so glimmering with dew, if one were really able to catch the thing itself?

No one of the worlds of this play can be truly understood or located until we know its relation to the moon. And, after all, in so relativistic a play as this one, all worlds may very well revolve around the moon.

Literary Technique in the Last Quarter of the Twentieth Century

Tom Wolfe

I just want to make a few remarks about a side of literary technique that is never written about and seldom talked about. It is one that most writers begin to understand only late in the game, if ever. If ever, as I say . . . for here I think we may have the answer to why this, the last quarter of the twentieth century, is the dreariest period of the century for such major forms as the novel and the play.

I think most writers go through the same stages, in terms of technique. The first I think of as the musical stage, in which the young writer is mainly fascinated by his ability to put pleasing, sonorous, rhythmical, or strange strings of words together. At about age thirteen, as I recall, I became intrigued by words that began with *j*. They looked marvelous to me . . . *jaded* . . . *jejune* . . . I didn't even know how to pronounce "jejune"—in fact, to this day I have never heard anyone use the word in conversation—but I put it in writing every chance I had. This one word began to take over entire passages, entire narratives. I wrote a short story in which everything was jejune and everybody was jejune . . . Pretty soon it became a noun as well as an adjective . . . "The jaded jejune of his hopes," that sort of thing . . . and finally it became a verb as well. People were jejuning each other all over the place and were in turn being ruthlessly jejuned by the jasmine jugate jinn of their own fantasies, and so forth and so on. It was not long after that I wrote my first poem. It was called "Owed to an Aesthete" . . . o-w-e-d . . . I considered that word play and a half . . . and it went:

> Your only faintly saffron suns
> Your nicely nipponesian nudes
> Your limply purslane slyped-up dung
> From your exema'd face exudes.

Nevertheless!—that example notwithstanding!—I think that this early musical stage of technique accounts for the fact that so many outstanding poets have done their best work while quite young. Poetry is the music of literature . . . in that like music it can have a nonrational but very sudden and powerful effect upon the mind. You will find a poet such as Shelley at the height of his powers, writing *Alastor* by day . . . and in the evenings sneaking hunks of bread off the table and rolling them into doughballs and flicking them surreptitiously into the face of his father-in-law. Nothing very strange about that . . . they just happen to occur at the same time, the two things, the marvelous surge of musical talent and the season of the rising sap.

The second stage comes when the young writer discovers that, for better or worse, the main arena in literature is prose. It is here that the greatest status is to be attained; that is what he finds out. This has been so for about 120 years, I would say. At this point many young writers are attracted to "poetic" prose or else to prose written after the manner of myths or fables. I can remember that I decided at this stage to write what I thought of as "crystalline" prose, prose that would shimmer like crystals. It would ring in your ears like the music of Richard Strauss. It would be timeless. It would seem as ethereal in the twenty-fifth century as in the twentieth. I considered that an advantage if one intended to become one of literature's immortals. Unfortunately, I can recite to you none of my timeless prose. I abandoned most of these efforts on the morning after. Today I see young writers, at this stage, tremendously attracted to the work of writers such as Tolkien, Hermann Hesse, Kafka, Borges, García Marquez, and Zamyatin. All of them write modern fables, although Zamyatin's range goes far beyond the fable.

What is the appeal of the fable to the young writer? I think it's this: the fable form avoids the problems of realism.

When you're at that age, when you're in your late teens or early twenties and you want to write, you want to feel that the only thing that matters is your genius. The material, the content of the writer's work, is merely the clay, the wax, that Himself is going to use. It is very hard for a young writer to come to grips with the realization that the material he finds—the subject matter—may account for 50 percent or more of his success . . . and of what comes to be known as his talent. A young writer does not want to believe that. He is apt to find that he is simply not very good at analyzing the world around him and selecting material from it. He doesn't know much about it. It becomes far more convenient to write a sort of cynical or ironic whimsy patterned after Borges or Kafka. It becomes quite easy to discount realism, if there is any way to justify doing so. In the late 1940s and early 1950s, when I was in college, it was hard to avoid realism, because it was still so much in vogue in the literary world generally. So practically everyone was forced to enter stage three—writing realistic prose—fairly early on. The typical and natural solution was to write about your own life, poignantly if possible. This became more than just a solution, however. It was an article of faith at that time: namely, that the only genuine, legitimate, and truly profound material for the great novelist was the substance of his own life. Practically every highly praised first novel of the period was autobiographical: whether it was a war novel, such as *From Here to Eternity* or *The Naked and the Dead,* or a novel of school life, such as *End as a Man,* or the great picaresque novel of the fifties, Jack Kerouac's *On the Road.* When I was doing research on *The Electric Kool-Aid Acid Test*, I met Neal Cassady, who was the hero, under the name Dean Moriarty, of *On the Road.* "It used to amaze us," he told me.

> Jack and me and everybody would take these wild rides back and forth across the United States, in these '46 Chryslers with the kickdown gears and whatever, and we'd start drinking and smoking and swallowing everything we could get our hands on, and when we got through everything we'd ever heard of, like we'd smoke Oriental rugs and eat dried creosote and swallow mildewed jute pellets, and end up absolutely wrecked and vomiting and Jack would crawl off into some flophouse, and we'd figure he was just sleeping it off, but in fact he would be in there with a typewriter, writing down everything that had happened, everything we had done. These things came out as his novels, and insofar as any of us could tell, he changed absolutely not one thing except the names.

Such was the mental atmosphere of the realistic novel fifteen or twenty years ago. In many cases it was nonfiction with the names changed. And I think this was the chief cause of what was notorious at the time as the "curse of the second novel." Without realizing what the process was, many talented first novelists had ransacked the first twenty years or so of their lives for material for one novel. When it came time for the second novel, they had lived only two or three years in the meantime and were absolutely baffled as to what to write about. Norman Mailer and James Jones were two in a long line of novelists of the period who had this problem and never really found a way out of it. Today we see something of the same thing plaguing Philip Roth, who I happen to think is the most naturally gifted novelist in the country. Roth has wound up continually ransacking and reransacking the material of his early life. *Portnoy's Complaint* was a brilliant book, in my opinion, but *My Life as a Man* and *The Professor of Desire* are rewrites of the same material. They are brilliant rewrites, for that matter—but here we run into the fact that, as I mentioned earlier, content is a big part of what we think of as talent or genius, and the material becomes thinner and less fresh, less novel, with each reuse.

When you think about it, it's a bit uneconomical to have to spend twenty years of your life to get material for one novel or even to spend five years of daily living to get new material for a second book. It reminds me of the marvelous Charles Lamb story called "A Dissertation on Roast Pig." A Chinese lout by accident burns down his house. In the ruins he finds the roasted carcass of a pig. It's delicious; it's the first roast pig he has ever had. When the passion for roast pig overcomes him again, he burns down his new house, first putting a pig inside, of course. Well, there I see the novelists of the forties and fifties trying to get tasty material out of their own lives.

In the 1960s a tremendous change in literary fashion seemed to solve the problem for the young writers of that period. The modern fable came into vogue. It became quite all right—quite desirable, in fact—for the young writer to remain in stage two, the "timeless" stage, and ignore the problems of realism altogether. The New Fabulism, exemplified by writers such as John Barth, Donald Barthelme, Thomas Pynchon, Richard Brautigan, and John Gardner, was the reigning form. The typical New Fable was a short story by Raymond Kennedy entitled "Room Temperature." It concerned a man named Jack who was living as a hermit in a shack in the woods in the dead of winter without plumbing, electricity, or any other apparatus of modern civilization. He is evidently happy to be removed from society, but we are told nothing of his background. Nothing in what he says or thinks betrays any ethnic, national, or class origin. We don't even know what part of the earth he is in, except that there is a lot of snow. Jack is possessed by a nameless dread. Soon an Inexplicable Visitor shows up, a man named Dick who has been beaten up in the city and dumped out here in the snow with no clothes on except for one shoe. Not the least bit dismayed by the way they stomped him in the city, Dick wants to return as soon as possible. Hermit Jack has just saved Dick from freezing to death, but Dick has an inexplicable attitude toward him. He orders Jack about his own shack and tells him he wants him to return to the city with him, apparently as a servant. Hermit Jack doesn't want to, but he finds himself inexplicably tagging along behind Dick out in the snowy wastes. The extreme cold is too much for him, and he slumps into the snow and begins to freeze to death . . . as Dick heads on back to civilization without so much as offering him a warm goodbye. As the story ends, Hermit Jack is alone in the snow, frozen stiff and dying.

These elements—the Hermit or Isolated Character, the Elemental Terrain (woods, snowy wastes, sea, desert, swamps), Lack of Background, Lack of Realistic Dialogue, Inexplicable Visitors, Inexplicable Attitudes, Inexplicable Forces, Frozen Death (or Paralysis)—plus an atmosphere of futility, meaninglessness, imminent and pointless disaster—these elements recurred continually in the New Fabulism. Not merely solitude, but Catatonic Solitude, became extremely fashionable, culminating in a story by Robert Coover that began: "In order to get started, he went to live alone on an island and shot himself."

So this century—this century which has seen wars so all-involving that they are known as world wars, this century in which man has perfected the means with which to obliterate himself but also the means with which to reach the stars, this century which has seen the growth of huge metropolises, tumultuous collisions of the races, and such crazy pileups of wealth that by 1968 every forty-eight-year-old vinyl-wallet manufacturer in America was out on the discotheque floor with his shirt unbuttoned down to his sternum and a lot of brutal chainwork around his neck and his red eyes beaming out of his walnut-shell eyelids, doing the Watusi, the Hully-Gully, and the New Boogaloo until the onset of dawn or saline depletion, whichever came first—this is the century that our most ambitious young writers chose to treat, in the words of the title of Gabriel García Marquez's book, as *One Hundred Years of Solitude*. In all the publishing houses they were waiting for the great novels that the rising generation of writers would write about the war in Vietnam, the protest movements, the hippie world, race, class, sex, the new ways of life in America—and these novels were never written. Not a single first-rate novel has come out of the war in Vietnam; and precious few of any sort. The rising generation the publishers were waiting for never rose.

A parallel development occurred in the theater. It was illustrated most strikingly by the career of Edward Albee. Albee became famous through the success of *Who's Afraid of Virginia Woolf?*, which was in most respects quite a realistic slice of life among American intellectuals in the 1950s. Just then the fashion in the American theater changed from realism of this, the Tennessee Williams sort, to the European fabulist style of Pinter and Beckett. Albee became determined to write "timeless" plays like theirs. Starting with *Tiny Alice* and *A Delicate Balance* his work became increasingly abstract and fablelike . . . and windier and emptier and less and less successful, even among critics. The fashion was so strong, however, that Albee was unable to break out of it.

Supporting the new fashion for fables was a body of theory that had two main arguments. One was that realism was an approach that had been done to death and was now exhausted. The other was summed up by William Phillips, the editor of the *Partisan Review:* "Realism is just another formal device, not a permanent method for dealing with experience." In my opinion precisely the opposite is true. The introduction of realism into literature by writers such as Richardson, Fielding, and Smollett in the eighteenth century was like the introduction of electricity into machine technology. It was not just another device; it raised the state of the art to a new plateau. The effect of realism on the emotions was something that had never been conceived of before. No one was ever moved to tears by reading about the unhappy fates of heroes and heroines in Homer, Sophocles, Molière, Racine, Sydney, Spenser, or Shakespeare. But even the impeccable Lord Jeffrey, editor of the *Edinburgh Review,* had confessed to weeping, blubbering, snuffling, boohooing, over the death of Dickens's Little Nell in *The Old Curiosity Shop.* One doesn't have to admire Dickens, or any of the other writers who first demonstrated this power, in order to appreciate the point. For writers to abandon this unique power simply because it had already been used— this was one of the more intriguing literary follies of the 1960s.

Publishers began to give up on the New Fabulism in the early 1970s for the simple reason that it did not sell. It bored readers to the point of skull implosions. Now you began to see the New Fabulists backing into realism . . . while paying homage to fabulism. E. L. Doctorow started the trend with his book *Ragtime,* in which he writes a typical modern fable but populates it with real people from recent history. The aforementioned Robert Coover then tried the same thing in *A Public Burning,* a rather naive and amateurish fable populated with real figures from the era of the Rosenberg spy case. In *October Light* Gardner starts off with a

typical modern fable of solitude in the wilds. It's a story of a brother and
sister who hate each other. They're shut up in a farmhouse. One—the
sister, I believe—locks herself in a room, where she discovers a paper-
back novel. Gardner now prints the novel she finds: a book in which the
rules and conventions of the New Fabulism are freely transgressed. It
was by far the most popular thing he had ever written.

Today critical standards and theories in the literary world are rather
gloriously confused. In the fog I see writers sneaking toward realism in
greater numbers. And I see playwrights beginning to discover the value
of *reporting* as a means of gathering material for serious literature. Playwrights are actually following the lead of screenwriters, who have found
that in a medium so dependent upon dialogue it is often necessary to go
out and listen to the real thing in order to make it work; i.e., it becomes
necessary to do reporting. Novelists have been slower in discovering
how this works, and it is ironic. To the great nineteenth-century novelists, reporting was a standard technique. They adopted procedures that
today are associated only with "investigative reporting" by newspapermen. Dickens wanted to gain an inside look at the infamous Yorkshire
boarding schools, where families farmed out their children for years at a
time so as not to have to bother with them. So he presented himself as
the agent for a father trying to park one of his sons in this manner, toured
the schools, and wrote down his findings each night in a notebook, like
any good reporter. When Balzac came to a point in a novel where he
needed to write, say, a scene about a socially correct funeral in the
countryside . . . he would stop writing and go seek out a socially correct
funeral in the countryside . . . and take notes on it and then come back
and write the scene. Zola wrote many of his books serially, just as
Dickens did. Often he would spend two weeks of the month in reporting
and two weeks on writing the installment. He would decide—in *Nana*—
that he wanted a scene at the races. So he would head off to Longchamps
and take notes. The result—as you will remember, if you have read *Nana*
—is something far richer than simply convincing detail, although that is
there. The detail itself, obtained through reporting, enables Zola to take
off on flights of extraordinary technical virtuosity. But let me give you
an example from another part of *Nana*. Nana, of course, is a courtesan,
and Zola wanted to have authentic information about such a woman. So
he obtained an introduction to a famous Paris courtesan of his day and
went to her house. He found, to his disappointment, that she was far too
sophisticated, too urbane a woman to be used as a model for Nana. But

while in her house he had a look at her bed. It had been created by goldsmiths at a cost of about $75,000 in today's terms. Out of its four golden posts came marvelous priapic figures with shanks akimbo. The sight of that bed became for Zola a metaphor for the entire Second Empire in France and resulted in one of the most powerful images in French literature.

What I am saying is that it was *through reporting* that the great writers of the nineteenth century were able to come up not only with slices of life but also with the most important insights, the most arresting symbols, the most powerful material in prose literature. They did not labor under the illusion that profundity was to be found only in the inspection of one's own immediate existence. They seemed, rather, to believe the opposite: profound knowledge was to be obtained only through moving out from one's own circle and reporting on the world beyond. We are in a period today in which there is seldom a major novel with more than one interesting character portrayed, and this one character is usually the alter ego of the author himself. This is the great limitation of Saul Bellow's work. His books are filled up with the swollen figure of the protagonist in the foreground—obviously himself under another name—with little stick figures dotted around in the small space that is left. The challenge that Zola, Balzac, Dickens, Thackeray, Dostoyevski, Tolstoy, Gogol—and Faulkner—routinely accepted was that of entering into the hides of characters utterly unlike themselves and bringing them alive, a full cast, in each novel. The key—this they understood as something obvious, as a matter of routine—was reporting.

Actually, I suppose I should keep quiet about this business of reporting. It is partly due to the general obtuseness of novelists and playwrights in this area that journalists have had such a field day in American writing over the past fifteen years. This has been perhaps the first period since the 1830s in England when the literary history of any major country has been dominated by journalists, aesthetically as well as in popular appeal—and the difference has been in the least understood side of literary technique, which is the use and the necessity of reporting. Ah, but this brings me dangerously close to a topic which I swore five years ago I would never publicly expound upon again . . . the New Something-or-other . . . and so I will stop now.

Making Up Stories

Joan Didion

Let me present you with a chain of associations.

I am delivering the 1979 Hopwood Lecture at the University of Michigan in Ann Arbor, Michigan, near the city of Detroit.

When Detroit is mentioned I think reflexively of my father. I have never before yesterday been in Detroit but my father was stationed there, the last year of World War II. When he came home to California from Detroit he brought me three handkerchiefs of a very heavy silk twill, one brown, one orange, the third a quite brilliant emerald green. He had bought these handkerchiefs at the J. L. Hudson Company and the saleswoman had told him that "all the young girls" were wearing them, knotted around the neck.

I was undone by this present, for several reasons: one was that I was only ten, and overcome that my father should consider me a "young girl," should buy me a grown-up present, a present of something "in fashion." The pieces of silk seemed to me incredibly glamorous and beautiful, and they were rendered even more so by the fact that this was the first time my father had ever had occasion to buy me—all by myself, without my mother—a present.

I remember that we sat down to lunch.

I remember that we had cracked crab, although there remains some question about this. I may have invented the crab, you never know.

I definitely remember that we had iced tea, in a silver pitcher, because I picked up this pitcher to pour myself some tea—more evidence that I was grown up, a "young girl" instead of a little girl—and I spilled it.

This spilling of the tea was a very fraught moment—anyone old enough to wear silk handkerchiefs knotted around her neck and drink iced tea was too old to drop the pitcher—and I remember bolting from the table, running to my room, and locking the door.

We can call that story "Homecoming," or we can call it "Family Life," or we can call it "Detroit and Other Sorrows."

It is not a story I will ever write.

Similarly: When the Hopwood Awards are mentioned I think reflexively of being an undergraduate at Berkeley and wishing that Avery Hopwood had left that famous one-fifth of his estate to the University of California instead of the University of Michigan. I wanted to win a Hopwood Award. I wanted to win one not only because the very word *Hopwood* had a big-time national sound to it, a kind of certification that the winner was on the right track, but also because the prize was money, cash, and I needed it.

I hear the word *Hopwood* and I think of Corinne Benson, who was my roommate one year at Berkeley. Corinne was from Marin County and she turned on the radio to a certain station every night at midnight in order to hear the sign-off, which was a male tenor singing "The Bluebird of Happiness." She had blonde hair and blue eyes and many, many powder blue sweaters to match her eyes, many sweaters and many dresses and many different-sized bottles of the particular perfume she always wore.

She lent me one of her dresses one night, to wear on a date to San Francisco.

This date was with someone I had met in a writing class. In other words he was "literary," as I wanted desperately to be, and had no car. We went from Berkeley to San Francisco on the F train and we ate the inevitable coq au vin at the inevitable French family restaurant and we saw a play, the inevitable Restoration comedy.

I do not now remember the play but I remember the dress and I remember this boy reading Dylan Thomas out loud to me on the F train back to Berkeley. He gave me a gloss on every line he read. For example:

"*It was my thirtieth year to heaven,*" he would read. And then he would turn to me and say: "It was his thirtieth birthday."

And I would nod.

He liked the dress, and asked why I never wore it, and I was too embarrassed to say that it was not mine. I was so young that I imagined it shameful to let anyone know that you cared enough about him to borrow a dress.

"*Altarwise by owl-light in the half-way house,*" he would read, and then interpret it. I recall thinking that if we only had Hopwood Awards at Berkeley we might each win one, this boy and I, and winning a Hopwood Award would give me enough money to buy a dress exactly like Corinne's, and give him enough certification, enough confidence, to ride

across San Francisco Bay without feeling impelled to improve the moment by giving me an interlinear translation of Dylan Thomas. Had he
known what I was thinking he would have called me bourgeois. This is
another story I will never write.

This kind of associating never stops.

Corinne Benson, the trace of her perfume in the borrowed dress, the
particular brilliant colors of those silk handkerchiefs from J. L. Hudson,
the flicker of the lights on the F train at night, coq au vin, iced tea, and
the way the moisture condenses on the outside of a silver pitcher: these
are only the skim off the top of all that floods through my mind when I
hear the words *Detroit* or *Hopwood Awards*.

For example, by a chain of associations too tedious to reconstruct,
Corinne Benson leads me directly to watching *Splendor in the Grass*
on television, with a drunk psychiatrist from Louisville, in the Faculty
Club at Berkeley on the night Saigon fell in 1975. The Faculty Club
at Berkeley leads me to the stone tower Robinson Jeffers built at Carmel. Carmel leads me to the ordination of a Jesuit priest, a summer
afternoon in Sacramento, and the ordination leads me to Sante Fe and
to New Haven and to the murders in Beverly Hills of Sharon Tate
Polanski, Jay Sebring, Voitek Frykowski, Steven Parent, and Abigail
Folger.

To give you the connections that take me from Detroit to those five
murders in California would be to give you a story of my whole life, and
I say "a story" rather than "the story" deliberately.

I say "a story" because only part of that story would be true.

Some of the story would be a trick of memory.

Elizabeth Hardwick has written a novel, *Sleepless Nights*, in which
the subject is memory, and in this novel she wrote: "Sometimes I resent
the glossary, the concordance of truth, many have about my real
life . . . I mean that such fact is to be a hindrance to memory."

Some of what all of us remember is automatic improvisation, a
scenario invented to link puzzling and contradictory scenes. When we
tell someone a dream we try, in spite of ourselves, for a certain
coherence, a dramatic shape: we interpret the dream, as we tell it, and
filter out those details which seem to lead nowhere. We think of our
dreams as stories, but they are not, at least until we tell them.

In fact the way we think in dreams is also the way we think when we
are awake, all of these images occurring simultaneously, images opening
up new images, charging and recharging, until we have a whole field of

image, an electric field pulsing and blazing and taking on the exact character of a migraine aura.

All of us have this going on in our heads, all the time, this incessant clatter, this charging and recharging.

Usually we sedate ourselves to keep the clatter down. And when I say that we sedate ourselves, I don't necessarily mean with drugs, not at all. Work is a sedative. The love of children can be a sedative. Planting a garden, locking the doors, cooking dinner, arranging the tulips in a certain glass and placing the glass so that the water catches the light: anything that successfully focuses our attention is sedative in effect.

Another way we keep the clatter down is by trying to make it coherent, trying to give it the same dramatic shape we give to our dreams; in other words by making up stories.

All of us make up stories.

Some of us, if we are writers, write these stories down, concentrate on them, worry them, revise them, throw them away and retrieve them and revise them again, focus on them all of our attention, all of our emotion, render them into objects.

It is very common for writers to think of their work as a collection of objects. A novel, to a writer, is an object. A story or an essay is an object. Every piece of work has its own shape, its own texture, its own specific gravity. This perception of the work as an object is not usually shared by the reader of it, and seems to be one of the principal differences between writers and people in other lines of sedation.

The point of making the object is to give the clatter a shape, to find the figure in the carpet, the order in the disorder.

Robert Penn Warren once described fiction as "an attempt, however modest and limited, to make sense of experience, to understand how things hang meaningfully together."

Joseph Heller described the conception of *Catch–22* this way: "I was lying in bed when suddenly this line came to me: 'It was love at first sight. The first time he saw the chaplain X fell madly in love with him.'" The "X" turned out to be Yossarian, but Heller didn't have the name, didn't even know that this "X" was in the Army. "The chaplain wasn't necessarily an Army chaplain," he said. "He could have been a prison chaplain. I don't understand the process of imagination though I know that I am very much at its mercy. The ideas come to me in the course of a controlled daydream, a directed reverie."

Cocteau described his work as deriving from "a profound indolence, a somnolence in which we indulge ourselves like invalids who try to prolong dreams."

Saul Bellow said, when someone asked him what he thought about winning the Nobel prize, "I don't know, I haven't written about it."

There you are. I have never heard a more succinct statement of the way writers think. The act of writing is for a writer the process of thinking, of plugging into that electrical field of image and making an object out of the flash and the clatter.

I don't mean at all that this object comes "naturally," any more than a piece of sculpture comes "naturally." You don't find a novel or a story lying around in your unconscious like a piece of driftwood. You have to hammer it, work it, find the particular grain of it.

Nor do I mean to say that we write out of our "experience," whatever that means. Someone is always saying to young writers that they should "write from experience." As it happens I get copies of a lot of composition textbooks, and the worst of them feature sample "themes," sample papers written on "The Night Fresno Beat Bakersfield" or "The Day I Learned I Made All-State Tackle."

These textbooks present the sample theme, and then they show ways the theme might be improved, usually by inventing some kind of "action" lead, something along the lines of "The clock was running. The ball was arcing into Fresno territory."

The trouble with this is that it is based on a very limited and literal view of experience. The advice that a writer write from experience is obviously good advice, but it is advice devoid of real meaning, since it does not define experience, or defines it as something that happened, as having actually been on the fifty-yard line on the night Fresno beat Bakersfield.

Experience is something quite different. Joseph Conrad wrote his great South American novel, *Nostromo*, out of "experience," and yet he had never in his life set foot in South America. He had once, as a very young man, shipped on a freighter that called at a few ports on the west coast of Mexico, had been told a story in one of them, and—out of those few hours ashore in Mexico twenty or twenty-five years before—he had made that novel that remains today all anyone needs to know in order to apprehend South America.

Henry James addressed himself to this question of experience. He answers a contemporary who advised that "a young lady brought up in a quiet country village should avoid descriptions of garrison life" by saying, in effect, no, not at all, you have it wrong. A young lady brought up in a quiet country village can apprehend everything about garrison life by glancing once through a window of Knightsbridge Barracks in London. If—and this was of course James's famous phrase—she is "one of the people on whom nothing is lost." Let me quote James:

> I remember an English novelist . . . telling me that she was much commended for the impression she had managed to give in one of her tales of the nature and way of life of French Protestant youth. She had been asked where she learned so much about this recondite being, she had been congratulated on her peculiar opportunities. These opportunities consisted of her having once, in Paris, as she ascended a staircase, passed an open door where some of the young Protestants were seated at a table round a finished meal. The glimpse made a picture; it lasted only a moment, but that moment was experience.

"That moment was experience."

We have all had such moments.

We retrieve them from that field of image that assaults us every day we live.

In the spring of 1975 I was teaching at Berkeley, just for a month and just one class, which met two days a week from four to six in the afternoon. I was in the middle of writing a novel that spring, and all day I would sit in my room at the Faculty Club. This room was just a room: twin beds, a desk, a straight-backed chair and a rented typewriter. I would get up very early and go out for breakfast and then I would come back to this room and sit at the desk and make up the novel. Tell myself the story. Entrance myself, in the literal sense of the word *entrance*.

Then at night a curious thing would happen. I would go out to dinner, or to a lecture, and I would listen to people talk about novels.

Everywhere I went, people were talking about novels.

Finished novels. Famous novels.

Just on the face of it, this was intimidating in the extreme: the main thing a writer wants to keep out of his or her mind is the idea that anybody else has ever written a novel.

But it was intimidating for another reason as well.

Everyone to whom I was listening at Berkeley that spring talked about novels as if the novelist—whether it was Dickens or George Eliot or Scott Fitzgerald—had known precisely what he or she was doing before setting out, as if the novel were schematic, and entirely planned.

If this was true, then I was in bad trouble.

I particularly remember a kind of amiable argument I was having one night with some people from the English Department. Someone had mentioned *The Last Tycoon*, and everyone was pointing out ways in which it didn't work, ways in which it seemed to them a flagrantly bad novel.

There was the "imbalance" of it.

There was the rather creaking deus ex machina aspect to the plot.

I didn't disagree with anything they said, but I still thought that *The Last Tycoon* was a brilliant piece of work, and they didn't.

Finally I realized what the argument was about, what the difference in our thinking was, and it was quite a radical difference. They were looking at *The Last Tycoon* not as a fragment of a novel in progress but as the first third of a novel for which we were simply missing the last two-thirds. In other words they saw that first third as completed, frozen, closed—the interrupted execution of a fully articulated plan on Fitzgerald's part—and I saw it as something fluid, something that would change as he discovered where the book was taking him.

They saw a novel as a plan carried out.

I saw a novel as an object discovered.

They saw the process as an act of intelligence.

I saw it as a mystery.

They saw the writer as someone who has a story to tell and writes it down.

I saw the writer as someone who discovers the story only in the act of making it up.

The novel I was working on during that spring in Berkeley had begun in 1971 as a book about a woman who was traveling through Mississippi and Louisiana with her ex-husband, who was dying. The novel was to take place entirely in motel rooms off interstate highways.

In Holiday Inns, in Ramada Inns. In Howard Johnson's.

It was to be a novel without event.

It was to be told in a flat third person.

By the time I was working on this novel in Berkeley in 1975—the novel was *A Book of Common Prayer*—it had taken quite a different shape. It had become a novel which took place largely in a Central American republic named Boca Grande and—far from being without event—

involved bombings, a highjacking, a revolution and a number of other theatrical—not to say melodramatic—events. And it was told not in that "flat third person" but in the first person, by a sixty-year-old woman named Grace Strasser-Mendana, born Grace Tabor in Denver, Colorado. Grace Tabor went down to Latin America as an anthropologist. Grace Tabor retired as an anthropologist and married into the Strasser-Mendana family, which ran Boca Grande. Grace Tabor was dying of pancreatic cancer, and she was to tell us the story of the woman who traveled with her ex-husband through Mississippi and Louisiana.

You could call this telling the story the hard way. I would call it telling myself a story that incorporated all of the images I was getting at the time.

Once in the late sixties I took a series of psychiatric tests, one of which was the Thematic Apperception Test. The Thematic Apperception Test, or "TAT," is the one in which the subject is shown a series of drawings and asked to make up a story based on each drawing. I recall resisting this test. I remember telling the doctor that of course I could make up stories, but he would be misguided to think that he knew more about what the stories revealed than I did, because I made up stories for a living.

He persisted, and I took the test.

One of the pictures was of a woman, not smiling, standing on some kind of raised ground—alone—and gazing down to where a group of men were very busy building a bridge or a culvert or maybe just tilling a field, some kind of basic physical work.

I remember that the story I made up to "go" with this drawing had to do with an American woman who had become involved with the revolutionary forces in Cuba during the early days of the revolution, and had since become disillusioned, and isolated in Cuba.

The doctor of course wanted to know "why" she was disillusioned, and I remember saying quite sharply "because that's the story I'm telling you."

We didn't get much further than that—we were proceeding, after all, from radically different points of view—but in fact I was more interested in this story than in any of the other stories I made up that day, and it occurred to me some years later, when I was making up the story that had begun as a trip through Mississippi and Louisiana and had evolved into a revolution in Central America, that the story had actually been in my mind for all that time.

I am going to read you some of the notes I made during the time that this novel about the trip through the South was in the process of evolving into *A Book of Common Prayer*. These notes were all in certain notebooks I had, and I am going to give them to you in the order in which they were made.

> She goes out to the airport and watches the planes take off. Arousing uneasy glances in the Panama airport, out there in the morning when the midnight Avianca from Mexico comes in. Drinking tea in the coffee shop at the Cartagena airport, making them boil the water before she will put the tea bag in.
>
> Arrival of mail, magazines, seed catalogues. Projects to make money and fame. Correspondents. Walking downtown in Cartagena in the midday blaze. Cracks and ruts in the sidewalk. Dinner alone in the Capilla del Mar.
>
> Unfitted for the heat. Frequent fevers, illness, occasional unsatisfactory liaisons with locals, who misapprehend her.
>
> IF THIS IS THE FRAME FOR THE SOUTHERN STORY THEN THE SOUTH MUST HAVE UNHINGED HER IN CERTAIN KEY WAYS.
>
> During the troubles in Boca Grande she dreamwalks her way into danger. Incapable of believing that it can touch her. Una norteamericana. Self-delusion. Herded into the bull ring.
>
> Argument with local druggist or doctor during bout of fever. Paregorina.
>
> The Miami Herald is what she reads.
>
> Official functions, rum and quinine. Whenever the USIS man is invited, so is she.
>
> SOUTH AMERICAN PART IN PRESENT TENSE, SOUTH IN PAST? MAYBE TWO NOVELLAS, PUBLISHED TOGETHER?
>
> Death very casual.
>
> FIRST LINE: HERE IS WHAT HAPPENED.
>
> FIRST CHAPTER HARD THIRD SUMMARY. THEN ALTER-

NATING CHAPTERS. LAST CHAPTER SOUTH AMERICAN
BUT BEGINS: "WHEN IT HAPPENED . . . " VERY HARD
LINE THIRD PERSON.

WHO IS THE THIRD PERSON? MAYBE YOU DON'T
KNOW WHO IT IS UNTIL 2/3 THROUGH?

"HERE IS WHAT HAPPENED: SHE LEFT THE FIRST MAN,
SHE LEFT THE FIRST CHILD, SHE WENT TO THE SEC-
OND MAN, SHE LOST THE SECOND CHILD, SHE DIED.
IN SUMMARY. SO YOU KNOW THE STORY. IN FACT
THE STORY HAD COMPLICATIONS, BUT ONLY FOR
THE LIVING. IF YOU HAVE EVER MADE THEM BOIL THE
WATER TWENTY MINUTES BEFORE YOU PUT THE TEA-
BAG IN YOU WILL KNOW WHAT I MEAN. FEVER IS RAM-
PANT."

Cataloguing the flora and fauna. Writing to the British resident in
Honiara, Guadalcanal. Reading the Pacific Islands Monthly. Devis-
ing a scheme to ship Christmas trees to Caracas.

When the ice melted in the Thermos bottles in the hotel rooms it left
flecks of white in the water. She imagined as she drank it that the
flecks were the salmonella typhosa, salmonella paratyphosa, salmonella shigella, but of course she knew that you could not see bacte-
ria with the naked eye. Unless your eyes were very good. She is
always planning to go home. She takes lessons in Spanish, Castilian
Spanish, from a very old woman.

Since the inception of the Nobel Prize in science there has been only
one given to a South American. This was given to an Argentinian
doctor in 1947. Later, under Peronist charges of incompetence, he
resigned from the university.

The Argentinian neurosurgeon who cannot practice in New York
or Buenos Aires. At the family compounds his wife is stopped at the
gate by his brother, with a machine gun. Kidnapping insurance. His
brother tries on military helmets all day, and on visits to New York
tries to sell vicuna blankets.

The illuminated Christ on the hillside had been the idea, but there
was no hillside in Boca Grande, was no hill. The Opera, the Botani-
cal Garden, the race track, the Jockey Club. The sentries with

tommy guns patrolling the presidential palace. Asylum was available in Boca Grande, but no deposed president had ever availed himself of it.

The preference for speaking French among Boca Grande's three or four first families. The money in European banks. American oil, the National City Bank, Brown Brothers Harriman, United Fruit.

American covers. Americans come down to do "research," come in "study groups," to study "behavioral patterns."

There had once been a railroad line built in Boca Grande but the contracts for its construction had been let to two competing companies, and upon completion it was found that they had built track of different gauges, so the track went unused and grew over.

The prescription for depression is "removal to a hill station," but we have no hill stations in Boca Grande.

LA REPUBLICA DE BOCA GRANDE: a Spanish colony from 1525 to 1823. Independent since 1942. 28 constitutions as an independent nation. When Boca Grande was a Spanish colony it was governed from Guatemala City or Colombia by a captaincy general. Brief period as one of the United Provinces of Central America. A member of the United Nations, the OAS, and the Central American Common Market. Myriad aid offices with acronyms, all the American ones plus the International Bank for Reconstruction and Development and the Central American Bank for Economic Integration. In the early nineteenth century Boca Grande resisted an annexation attempt by Mexico. Gastrointestinal infection is the leading natural cause of death. Rainy season from June to October. There is nothing left of Boca Grande's colonial period because of an earthquake in 1900.

Let me describe Charlotte's appearance. Find the character clues here. A woman of medium height, extreme and volatile thinness, a pronounced pallor, and pale red hair which curled in the damp heat and stands out around her face. She has a tendency to drop her head slightly, as if the weight of her hair is more than she can carry. Her body has a tendency to retain water and since adolescence she has taken a diuretic, but has been told not to take it in the tropics, so that when she is tired her ankles seem thick. Her expression startles by its openness, as if she sees someone about to hit her. She is 40 years old but this naked and rather unfinished expression gives the impression of a somewhat younger woman. She wears expensive shoes and the careless observer might take her to be vain about her feet, but this is not so: in fact she believes her feet ugly and tries to hide them when she is seated. She has for 15 years carried the same Hermes handbag, day and evening, now in need of repair but the lifetime guarantee is useless in Boca Grande and she will not spend money to have it repaired, because it is guaranteed. This is the kind of conundrum she frets over. She wears expensive discreet clothes which on her manage to look flamboyant, and there is always something slightly askew: a hem about to come out, a seam with a quarter-inch split, a minute stubborn stain, a trace of powder on the chiffon blouse. What is this woman doing in Boca Grande?

Well, of course, there it was: there was the question I had to answer. There was the "story." What was this woman doing in Boca Grande?

During the time I spent answering that question, making up the story, I lived in Boca Grande. Everything I heard or saw or thought about—all the clatter, all the images—was framed by this imaginary country, by the light there, the weather there.

For a long time after I finished that novel, I continued living in Boca Grande. I couldn't let it go. I knew too much about it. I knew for example how to run a copra plantation, I had taught myself how. I knew that if you try to crowd 200 palms to the acre you are going to get a low yield, I knew not to plant near salt water, I knew about the particular varieties of scale and fungus that afflict coconut palms.

In other words I had, for a while, made the world hang meaningfully together, made all the images coherent, and it was hard to give that up.

It is still.

So I am making up another story.

And teaching myself the economics of the sugar business.

Imagined Life

Maxine Hong Kingston

One summer in Hawai'i, John Hawkes and I taught writing seminars in adjoining classrooms. I told my students: Don't worry about form; write any old thing, and it will naturally take shape. It will be a classical shape—a sonnet, an essay, a novel, a short story, a play—of its own accord. Do you think that Petrarch cooked up fourteen lines and an *abbaabbacdcdcd* rhyme scheme capriciously? After stating a problem, the human mind inevitably mulls on it, looks at its complexities, and comes to a new understanding. At its most efficient, the mind does this in fourteen lines, and when the resolution is especially neat, it makes a couplet. Like a computer program, a sonnet is one of the natural patterns of the brain. And iambic pentameter is the normal rhythm of the English language. I told the students to copy and tack over their desks some advice from Lew Welch:

> When I write, my only concern is accuracy. I try to write accu-
> rately from the poise of mind which lets us see that things are
> exactly what they seem. I never worry about beauty; if it is accurate
> there is always beauty. I never worry about form; if it is accurate
> there is always form.

Write about any old thing that has been obsessing you for years, then step back and see what shape the words are tending toward; then use that recognizable structure for guidance as you rewrite. For example, if some of the lines are iambic tetrameter with a syllable left over, see what happens if you push the line out another half a foot. Maybe there will be a concomitant extending of thought. Or shorten the line and see if you like the closer, thicker effect. You short story writers, sustain a scene for one more page; the characters may have to perform a culminating deed, and the scene then must yield its drama.

Meanwhile, in John Hawkes's seminar, I imagined wonderful goings on. Better goings on. In college, my husband and I had written a series of papers on Hawkes's *The Beetle Leg, The Blood Oranges, The Cannibal, The Lime Twig,* and *Second Skin.* And I had just read *Travesty* in preparation for meeting Hawkes. He must be telling his students miraculous things that I didn't dare fool with. That I didn't even know about. While I dealt with form, he must be counseling imaginations. I could almost hear him speaking like the narrator in *Travesty: "Imagined life is more exhilarating than remembered life."* In Italics. Repeating. *"Imagined life is more exhilarating than remembered life."*

> Somewhere there still must be
> Her face not seen, her voice not heard.

I picture John Hawkes listening to students' lives, their loves, figuring out how to strengthen them, probing at sources of power. Helping people find bottomless pitchers of cream and the other sides of walls.

Every time I have taught a class or a workshop, the most forbidding student in there has been somebody who signs up for the course because she's "blocked." That summer, there was again such a woman. It's always a woman, and she is always too nicely dressed. I tried talking her into switching from my course to John Hawkes's, but she wouldn't go. It was too late anyway; she'd already handed me her IBM card, which I'd turned in to the office. Also, it was at the last of the course that she admitted to being "blocked." Like other troubled writers in previous classes, she had shown me work she had done years ago, and fooled me. If I come across such a woman again, I will pretend to be John Hawkes and tell her to wear wanton dresses and to brush her hair more loosely. Then I am going to tell her that what's wrong with her is that she believes that a writer only exposes lives—when what a writer really does is imagine lives. To imagine a life means to take such an interest in someone that you suppose about him. You conjecture about him. You care what he eats and about whatever he is doing. "Stands he or sits he? Or does he walk? Or is he on his horse?"

"But—," says the "blocked" lady, who begins too many of her sentences with "but." "But I don't have a problem with romantic fantasizing." No, her problem is in the real world, and it is with real people. Each one of my "blocked" ladies has said she can't write because she is afraid of hurting her friends and relatives. "What does your mother think about your book?" she keeps asking me. "What does your father think?"

Well, like everybody else of my generation who majored in English, I was trained in the New Criticism, and I didn't like that kind of question.

All right. To make your mother and your scandalous friends read about themselves and still like you, you have to be very cunning, very crafty. Don't commit yourself. Don't be pinned down. Give many versions of events. Tell the most flattering motives. Say: "Of course, it couldn't have been money that she was after." In *The Woman Warrior*, my mother-book, the No Name Woman might have been raped; she might have had a love affair; she might have been "a wild woman, and kept rollicking company. Imagining her free with sex. . . ." Imagining many lives for her made me feel free. I have so much freedom in telling about her, I'm almost free even from writing itself, and therefore obeying my mother, who said, "Don't tell."

Forget "definitive." The reason that John Hawkes finds imagined life more exhilarating than remembered life is that imagined life is not set.

The blocks that my father put in my way took more craftiness to break than my mother's. A consequence for my mentioning immigration papers could be his deportation. The Immigration and Naturalization Service demands consistency in the life story of a China Man. So, in my father-book, *China Men*, I used the very techniques that the men developed over a hundred years. They made themselves citizens of this country by telling American versions of their lives. My father has three or four stories about how he happens to be in America in spite of the Exclusion Laws and history and common sense. In "The Father from China," the illegal father sailed to Cuba, where he had his friends nail him up in a crate to stow away to New York Harbor. The last sentence of that story goes like this: "Of course, my father could not have come that way. He came a legal way." The legal father landed at the immigration station on Angel Island, where the imprisoned men wrote poems on the walls. They spent their time memorizing stories to tell at hearings. Some even had paper and wood models of the village they had supposedly come from so that all the people from that village could describe it the same way. Those who bought papers from American citizens memorized other men's lives.

In a third story, my father was born here. If you're born in America, you're automatically a citizen. So, my grandfather ran out of the San

Francisco Earthquake and Fire with a newborn baby in his arms. It was a magical birth since my grandmother was in China at the time. Coincidentally, this happened when the San Francisco Hall of Records burned to the ground. That means that everyone who wants a birth certificate can say, "All records of my birth were burned in the San Francisco Earthquake and Fire." "Every China Man was reborn out of that fire an American."

A fourth way that my father is legal is that his father had bought for a bag of Sierra gold a Citizenship Paper from a Citizenship Judge. So, we are Americans many times over. Even more times over: The brothers in Vietnam got top security clearances.

You see how people have imaginations out of necessity. I didn't have to make up ways for telling immigration stories.

My father doesn't say, "Don't tell." He doesn't say much at all. The way to end the silence he gave me was to write this sentence: "I'll tell you what I suppose from your silences and few words, and you can tell me that I'm mistaken." You may use that sentence yourself if you like. Copy it down and see what comes next.

My father is answering me by writing poems and commentary in the margins of my books. The pirated translations have wide margins. Writing commentary is a traditional Chinese literary form. You can break reader's block by writing well.

Yes, the imagined life is so exhilarating that householders go in quest of new lands—the Gold Mountain and China. The Gold Mountain is a land of gold-cobbled streets, and it is also a country with no war and no taxes; it is governed by women. Most of us are here in America today because somebody in our families imagined the Gold Mountain vividly enough to come looking for it. I guess most people think they've found it, and "Gold Mountain" is synonymous with "United States of America." But we aren't peaceful; taxes are due the day after tomorrow; and women aren't in charge. You see how much work we have ahead of us— we still have that country to find, and we still have its stories to tell. Maybe those "blocked" ladies don't know: There is work that belongs to all of us, and they can't quit.

I haven't seen China yet. I didn't want to go there before finishing my two books because I was describing the place that we Americans imagine to be China. The mythic China has its own history, smells, flowers, one hundred birds, long-lived people, dialects, music. We can taste its sweetness when our grandmother sends us invisible candy. The place is so real that we talk about it in common, and we get mail from there. As real as the Brontës' childhood cities. As real as Dungeons and Dragons. If I had gotten on a plane and flown to the China that's over there, I might have lost the imagined land.

I have a Boston cousin, and a Foster City cousin who went back to our home village. They report separately that there were hardly any people about. It's like Roanoke. What to make of such "airy nothing"?

Now, I don't want to leave you with the impression that to imagine life means that you only invent ways to befuddle and blur and to find what is not there. To live a true human life today, we have to imagine what really goes on when we turn on the machines. "The Brother in Vietnam" warns about how easy it is to operate an instrument panel and not see the people far away dying horribly. That story is gray like an aircraft carrier—no red, green, and gold dragons in the riggings. No red blood. We deliberately weaken and divert our imaginations to be able to bear a world with bombs.

We went to a movie where the attendants gave each kid a free picture of an atomic bomb explosion. Smoke boiled in a yellow and orange cloud like a brain on a column. It was a souvenir to celebrate the bombing of Japan. Since I did not own much, I enjoyed the ownership of the V-J picture. At the base of the explosion, where the people would have been, the specks didn't resolve into bodies. I hid the picture so the younger children could not see it, to protect them against the fear of such powerful evil, not to break the news to them too soon. Occasionally, I took it out to study. I hid it so well, I lost it. I drew billows and shafts of light, and almost heard the golden music of it, the gold trumpets and drums of it.

The yearning for beauty can prettify reality, and sometimes imagination has to restore us to terror.

(Do you have any friends—I do—who believe that they are poets because they have imagination and poetic feelings even though they don't write at all? I don't like telling them so, but it seems to me that imagination is one thing and writing is something else, a putting-into-words. Words pin down the once-seen, and reproduce it for readers. That's why I'm quoting from my books so much—I need those words to call forth other realities. The New Critics seem to be breathing over my shoulders and saying, "Cut it out." The work is supposed to be a self-contained whole, speaking for itself. There's not supposed to be an imagination apart from the work. But I know there is one. Words are only the known world—La Terra Conoscivta—beyond which the old maps showed Arabia Deserta, the Great American Desert, Red Cloud's Country, the unattached Territories, the Badlands, Barbaria, the Abode of Emptiness, the Mountains of the White Tigers, the Sea of Darkness—sea serpents and mermaids swam there—"strange beasts be here."—Nada ou Nouvel, whence the four winds blew. And the space maps show the Hyperspace Barrier, areas of Giants, Supergiants, Dwarfs, Protogalaxies, Black Holes—infinite areas named with a word or two.)

The Brother in Vietnam, who has some imagination left, refuses to go to language school because he can picture scenes in which he would use the *Vietnamese Phrase Book:*

Welcome, Sir. Glad to meet you.
How many are with you? Show me on your fingers.
Are you afraid of the enemy? Us?
Do you believe in
(1) U.S. victory?
(2) annihilation of Bolshevism?
Are you afraid? Why?
If we cannot trust a man,
(1) wink your eye
(2) place your left hand on your stomach
(3) move your hand to the right, unnoticed, until we note your signal.

And because he knows languages, the brother cannot go wholeheartedly to war against people who have the same words as the Chinese for "happiness," "contentment," "bliss," "orchid," the same pun on "lettuce" and "life," the same words for things that matter, "study," "university," "love." The young men in the Vietnam story have reader's block.

As a passenger on a bombing run, the Brother in Vietnam tries his best to see.

> Even using binoculars, he did not see much of the shore. Hanoi was an hour away by plane. He did not see the bombs drop out of the plane, whether they turned and turned, flashing in the sun. During loading, when they were locked into place, they looked like neatly rolled joints; they looked like long grains of rice, they looked like pupae and turds. He never heard cries under the bombing.

We approach the truth with metaphors.

> All that he witnessed was heavy jungle and, in the open skies, other planes that seemed to appear and disappear quickly, shiny planes and their decals and formations. The bombs must have gone off behind them. Some air turbulence might have been a bomb ejected.

When a pilot did not show up in the chow line, it was up to the other men to imagine his death.

> John Hawkes approaches God with metaphor:

> . . . and I heard what she was saying: "God snapping him fingers," she said, and that sudden moment of waking was just what she said, "God snapping him fingers," though it was probably Edward breaking a twig or one of the birds bounding a bright seed off the smooth green back of a resounding calabash.

> Now, I have told you those things about imagination that I'm sure of, and I have shown ways that words hold the imaginary; the book opens like hands parting, presenting you a surprise. But there are properties of the imagination which I don't understand at all. I hope that one of you will delve into the following, and let the rest of us know:

> How is it possible that the writer can suddenly and effortlessly become now this character and now that one, see through his eyes, her eyes, speak with his voice, her voice, make the reader view the world with the soul of another? I can see a room, a forest, a street, from a very particular character's angle of vision, and there are details as definite as if

I were watching a movie with point-of-view camera directions. What is the process that makes this—what is it? empathy? voodoo?—happen? If the "blocked" writer can't do this anymore, how can I show her how it's done? In voodoo, creatures exchange souls. But there are exercises and rites in voodoo, whereas in writing, the inhabiting of another person seems to happen spontaneously. Would it do us good to study with voodoo priestesses?

What about interest? How is it that interest is an emotion in me, and, I presume, in other writers. There are things, people, images that seem to have no significance in the world but are obsessionally interesting to me. And there are major current events, wars, assassinations that you would think every informed person should care about, and I cannot work up an interest. For about thirty-five years, I glimpsed a sharp white triangle. It looked like a shark's tooth or a corner of paper or a creased pantleg. I felt great fear and energy whenever I beheld it. I beheld it and beheld it until I found the story of it. That white triangle turned out to be *China Men,* and appears contained in that book as the creased pantleg of a Navy officer looking for the stowaway father. Where did that image come from? Why is it full of radiation—stories ramifying from it? How do you recognize this white triangle when it appears? How do you evoke one?

And that snap—God's fingers? a bird? a twig?—how and why did John Hawkes hear that snap?

Perhaps it does some good just to be aware of these writer's figments. Wanting them and wanting to write well may help them come.

Voodoo and white triangles. No wonder Shakespeare compared the lunatic, the lover, and the poet.

> The lunatic, the lover, and the poet
> Are of imagination all compact
> One sees more devils than vast hell can hold,
> That is, the madman; the lover, all as frantic,
> Sees Helen's brow in a brow of Egypt.
> The poet's eye in a fine frenzy rolling,
> Doth glance from heaven to earth, from earth to heaven;
> And as imagination bodies forth
> The forms of things unknown, the poet's pen
> Turns them to shapes and gives to airy nothing
> A local habitation and a name.

Everybody knows about being a lover, so I'll just talk about madness. Haven't you tried to go mad? What a relief it would be. You could act any way you please. Say anything to anybody. But don't give in to madness. It binds too tightly. Moon Orchid, who couldn't speak English, imagined that the Mexicans plotted against her. She was talking-story as fast as she could, putting into words what the people around her were doing. And she kept repeating the same crazy stories over and over.

The lunatic exaggerates evil, and the lover exaggerates beauty. The poet, though, makes things real. I like that plain word *local*—and take it to mean the mundane, the ordinary. In the formless universe, the poet makes us at home.

Here's how John Hawkes ends *Second Skin:*

Now I sit at my long table in the middle of my loud wandering night and by the light of a candle—one half-burned candle saved from last night's spectacle—I watch this final flourish of my own hand and muse and blow away the ashes and listen to the breathing among the rubbery leaves and the insects sweating out the night. Because now I am fifty-nine years old and I knew I would be, and now there is the sun in the evening, the moon at dawn, the still voice. That's it. The sun in the evening. The moon at dawn. The still voice.

What's it? What still voice? We have to learn to hear it.

Finally, remember the most common use of imagination, its fantastic and magical power to turn the order of things upside down. I wrote about a tribe of musical barbarians, who played reed flutes and fought with bows and arrows. So I invented for them a nock whistle to attach to their arrows; the archers shot terrifying sounds through the air. Then, my book finished, I went to a Chinese archaeological exhibit, and there, in the last case before the exit—I was just about to leave but turned back—behind the glass was a nock whistle. I believe that I caused it to appear on earth. Just as, because my husband and I wrote many papers about him, one day John Hawkes appeared at our door and said, "Hello, my name is Jack. And this is my wife, Sophie."

The Hazards and Sources of Writing

Norman Mailer

There's nothing more boring than a speaker who starts to talk about a writing award and quickly reveals that he knows nothing about it. But it so happens that the Hopwood Awards really do have a well-deserved fame because they were the first significant college literary awards in the country. In the years when I went to Harvard, from 1939 to 1943, we always used to hear about them and wish we had awards of that sort at Harvard, at least those of us who were certain we were going to be writers. In 1946, the year I got out of the Army, I lived in a brownstone in Brooklyn Heights and in the same brownstone, which had only four apartments in it, lived Arthur Miller. I soon learned from his and my friend Norman Rosten that Miller had won a Hopwood Award. That was the first thing I knew about him. He had a play on Broadway that year called *All My Sons* and that was the year he was writing *Death of a Salesman* and I was writing *The Naked and the Dead*. We used to meet occasionally in the hall when we went down to get our mail. Those days Miller was a shy man and I was fairly shy myself and we would just mutter a few words to each other and try to be pleasant and then go our separate ways. I think I can speak with authority about Miller's reaction, I know I can about my own: each of us would walk away and say to himself, "That other guy, he ain't going to amount to nothin'."

It's an anecdote about another writer that introduces my talk today. Kurt Vonnegut and I are friendly with one another, but wary. There was a period when we used to go out together a great deal because our wives liked each other and Kurt and I would sit there like bookends. We would be terribly careful with one another; we both knew the huge cost of a literary feud so we certainly didn't want to argue. On the other hand neither of us would be caught dead saying to the other, "Gee, I liked your last book" and then be met with a silence because the party of the second part could not reciprocate. So we would talk about anything else, we would talk about Las Vegas or the Galápagos Islands. We only had one literary conversation and that was one night in New York. Kurt looked up and sighed, "Well, I finished my novel today and it like to killed me." When Kurt is feeling heartfelt he speaks in an old Indiana accent which I will do my best to reproduce. His wife said, "Oh Kurt, you always say that whenever you finish a book" and he replied, "Well, whenever I finish a book I do say it and it is always true and it gets more true and this last one like to killed me more than any."

Before I talk about the ways in which books kill you I want to tell you one final story that has obsessed me for a long time. I have pondered this story for years and just the other day while thinking about it I came up with a new idea. So I'll tell you the story the way I used to tell it and only then will add the new thought. The story is that the distinguished painter Robert Rauschenberg was once given a gift of a pastel from Willem de Kooning. Rauschenberg, with de Kooning's permission, erased the pastel and then signed it *Pastel by de Kooning Erased by Robert Rauschenberg* and then he sold it. To be crude about it, that story fried one half of my mind because I thought, there's something profound here but I can't get ahold of it. And then the light came to me. I said, "Of course, what Rauschenberg was saying is that the artist has the same right to print money as the financier. Money is nothing but authority imprinted upon emptiness" and laid the story to rest and was totally content until the other day when I thought, wait a minute, maybe the person who bought the pastel was neither a gambler nor even someone who is so aware of chic in painting that he knew he would make a profit from it. Maybe if a truly talented painter erases the work of another truly talented painter, there's a resonance, an echo, in the lost work. If Fidel Castro had executed Charles de Gaulle, let's say, and buried him himself that would not be ordinary burial ground. There would be an aura about the place. Students of the occult would pay great attention to it and I thought maybe that's what was going on here—that some echo of de Kooning's original work might be *illuminating* the person who purchased it. Now I am obsessed with the story again because one of two possibilities exists: either the act was an outrage or it advances art significantly. I will ask you to hold this story in suspension until the very end of my remarks when its meanings will either strike you powerfully or not. As a professional speaker I know that the worst thing you can ever do is introduce some notion that's subtle and profound to an audience at the beginning of your talk because they think of nothing else for the rest of the time that you are up there, or at least half their mind ponders it while they pretend to listen to you. But certain saws are useful when you come to the state of Michigan and one of them is that there is no fool like an old fool. I am always trying out this premise: can you get your audience interested in something and then proceed to desert the topic and never come back? So keep in mind my story about Rauschenberg while I speak more formally on "The Hazards and Sources of Writing."

When we contemplate the extraordinary terrain, psychologically speaking, that extends across the profession of novel writing it may help to divide this region of endeavor into three self-contained lands. We could speak of the techniques of novel writing, that is, plot, point of view, pace, novelistic strategies, or whatever else can reasonably be taught in a classroom. All of these are elements appropriate to the first territory—techniques—but I will not speak of that today. For all I know, many of you are able to expatiate on these matters with more brilliance than myself. I am an old student of writing, not a young one. I have a tendency to mumble about technical matters like an old mechanic: "Let's put the thingamajig before the whoosits here" is how I usually state the deepest literary problems to myself. Therefore, I am going to move over to the second and third parts of this admittedly arbitrary division of the subject. I am going to speak of the psychology, or maybe it is closer to say the existential state, of the novel writer once he has passed his apprenticeship—and to avoid tremendous amounts of trouble for the rest of this occasion, let me say that I am going back to the old English tradition of using the possessive pronoun *his* to indicate all of human-kind. The apprenticeship of an established writer is subject to all the hazards of his profession, those perils of writer's block and failing energy, alcoholism, drugs, and desertion. For many a writer deserts his writing to go into a collateral profession in advertising or academia, trade journals, publishing . . . the list is very long. What is not routine is to become a young writer with a firmly established name. Luck as well as talent can take one across that first border. Some do surpass the trials of learning technique and commence to make a living at our bizarre profession. It is then, however, that less-charted perils begin. I would like to speak at length of the hazards of writing, the cruelties it extorts out of the mind and flesh and then if we are not too depressed by these bleak prospects, go over to the last of these three lands, which is comparable to heaven or to Atlantis or at least to a kingdom beneath the sea for it resides in no less a place than the mysterious dimension of our unconscious: the source land of all our projects, the essence of our aesthetic flights, and no human, no matter how professional, can speak with authority of what goes on there. We are only going to wander at the edges of such a magnificent region and be satisfied, I hope, with the quickest glimpses of its wonders and mysteries. No one can explore the mystery of novel writing to its deepest source.

Let me speak first of the hazards. I know something of them and I ought to. My first story was published after all more than forty years ago and the first novel I wrote that saw print is going to be thirty-six years old in a month. Obviously for a long time I have been accustomed to thinking of myself as a writer, even as others see me that way. So I hear one lament over and over from strangers: "Oh, I too would have liked to be an author." You can almost hear them musing aloud about the freedom of the life. How felicitous to have no boss and face no morning rush to work, to know all the intoxications of celebrity—how they long to satisfy the voice within that keeps saying, "What a pity that no one will know how unusual my life has been! There are all those secrets I cannot tell!" Years ago I wrote, "Experience, when it cannot be communicated to another must wither within and be worse than lost." I often ponder the remark. Once in a while your hand will write out a sentence that seems true and yet you do not know where it came from. Ten or twenty words seem able to live in balance with your experience. It may be one's nicest reward as a writer. You feel you have come near the truth. When that happens you can look at the page years later and meditate again on the meaning, for it goes deep. So I think I understand why people want to write. All the same, I am also a professional and so there is another part of me, I confess, that is ready to laugh when strangers tell me of their aspirations. I am not free of the scorn of a veteran prize fighter who hears someone say, "I'd like to flatten that bully." The speaker does not know how many years of discipline and dull punishment must be given over to the ability to throw a good punch at will. I say to myself, "They can write an interesting letter so they assume they are ready to tell the story of their lives. They do not understand how much work it will take to pick up even the rudiments of narrative." If I believe that the person who has spoken to me in this fashion is serious I warn them as gently as I can. I say, "Well, it's probably as hard to learn to write as to play the piano." Then if their only reason for wanting to be a writer is to pull in some quick success they get depressed and that's OK with me. One shouldn't encourage people to write for too little. It's a splendid life when you think of its emoluments but it is death to the soul if you are not good at it.

Let me keep my promise, then, and go on a little about the negative part of being a writer. Those few of you here who don't see yourselves as potential writers may then feel less wistful, for if you still have not discovered whether you are talented enough to tell your private tale, you will at least have escaped an awful pressure. To skip at one bound over all these fascinating and (as today) happy years when one is an apprentice writer and learning every day, at least on góod days, there is in contrast the abominable pressure on the life of the professional novelist. For soon after you finish each hard-earned book the reviews come in and the reviews are murderous. Contrast an author's reception to an actor's. With the notable exception of John Simon, theater critics do not often try to kill performers. I believe there is an unspoken agreement that thespians deserve to be protected against the perils of first nights. After all, the actor is daring a rejection that can prove as fearful as a major wound. For sensitive human beings like actors a hole in the ego can be worse than a hole in the heart. Such moderation does not carry over, however, into literary criticism. *Meretricious, dishonest, labored, loathsome, pedestrian, hopeless, disgusting, disappointing, raunchy, ill-wrought, boring*—these are not uncommon words for a typical review. I still remember, and it is close to thirty years ago, that my second novel, *Barbary Shore,* was characterized by the massive authority of the reviewer at *Time* magazine as "paceless, tasteless, and graceless." I am still looking forward to the day when I meet him. You would be hard put to find another professional field where criticism is equally savage. Accountants, lawyers, engineers, and doctors do not often speak publicly in this manner.

Yet the unhappiest thing to say is that our critical practice may even be fair, harsh but fair. After all, one prepares a book in the safety of the study and nothing short of your self-esteem, your bills, or your editor is forcing you to show your stuff. You put your book out, if you can afford to take the time, only when it is ready. If economic necessity forces you to write somewhat faster than is good for you—well, everybody has their sad story. As a practical matter not that much has to be written into the teeth of a gale and few notes need be taken on the side of a cliff. An author usually does his stint at the desk, feeling not too hungry and suffering no pains greater than the view of his empty pad of paper. Now granted that white sheet can look as blank as a television screen when the station is off the air, but that is not a danger, merely an awesome presence. The writer, unlike more active creative artists, works in no immediate peril. Why should not the open season begin so soon as the work comes out? If talented authors were to have it better than actors in all ways, there would be a tendency for actors to disappear and talented authors to multiply, so the critics keep our numbers down.

In fact, not too many good writers do remain productive through the decades. There are too many other hazards as well. We are jerked by the media in and out of fashion and each drop from popularity can feel like a termination to your career. Such insecurity is no help to morale, for even in the best periods every writer always knows one little terror. *Does it stop tomorrow? Does it all stop tomorrow?* Writing is spooky. There is no routine of an office to keep you going, only the white page each morning and you never know where your words are coming from, those divine words. So your professionalism at best is fragile. You cannot always tell yourself that fashions pass and history will smile at you again. In the literary world it is not easy to acquire the stoicism to endure, especially if you've begun as an oversensitive adolescent. It is not even automatic to pray for luck if it has been pessimism itself which gave force to your early themes. Maybe it is no more than blind will, but some authors stay at it. Over and over they keep writing a new book and do it in the knowledge that upon its publication they will probably be savaged and will not be able to fight back. An occasional critic can be singled out for counterattack, or one can always write a letter to the editor of the book section, but such efforts at self-defense are like rifle fire against fighter planes. All-powerful is the writer when he sits at his desk, but on the public stage he may feel as if his rights are puny. His courage, if he has any, must learn to live with the bruises left by comments on his work. The spiritual skin may go slack or harden to leather, but the honor of his effort to live down bad reviews and write again has to be analogous to the unspoken, unremarked courage of people who dwell under the pressure of a long illness and somehow resolve enough of their inmost contradictions to be able to get better. I suppose this is equal to saying that you cannot become a professional writer and keep active for three or four decades unless you learn to live with the most difficult condition of your existence, which is that superficial book reviewing is irresponsible and serious literary criticism can be close to merciless. The conviction that such a condition is fair has to take root deep enough to bear analogy to the psychology of a peasant who farms a mountain slope and takes it for granted that he was meant to toil through the years with one foot standing higher than the other.

Every good author who manages to forge a long career for himself must be able, therefore, to build a character that will not be unhinged by a bad reception. That takes art. Few writers have rugged personalities when they are young. In general, the girls seldom look like potential beauty contest winners and the boys show small promise of becoming future All-Americans. They are most likely to be found on the sidelines commencing to cook up that warped, passionate, bitter, transcendent view of life which will bring them later to the attention of the American public, but only later. The young writer usually starts as a loser and so is obliged to live with the conviction that the world he knows had better be wrong or he is wrong. On the answer depends one's evaluation of one's right to survive. Thanks to greed, plastics, mass media, and various abominations of technology—lo, the world is wrong. The paranoid aim of a cockeyed young writer has as much opportunity to hit the target as the beauty queen's wide-eyed lack of paranoia. So occasionally this loser of a young writer ends up a winner, for a while. His vision has projected him forward, he is just enough ahead of his time. But dependably that wretched, lonely act of writing will force him back. Writing arouses too much commotion in one's psyche to allow the author to rest happily.

It is not easy to explain such disturbances to people unless they do write. Someone who has never tried fiction will hardly be quick to understand that in the study a writer often does feel godlike. There he sits, ensconced in judgment on other people's lives. Yet contemplate the person in the chair; he could be hung over and full of the small shames of what he did yesterday, or what he did ten years ago. Those failures of life, those flashes of old fiascos, wait like ghosts in the huge house of the empty middle-aged self. Sometimes the ghosts even appear and ask to be laid to rest. Consciously or unconsciously, writers must fashion a new peace with the past every day they attempt to write. They must rise above despising themselves. If they cannot, they will probably lose the sanction to appear like god to themselves and render judgment on others.

Yet the writer at work must not tolerate too much good news either. At his desk it is best if he does not come to like himself too much. Wonderfully agreeable memories may appear on certain mornings, but if they have nothing to do with the work they must be banished or they will leave the writer too cheerful, too energetic, too forgiving, too horny. It is in the calm depression of a good judge that one's scribblings

move best over the page. Indeed, just as a decent judge will feel that he
has injured society by giving an unfair verdict, so does an author have to
ask himself constantly if he is being fair to his characters. For if the writer
does violate the life of someone who is being written about—that is,
proceeds in the ongoing panic of trying to keep a book amusing to
distort his characters to more comic, more corrupt, or more evil forms
than he secretly believes they deserve—then he may be subtly injuring
the reader. That is a moral crime. Few authors are innocent of such a
practice; on the other hand not so many artists can be found who are not
guilty, also, of softening their portraits. Some novelists don't want to
destroy the sympathy their readers may feel for an appealing heroine by
the admission that she shrieks at her children. Sales fly out the window.
It takes as much literary integrity to be tough, therefore, as to be fair.
The trail is narrow. It is difficult to keep up one's literary standards
through the long slogging reaches in the middle of a book. The early
pleasures of conception no longer sustain you; the writer plods along
with the lead feet of habit, the dry breath of discipline, and the knowledge that on the other side of the hill the critics—who also have their
talent to express—are waiting. Sooner or later you come to the conclusion that if you are going to survive you had better, where it concerns
your own work, become the best critic of them all. There is a saying
among boxers that the punch you see hurts less than the one you never
came to see. An author who would find the resources to keep writing
from one generation to the next does well to climb above his own ego
high enough to see every flaw in the work. Otherwise he will never be
able to decide what are its true merits.

Let yourself live, however, with an awareness of your book's lacks
and short-cuts, its gloss where courage might have produced a little real
shine, and you can bear the bad reviews. You can even tell when the
critic is not exposing your psyche so much as he is turning his own dirty
pockets out. It proves amazing how many evil reviews one can digest if
there is a confidence that one has done one's best on a book, written to
the limit of one's honesty, even scraped off a little of one's dishonesty.
Get to that point of purity and your royalties may be injured by a small
welcome but not your working morale. There is even hope that if the
book is better than its reception, one's favorite readers will come eventually to care for it more. The prescription, therefore, is simple: one must
not put out a job that has any serious taint of the meretricious. At least
the prescription ought to be simple, but then how few of us ever do

work of which we are not in fact a bit ashamed. It comes down to a
matter of degree. There is that remark of Engels to Marx, "quantity
changes quality." A single potato is there for us to eat, but ten thousand
potatoes are a commodity and have to be put in bins or boxes. A profit
must be made from them or a loss will certainly be taken. By analogy a
little corruption in a book is as forgivable as the author's style, but a
sizable literary delinquency is a diseased organ, or so it will feel if the
critics begin to bang on it and happen to be right for once. That will be
the hour when one's creditors do not go away. I wonder if we have not
touched the fear that is back of the writing in many a good novelist's
heart, the hazard beneath all others.

Now this much said we might quit with the agreeable moral instruction that one must do one's best to be honest. If I had any common
sense I would thank you and leave the podium. Unfortunately, there is
more to be mentioned about writing. Like love, one never comes to
understand it altogether; there's always room to expound some more.
The act of writing is a mystery and the more you labor at it, the more
you become aware that it is not answers which are being offered after a
life of such activity so much as a greater appreciation of the scope of the
literary mysteries. The ultimate pleasure in spending one's days as a
writer is the resonance you can bring afterward to your personal experience. So the mystery of the profession—where those words come from
and how to account for their alchemy on the page—not only arouses
terror at the thought of one's powers disappearing, but also inspires the
happiness that one may be in contact with the source of literature itself.
Now, of course, we cannot talk directly of such prodigious matters; it is
enough to amuse ourselves with approaches to the problem. In my late
childhood, for example, which is to say in my college years, students
used to have one certainty. It was that environment was all; one was the
product of one's milieu, one's parents, one's food, one's conversations,
one's dearest and/or most odious human relations. One was the sum of
one's own history as it was cradled in the larger history of one's time.
One was a product, and if one wrote novels, they were merely a product
of the product. With this working philosophy I did one book—it happened to be *The Naked and the Dead*—which was wholly comfortable to
me. I would not have known at that hour what an author meant by
speaking of any of his works as uncomfortable. *The Naked and the Dead*
seemed a sure result of all I had learned up to the age of twenty-five, all I
had experienced and all I had read. My characters had already been

conceived and put in file boxes before they were ever on the page. I had hundreds of filled-out file cards before I ever began to write. The novel itself seemed merely the end of a long active assembly line and I felt able to account for each part of it.

Since its immediate success catapulted this author into another existence altogether, however, such a comfortable view of literature was soon lost. You will forgive me for now proceeding to go on a bit about my own works. It's because I am an authority on the conditions under which they were written. It is the only matter on which I am an authority and if I were to talk on the novels of other authors in the same vein I would merely be speculating on how they were written. So let me say that the next book on which I embarked after *The Naked and the Dead* was such a mystery to me that to this day I do not comprehend it. I can tell you what it is about, what I was trying to say, but do not ask me where *Barbary Shore* came from. I used to feel as if this second novel was being written by someone else. Where *The Naked and the Dead* had been put together with all the solid agreeable effort of a young carpenter constructing a decent house while full of the practices, techniques, and wisdom of those who built houses before him, *Barbary Shore* might as well have been dictated to me by a ghost in the middle of a forest. Each morning I would sit down to work with no notion at all of how to continue. My characters were strangers to me and each day after a few hours of blind work (because I never seemed to get more than a sentence or two ahead of myself) I would push my plot and people three manuscript pages further forward into their eventual denouement, but I never knew what I was doing nor where it came from. It's fortunate that I had heard of Freud and the unconscious; if not I would have had to postulate such a condition myself. An unconscious was the only explanation for what was going on. Of course, given my distraught state I might well have been committed the moment I started to babble about this unconscious, if not for the happy fact that everyone around me was also aware of the now-established theories of the good doctor from Vienna. I was left aware, however, of two presences cooperating in the production of a literary work, and the second had the capacity to take over the act of authorship from the first.

Since then I have not written a novel which has not belonged to one category or the other. Some, of course, have belonged to both. They have come out of the deepest parts of my unconscious but have also been the obvious result of long and painstaking conscious preparations. *The*

Deer Park and *Ancient Evenings* are fair representatives of this mixture of categories, and then there was my novel *The Executioner's Song* which was so close to the facts of a real event that many would argue that it was not a novel at all. Obviously it was as much a part of the same family of books as *The Naked and the Dead.* At the other extreme is *Why Are We in Vietnam?* That was a work which not only emerged out of some obscure part of me but was also not in my style. Indeed not even in a voice remotely like my own. I can never read it aloud with success. When I try to, I'm tempted to ask for an actor to step up from the audience who can do it better than I can. Yet I wrote it in three happy and confused months. Some novels take years, and some novels shift the weights and balances of your character forever by the act of writing them, but this work took only three months and passed through me with the strangest tones. Never before or since have I been remotely as funny. The work was wild and comic to an extreme. I used to go in each morning and the voice of my main character, a highly improbable sixteen-year-old genius—I did not even know if he was white or black; he claimed to be one or the other at different times—would commence, he would travel through my mind and emerge. I had no idea where he came from nor where he was going. I felt like a spirit medium; I needed only to have the decency to appear at my desk at the regular time and (I cannot call him He) It would begin to speak. I thought of the book afterward as a gift, for compared to others I hardly had to work at all.

Sometimes when I am feeling tolerant to the idea of karma, demiurges, spirits of the age, and the intervention of angels, saints, and demons, I also wonder if being a writer over a long career does not leave you open to more than one origin for your work. In a long career one may come forth with many books that are products of one's skill and education, of one's dedication, but I also wonder if once in a while the gods do not look about and have their own novels to propose and peer down among us and say, "Here is a good one for Bellow" or "That would have been a saucy dish for Cheever, too bad he's gone" or, in my own case, "Look at poor old Mailer worrying about his job again. Let's make him the agent for this absolutely wicked little thing about Vietnam." Who knows? we may be sturdy literary engineers full of sound literary practice or, as equally, unwitting agents for forces beyond our comprehension. It matters less than the knowledge that our books can come from more than one wondrous place. After all, it is not so depressing to think that with all our hungers we can also have the fortune to be handed in passing a few gifts we do not deserve. How agreeable to feel kin to the force that put paintings on the walls of caves, set stonecutters to exactitudes that would permit gothic arches, gave the calculus to Newton's age and space travel to ours. No, it is not so ill to sense that we are also heir to emanations from some unaccountable and fabulous source. Nothing lifts our horizons like a piece of unexpected luck or the generosity of the gods.

The Beliefs of Writers

E. L. Doctorow

All writers relish stories from the lives of the masters. We hold them in our minds as a kind of trade lore. We hope the biography of the great writer yields secrets of his achievement. As many writers as Hemingway inspired to write he probably inspired to hunt or to box. I imagine many of them crouching this very moment in their duck blinds. Writers always want to learn how to live as a means of bringing out the best they have in themselves.

The master's life I've been thinking about lately is Tolstoy's, in particular his crisis of conscience at the age of fifty. Always at the mercy either of his passions or his ethics, Tolstoy lived in a kind of alternating current of tormented resolution. The practice of fiction left him elated and terribly let down. It's said that he had to be prevented from throwing the finished manuscript of *Anna Karenina* into the fire. In any event, at the age of fifty he decided that his life lacked justification, that he was no better than a pander to people who had nothing better to do with their time than to read. And he gave up writing novels.

Of course, his resolve did not seem to cover the shorter form and over the years he lapsed into the composition of a few modest pieces— "The Kreutzer Sonata," "The Death of Ivan Ilyich"—but for the most part he employed his position and his talents to militate against some of the overwhelming misery of life under the Czar. He indulged a prophetic voice. He preached his doctrine of Christian nonviolence. He wrote primers designed to teach the children of peasants to read.

Now theoretically, at least, there is for every writer a point at which he or she might come to the same conclusion as Tolstoy, a point at which circumstantial reality overwhelms the very idea of art or seems to demand a practical benefit from it; when the level of perceived or felt communal suffering or danger makes the traditional practice of literature for traditional purposes, intolerable. But even a casual examination of literary history finds a readier disposition for this crisis of faith in Europe, where the passion of art has often been a social passion. So in

Russia we have not only the example of Count Tolstoy stomping around in his peasant boots but the young Dostoyevski and his circle arguing everything about fiction except its enormous importance to history and human salvation. And in France we have Sartre and Camus, among others, conceiving a response to the moral devastation of World War II, a literary Resistance that includes drama, allegory, metaphysics, and handing out pamphlets in the streets.

With certain exceptions, American writers have tended to be less fervent about the social value of art and therefore less vulnerable to crises of conscience. The spiritual problems of our writers are celebrated but of a different kind from those having to do with the problem of engagement. Our nineteenth-century masters lived in sparse populations. Forests, the sea, the prairie, were images of terrifying freedom. So we've been brought up on solitude as much as society. We have a different faith to lose. I think of the despair of Hemingway, for instance, that led him to turn one of his shotguns on himself, or Faulkner's and Fitzgerald's that led them to drink themselves into ruin. The problem as they lived it was a torment of success or failure but in any event some recognition of mortal limits, some inconsolability of rugged individualism formulated entirely as a private faith. Tolstoy, we should remember, lived to write his last novel, *Resurrection,* when he was in his seventies. His ego is no less colossal but our American masters thought with theirs to hold up the earth and sky.

So in thinking about Leo Tolstoy's attitude, I'm very much aware of its foreignness. We have had one decade in our own literary history, the 1930s, when politics and art, engagement, seemed to be on everyone's mind, but we take this period as a time of misfired artistic energy, of duped intellectuals and bad proletarian novels. Having been turned ideological, we suffered for it, or so the lesson goes. American novelists since then have tended to cast themselves resolutely as private citizens and independent entrepreneurs. There is certainly no tradition among us for serving our country as senators and ambassadors like our European and Latin American colleagues. Our ancestry reveals an occasional customs inspector. We see the public value of our work as an accident of its private diction. Our attitude is expressed succinctly by the naturalized American poet W. H. Auden, who said a writer's politics are more of a danger to him than his cupidity. We worry that if a work is formed by ideas exterior to it, if there is some sort of programmed intention, a set of truths to be illustrated, the work will be compromised and we'll produce not art but polemic. We want our novels pure. We dislike about *War and Peace* that Tolstoy lectures us on history. He was always that way, we think, not just after the age of fifty.

Oddly enough, the aesthetic piety just described places the artist's idea of himself centrally in the American heartland. The notion that we are the independent entrepreneurs of ourselves is a national heritage. Irving Howe, among others, has pointed out that working people in the United States, unlike their European counterparts, refuse to identify themselves as a class. They tend to define themselves not by their work but by what they own from their work, the property they've accumulated, their ethnic background, their social activities—by anything, in short, that points up their distinction from the larger community. For the independent entrepreneur of himself, there is upward mobility, at least across generations, and there is the road—he can hit the road when things go bad, pull up stakes, move on. All this including the writer's idea of what he can allow in his art and what he cannot expresses our great operative myth of individualism.

We are thought as a country to be nonideological and nonsystematic in the way we go about conceptualizing our problems and solving them—or not solving them. We are chronically and by nature suspicious of systematic solutions. We're pragmatists. We like to go out in the barn of the Constitution and tinker. Writers no less than blue-collar people share the national aversion for the intellect, for the passion of the intellect, and the voices we find for our books are a shade more ironical and less epic than the Tolstoyan basso profundo. In preference to the Olympian view from the mountain we settle for the authority of the egalitarian witness, the pragmatic deposer of what he can confirm with his own eyes and ears.

If there was a moment when this piety of literary practice was set to harden, perhaps it was in 1940 with the publication of Hemingway's *For Whom the Bell Tolls*. What preceded it was a decade of intense debate carried on both within the work of novelists and critics and outside it in journals and in symposia or conferences. Almost no serious work of the era was not informed by the presumption of social crisis. Confronted with the miseries of the Depression, and the rise of the modern totalitarian state, writers and artists and intellectuals argued the alternatives to industrial capitalism. We are told this in Malcolm Cowley's book *And I Worked at the Writer's Trade*. The spirit shared inescapably by every American artist was the longing for ideal community. Among writers this spirit moved as much in the thought of conservative Southern Agrarians like John Crowe Ransom and Allen Tate, who could project a utopia based on the civilities of Southern farm life; or T. S. Eliot, behind whose Waste Land lay a golden, God-lit medieval city; as in the more numerous prophets of the varieties of Marxian socialism.

And outside the books the value and justification of literature, of any art, came into furious debate. Whatever position a writer took, from formalism to communism, the need to take some position was inescapable. The writer's destiny was to be confronted with his conscience, to find his place, draw his lines. Commitment—to what? Engagement—of what sort? The process was both brutal and complicated. The world didn't stay still but moved along. History contaminated pure thoughts, the right causes got mixed up with the wrong people, ideals gave away to expediency, and hateful writers did good work and noble writers did lousy work. But everyone—good writers, bad writers—seemed to be in touch with what was going on in the world.

Hemingway himself had published a novel in 1937, *To Have and Have Not,* in which the Hemingway hero, a smuggler off the Florida coast, came as close as he ever had to articulating a communal sentiment. His name in this book is Harry Morgan and he's made to say "A man alone ain't got no bloody fucking chance." This is a monumental insight coming from the younger sibling of the romantically self-involved expatriates of the earlier novels.

Hemingway's next novel was to take place in Spain at the time of the civil war. He had seen the war firsthand, he was more worldly and more in touch with things than either Faulkner or Fitzgerald. Though he was a Loyalist, he deeply mistrusted and came to detest the Communists who ran things for the Loyalist side. This judgment, which turned out to be sound, was not unlike that of George Orwell in *Homage to Catalonia.* But it was Orwell, the European, who took what he learned to the point of revelation, the political prophecy of *Nineteen Eighty-Four.* We find by contrast in *For Whom the Bell Tolls* that a man alone may have no bloody fucking chance but it can be very beautiful that he hasn't. The Hemingway hero is now named Robert Jordan and he's a young American volunteer on the Loyalist side, a demolitions expert who is coming to the mountains to blow a bridge held by the Phalangists. He ends up dying alone, heroically, having taken over the leadership of the partisan band he's joined, and sent them away to live on, his own code of honor the only enduring value of The Civil War of the Spanish people. The most

international of American writers, was, morally speaking, an isolation-
ist. War is the means by which one's cultivated individualism can be
raised to the heroic. And therefore, never send to ask for whom the bell
tolls; it tolls: so that I can be me.

Now before you or I overread my claim, or what it is I'm getting to,
let me take a moment to clarify something. I mean not to make pronouncements about literature but to speak of literary belief, which is
something else than literature. Literary belief is the culture of presump-
tions and ideas that govern those of us who make literature our lives as
writers. So I do not intend here to contrast Realism and Experimentalism
or to speak of the Romantic tradition or the influences of Modernism or
any of that sort of thing which properly is the province of the literary
critic and historian. What I'm doing is thinking out loud about where we
are now, all of us, in our practice of fiction and perhaps how we got here.
What do we believe about our writing, our calling, what do we think its
possibilities are? In a catalogue of publications by the University of
Chicago Press, I recently noticed a title that interested me, *The Soviet
Novel: History as Ritual,* by Professor Katerina Clark. The copy advises
that Professor Clark's study of the Soviet novel turns on the idea of its
serving as a repository of official myths. Knowing the fate of dissident
Soviet authors and meeting them now in numbers in this country, it
seems a reasonable claim and I look forward to reading the book. But I
warrant that some of the serious works of American fiction, no less than
our kitsch, in some ways serve as repositories for our myths, though of
course not by direction and of course our myths are not official, at least
not until recently. And a consideration of Hemingway now fifty or sixty
years later has to include the possibility that his popularity with the
public and among young writers was in part due to his service as a
repository of American myth. The entrepreneurial self had come in for
some rough treatment from Melville in *Moby-Dick* and from Dreiser in
Sister Carrie. But Hemingway found its most romantic face. Withdrawal
from society, distrust of it, despair of it, has been preponderant in our
fiction ever since Robert Jordan withdrew from life and love and looked
out over the barrel of his rifle on the last page of *For Whom the Bell Tolls.*
It is as if given the self, nothing but the self—not God, not the state,
love, or any conviction of a universal order—we have made ourselves its
annotators. We may have rejected Hemingway's romance—the self has
become absurd, blackly humorous, and, finally, shattered and fragmentary—but, and this is the point, it is ours.

Surely we can say of contemporary fiction without fear of contradiction that it suffers from a reduced authority, certainly for its readers
who seem to be reading less of it. It may be that the most avid readers of
new fiction in America today are film producers, an indication of the
trouble we're in. But what is more peculiar is the reduced authority of
fiction in the minds of writers themselves, who seem to want to take on
less and less of the world with it. This is an impression, of course,
nothing more. And even as I test it in my mind with several significant
exceptions, it nevertheless seems valid to say that there is a timidity to
serious fiction now, some modesty of conception and language, that has
pulled us back from its old haunts. There seems to be a disposition many
of us have to accept some rule largely hidden, to circumscribe our analysis and our geography, to come indoors and lock the door and pull the
shades and dwell in some sort of unresounding private life.

Of course, fiction as traditionally practiced has always dealt with
private life. High seriousness in literature is attached to the belief in the
moral immensity of the single soul. If the artist is lucky or a genius, the
specific creation of his belief, Emma Bovary, Carrie Meeber, Stephen
Dedalus, Jay Gatsby, Joseph K., implicates the universe. We become
more who we are in the imposition on ourselves of these morally illuminating fictive lives. But of these characters I've listed, the books in
which they find their animation make society at large the antagonist,
whether as middle-class provincialism, religious culture, or government
bureaucracy; the fate of these individuals issues from their contention
with or concession to the vast world around them. And the geography of
the book is vast. The heroine of *Sister Carrie* is, like her lover Hurst-
wood, a soul dominated by the material lures of the big city. We witness
her sentimental education, not in the emotions of love for which neither
she nor anyone else in the book has endurance, but in the emotion of
social and economic advancement. There's no claim in Dreiser for the
consistent government of the human mind, exactly the sentimentalism at
the root of so many well-written, fashionably ironic novels of private life
done today. And so our awareness moves out concentrically over
Chicago, over New York, over the whole United States. And then it
keeps going.

It is that moving outward, that significant system of judgment,
missing in much of our work today. Of course, we have now a considerable history of this reduced literature and of course it's not exclusively
American. An early retreat was sounded in the 1950s by Robbe-Grillet.

But it's the American phenomenon I'm trying to understand and locate: an exhaustion of the hope that writing can change anything, or the discovery that all the wickedness is known and thoroughly reported, that all the solutions to the wickedness are known, that nothing changes, it all goes on with only the freshness of expression lost, and the power of the art. Some sort of raging, amoral system inside of which the artist is only astute in the act of withdrawal.

There are many exceptions to this generalization, of course. We've had novels about Vietnam. And certainly it is less true as applied to black writers and to writers who are feminists. Yet it is true for all of us that rather than making the culture, we now seem to be made by it, even when we are being traditional novelists reporting on what we see and making a morally comprehensive world. Somehow in this post-modernist time we have been cowed. We lack some rage of imagination, the imperial earth-shaking intention on the one hand, that—the world not responding properly—would cause us to give up our writing altogether on the other. So that, with Tolstoy, we would rail against art as we had before railed against life.

And there's a corresponding drift among critics. I think of the few works by my contemporaries which are examples of political fiction. They only accentuate the prevailing rules. There is no poetics yet devised by American critics that would treat engagement as anything more than an understandable but nevertheless deplorable breakdown of form. It is my impression, perhaps unjustified, that for some segments of our critical community, the large examination of society within a story, the imposition in a novel of public matters on private life, the lighting of history within an individual, places a work in aesthetic jeopardy. Thus the social novel is seen always as ideological. In fact, if the subject of the novel is of a certain sort, if the novel is about a labor union organizer, for example, or a family on welfare, it is assumed to be political, that is, impure, as for example a novel about life in prep school is not. Political is always to be distinguished from what entertains. The CIA novels of William Buckley are thought to entertain. Whereas some many months ago in the *New York Times Book Review*, a critic, Robert Alter, said of Joseph Heller's novel *Catch-22* and a novel of mine, *The Book of Daniel*, that they were flawed by a spirit adversarial to the Republic.

The final distinction is, of course, between political and literary, a quaint distinction and probably a source of amusement to writers in other parts of the world, Nadine Gordimer in South Africa, for example,

or Milan Kundera of Czechoslovakia, Günter Grass of West Germany,
García Marquez of Colombia, and it would have given a good laugh to
Stendhal, Dickens, Dostoyevski, and Malraux. I think it is no slander to
suggest that some of our critics are more likely to accept the political
novel and even acclaim this or that example as long as it is written by
a foreigner about a foreign country. This is analogous to President
Reagan's support of workers' movements as long as they are in Poland.

Let's get back for just a moment to the 1930s. No one could seriously want the thirties to be held up as any kind of model age. There is
nothing remotely desirable that I can see in Depressions or Crystal
Nights or show trials. I don't imagine the purpose of history is to inspire
art. I don't agree with Faulkner that "Ode on a Grecian Urn" is worth
any number of old ladies—or old men. I don't think Faulkner is worth
the antebellum South, and I would rather not have had Kafka at the price
of twentieth-century European carnage. But in trying to locate contemporary American writing I look at the thirties, that supposedly meager
decade of misfired artistic energy and of duped intellectuals and bad
proletarian novels, and I see: not just Faulkner and Hemingway and
Fitzgerald and Thomas Wolfe but James T. Farrell, Katherine Anne Porter, Richard Wright, Nelson Algren, William Saroyan, John Steinbeck,
John Dos Passos, Nathanael West, Dorothy Parker, Edward Dahlberg,
Dalton Trumbo, Horace McCoy, Erskine Caldwell, Lillian Hellman,
James Agee, Edmund Wilson, Daniel Fuchs, Henry Roth, Henry Miller.
For starters. A literature of immense variety and contention, an argu-
ment from every side, full of passion, excessive, self-consuming.

Literary life in the present is, by comparison, decorous. It's very
quiet today. Is it because our society is sunlit and perfect? Are all our
vampires staked through the heart? Or have we, as writers, given up our
presumption of the authority of art, of the central place of the sustained
narrative critique in the national argument?

Alfred Kazin has an idea about the thirties that might be appropriate
here. "That crucial period," Kazin says, "turned out to be stronger in
counter-revolution than in revolution, in the power of the state than in
the apostolic freedom of the individual soul." He goes on to say, "Orthodoxy was becoming the norm in the '30s, not radicalism. The period that
seems so easy to sentimentalize as one of struggle against poverty and
oppression actually saw the triumph of Fascism in Germany and Spain,
the unchecked dominion of Stalinist terror over what was radical in
Communism itself. In this country the statism seemingly necessary for

the crisis legislation of the New Deal was soon with Pearl Harbor to hammer out social regimentation and forms of intellectual control that many Americans now regard as the norm."

Of course, I'm taking his remarks out of context. But if Kazin is right—and listening to the shrill voices of conservatism in culture as well as everything else, how can we doubt it?—then we have some suggestion of the ultimate dependence of the artist upon the people he would speak for. And why not? We conceive the work of art as the ultimate act of individuation, but it may be seen also as a production of the community. Narrative is the art closest to the ordinary daily operation of the human mind. People find the meaning of their lives in the idea of sequence, in conflict, in metaphor, and in moral. People think and make judgments from a confidence of narrative. You will note that anyone at any age is able to tell the story of his or her life with authority. The narrative mode of thought comes naturally to everyone, as for instance mathematical or scientific reasoning does not. One imagines in the dawn of prehistoric human life that storytelling did not have to be invented as, say, counting or the wheel. In one sense a novel is nothing more than an intricate construct of opinions. Opinions are the novel's molecules and altogether these opinions, judgments, facts, yield a worldview. These opinions, furthermore, are maintained by means of sensual evocation as much as by intellect. Every sense we have is stimulated by the vicarious instrumentation of words; and we derive from the prose we read a harmony of judgments, both explicit to our mental selves and intuitive and felt, that very nearly evokes the way each of us in every minute of consciousness composes the world in order to make sense of it.

Everyone, all the time, is in the act of composition, our experience is an ongoing narrative within each of us. The critic Isaac Rosenfeld once said every life has a theme. That's a literary word, theme. The theme of a life as a book is the disinterested central judgment we make of it. The novel duplicates the temporality of life and the authority for the telling of the novel is most often the death of its characters—the same authority, in the words of the great critic Walter Benjamin, "which even the poorest wretch in dying possesses for the living around him."

Thus, ironically, in our withdrawal, our nonpolitical pragmatic vision of ourselves and our calling, we may be expressing the general crisis of our age. We are writing as we live, in a kind of stunned submission to the political circumstances of our lives and the establishmentarian rule of our politicians. We are being bought off by our comforts while great moral outrages are committed in our name. As two superpowers hold the world hostage, a statist ideology encroaches on the realm of individual thought.

I would not mean to imply that the problems of writers under these circumstances are not the least of America's problems. But the coercion of Realpolitik, the ideology of Cold War, and the shadow of the bomb may have robbed us of the passion of our calling, which is the belief that writing matters, that there is salvation in witness and moral assignment. These days many of our best writers do a kind of passive prophecy. They concentrate on the powerlessness or haplessness of our lives, and the inappropriateness of our public places for human life or the inadequacy of our culture for the conduct of human emotion. An inadvertent social critique comes off their pages without that level of rage that would drive them to and fro, like Leo Tolstoy, from art to the conviction that nothing is more important than teaching the children of the poor to read. The young writer today who picks up tonally, philosophically, on the Hemingway romance, is in danger of misperceiving the predominant condition of things, which is that the future for any of us is not individual. As independent entrepreneurs of ourselves with no control over our destiny, we may be failing the task. How will we be able to stay true to the changing nature of our lives if we hold to a myth that is being nullified by history? If our response to what is going on today were appropriate, it would probably produce books of a grubbier, sloppier and more energetic sort than we are doing. Books with less polish and self-consciousness, but about the way power works in our society, who has it, and how it is making history. In order to begin to rebuild our sense of ourselves, we may have to go back to childhood, to the past, and start again. In order to reclaim our society, we need the words to find it. If we make that effort everything I've been pondering here may not be an end but a beginning. And that should dilate your nostrils, young writers, and give you a scent of the chase.

Beginnings

Joyce Carol Oates

> I will maintain that the artist needs only this: a special world of which
> he alone has the key.
>
> —André Gide

I begin with the proposition that the impulse to create, like the impulse
to destroy, is utterly mysterious. That it is, in fact, one of the primary
mysteries of human existence. We can't hope to explain it but we can't,
evidently, resist speculating about it.

Two general theories about the genesis of "art."

— It originates in play: in experiment, improvisation, fantasy; it
remains forever, in its deepest impulse, playful and spontaneous,
a celebration of the (child's?) imagination.
— It originates out of the artist's conviction that he is born damned;
and must struggle through his or her life to achieve redemption.
By way of art.

If these theories appear to contradict themselves, to the point, very
nearly, of comedy—so, as Walt Whitman would say, they contradict
themselves. Sometimes one is obviously true; sometimes, the other.

In his classic essay *The Structure of Scientific Revolutions* (1962) the science
historian Thomas Kuhn makes the point that "discovery," in terms of
single, discrete, and readily identified dates, let alone "discoverers," is
highly misleading. Scientific discoveries are, in a historically real (if poetic) sense, there to be discovered. Not only are scientific theories developed, frequently, by more than one individual, not inevitably in communication with other individuals, but there is often a good deal of
ambiguity about when "discovery" itself takes place. Despite our pre-
dilection for believing in isolated and inspired genius, genius *sui generis,* it
is not often the case that scientific revolution has to do with the individual. There may be heroism, and heroes, but the drama—the evolution of
scientific discovery—would have taken place in any case.

In the world, or worlds, of art, very different phenomena may be observed. Not only is the work of art uniquely identified with a single individual, but, if we look closely, it is frequently the case that, from that individual's perspective, the work of art is in itself unique, and perplexing in terms of its origins. Just as our historical beginnings are utterly mysterious—why are we born? why when and as we are?—so too are the beginnings of works of art and of "artists." Conception (in contrast to the fully public fact of birth) suggests not only the unknowable but the forbidden: our birth dates are matters of public record but our dates of "conception" are permanently shrouded in mystery. Consciousness dominates our thinking about works of art as well as artists, even as we know that the genesis of any creation (in contrast to its execution) must derive from unconscious sources.

Ornamental qualities in prose fiction are invariably the consequence of authorial deliberation and strategy while more powerful qualities— the primitive force-fields that generate "theme" (or obsession)—are clearly given. The storyteller experiences the ravishing phenomenon of stories being told through him and by way of him; his single voice generating any number of singular "voices." Is it magic? Is it psycho-pathology? Is it supremely normal? In Plato's *Ion* Socrates says, "God takes the mind out of the poets, and uses them as his servants, and so also those who chant oracles, and divine seers; because he wishes us to know that not those we hear, who have no mind in them, are those who say such precious things, but God himself is the speaker, and through them he shows his meaning to us. . . . These beautiful poems are not human, not made by man, but divine and made by God; and the poets are nothing but the gods' interpreters, possessed each by whatever god it may be." But this is a logic hostile to the individual; a logic in denial of the wide play of personality that characterizes creative work. For if there is any single quality which we associate with art it is the individual, the personal, the unique, the inimitable. One might add: the inevitable. In many writers it comes to seem over a lifetime that a complex and essentially unknowable drama is working itself out by way of the individual; yet, so far as the individual is concerned, each experience is immediate and singular. And the act of writing itself is likely to be felt as purely and radiantly subjective: "the exalted sense of being above time and death which comes from being again in a writing mood" (Virginia Woolf, *Diary*, September 8, 1934).

After the completion of an ambitious project the writer may try to pass judgment on it, "objectively"; he may try to analyze it as a reader; or probe his own motives for writing. "The port from which I set out was, I think, that of *the essential loneliness of my life*—and it seems to be the port also, in sooth, to which my course again finally directs itself! This loneliness—what is it still but the deepest thing about one? Deeper, about *me*, at any rate, than anything else; deeper than my 'genius,' deeper than my 'discipline,' deeper than my pride, deeper, above all, than the deep counterminings of art" (Henry James in a letter of 1900). Though such analyses are often astute and startling—recall James Joyce explaining that the labyrinthine *Ulysses* was written "to preserve the speech of my father and his friends"—it surely cannot explain the depth, or the subtlety, or the stark originality, or genius, of a work. Virginia Woolf noted that the writing of *To the Lighthouse* seemed to have laid the ghosts of her father and mother, of whom she used to think constantly: "I believe this to be true—that I was obsessed with them both, unhealthily; and writing of them was a necessary act" *(Diary,* November 28, 1928). It remains a surprising (and disturbing) fact to many literary observers, that writers should, upon occasion, write so directly from life; that they should "cannibalize" and even "vampirize" their own experiences. But this species of creation is surely inevitable? entirely natural? The artist is driven by passion; and passion more powerfully derives from our own experiences and memories. Writers as diverse as William Butler Yeats, Marcel Proust, August Strindberg, D. H. Lawrence, Ernest Hemingway, even, to a less obsessive degree, Thomas Mann, Willa Cather, Katherine Anne Porter—all were writers of genius whose imaginations were not constrained but positively energized (in Strindberg's case one might say "demonized") by specific events in their lives.

Strindberg, for instance, used not analogous but exact details from his family life, and in particular from his three marriages, for his fiction and plays; his biographer Olof Lagercrantz has noted that he went so far as to create domestic traumas in order to "rectify" his literary material, and, with the passage of time, developed an intuitive symbolist method of creation, in which individuals no longer seemed to exist save as emanations of meaning—*his* meaning. Equally dependent upon his own life—upon what he called "passional" experience—D. H. Lawrence directly fictionalized his own experiences as "son" and as "lover" in virtually all his novels and poetry, from *The White Peacock* to *Lady Chatterly's Lover* and *Pansies.* Thomas Mann was so "excessively precise" in recording his origins and family life in *Buddenbrooks* and *Tonio Kröger* that he directed a French translator to consult these works of fiction for a biographical portrait. And there falls across much of Albert Camus's work, however obliquely, and allegorically transformed, the presence of the "silent, uncomplaining figure of [my] deaf mother" who instilled in her son fiercely contending emotions of sympathy and helplessness.

Yet how many people, writers or otherwise, have been haunted by families to no productive end. . . ! Clearly the powerful unconscious motives for a work of art are but the generating and organizing forces that stimulate consciousness to feats of deliberation, strategy, craft, cunning.

To be *inspired:* we know what it means, even how it sometimes feels, but what is it? Filled suddenly and often helplessly with renewed life and energy, a sense of excitement that can barely be contained; but why some things—a word, a glance, a scene glimpsed from a window, a random memory, a conversational anecdote, the shard of a dream—have the power to stimulate us to intense creativity while others do not we are unable to say. The early Surrealists believed in the empirical world as a "forest of signs"—a rich, largely unexplored region of message-forms that lay behind the apparent irrationality of the surface: just as meanings lay behind the apparent irrationality of the dream. Images yield themselves to those who *see*—like Man Ray wandering through Parisian streets with his camera, forcing nothing, anticipating nothing, but leaving himself open to document *disponibilité,* or availability; or chance. Surrealism's most striking images were, at the outset, purely ordinary images, decontextualized and made strange—as Lautréamont said, "Beautiful as the chance encounter of a sewing machine and an umbrella on a dissection table."

No less open to *disponibilité* was Henry James, who listened avidly to dinner table conversation in London social circles—for years the popular novelist dined out as many as two hundred times in a single season. He heard, and overheard, any number of gossipy tales; yet chose to write *The Sacred Fount, The Turn of the Screw, The Aspern Papers, The Spoils of Poynton.* (Having heard approximately half of the riveting anecdote that would provide the comical plot of *Spoils* James asked not to be told the rest: he didn't want his imagination contaminated by mere factual truth.) In revisiting Washington Square after years of absence from the United States James claimed to have "seen" the ghost of his unlived American self—and wrote that remarkable ghost story, "The Jolly Corner," in which the unlived self, the other James, is both realized and exorcized. After the violent Dublin insurrection of Easter 1916 William Butler Yeats was indignant with the Irish rebels for sacrificing their lives, needlessly, he thought; yet for days he was haunted by a single mysterious line of poetry—a line repeating itself again and again—until finally his great poem "Easter 1916" organized itself around that line: "A terrible beauty is born."

> I write it out in a verse—
> MacDonagh and MacBride
> And Connolly and Pearse
> Now and in time to be,
> Wherever green is worn,
> Are changed, changed utterly:
> A terrible beauty is born.

Karen Blixen, writing under the carefully chosen pseudonym "Isak Dinesen" ("Isak": one who laughs) transmogrified personal experience, a good deal of it bitter, into apparently distant, if not mythical images; yet the biographical element in her work is consistent if one knows how to decipher the clues. For instance, in a late parable, "The Cardinal's Third Tale," of *Last Tales,* a proud virgin contracts syphilis by kissing the foot of Saint Peter's statue in the Vatican after a young Roman worker has kissed it before her—a detail that aroused a good deal of negative criticism for its apparent "frivolity" since, at the time of the book's publication, the secret of Dinesen's own syphilis, also "innocently" contracted, was not generally known. Young Jean-Paul Sartre was so profoundly struck by the hallucinogen-induced vision of a tree's roots that *La Nausée,* his first novel, virtually shaped itself around the hieratic image; an image that has consequently come to represent, however misleadingly, the Existentialist preoccupation with things in their mysterious and usually malevolent *thingness.*

In 1963 the poet Randall Jarrell received a box of letters from his mother, including letters he himself had written at the age of twelve in the 1920s; he immediately embarked upon what was to be his last period of creativity—virtually plucking poems, his wife has said, from the air. The title of the book says it all: *The Lost World.* Before this, Jarrell had been inactive; after this, he sank into depression. He died in 1965. The poet Theodore Weiss, having written a twenty-line poem, was inspired to work on it in subsequent days—and months—and, finally, years: twenty years altogether. Each line of the poem mysteriously "opened out into a scenario" shaping itself finally into Weiss's first book-length poem *Gunsight*. Eudora Welty was moved to write her early story "Petrified Man" by hearing, week after week, the most amazing things said in her local beauty parlor in Jackson, Mississippi—in this story the writer effaces herself completely and allows the voices to speak. While driving in the Adirondacks E. L. Doctorow happened to see the sign "Loon Lake"—in which everything he felt about the mountains ("a palpably mysterious wilderness, a place full of dark secrets, history rotting in the forests") came to a point. And there suddenly was the genesis, the organizing force, for his novel *Loon Lake:* "a feeling for a place, an image or two."

For John Updike inspiration arrives, in a sense, as a "packet of material to be delivered." In 1957, revisiting the ruins of the old Shillington, Pennsylvania, poorhouse, a year or two after his grandfather's death, Updike found himself deeply moved by the sight: "Out of the hole where [the poorhouse] had been there came to me the desire to write a futuristic novel"—a memorial effort cast in the form of a parable of the future. So Updike's first novel *The Poorhouse Fair* was conceived—the very antithesis of the typical "autobiographical" first novel. Norman Mailer's first novel, *The Naked and the Dead,* was, by contrast, a wholly deliberate effort, "a sure result of all I had learned up to the age of twenty-five." Mailer's characters were conceived and put in file boxes long before they were ever on the page; he had accumulated hundreds of such cards before he began to write, by which time "the novel itself seemed merely the end of a long active assembly line." But Mailer's second novel, *Barbary Shore,* seemed to come out of nowhere: each morning he would write with no notion of how to continue, where he was going. Where *The Naked and the Dead* had been put together with all the solid agreeable effort of a young carpenter constructing a house, *Barbary Shore* "might as well have been dictated to me by a ghost in the middle of a forest." Similarly, *Why Are We in Vietnam?,* Mailer's *Huck Finn,* was written in a white heat of three ecstatic months dictated in a sense by the protagonist's voice—"a highly improbable sixteen-year-old genius—I did not even know if he was black or white." Joseph Heller's novels typically begin with a first sentence that comes out of nowhere— independent of theme, setting, character, story. The opening line of *Catch-22*—"It was love at first sight. The first time he saw the chaplain, ———fell madly in love with him"—simply came to Heller for no reason, could not be explained, yet, within an hour and a half, Heller had worked out the novel in his mind: its unique tone, its tricky form, many of the characters. The genesis for *Something Happened* was the inexplicable sentence "In the office in which I work, there are four people of whom I am afraid. Each of these four people is afraid of five people." And though, a minute before, Heller knew nothing of the work that would absorb him for many years, he knew within an hour the beginning, middle, and ending of the work, and its dominant tone of anxiety.

Such visitations are experienced as mysterious at first—indeed, often anxiety-provoking—but, in retrospect, as fate. Francine Gray's moments of inspiration have been similarly sudden and unexpected: seeing a photograph of the Jesuit priest Philip Berrigan pouring a vial of blood over draft documents in the 1960s led to the writing of her passionate book of nonfiction, *Divine Disobedience;* the observation of a solitary fellow tourist on a Russian trip was the germinating stimulus for *World Without End;* a visit to an ailing relative in a hospital, and the observation of another close relative as he regarded himself in a mirror, constituted the emotional nexus of *October Blood.* Joan Didion began *Play It as It Lays* with no notion of "character" or "plot" or even "incident." She had only two pictures in her mind: one of empty white space; the other of a minor Hollywood actress being paged in the casino at the Riviera in Las Vegas. The vision of empty space suggested no story but the vision of the actress did: "A young woman with long hair and a short white halter dress walks through the casino at the Riviera at one in the morning. She crosses the casino alone and picks up a house telephone. I watch her because I have heard her paged, and recognize her name: she is a minor actress I see around Los Angeles but have never met. I know nothing about her. Who is paging her? Why is she here to be paged? How exactly did she come to this? It was precisely this moment in Las Vegas that made *Play It as It Lays* begin to tell itself to me."

In his *Paris Review* interview of 1976 John Cheever speaks of the way totally disparate facts came together for him, unbidden: "It isn't a question of saving up. It's a question of some sort of galvanic energy." The writing itself then becomes the difficult effort to get the "heft" right—getting the words to correspond to the vision. Surely one of the strangest of all literary conceptions is that of John Hawkes's *The Passion Artist.* In a preface to an excerpt from that novel in Hawkes's anthology *Humors of Blood & Skin* Hawkes relates how, when he and his wife were spending a year in southern France, he found himself inexplicably unable to write, in the midst of a profound and paralyzing depression; "whenever I entered our house I thought I saw my father's coffin. . . . I had this vision even though both my parents were buried in Maine. Each morning I sat benumbed and mindless at a small table. Each morning Sophie left a fresh rose on my table, but even those talismans of love and encouragement did no good. All was hopeless, writing was out of the question." Then came an invitation for lunch. Hawkes was told a lively bit of gossip about a middle-aged man who went one day to pick up his young daughter at a school in Nice, only to discover accidentally from one of the child's classmates that the daughter was an active prostitute, already gone that day from the playground to a sexual assignation. Hawkes listened to the anecdote; saw himself walking toward a lone girl and some empty playground swings. . . . One or two further associations, seemingly disjointed, and he had the plot of what would be *The Passion Artist.* The paralysis had lifted.

The most admirable thing about the fantastic, André Breton says, is that the fantastic does not exist: everything is real.

In *A Portrait of the Artist as a Young Man* Stephen Dedalus explains the Joycean concept of the "epiphany": "A sudden spiritual manifestation, whether in the vulgarity of speech or of gesture or in a memorable phase of the mind itself. He believed it was for the artist to record these epiphanies with extreme care, seeing that they themselves are the most delicate and evanescent of moments." That Joyce's concept of one of the most potent motives for art has become, by now, a critical commonplace, should not discourage us from examining it. In his own practice the young Joyce, in his late teens and a student at University College, Dublin, began to collect a notebook of "epiphanies" fueled by the ambition not only to write but to write works of genius. He collected approximately seventy epiphanies—sudden and unanticipated moments of "spiritual manifestation"—of which forty survive. Many were to be used with little or no change in *Stephen Hero* (Joyce's early uncompleted novel) and in *Portrait;* the stories of *Dubliners* are organized around such revelations, rather like prose poems fitted to a narrative structure. It might be said that *Ulysses* is a protracted celebration of epiphany fitted to a somewhat over-determined intellectual (Jesuitical?) grid: a short story tirelessly inflated to encompass the cosmos. (In fact, *Ulysses* had its formal genesis in a story for *Dubliners* titled "Ulysses," or "Mr. Hunter's Day,"—a story that, according to Joyce, never got beyond its title.) The epiphany has significance, of course, only in its evocation of an already existing (but undefined) interior state. It would be naive to imagine that grace really falls upon us from without—one must be in spiritual readiness for any visitation.

Yet is the writer in truth the triumphant possessor of a secret world to which (in Gide's words) he alone has the key?—or is he perhaps possessed by that world? The unique power of the unconscious is that it leads us where it will and not where we might will to go. As dreams cannot be controlled so the flowering of any work of art cannot be controlled except in its most minute aspects. When one finds the "voice" of a novel the "voice" becomes hypnotic, ravishing, utterly inexplicable. From where does it come? where does it go? As in any fairy tale or legend the magic key unlocks a door to a mysterious room—but does one dare enter? Suppose the door swings shut? Suppose one is locked in until the spell has lifted? But if the "spell" is a lifetime? But if the "spell" *is* the life?

So, the familiar notion of a "demonic" art, the reverse in a sense of Plato's claim for its divine origin—yet in another sense identical. Something *not us* inhabits us; something insists upon speaking through us. To be in the grip of a literary obsession is not so very different from being in the grip of any obsession—erotic love, for instance, in its most primary and powerful state. Here the object of emotion is fully human but the emotion has the force of something inhuman—primitive, almost impersonal, at times almost frightening. The very concept of the "brainstorm": a metaphor nearly literal in its suggestion of raging winds, rains, elemental forces. The extravagance of William Blake's visions, for example; the ecstasy of Kafka in writing his early stories—writing all night! tireless! enthralled!—no matter that he is in poor health and physically exhausted. "Odd how the creative power at once brings the whole universe to order," Virginia Woolf observes (July 27, 1934), but she might have gone on to observe that the "universe" is after all one's own very private and unexplored self: "demonic," "divine."

The genesis of Mary Shelley's *Frankenstein* is nearly as primitive as the appeal of that extraordinary work itself: after days of having failed to compose a ghost story (in response to Lord Byron's casual suggestion) the eighteen-year-old Mary Wollstonecraft Godwin Shelley had a hypnogogic fantasy in her bed—"I saw the pale student of unhallowed arts kneeling beside the thing he had put together. I saw the hideous phantasm of a man stretched out and then, on the working of some powerful engine, show signs of life. . . . His success would terrify the artist; he would rush away [hoping] this thing . . . would subside into dead matter. He sleeps; but he is awakened; he opens his eyes; behold the horrid thing stands at his bedside, opening his curtains." One of the central images of *Frankenstein* is that of a stroke of lightning that seems to issue magically in a dazzling "stream of fire" from a beautiful old oak, blasting it and destroying it: a potent image perhaps for the violence of the incursion from the unconscious that galvanized the author's imagination after a period of strain and frustration. (It cannot have been an accident that *Frankenstein,* telling of a monstrous birth, was written by a very young and yet-unmarried pregnant woman who had had two babies with her lover already, only one of whom had survived.) Following this waking dream of June, 1816, Mary Shelley had her subject—spoke in fact of being "possessed" by it. So too the brilliantly realized vision of the monster comes to us with such uncanny force it is difficult to believe that it owes its genesis to so very personal an experience—and did not evolve from a collective myth. *Frankenstein; or, The Modern Prometheus* was published in 1818 to immediate acclaim; yet with the passage of years the novel itself has receded as an art-work while Frankenstein's Monster—known simply and inaccurately as Frankenstein—has achieved dominance. The nightmare vision ends as it began, with a curious sort of impersonality.

The writer commonly writes to articulate a mystery he seems in a way to understand: the most paradoxical of situations. His vision is experienced as a totality but can be narrated only by slow painstaking degrees, as if one were trying to assemble a vase broken into thousands of pieces. In the afterword to *Memoirs of Hadrian* the author Marguerite Yourcenar speaks of her moment of inspiration when, in 1927, as a young woman, she happened to come upon a sentence in a published volume of Flaubert's correspondence—"Just when the gods had ceased to be, and the Christ had not yet come, there was a unique moment in history, between Cicero and Marcus Aurelius, when man stood alone." Yourcenar then adds: "A great part of my life was going to be spent in trying to define, and then trying to portray, that man existing alone and yet closely bound with all being." Partly due to interruptions in the author's life and partly because she felt inadequate to the task—"There are books which one should not attempt before having passed the age of forty"—*Memoirs of Hadrian* required twenty-seven years to write: it was finally published in 1951.

Why the need, in some rising very nearly to the level of compulsion, to verify experience by way of language?—to scrupulously record and preserve the very passing of Time? "All poetry is positional," Nabokov notes in his autobiography *Speak, Memory,* "—to try to express one's position in regard to the universe embraced by consciousness is an immemorial urge. The arms of consciousness reach out and grope, and the longer they are the better. Tentacles, not wings, are Apollo's natural members." For Nabokov as for many writers—one might say Boswell, Proust, Virginia Woolf, Flaubert—surely James Joyce—experience itself is not authentic until it has been transcribed by way of language: the writer puts his imprimatur upon his (historic) self by way of writing. He creates himself, imagines himself, sometimes—recall Walter Whitman changing his name to Walt Whitman, David Henry Thoreau changing his name to Henry David Thoreau—re-names himself as one might name a fictitious character in a work of art. And the impulse can rise to the level of a sacred obligation, at least in a young author's ambition: "There is a certain resemblance between the mystery of the Mass," says James Joyce to his brother Stanislaus in a letter, "and what I am trying to do . . . to give people a kind of intellectual or spiritual pleasure by converting the bread of everyday life into something that has a permanent artistic life of its own . . . for their mental, moral, and spiritual uplift." (One is tempted to note here in passing that it was for their "mental, moral, and spiritual" preservation the citizens of Dublin suppressed Joyce's *Dubliners* and in effect drove him into his life's exile in Europe.)

No one has analyzed the complexities of a writer's life so painstakingly as Virginia Woolf in her many volumes of diaries and to a lesser extent in her correspondence. The slow evolution of an idea into consciousness; the difficult transcription of all that is inchoate, riddlesome; the sense of writing as a triumphant act; the necessity of surrendering to the unconscious (the "subconscious" as Woolf calls it, imagining it as "her"); the pleasure in language as sounds, beats, rhythms—Woolf writes so meticulously about these matters because she is trying to understand them. In a letter to Vita Sackville-West of September 8, 1928, she says:

> I believe that the main thing in beginning a novel is to feel, not that you can write it, but that it exists on the far side of a gulf, which words can't cross: that it's to be pulled through only in a breathless anguish. Now when I sit down to write an article, I have a net of

words which will come down on the idea certainly in an hour or so. But a novel . . . to be good should seem, before one writes it, something unwriteable; but only visible; so that for nine months one lives in despair, and only when one has forgotten what one meant, does the book seem tolerable. . . .

And of style:

Style is a very simple matter, it is all rhythm. Once you get that, you can't use the wrong words. . . . This is very profound, what rhythm is, and goes far deeper than words. A sight, an emotion, creates this wave in the mind, long before it makes words to fit it; and in writing . . . one has to recapture this, and set this working (which has nothing apparently to do with words) and then, as it breaks and tumbles in the mind, it makes words to fit in. . . .

One thinks of the young Ernest Hemingway writing each morning in a Parisian cafe, groping his way into what would be his first book, *In Our Time:* writing at first with extreme slowness and difficulty until he set down his "one true sentence"—usually a brief declarative sentence—and could throw the earlier work away, and begin his story. One thinks of Theodore Dreiser composing, as he claimed, much of *Sister Carrie* in a trance—that masterpiece of "American naturalism"; and of William Faulkner's composition of his greatest novel, which began with a troubling and inexplicable image (the vision of a little girl with muddy underpants climbing a tree outside a window) and slowly expanded into a long story that required another story to amplify it, which in turn required another, which in turn required another, until Faulkner had four sections of a novel he had not, in the most literal sense, thought to write. *The Sound and the Fury* was published in 1929; but it was not until two decades later when Malcolm Cowley edited *The Portable Faulkner* that Faulkner added the Appendix—that remarkable document that is, of course, always published as an integral part of the novel.

"I am doing a novel which I have never grasped. . . . There I am at p. 145, and I've no notion what it's about. I hate it. Frieda says it's very good. But it's like a novel in a foreign language I don't know very well— I can only just make out what it is about." So D. H. Lawrence writes in a letter of 1913 in reference to his work-in-progress *The Sisters.* So vague and unformed was the young author's sense of his novel in its early "crude fermenting" he had intended it to be a pot-boiler of a kind: the novel that would eventually become *Women in Love*. He made several false starts in its composition before realizing that he must give his heroine some background: this background rapidly evolves into the germ of a new, separate novel about three generations of Brangwens—a social history of the English Midlands from before the industrial revolution to approximately 1913. In short, the "background" for the heroine of *The Sisters* became *The Rainbow*, published in 1915. (*Women in Love* was published in 1920: the two novels are radically different in structure, style, narrative voice, and tone.)

Is it as a consequence of Lawrence's method of composition, or in defiance of it, that he published within a few years two of the great novels of the twentieth century, *The Rainbow* and *Women in Love*? Lawrence was the most intuitive of writers yet he was willing to write numerous drafts of a work and even to throw away as many as one thousand pages, as he claims to have done with *The Rainbow*. His deep faith in himself allowed him the energy to experiment in following his voice and his characters where they would lead; temperamentally he was the antithesis of James Joyce, who imposed upon his work a purely intellectual scheme meant to raise it to the level of the symbolic and the archetypal. "Don't look for the development of [my] novel to follow the lines of certain characters," Lawrence says in a letter of 1919, "—the characters fall into the form of some other rhythmic form, as when one draws a fiddle-bow across a fine tray delicately sanded, the sand takes lines unknown."

The sand takes lines unknown. What more beautiful and precise image to suggest the very imprecision of the creative enterprise?—the conjunction between inner and outer forces we try in vain to understand and must hope in the end only to embody?

Postscript

On the genesis of my novel *Marya: A Life*.

In 1977 I wrote a short story, very short, deliberately spare and uninflected, I decided to call "November Morning." It was about a boy of eight whose father has been killed, though the boy himself doesn't quite understand what has happened. He is taken to see his father's corpse, in a county morgue; but his father has been so badly beaten or mutilated (it isn't clear which, to the reader), that the boy doesn't seem to recognize him. The story is told not by the child but by way of his limited consciousness and his reluctance to understand what has happened in his family. The setting of the story was rural: naturalistic but dream-like. The time was several decades ago.

I finished "November Morning" in a few days, and sent it to my agent. Though I went on to other projects I found that I was still thinking about the story, haunted by it, as if I hadn't really finished it. My practice as a writer might be defined as an active pursuit of "hauntedness": I can't write unless I am preoccupied with something, sometimes to the point of distraction, or obsession. But rarely am I haunted by a piece of writing, after I have finished it. . . . Though the story was accepted by a magazine, I decided I didn't want it published in that form; but when I tried to withdraw it from publication I learned that I had waited too long. So the story, incomplete, teasingly "wrong," was published.

The test of a work's integrity is its appearance in print: you know then, if you didn't know beforehand, if it is honest or not.

(Cocteau said that writing is a force of memory which is not understood. Certainly there are times when the prospect of writing leaves me virtually faint with longing; a yearning, a desire so palpable it's almost physical, bound up in some complex, undefinable way with memory. This yearning can't be satisfied except by the head-on plunge into work, in which, somehow, God knows how, raw instinct and critical acuity come into some sort of equilibrium. People who don't write might think it is easy. Or, considering me, as a writer labeled "prolific," that it is easy for *me*: but nothing is farther from the truth. Writing is not easy for most writers nor is it easy for me.)

So I rewrote the story another time. At some point it struck me that the protagonist should have been a girl, and not, as I'd thought, a boy. And that would make all the difference.

Except for the bare outline of the plot everything was recast entirely: tone, texture, rhythm, the silences and spaces between words. Immediately I had my "real" character; I knew her thoroughly; Marya, Marya Knauer, eight years old as the story opens but already in my imagination an adult woman—the thirty-six-year-old woman she would be when the novel ends. (I seemed to know too that Marya's story could not be eight pages long but would be novel-length. Many pages, many years, many experiences would be necessary to bring her into focus and to the culminating point of her life.) I had the ending, now; the final image; I had a number of scenes, "dramatic interludes," in the middle; I saw, or seemed to see, the ghostly outlines of characters whom Marya would encounter, who would act upon her in crucial ways, if not radically alter her life. Most of all I "saw" Marya—a girl, and then a woman, with a face not unlike my own yet not my own: kin of some kind, perhaps sisterly, but unknown to me.

It wasn't until I had finished a first draft of the novel that I learned, by chance, that the story I believed I had invented recapitulated an incident in my mother's early life. Not my father, of course, but her father had been murdered; not I, but my mother, had been "given away" after her father's death, to be brought up by relatives. Marya is eight years old at the time of the event that changes her family's life; my mother was an infant of six months. Somehow, without knowing what I did, without knowing, in fact, that I was doing anything extraordinary at all, I had written my mother's story by way of a work of prose fiction I had "invented" . . . .

The Prose Sublime: Or, the Deep Sense of Things Belonging Together, Inexplicably

Donald Justice

There must be in prose many passages capable of producing a particular kind of aesthetic reaction more commonly identified with poetry. Unlike the classical sublime of Longinus, the prose sublime I have in mind would only in the simplest case depend for its effect on images or fine language; and those purple passages which, because they do so, are generally singled out for notice need not much concern us. In any case, the reaction to prose as to poetry proves in experience to be much the same, a sort of transport, a *frisson,* a thrilled recognition, which, "flashing forth at the right moment," as Longinus has it, "scatters everything before it like a thunderbolt."

In respect to poetry more than one effort has been made to pin down the very physiology of this reaction, albeit too personal and eccentric to be taken as universal. The report goes that Dickinson would feel, physically, as if the top of her head were taken off; her whole body grew so cold it seemed no fire could ever warm it. Housman's testimony is more circumstantial still. His skin, as he shaved, might bristle so that the razor ceased to act; a shiver would run down his spine or he would feel "a constriction of the throat and a precipitation of water to the eyes"; or something might go through him like a spear, and the seat of that particular sensation was "the pit of the stomach." We might suppose that physical sensations so violent and, it would seem, verging on the pathological, would be enough to discourage all reading, but it is not so. We ourselves may have been spared the specific symptoms, but the remarkable similarity of such accounts remains impressive. Perhaps this much could be said, that some sense of elevation or elation may be felt which does not, for every reader, register itself in terms so physical. All the same, the illusion of something physical may be left behind, a shadow or tint not unlike the spreading of a blush, a suffusion of something warm and flowing just beneath the surface. Has

364

not everyone felt something of the kind? The cool-minded R. P. Black-mur admits to "moods when the mere movement of words in pattern turns the shudder of recognition into a blush and the blush into vertigo." But however such feelings should be described matters less than the question of what it is that calls them forth.

The obvious place to look is just where everyone has always looked, in a prose which depends for its power primarily on the quality and distinction of its language. For there can be no doubt that fine prose of itself can and does give pleasure, and pleasure of the very kind to which poetry is normally thought to have first claim. The type of prose gener-ally offered by way of example, however, would compromise the purity of the inquiry—prose that aims to be poetical: Pater or Doughty, per-haps, or self-consciously experimental work like *Tender Buttons* or *Fin-negans Wake*. What this says of general ideas about poetry is too embarrass-ing and Victorian to pause over. We must try to find what we are looking for in a prose that does not aspire to the condition of poetry but is content to remain itself. Let us consider a passage not excessively familiar, one to which nothing of story and almost nothing of character can be adduced to explain its success: a specimen of prose pure and simple.

In the spring mornings I would work early while my wife still slept. The windows were open wide and the cobbles of the street were drying after the rain. The sun was drying the wet faces of the houses that faced the window. The shops were still shuttered. The goat-herd came up the street blowing his pipes and a woman who lived on the floor above us came out onto the sidewalk with a big pot. The goat-herd chose one of the heavy-bagged, black milk-goats and milked her into the pot while his dog pushed the others onto the sidewalk. The goats looked around, turning their necks like sight-seers. The goat-herd took the money from the woman and thanked her and went on up the street piping and the dog herded the goats on ahead, their horns bobbing. I went back to writing and the woman came up the stairs with the goat milk. She wore her felt-soled cleaning shoes and I only heard her breathing as she stopped on the stairs outside our door and then the shutting of her door. She was the only customer for goat milk in our building.

Intense clarity; one-dimensional—everything rendered on a single plane. Whatever beauty the passage has—and it has as much as any passage of this scope can probably bear—depends less on the words themselves and the care taken with them than on this very sense that great care is in fact being taken. This leads to a strong sense of the author's presence as manifested in the style, a style that seems to come directly from the character of the author and is, practically speaking, indistinguishable from it. With Hemingway this sense of the author is rarely, if ever, absent, but that is just the point.

The author here would be felt as present even without the personal pronoun. He is present in the weight of the words picked out and the rhythms of the composed and modeled phrases, as much as in the attitudes and affectations of the Hemingwayesque. To pick up *A Moveable Feast* for the first time, as I did not long ago, years after its original publication, was to be astonished all over again, as in adolescence, by the prose. I found myself content to read through it as if it had no subject, as though the malicious gossip and tall tales were nothing more than an excuse for the exercise of the famous muscular style. The old I. A. Richards distinction between tenor and vehicle seemed to reverse itself. The subject had become mere vehicle; the true tenor—that is to say, what was being articulated by means of all the beautiful, fierce detail— turned out to be the style itself.

Of course that is exaggeration. Yet if the prose sublime is here at all it seems lodged first in this way of using language and only then, though inseparably, in the picture this language brings into such clear and changeless focus. Technically speaking, this may in some sense always be true or partly true, but it is rarely so decisively true as here, and this rarity in itself becomes a factor in the reader's admiration.

But beneath the surfaces of language, beyond even style or Blackmur's "mere movement of words in pattern," there must be other deeper and more hidden sources for the mysterious yet familiar feelings we are trying to trace. A certain idealizing tendency in the criticism of the past might lead us to assume that the most fundamental source of all would lie in what James calls a "deep-breathing economy and an organic unity"; but in practice no example can ever be adequate to the task of representing that. I must doubt, in any case, whether an organic unity can be maintained except by an uncritical assertion of faith and, as for economy, what we instead constantly find ourselves overwhelmed by in novels is just the generosity of their wastefulness. Often enough the reasons for what comes through as the richest life and most sounding harmony in novels never do become clear, though with our favorite authors we learn to trust that somehow, anyhow, everything must, in a sense, belong. When the reasons do too obtrusively loom up, it is right to suspect that some scheme of the author's is being imposed upon the reader.

According to Percy Lubbock, James's great interpreter, the reader of a novel finds it impossible to retain what Lubbock calls "the image of a book" entire. It must be nearly as hard for the author to manage this trick himself. Always, says Lubbock, "the image escapes and evades us like a cloud." Yet it does not entirely escape. In our memory there remains forever some image of the novel called *Madame Bovary,* and it is not at all the same as the remembered image of *War and Peace* or *The Wings of the Dove.* Ours are doubtless only phantasmal images of the whole—we could never, like a Borgesian character, become the true author of any of these novels—but these cloudy images have still enough of the contours of a wholeness about them to enable us to think of each one individually and quite distinctly.

And is wholeness the question anyhow? More vivid and alive, certainly, are those broken-off pieces of the whole which continue to drift across our consciousness more or less permanently, fragments though they are. In novels these pieces had once figured as scenes or the mere details of scenes; or as characters, characters in the end perhaps independent of the acts by which we had come to know them; or sometimes, though rarely, as a mere phrase or formula: "Hurrah for Karamazov!" Aside from whatever cloudy sense of the whole the reader may have held onto, such pieces are pretty much all that is left to prize, and there need be no embarrassment in conceding this simple truth.

I have said enough to indicate my belief that it would be futile to seek out the prose sublime in any large idea of artistic unity. Such ideas come to seem, in the light of experience, artificial, faintly theological. Even with the old Coleridgean formula—*unity in variety*—it might be well to emphasize, for a change, the uncanonized term of the pair, *variety.* For one form of the aesthetic reaction we are trying to understand seems to occur just at that point when we grow aware that an ever-present and powerful sense of variety has begun to yield to what may never become more than a provisional sense of unity. A number of different things being put more or less together, one after the other, circling, recurring, veering off, they are seen to make a fit, perhaps quite unexpectedly, to be part of some larger but undefinable complex. There comes over us then a deep sense of things belonging together, inexplicably. Joyce's "basic patterns are universal," observes Blackmur, "and are known without their names." Universal patterns concern me less than patterns of the occasion and, indeed, of so many changing occasions if we had the time to look for them that we could never expect to invent names to cover them all. Something of the mystery in the act of recognition, at which Blackmur hints, is probably always present.

There is a pattern familiar in modern poetry that may point to a similar, if less obvious, pattern in prose. It involves the simple juxtaposition of seemingly unrelated things. Take Pound's "In a Station of the Metro."

> The apparition of these faces in the crowd;
> Petals on a wet, black bough.

A rather high degree of likeness, based here on visual resemblance, is clearly intended, but the connection is never stated as such. It is a disposition of objects or perceptions, or of objects taking the place of perceptions, that is found here and there in Chinese poetry as well, a type of parataxis in which the implication of likeness is carried by the arrangement itself.* Nor should the expository importance of Pound's title escape notice; it forms the bottom note of a triad, so to speak, the three notes of which are set vibrating together in a next chord. To register, further, the social and emotional distance between a modern, urban Metro station and the timeless pastoral of petal and bough is to see how the poem offers one more version of what Dr. Johnson long ago described as the "discovery of occult resemblances in things apparently unlike."

If we examine now a passage in prose, a long paragraph which likewise involves "things apparently unlike," we may catch something of the same pattern in action, though here less plainly laid out and therefore more elusive. The paragraph comes from the novel *Poor White,* by Sherwood Anderson, and it is chosen because, being unfamiliar, it has a chance to show freshly whatever force it may have. It is no more than a

---

*A line from Li Po, cited in Wai-lim Yip's *Chinese Poetry:* "Floating cloud(s): wanderer's mood." Yip compares this technique to the montage of Eisenstein, but the comparison should not be pushed too far, if for no other reason than the fact that in cinema, after the pioneer days, montage of this type came to seem arty and theoretical in a way that it does not yet seem in poetry or in prose, where it remains a practical resource. Pound calls the arrangement, or something like it, "planes in relation," and the analogy to sculpture and perhaps painting seems more persuasive than the one to cinema.

broken-off piece of a whole, but a whole in this case that really cannot be said to exist, a novel which survives, if it does, only in pieces, perhaps by now only in this very piece. Anderson seems never to have had a thought longer than thirty pages or so, and in the novel this paragraph rises toward whatever life and beauty it possesses out of a context truly flat and torpid. The plot is not important; there is practically no plot anyhow; Anderson did not like plot.

And then in Turner's Pike something happened.* A farmer boy, who had been to town and who had the daughter of a neighbor in his buggy, stopped in front of the house. A long freight train, grinding its way slowly past the station, barred the passage along the road. He held the reins in one hand and put the other about the waist of his companion. The two heads sought each other and lips met. They clung to each other. The same moon that shed its light on Rose McCoy in the distant farmhouse lighted the open place where the lovers sat in the buggy in the road. Hugh had to close his eyes and fight to put down an almost overpowering physical hunger in himself. His mind still protested that women were not for him. When his fancy made for him a picture of the school teacher Rose McCoy sleeping in a bed, he saw her only as a chaste white thing to be worshiped from afar and not to be approached, at least not by himself. Again he opened his eyes and looked at the lovers, whose lips still clung together. His long slouching body stiffened and he sat up very straight in his chair. Then he closed his eyes again. A gruff voice broke the silence. "That's for Mike," it shouted and a great chunk of coal thrown from the train bounded across the potato patch and struck against the back of the house. Downstairs he could hear old Mrs. McCoy getting out of bed to secure the prize. The train passed and the lovers in the buggy sank away from each other. In the silent night Hugh could hear the regular beat of the hoofs of the farmer boy's horse as it carried him and his woman away into the darkness.

---

*To identify: Hugh is the inarticulate, dreamy hero; Rose McCoy is his landlady's schoolteacher daughter, who boards elsewhere; Mrs. McCoy is the widow of a railwayman named Mike; and Turner's Pike is a road leading out of a small Midwestern town about the turn of the century.

Perhaps we must be told that the railwaymen have worked up a custom of tossing out chunks of coal for the widow McCoy as they pass—times are hard; but we should be able to guess that Rose and Hugh, vague longings aside, are fated never to get together. Something of all this is probably implicit in the tone of the passage, in the emotional sense the scene does in its own way make. Yet it would be hard to find in these "things apparently unlike" very much that we could call resemblance, occult or not. Not everything is reducible to metaphor; there is more to our search than the uncovering of hidden likenesses. The mind recognizes readily enough how the parts of a poetic image fit together—often enough just the two halves of it, side by side—but in prose there is ampler room for maneuver. Any mixing of contraries may stop short of parallel or symmetry; it is the mere act of combining that seems to make the figure. Two or more things being put into play together are found, as by a sort of grace, to coexist somewhat harmoniously. In the Anderson passage the testing moment when this must be recognized or missed arrives with the chunk of coal, which has nothing whatever in common with moonlight or lovers in a buggy. The point is not just that the author states no connection; neither is any particular likeness implied, and it is in just this way that its pattern, if it has one, is markedly different from the Metro Station pattern. There is only the sentence in which the discord is resolved: "The train passed and the lovers in the buggy sank away from each other." The experience has the character of a ceremonial, small mystery; and I would add that what we experience seems to involve a perception of time. It is a classic instance of things coming together even as they pass, of a moment when things may be said to associate without relating. The feeling raised by this perception is one of poignancy; perhaps that is the specific feeling this type of the prose sublime can be expected to give rise to. Made up of unspoken connections, it seems also to be about them. Probably it is not peculiarly American, but I can recall nothing in European novels, not even in the Russians, which evokes and gives body to this particular mood.*

This may come in the end to nothing but one more attempt to deal with what is after all inexpressible. Yet something remains. Incidentally, no one can have read through many pages of Anderson without having been struck by the frequency in his prose of this word *something:* "And

---

*A more complicated and sustained example, again from forgotten Anderson, is chapter 12 of his *Dark Laughter,* but it is far too long to quote here.

then in Turner's Pike something happened." The quintessential predicament for any character in Anderson is this: he (or she) wanted something and did not know what it was. It may be the universal predicament, for that matter. In any case, it resembles the predicament the reader of Anderson finds himself in, for he sees and seems almost to understand something without knowing what it is. Not that this feeling is brought about only by the sort of pattern we have been considering; it is rather that such a pattern can, like patterns more clearly universal, also be known, though without its name, for indeed it has none.

In a brilliant essay entitled "Techniques of Fiction," Allen Tate refers to what he calls the "actuality" of a scene in *Madame Bovary*. It is the scene in which Emma, having received a letter of farewell from her lover, dashes up to the attic in a panic; there the sound of her neighbor Binet's lathe turning comes to her; the sound seems to draw her down toward the street, toward the death she already halfway desires. It is this purely coincidental detail of the lathe, which in no foreseeable way has anything to do with Emma's fate, that confers the sense of "actuality" on the scene for Tate. What he calls "actuality" is only a more philosophical or theological way of designating the aesthetic moment when things associate powerfully together without apparent reason; others have used the term "dramatic correlative" for such a connecting, an echo no doubt of Eliot's "objective correlative." Presumably the novelist, by identifying the process, might make use of it at will, though it does not show up as a device in the pages of *The Rhetoric of Fiction*. Nor in the Anderson passage is any sense of actuality which it happens to possess so much built up and managed as it is simply taken for granted, either naively or confidently—rather, let us say, with the very confidence which can be one of the great assets of the naive writer.

Such moments are akin to the Joycean epiphany or to the "frozen pictures" of novels, moments at which the action, pausing, gives way to a held picture, something like the cinematic freeze-frame or a fermata in music; the picture in itself seems to represent, almost abstractly, some complex of meaning and feeling.* When Prince Andrey, wounded,

---

*Stage tableaux work a little in this way, especially at curtains, though a sense of contrivance can compromise the purity of the effect. Moreover, whatever expressive tableau the director arranges is often accompanied by a speech which seems to "interpret" the meaning of the picture, as in the last moments of *Uncle Vanya*, for instance. One thinks in the worst cases of the titles which in Griffith accompany the screen image.

looks up at the "lofty" and "limitless" sky, the effect is of a kind of summation, the meaning of which can be and, as it happens, is stated: "Yes, all is vanity, all is a cheat, except that infinite sky." The Joycean epiphany seems likewise to be a form of revelation or insight; the meaning in wait around the last turned corner of narrative is suddenly illuminated by a flash of understanding: "Gazing up into the darkness I saw myself as a creature driven and derided by vanity; and my eyes burned with anguish and anger." This is very beautifully said, and we may for a moment wonder, as Longinus might have wondered, if the effect is not grounded in the flash of style as much as in the flash of understanding; yet both are present.

In Anderson there is not the same push toward meaning; the rendering exhausts the interpretation: "The train passed and the lovers in the buggy sank away from each other." This has everything the Joycean epiphany has except for the crucial flash of understanding; and the plain style of it I find quite unofficially beautiful as well. Such a passage seems hardly to bother with understanding at all; it is a passage of unspoken connections, unnameable affinities, a tissue of association without specified relations. As far as I know, this last species of the prose sublime, being so elusive, has not previously been isolated and identified.

In it, connections, if any, remain unstated; likewise meanings. As used to be remarked of poems, such passages resist paraphrase. Their power is hidden in mystery. There is, at most, an illusion of seeing momentarily into the heart of things—and the moment vanishes. It is this, perhaps, which produces the aesthetic blush.

The Russian Heroine:
Gender, Sexuality, and Freedom

Francine du Plessix Gray

In December of 1979, the first feminist text since the 1920s was made public in the Soviet Union. A *samizdat* pamphlet called *Almanac: Woman and Russia,* it was issued in Leningrad in an edition of ten typewritten copies. Along with a few poems and short stories by women, it included essays concerning the overburdening of the nation's working mothers, the pitiful state of Soviet day care centers, the flaws of Soviet gynecology, and the misogynous views of women in Soviet society and media. Notwithstanding the blandness of these grievances, which these days are vociferously aired in the official *glasnost'* press, the *Almanac*'s authors were subjected to intensive harassment by the KGB; a few months later, four of them were expelled from the Soviet Union and forced to emigrate abroad.

It is to them that I dedicate this essay, to Tat'iana Goricheva, Natalia Malakhovskaia, Tat'iana Mamonova, and Iulia Voznesenskaia, to their modest attempt to offer Russian women a voice and a room of their own. For the same government that boasts of having pioneered women's equality in 1917 has remained rabidly hostile to any women's movement not directly under its control. And the *Almanac* contributors were brutally separated from kin and motherland for having acted on a premise which our generation of Western women has the luxury of taking for granted: on the premise that like any other oppressed group, we must go through a phase of spelling out our distinctness in order to merge with the mainstream of society, in order to pass from exile to power.

So it is in a mood of joyful subversion that I attack a theme which Soviet audiences would still condemn as "feminist bourgeois deviationism"—women and Russian prose fiction. I would like to consider women both as authors and as protagonists, women as participators in the craft of fiction and as symbols in a national genre which until recently remained a very male domain. For it is essential to note that of the novelistic traditions that have most enriched Western culture—British, French, American, Russian—Russian fiction is the only one that has not been profoundly marked by the female imagination, the only one in which no novel or short story crafted by a woman has yet endured beyond its time and remained a classic.

Eighteenth- and nineteenth-century Russian literature did yield some marvelous memoirs, diaries, and autobiographies penned by women, notably those of Ekaterina Dashkova, Nadezhda Sokhanskaia, and Nadezhda Durova; one good poet, Aleksandra Pavlova; a handful of fiction writers briefly in vogue in their day like Elena Gan, Evgenia Tur, Elena Zhukova. In our own century Russian culture has had some interesting contributors to the Modernist movement, such as Zinaida Gippius, Zinovieva Annibal, Nadezhda Teffi; it has offered us two of the most sublime poets of the century, Anna Akhmatova and Marina Tsvetaeva; and two of the most admirable memoirs of Stalin's gulags, Evgenia Ginzburg's and Nadezhda Mandelstam's.

Yet until the remarkable flowering of Russian women's fiction that occurred in the mid-1960s, which I plan to explore later in this essay, the great novelistic tradition of Russia has had no Lady Murasaki or Madame de Staël or Madame de La Fayette: it has had no Aphra Behn, no Jane Austen, no George Eliot or Brontë sisters or Virginia Woolf, none of those wondrous chroniclers of the female sensibility who have transfigured the novel form. And compared with Great Britain, America, or France, where popular women's novels, however wretched their quality and transient their vogue, profoundly affected their nation's cultures, Russian women's prose has had very little impact. One need only recall the enormous influence of women's fiction on the feminization of nineteenth-century America, and of pulp romances—the origins of young Emma Bovary's corruption—on the collective psyche of France, to realize the marginality of women's literature in the Russian Empire.

There have been vast differences between the status of women in Russia and in Western Europe which might be relevant. One cannot overlook the impact, for instance, of the Mongol occupation of Muscovy in the thirteenth century, which imposed a Moslem-style segregation of the sexes for several centuries to come. In those very decades when the salons of Parisian women were the center of France's literary and political culture, virtually dictated men's tastes and restructured the mores of their nation, Moscow women, particularly in the boyar classes, were sequestered in *terems*—harems—on their houses' uppermost floors, where they were rigorously shielded from view and even ate separately from men. Peter the Great still outraged many of his subjects by holding Western-style mixed gatherings at his court, paving the way for the extraordinary ascendance of Catherine the Great, who remains an ambiguous role model because she was German. Russian women did have two privileges not granted to their Western peers—they could own land and serfs; but these joys were of little avail, for they were forbidden to travel, even from town to town in their own country, without a parent's or a husband's permission.

One might also note that Russian Orthodox Christianity was in many ways more oppressive of women than Roman Catholicism; that its misogyny was never counterbalanced by a tradition of chivalric love, or by the liberating secular influences of a Renaissance or an Enlightenment. The chauvinism of Byzantine Orthodoxy was reinforced by a folk culture uniquely abundant in sexist proverbs, such as "Long in hair, short in brains," or "Beat the wife to get better cabbage soup." Its theology remained totally deprived of that idealization of marital sex which prevails in many Roman Catholic countries; even within marriage, female sensuality was viewed as "the devil's gateway," a perilous force which every husband must tame and repress. It is the Orthodox Church that issued one of the most crudely misogynous documents of the Christian era—the famous *Domostroi,* or Law of the Home, distributed to Russian households in the sixteenth century at the order of Tsar Ivan III. A manual for family behavior which models marriage on the monastic ideal (a "perverted" and "abominable morality," the philosopher Nikolai Berdiaev calls this text, "a disgrace to the Russian people"), the *Domostroi* remains famous for its meticulous instructions on the manner in which husbands must beat their wives—"privately and politely"; and for its directives that wives "complain to no one" about such treatment, and guard all such abuse from public scrutiny.

Until the development of a liberal intelligentsia in the midnineteenth century, this repressive ethos, imposed by both Church and State, was bound to impede the very education of women. According to our eminent American historian Barbara Alpern Engel, there were only 4,000 women enrolled in any formal education in Russia in 1837.

Having cited, in a spirit of pure speculation, a few of the factors which might have inhibited the development of a substantial female literature, I proceed to the first item on my agenda—images of women in nineteenth-century Russian prose fiction—images crafted by a commu-

nity of men whose genius has seldom been surpassed. The subject is so
vast that I shall confine myself to two pervasive and intimately linked
nineteenth-century themes which are continued with some fidelity in
twentieth century Soviet literature: (1) a very ascetic, negative attitude
toward women's sensuality, and (2) the paradoxical idealization of
women that accompanies this denigration, and which led to the creation
of heroines considerably more powerful than their male counterparts.

Let me start with one of the most telling scenes in Russian fiction,
Natasha's name day party in *War and Peace,* part I, chapters 5 and 9. As
we are introduced to Natasha of the darting little steps and tossing curls
and adorable little lace-frilled legs, two features of this child-woman are
particularly striking: her forthright, penetrating, all-knowing gaze, and
the fragmentary, barely intelligible language in which she attempts to tell
her mother about her doll—"Do you see . . . My doll, Mimi. . . . you
see . . ." Part of Tolstoy's "implacable hostility toward women," to use
Gorky's phrase, is his degrading of women's intellectual potential, and in
particular of their linguistic skills. "Women," so Tolstoy wrote in his
journal, "do not use words to express their thoughts, but to attain their
goals." And so within two pages of her appearance Natasha's very in-
coherence, coupled with her singular insight into others, endows her
with that female gift, already evidenced by Pushkin's Tatiana, which will
remain a constant in Russian novelists' rendering of their many "earth
women": an uncanny grasp of reality which is based on pure intuition, an
instinctual, nonverbal keenness which is linked, in turn, to a redeeming,
close-to-the-soil Russianness.

We turn some twenty pages toward the crucial meeting I wish to
focus on in chapter 9: Tolstoy invites to Natasha's name day party another very familiar figure of Russian literature, the Formidable Woman
archetype. She appears in the guise of Maria Dmitrievna, a person of
immeasurable power in Moscow society who is referred to with fear and
respect by her friends as "the terrible dragon." Tall and stout, so the
author describes her, close to sixty years of age, upon entering the room
she leisurely rolls up her sleeves as if preparing for a fight. "Well, how's
my Cossack?" she booms out as she kisses Natasha and hands her a pair
of ruby earrings. And throughout the evening, disdaining the fashionable French banter of the Rostovs' salon, the dragon lady insists on only
speaking a very earthy brand of Russian. "You old sinner," she exclaims
to Count Rostov, Natasha's father, as he kisses her hand. "You're feeling
dull in Moscow? Nowhere to chase with your dogs?" Right then and

there, the near crudeness of her speech, "Cossack," "sinner" (*grekhovod-nik*), "dog-chasing," (*sobak goniat*), shines magnificently amid the inane glitter of the Rostovs' ballroom, challenging the torpor of that society both decadent and insecure—aping Western manners with the gauche eagerness of Asiatic princes—which the formidable "dragon" has come to defy.

The Rostovs' party will remain dominated by these two redemptive figures: mighty sixty-year-old Maria Dmitriovna and virginal Natasha, the only one wise and strong enough to stand up "fearless and gay," with "boldness and smartness," before her aging friend. The entire company admires the lightning bolts of intuition and impertinence that flow exclusively between them. And if we keep that scene firmly in mind, as we take leave of Natasha some 1,250 pages later in the novel's epilogue, Natasha now ill-kempt and straggly-haired in her soiled housecoat, grown fat "like a breeding-fish" from incessant childbearing, we sense that our heroine might herself become, in time, an archetype of the Formidable Woman. Her husband Pierre, by far the most vital male protagonist of the novel, has capitulated to his wife's primeval force. We are told that he is seriously henpecked ("under her heel," *pod bashmakom*, as the original goes) and has meekly submitted to her wishes "that every moment of his life belong to her and to the family." Such is the force of domestic tyrant Natasha that Pierre does not dare "speak smilingly to another woman" or even "dine at the club as a pastime," and is confronted with a tantrum of fibs and reprimands when he is a few days late returning from a business trip. This final Natasha is abundantly praised by Tolstoy for her very slovenliness and enduring plainness of speech, for disdaining the dangerous example of French women who continue to take care of their appearance after marriage, is extolled, in fact, for having ceased to be sexually enticing to her husband. In his epilogue which was Tolstoy's personal marriage manual, which set forth his grim view of marriage as both essential salvation and inevitable damnation, the author has set the model for generations of marriages in Russian and Soviet fiction.

The novel, better than any form that comes to mind, communicates the most unadmitted terrors, the core hangups of any society. And I began with these two paragons of excellence—young Natasha and aging dragon lady, redemptive pre-sexual virgin and mighty post-sexual matron—because their duet expresses a very Puritanical trait of Russian culture which has been crucial in the modeling of its fictional women: Russian heroines tend to incarnate perfection in either pre-pubescent youth or advanced age; sexual union is frequently seen as grotesque; mature, still sexual women must be severely curbed, are only safe when their energies are totally sublimated in that holiest of duties—motherhood; and throughout much of the Russian tradition, with the exception of Chekhov and Turgenev, women in love, even within marriage, tend to be a force that must in some way be neutralized. As Barbara Heldt puts it beautifully in her book *Terrible Perfection: Women and Russian Literature,* the plot revolves around what strategy various male heroes choose.

Tolstoy, as we see in *War and Peace*'s epilogue and even more cruelly in "Family Happiness," confines women to bovine reproductive doom. Lermontov's leading man Pechorin, of *A Hero of Our Time,* both conquers and fails by deceit. Turgenev's men capitulate to the female's superiority. Dostoyevski, who compares the erotic drive to "the sensuality of insects," offers his women spiritual regeneration. Gogol's men might prefer suicide to the moral perils of copulation or marriage. And all these protagonists must resolve a paradox central to Russian fiction: woman, whose body is such a threat to man's spirit, becomes his moral superior once her sexuality has been in some way curbed.

Take the case of Gogol, a devout Orthodox believer whose deep revulsion for women's flesh may not be equaled by any other literary genius in history. In his story "Ivan Fedorovich Shponka and His Aunt," the author manages to fuse the attributes of Natasha and Maria Dmitrievna, of harmless Virgin and admirable Post-Sexual Woman, into one Amazonic figure. The kind, magisterial Aunt Vasilia, who governs the life of the orphaned, timorous bachelor Ivan Shponka, "values her spinster's life more than anything else," and transcends all gender in her awesome androgynous skills. Giant in stature and endowed with "very manly hands," she shoots wild game and climbs trees like the ablest sportsman, rows boats "more skillfully than the fishermen themselves." Things go awry when Auntie Vasilia, suddenly craving a brood of children over whom to extend her rule, orders her tenaciously celibate nephew to get married. Ivan, terrified of abandoning his safely virginal living arrangement, swears to resist marriage to the end. And in the apocalyptic nightmare sequence of the final scene, his hallucinations lead him to see a monstrous, domineering wife in every inch of his room:

His wife was sitting on a chair . . . and then he noticed that she had the face of a goose. He looked the other way, and saw another wife, and she had a goose's face as well. He looked again and there was a third wife; he looked around, still another. . . . He took off his hat—and there was a wife sitting in it. . . . He took some cotton wool out of his ear—a wife was there too. . . . Then he had another dream, that his wife was not a person at all, but some kind of woollen material. He had gone into a shop . . . "What kind of material would you like, sir?" asked the shopkeeper. "Have some *wife*, it's the latest thing now! . . . Everyone's having coats made from *it*." The shopkeeper made his measurements and cut the wife up. . . . "That's very poor material," says the Jewish tailor to whom Ivan takes the fabric, "No one uses *that* kind of stuff for coats now . . ."

I've indulged in this passage, a landmark of the fantastic prose genre, because it expresses as poignantly as any that terror of the castrating, superior female which marks much of Russian fiction. In Gogol, misogynous dread has grown unleashed into virtual paranoia. The sexual politics of Lermontov's *A Hero of Our Time* take a more Westernized form, a jaded Casanovan revenge against every female whom the hero conquers. The most interesting seduction achieved by Lermontov's Pechorin is that of Princess Mary, for it displays several other crucial aspects of fictional males' inferiority complex before their female peers: the boredom, the cynicism, the rootless, Europe-aping decadence already embodied by Pushkin's Onegin, a Hamletic indecision and self-defeatism. In this particular section of *A Hero of Our Time*, the jaded, globe-trotting Pechorin is confronted by his former mistress—a married woman whom he has long ago abandoned—and by the proud Princess Mary, whom he also abandons as soon as he is certain that she is in love with him. During his courtship, Pechorin eloquently expresses that blend of narcissism, introspection, and self-hatred which plagues so many nineteenth-century Russian anti-heroes: "Why do I so stubbornly try to gain the love of a little maiden," Pechorin asks himself, "whom I do not wish to seduce, and whom I will never marry? Why this feminine coquetry? . . . I sometimes despise myself. . . . Is this not why I despise others?" After Pechorin has ravaged Princess Mary's life by killing her suitor and destroyed all chances she has for any future marriage, he visits her one last time and absolves himself in a typically Russian form of *mea culpa,* the sensuality of self-degradation: he humiliates himself by admitting her immeasurable moral superiority. "I am base in regard to you," he tells her; and the curtain falls soon after these words: "She turned to me as pale as marble. 'I hate you,' she said."

Could the forceful Russianness of Pushkin's Tatiana ever have delivered Onegin from his own feckless narcissism? Could any turn of fate have aided Madame Odintsova, the cool, kind, aristocrat of Turgenev's *Fathers and Sons,* to rescue Bazarov from his tragically didactic theorizing? Could any seductive woman ever have nudged Goncharov's Oblomov out of that greatest protective armor of the lethargic Russian male—his housecoat, *khalat?* There is one key word which describes the superiority of Russian heroines to a national community of anti-heroes and born losers. Crucial to generations of Russian literary critics, it is the concept of "wholeness," *tsel'nost.* This rich and loaded word connotes endurance, selflessness, patience, stability, resourcefulness, a capacity for communion with others, and above all, decisiveness. This female wholeness serves as a rebuke to the Hamletic escapism of various classes of Russian males, be he a parasitical *chinovnik* bureaucrat, a lazy country gent, or a disaffected intellectual such as Goncharov's Oblomov. Only Oblomov, to my mind, might stand above reproach: his monastic skepticism of power and worldly success, his uncompromising resistance to the corrupt bureaucracy from whose ranks he has deliberately dropped out, endows him with a kind of holiness—I have long wished to write an essay on the theme of *Oblomov: The Slob as Saint.*

Marianne of *Virgin Soil* is my favorite of Turgenev's women, and an admirable example of the way in which this great writer stages his choreography of born-loser male and kinetic female. Marianne, clearly modeled on that remarkable generation of women revolutionaries which included Vera Zasulich and Olga Liubatovich, is somewhat of an anomaly among Russian literary heroines. Unusually plain, squat, rather masculine, she is not chaste, nor is she endowed with any of the condescending diminutives of feminine charm that characterize even her noblest sisters (we are always asked to admire Anna Karenina's charming *little* hand, Masha's or Natasha's adorable *little* feet). Marianne, who suffers "for all the poor, the oppressed, the wretched in Russia," has espoused the cause of women's emancipation and the overthrow of the Tsarist regime. She finds common cause with Nezhdanov, an impoverished young nobleman, and the two militants fall in love as they join the *narodnik* movement together, "going to the people" to prepare them for revolution.

The novel is tragicomic in its descriptions of how these refined young aristocrats, to the bafflement of the abjectly conservative Russian peasantry (and with prophetic similarity to our own SDS a century later) masquerade in laborers' garb and vainly struggle to learn such rustic tasks as chopping wood and planting crops. But *Virgin Soil* achieves its true force by portraying the vastly different levels of vitality and decisiveness with which Marianne and her lover, Nezhdanov, dedicate themselves to revolution. Marianne echoes that gift for self-sacrifice already hailed as a sacred female trait in Nekrasov's poem "Russian Women," which portrayed the wives of the Decembrists, Princess Volkonskaia and Countess Trubetskaia, as they deliberately joined their husbands in Siberian exile. But instead of roughening his hands with labor, as Marianne does, Nezhdanov lies in bed pondering his indecisiveness; and part of his torpor is rooted in his self-hatred, his deep inferiority before Marianne. He sees her as "the incarnation of everything good and true on earth—of fatherland, happiness, struggle, freedom!" Finding himself unworthy of her, and of the revolution, he berates himself for being "a corpse, a half-dead creature . . . an honest, well-meaning corpse!" This self-denigration is fulfilled: Nezhdanov commits suicide out of a genuine and perhaps realistic despair at being another "superfluous man," at the impotence of his class, at the futility and doom he senses before any genuine political change. Resilient Marianne survives, marrying a true man of the people, of the virgin soil.

Leafing through Dostoyevski for a statement of his own beliefs in the natural superiority of the female, I find few more concise than the following excerpt from his journal: "In her [woman] resides our only great hope, one of the pledges of our survival. . . . Russian man has become terribly addicted to the debauch of acquisition, cynicism and materialism. . . . Barbaric Russia will show what a place she will allot to the little sister, the little mother . . . that self-renouncing martyr for the Russian man." Women's suffering as a source of national redemption: few prototypes of nineteenth-century Russian fiction better illustrate this central theme than Dostoyevski's idealized, curiously defleshed, virtuous prostitutes—prototypes featured by just about every nineteenth-century Russian writer—who confront men with the following paradox: "Look how far nobler than men all women remain, even in the most degraded state!"

Along with Dostoyevski's fallen women, the theme of the redemptive suffering female is best embodied by Maria Timofeevna in *The*

Possessed. A kind, feeble-minded cripple who is perpetually whipped and beaten by her degenerate brother, Maria Timofeevna is given several mystical and divine attributes. She is an incarnation of Sophia, the principle of Divine Feminine Wisdom, a concept which will become crucial to Blok, Sologub, the entire Symbolist movement, and on to Bulgakov and Pasternak. Like many of the "holy fools" of Russian literature, Maria Timofeevna is also endowed with the gifts of prophecy and vision; she possesses the greatest spiritual treasure of all, a gnostic insight into the dual identity of the Virgin Mary and of Russia's central pagan deity, Moist Mother Earth. This enables her to bear her suffering with the knowledge that for women, "every earthly anguish, every earthly tear, is a great joy," that through their very suffering they bear "the hope of the human race"—a notion that the Soviet state would amply exploit in its female Logo of the dedicated, all-enduring mother/citizen/worker/wife.

No meditation on the Russian heroine can end without a brief homage to Chekhov, perhaps the most humane portraitist of female character in the national pantheon, an author before whom we can do little but bow in silent and humble gratitude. It's worth noting that the heroine of Chekhov's "Lady with a Dog"—Anna Sergeevna—bears the same Christian name as the most masterfully portrayed and beloved heroine of Russian literature, Tolstoy's Anna Karenina. But Chekhov's Anna, created a generation after Karenina, is allowed to triumph over the tyranny of convention, and her adulterous liaison is described in as noble a light as marriage. In "The Darling," a scathing satire of women's abject dependence on men's love, and in countless other works, Chekhov can be seen as one of the first true feminists. Along with Henry James, he is perhaps the first great Western writer to forgo any form of biological determinism, and to praise (with what subtlety and compassion!) the valor of women who leave the roles prescribed them by society. It is in part this sense of wasted energy, of a female potential constantly thwarted by convention, which gives his work its sense of irony and impending doom, of an Empire's end.

The relationship of Russian women to Western Slavists increasingly resembles that of birds to ornithologists. Due to their long cultural isolation and to their distaste for any gender-oriented analysis, which might threaten the class-analysis prescribed by Marxist theory, our Soviet peers are no more aware of the growing feminist literature being written about them in the West than scarlet tanagers are aware of Roger Tory Peterson.

Before linking the nineteenth-century Russian heroine to some of her twentieth-century descendants, I want to mention one very ambitious recent contribution to the fields of Slavic and feminist studies: *Mother Russia*, by the American Slavist Joanna Hubbs. Boldly merging archeology, art history, folklore, and comparative mythology, this book touches on many social and historical factors relevant to my themes—the male's archaic awe and terror before female power, the prevalence of forceful women over relatively weak men in the Russian fictional imagination.

A few of the author's observations: the religion of the early Slavs was strikingly lacking in any dominant male gods. Powerful Woman archetypes abound to a far greater degree in Slavic folklore than in most other cultures: *Polianitsy*—Amazonic heroines of early Russian epics; *rusalki*—virginal, often malicious water deities; and particularly *baba yaga* —an unmarried, prescient old witch who embodies female wisdom at its most punitive and wrathful. Hubbs also suggests that the ascetic streak in Russian culture, its dread of female sexuality, might be traced to the unusually powerful network of Amazonic and matriarchal patterns against which the Byzantine Church had to contend. For Russia is a region in which woman-centered social orders, and pre-Christian cults of the Great Goddess, seem to have lingered far longer than in most other societies—cults which the Church redirected most successfully into a particularly fervent worship of the Virgin Mary, which, in turn, helped to forge the national theme of Mater Dolorosa, of woman's compassion and suffering as a source of human redemption.

Before we turn to the Revolution, two more suggestions of my own about the Powerful Woman syndrome in Russian literature and society: could we agree that the deepest traditions of Russian culture—the higher value of the life of the spirit, of *dukhovnye tsenosti*—are far more feminine than those of most other nations? (Compare them, for instance, to the very masculine, pragmatic, utilitarian German ethos.) And might it be that centuries of immutable autocratic rule, unallayed by any tradition of popular democracy or collective action, have a far more punitive impact on the self-esteem and willpower of men than of women? (Women were not allowed to act anyhow, and kept right on ruling over their little domestic kingdoms.)

Upon the Revolution of 1917, when Moscow the Third Rome was transfigured into Moscow the Third International, the Bolshevik regime became the first government in history to inscribe women's emancipation into its constitution. And the Soviet Founding Fathers predicted that the overthrow of capitalism would abolish "the old bondage" of the nuclear family and assure women full equality at home and at the workplace.

Since these utopian promises were offered, the Russian literary heroine has passed through roughly three phases: (1) the brief bacchanal of artistic freedom that lasted until the late 1920s, during which her struggle to be reborn as the New Socialist Woman was portrayed in often turbulent terms; (2) the period of Socialist Realism (jargon: *lakirovka,* the great varnishing) which lasted from 1934 until the death of Joseph Stalin, during which most of the heroine's psychological conflicts were carefully shielded from view; (3) a growing acknowledgment, first expressed during the Khrushchev thaw, and stated with increasing rage and despair in our own days, that the Revolution liberated women into the *double* duty of work and home; that the Leninist ideal of freeing working women from domestic drudgery, or of effecting that "radical reeducation" of the male psyche promised in 1917, was all a pipe dream and a lie.

In the refreshingly depraved years which immediately followed the Revolution, that long-suppressed Dionysiac, erotic trait of Russian culture which had come to the fore in the first decades of the century had its last Indian summer. And it's interesting that during this period, the 1920s, our central motif—the dreaded devouring female—grows to more monstrous proportions than ever. She returns in the grotesquely sluttish widow who engulfs the protagonist of Iurii Olesha's *Envy* (1927). She returns with truly demonic force in Isaac Babel's fable *The Sin of Jesus* (1921) as a constantly pregnant "slut" whose lust is so fiendish that she suffocates (in bed, of course) an angel sent to her by God to protect her from her own lechery and that of mortal men.

For Soviet heroines of the 1920s had many promiscuous incarnations which a decade later might have doomed their creators to the Gulag. The drugged, alcoholic ingenue of Sergei Malashkin's *The Moon's on the Right Side* (1926) can't even remember how many dozens of lovers she's had—as she explains, saying "no" to the *tovarishchi* might be considered bourgeois. The heroine of Nikolai Bogdanov's *The First Girl* (1928) is a member of Komsomol, the Young Communist League, who has spread venereal disease "in the performance of duties to the comrades," and is murdered by her best friend in order to save the organization from scandal.

Incarnations of the Amazon Woman are not solely negative in this decade. She appears in heroic form in Aleksei Tolstoy's *The Viper,* in which a pampered aristocratic debutante grows to be a tough, disciplined soldier who handles guns and horses better than any man in the regiment. She is equally valorous in the fictions of the first and last great Soviet feminist, Aleksandra Kollontai, whose heroines advocate total emotional independence from men. She is tragic in Fyodor Gladkov's *Cement* (1925), whose protagonist, Dasha, immolates her life so totally to the State and to the emancipation of women that she even sees the death of her daughter in a government children's home as a noble sacrifice.

But in the following decades women were to be tightly refettered, both in literature and in life. Let's not forget that the Soviet State looks on Women, essentially, as producer and reproducer. Its commitment to equal rights has never been based on the individualistic, libertarian principles of Western feminism; it is anchored, rather, on utilitarian, patriotic factors—rapid economic growth, speedier construction of dams, dynamos, and tanks—which fluctuate vastly from decade to decade according to the State's needs. Witness what happened when Stalin's regime began its first Five Year Plan, and realized that rapid industrialization, contrary to Lenin's premises, did require the discipline of family life. Phase two of the Soviet heroine's incarnation—dictated by the Socialist Realist doctrines announced in 1934—became marked by a cult of motherhood, and a heightened ideal of female self-sacrifice, quite as exalted as it was under the tsars. These ideals were reinforced in the postwar years, when after the death of over 20 million soldiers and civilians (another 20 million, according to most estimates, had been lost to forced collectivization and Stalin's purges) one out of three Soviet households was headed by single women.

The literary model for the Socialist Realist portrayal of women, of course, was Maxim Gorky's *Mother,* an ironic prototype indeed seeing that it was written in 1906, much of it during a trip to the United States, and two decades before the author resettled permanently in the USSR after many long forays abroad. However clumsy a novel, *Mother* is riveting in its symbolism, in its recycling of archaic, ascetic Orthodox ideals of woman's mission into state propaganda. "Mother" is an illiterate working class woman who retains a saintly kindness throughout the brutal beatings of her alcoholic husband, and who after her early widowhood is regenerated and "raised from the dead," as she puts it, by the revolutionary activities of her bachelor son. Note the religious and monastic symbolism: her charismatic son, Pavel, Paul, gathers about him a band of apostles who all refuse marriage because "No revolutionary can adhere closely to another individual without distorting his faith." As Pavel is sent to exile—perhaps to death—in Siberia, the heroine states that she has gained "a resuscitated soul they cannot kill" by becoming, herself, a Socialist militant.

It is with the aid of these curiously mystical ideals that the literature of a militantly atheist state, in the Stalin era, forged its images of women: the notion that all personal joys and problems must be sublimated into that holier maternal unity which is the Socialist collective; the precept that the citizen's true spouse and parent is the Party and the Nation State (is it any wonder that Soviet Russia's divorce rate is so phenomenal, now dooming one out of three marriages?).

Under these premises, the heroine could only be shown as the resilient citizen who serves the state by holding a job as well as any man and taking care of the family as only a woman can. No chink in her armor was ever allowed to show, we were barely even permitted to enter into her home; the only truly uplifting fiction about this self-abnegating superachiever was to be set in the work collective, preferably on immense construction projects. During this hydro-electrification of Russian literature, all family conflicts were taboo; our heroine's traditional mate—the spineless anti-hero of *ancien régime* fictions—had been reborn as the provident, dedicated "positive hero," Socialist New Man: no more depressions, no more romantic Hamletic indecision, no more Oblomovian housecoats, and no more smarty-pants modernist metaphors not instantly lucid to the masses. Plus: all endings had to be happy, for women's life in the Socialist state, as the old Russian saying goes, was "a river of milk and fruit-jelly shores," "*Molochnaia reka, kissel'nye berega.*"

These lacquered sweets began to go sour as our heroine entered Phase Three of her incarnations, under Khrushchev's thaw. The ideological soul-searching of industrial and *kolkhoz* novels gave way to more personal life-problems; particularly in the writings of Vera Panova, perhaps the most popular woman writer of the post-Revolutionary years, we were offered fictional forays into the home which admitted—oh, revelation!—to difficult housing conditions, juvenile delinquency, even adulteries. Archetypal plot: the young careerist in love with her older colleague, such as the heroine of yet another woman's novel, Galina Nikolaeva's *A Running Battle*. After trysting for a few months in a cockroach-infested suburban room, the lover, declaring that "the era of socialism is ill-equipped for adultery," returns to his wife. The abandoned ingenue accepts a post in some distant province and nobly dedicates her life to work and the nation-state.

A brief word is in order about post-Revolutionary Soviet attitudes toward women authors. To use Simone de Beauvoir's paradigm of Woman as the Other, as the alienated creature solely defined, throughout history, by men's standards and men's needs: in life as in literature, Soviet women still experience a greater alienation and Otherness than women in any other developed nation that comes to mind. For notwithstanding its official policy of equal rights, the USSR remains a very Oriental society which segregates women into various forms of ideational harems rigidly controlled by the male power structure.

And so sexist biases against women writers on the part of Soviet male authorities, the crude gender stereotypes and the abusive language in which these biases are couched, have been chronically abysmal. Chauvinism may now be less overt than in 1946, when the Writers' Union expelled the sublime poet Anna Akhmatova with a motion of censure that labeled her "a nun and a fornicatrix." But to this day, praise offered women authors by male critics in the Soviet press is often accompanied by the following accolade, "This is fine writing, as if accomplished by a man's hand." And as of 1986, there were only a dozen women holding executive posts in the Writers' Union, as opposed to 360 men—even though a sizeable group of gifted women writers, for the previous two decades, had been quite altering the landscape of Soviet fiction.

This new wave of authors who came to the fore in the mid-1960s gained their place, in part, by stating some of the more subversive notions put forth by women since the 1917 Revolution: the notion that professional work is not the panacea for women's problems which the founding fathers had promised it to be; that the Bolshevik rhetoric of equal rights has only been a camouflage for the hardships of a double shift life; that the average Soviet workplace, in the recent words of novelist I. Grekova, is "a heart attack factory," "*fabrika infarktov.*"

These views were put forth with particular brilliance in Natalia Baranskaia's novella A Week Like Any Other (1967), the chronicle of a tormented, perpetually beleaguered Soviet working mother. Its heroine, Olga, is a young scientist so harassed by the double burden of career and motherhood that she constantly feels guilty of being a failure at both. Up every work day from 6 A.M. to midnight, she shares a chemistry lab with eight women colleagues who live in states of "constant anxiety, eternal rushing, fear" somewhat akin to hers. Written in the form of one week's diary entries, *A Week Like Any Other* expresses with unsurpassed poignancy the nightmares of Soviet women's daily lives: food shortages; eternal queues; passive husbands, either abusively drunk or buried in TV or newspapers, who never lift a finger to help out; indifferent doctors hastily attending children who constantly get ill from sloppily run nursery schools—illnesses which force women to stay home one day out of four and reduce their salaries to a paltry sum, so impeding the possibility of any meaningful career advancement that their work seems absurd.

As in most of contemporary Russian women's fiction, there is an ascetic, Amazonic streak in Baranskaia's writing. It is indicated that even though Olga and her husband "love" each other and seldom quarrel, their life is so harassed that sexual contact rarely occurs. It is equally clear that the most precious part of Olga's life, outside of her beloved children, is the daily support of the women friends in her work collective. The pressure of a woman friend's hand across Olga's cheek is the week's only reassurance, its only soothing moment.

For when the longed-for Saturday morning finally comes around, Olga, promising research scientist, makes five days' worth of soup, dusts the flat, scrubs its floors, does the week's heavy laundry, puts up dry fruit compote, grinds the meat for the weekend's hamburgers, irons, sews, has her weekly shampoo, and begins a nervous breakdown. As Olga works into Saturday evening while her spouse continues to read his magazines, she collapses into a sobbing fit; her children howl about her; her husband insultingly suggests that she quit working and sit home to mind the children—after all, she rebuts, *her* academic credentials, *her* professional standing, are equal to his. At week's end her marriage seems even more tense, her career more unmanageable than it was at the beginning of the week. Here, at last, is an utterly accurate portrait of Soviet women's reality, one bound to strike humility and meek gratitude into the heart of even the most combative Western feminist. There is an old Russian proverb, indicative of the sense of superiority bred into the nation's females, which goes: "Women can do everything. Men can do the rest." Baranskaia's generation seems to be saying, "Yes, we *can* do everything, but we don't *want* to any more."

Baranskaia is one of a dozen women authors who have greatly feminized Russian letters. Some of their writings, particularly those of I. Grekova, have already been widely translated and published abroad;

and most of these authors, who tend to work exclusively in the story form, *povest'*, rather than the novel, are included in three important collections of Soviet writing being issued in the United States this year: *Balancing Acts: Contemporary Stories by Russian Women,* published by Indiana University Press; *On the Golden Porch,* an anthology of stories by Tat'iana Tolstaia, issued by Alfred A. Knopf; and *The New Soviet Fiction,* Abbeville Press, which has splendid contributions by Tolstaia, Liudmila Petrushevskaia, and I. Grekova. The most striking single trait shared by this new crop of women authors is also its most common fault: they have returned with a vengeance to the nineteenth-century duet of Formidable Woman—Weak Male once tabooed by Socialist Realism. Their male protagonists are quite as spineless, as lethargic, as Oblomovian, as superfluous as the heroes of nineteenth-century fiction, and far, far less interesting and complex.

The indecisive lover of "Nothing Special," a splendid story by Viktoria Tokareva included in the Indiana anthology, admits to "his essential and beloved inertness," confessing that he will never be able to know happiness because "you have to work for it." Liudmila Uvarova's "Be Still, Torments of Passion" is the chronicle of a successful actress whose one lover was such an ineffectual wimp that she chose to live out the rest of her decades with two devoted women friends. The resourceful, larger-than-life heroine of Grekova's novella *The Hotel Manager,* who is left a widow conveniently early by her petty husband, finds emotional fulfillment in the love of her own widowed mother and of the resilient unwed mothers she befriends. And listen to the monologue of the male protagonist in Nina Katerli's "Between Spring and Summer," a gentle cardiac patient who is the only male employee in a work collective of bossy women engineers. "Equal rights, of course. But equality has turned out to mean . . . that a man was no longer the master of his home . . . that he was the least important person in it. What had happened to men? And where had these women come from who ran everything, whether at home or on the job?"

The males portrayed in these fictions, neither tender lovers nor dependable husbands, are not even forceful enough to be domestic tyrants; they are often endowed with those odious diminutives which nineteenth-century writers used to bestow on their heroines—they tend to have "limp little hands," "frail little feet," "thin little chicken necks." This is one of the worst flaws in these authors' craft: through their cardboard portrayals of men, their continual stereotyping of gender, they fall into that very same trap of biological determinism, traditionally indulged in by the male power structure, which has oppressed women for centuries.

These writers break totally with their classical male predecessors, however, by their creation of radically de-idealized heroines: perhaps they have learned that idealization is another way of neutralizing women's power, that men place us on pedestals in order to keep us in our place, the better to admire our suffering. Their heroines—be they alcoholic actresses, harassed single mothers, or widowed surgeons—project an unsparingly critical self-image of Soviet women as tough, modest, vulnerable, often vain, often embittered, and frequently at the end of their tether. They are chaste through dearth rather than choice; they have a striking lack of verbal communication with whatever men hover in their lives; they are self-sufficient, yet like many of their American peers, they are very lonely. Their curiously loveless, melancholy landscape is suffused with a Chekhovian mood of disillusionment; it is a requiem for a romantic happiness once dreamed of but never achieved. If there is one quote from classical fiction that might serve as its epigraph, it is the lament of Elena in Turgenev's *Rudin:* "We can't live without love . . . but who is there to love?"

Current women's fiction in the USSR shares many other features, and many limitations, with our contemporary women's letters. It tends to be familial and intimist, obsessively concentrated on the problems of what Soviets call *byt,* the details of everyday domestic life. Like our own shopping mall realism and name-brand fiction, Soviet women's writing is extremely bourgeois. It is very concerned with the acquisition of comforts and personal belongings, a fixation admirably satirized in Tat'iana Tolstaia's story "Fire and Dust." (Seeing the decades of dearth, heaven knows their consumer obsessions are far more pardonable than ours.) And as in our own literature, Soviet women's fiction is considerably less experimental in technique and far more apolitical than that of our male peers. Such grand Slavophilic themes as salvation-through-Russianness, or women's suffering as a source of national redemption, have remained an exclusively male domain, best embodied by Rasputin's heroic old villagers, and most sublimely so by the protagonist of Solzhenitsyn's "Matryona's House." Soviet women are *not* taken with the theme of redemptive suffering.

One more striking similarity between current Soviet women's writing and ours is its obsession with filial and maternal attachments, which are inevitably portrayed as far more precious than romantic ones. For motherhood, in Soviet literature and life, has far deeper mystical, social, and political dimensions than it does in the United States. Already linked, in tsarist times, to the cult of the Virgin Mary, in the Soviet era it is an act of faith that forges links with the mythical Socialist future, and also an investment against solitude. For the harassed young housewife of Baranskaia's *A Week Like Any Other* tends eventually to become a single, divorced woman whose life is concentrated on her child, her parents, her career and (with luck) a few women friends. The middle-aged heroine of Baranskaia's recent story "The Kiss," for instance, a single working mom with a grown, married daughter, is offered her first romantic interlude in over a decade; while setting a festive table for her longed-for lover she receives a phone call from her beloved daughter—the baby is sick, please Mama I need you; and without a pang of regret or of hesitation, ten minutes before her date is scheduled to arrive Mom packs up the dinner goodies into a shopping bag and takes the subway to attend to her darling Natasha. This literature is more than Amazonic; it is downright parthenogenetic.

There is one striking feature of Soviet women's fiction alien to ours—a prevalence of hospital settings. In her splendid introduction to the Indiana University Press collection, *Balancing Acts,* Elena Goscilo interprets the hospital syndrome as "a metaphorical microcosm of an ailing, segregated society in which women, its quintessential victims, join forces to struggle . . . against colossal incompetence, shoddiness, general indifference to their plight, and a tragic sense of isolation." The hospital and maternity wards repeatedly portrayed in the writings of Grekova, Uvarova, Varlamova, Tokareva, Petrushevskaia, indeed do give women a way of criticizing the scandalously corrupt state of Soviet medicine and other human services, the debasing indignities which they particularly inflict on women. But they are also literary ploys which enable fictional women to speak with utmost candor and bawdiness on their favorite topics—how to effect the *perestroika* of Russian men.

I shall end with brief eulogies to a few of my Soviet colleagues whose work I find particularly outstanding. First, the émigré writer Iulia Voznesenskaia, one of the true-life heroines to whom I dedicated this essay, who was exiled from her homeland for daring to say, a decade too early, that there are a few problems unique to women, and that there might be such a thing as feminine literature. Her *Women's Decameron,* published in a fine English translation, is a marvel of ribaldry modeled on the medieval Italian classic of the same name. Each of ten outspoken women in a Leningrad maternity ward—raunchy airline stewardesses, hilariously parodied Party workers—recounts crucial stages in her life: her first sexual encounters, her first heartbreak, the first of her nine abortions.

Liberated as it is by exile, *The Women's Decameron* is considerably more interesting in technique than most women's literature emerging from the USSR. For however fascinating and unprecedented they are as social documents, Soviet women's fictions cannot be admired for their formal innovations; on the intellectual and aesthetic level they remain provincial compared to the best of their European and American peers. They are often overly sentimental and lacking in irony; they tend still to work within the confines of a rather archaic realism; their breathless use of flashback gives the impression that they never heard of the technique until last year, which they may well not have. For who are their models? They work in a culture which has long been denied access to its own remarkable modernist tradition; in which the very forgers of European modernism—Joyce, Kafka, Beckett, Stein—are only beginning to be officially available; in which such universal classics of women's literature as Edith Wharton, Virginia Woolf, Colette, Simone de Beauvoir, and Doris Lessing remain untranslated or virtually unobtainable. And after so many decades of isolation and oppression, the Soviets' grasp of Western literary values is so garbled that university courses in American fiction often lump Hemingway, Faulkner, Margaret Mitchell, Leon Uris, Arthur Hailey, J. D. Salinger, and Jacqueline Susann into one semester's reading list.

Beyond the ones I've already discussed, several Soviet women's fictions rise above these limitations: the lyric energy of Liudmila Petrushevskaia; Viktoria Tokareva's barbed irony; the eminent narrative gifts of Nina Katerli and of Inna Varlamova, who have been admirably translated by Ardis Press; and most particularly the work of Tat'iana Tolstaia. She is the great-grandniece of Leo Tolstoy, the granddaughter of Aleksei, and a doyenne of the younger generation of Soviet authors. Tolstaia may be the only woman writer who shares with the male members of the Soviet avant-garde—Andrei Bitov, Viktor Erefeev—a postmodernist obsession with Russia's literary past. Her parodies of the most cherished themes of classical Russian fiction—the redemptive valor of woman's self-sacrifice, the duet of Formidable Woman and Indecisive Man—are effected with a black, mordant wit learned from her masters,

Platonov and Nabokov, whom she has been privileged to read for some decades in *samizdat*. The heroine of Tolstaia's story "Sonia," perhaps modeled on her namesake, the selfless spinster cousin in *War and Peace,* is a homely old maid whose saintly generosity is exploited and rendered ridiculous by her cynical friends. The hero of another tale, "Peters," is a plump wimp tyrannized by an archetypally powerful grandmother; after a few decades of attempted bachelorhood he ends up being dominated by an even more suffocating wife—shades of Gogol's Ivan Shponka.

The vigorous prose of Tat'iana Tolstaia and of several of her peers leads one to believe that Soviet women are finally gaining a voice and a room of their own in the creation of those uniquely redemptive worlds we call fictions; and that the freedoms of Gorbachev's *glasnost'* will soon enable them to express life's most quixotic lesson: the irony and anxiety of true freedom.